JE 19

THE AGE OF ADDICTION

THE AGE OF ADDICTION

How Bad Habits Became Big Business

DAVID T. COURTWRIGHT

THE BELKNAP PRESS OF

HARVARD UNIVERSITY PRESS

CAMBRIDGE, MASSACHUSETTS

LONDON, ENGLAND

2019

First printing

LIBRARY OF CONGRESS CATALOGING-IN-PUBLICATION DATA
Names: Courtwright, David T., 1952– author.
Title: The age of addiction : how bad habits became big business / David T. Courtwright.
Description: Cambridge, Massachusetts : The Belknap Press of Harvard University
   Press, 2019. | Includes bibliographical references and index.
Identifiers: LCCN 2018045844 | ISBN 9780674737372 (alk. paper)
Subjects: LCSH: Compulsive behavior. | Capitalism—Psychological aspects. |
   Capitalism—Moral and ethical aspects. | Hedonism. | Advertising—Psychological
   aspects. | Psychology, Pathological.
Classification: LCC RC533 .C678 2019 | DDC 616.85/227—dc23
LC record available at https://lccn.loc.gov/2018045844

For Shelby Miller, to whom nothing in this book applies,

and for John Burnham, to whom everything applies,

and who would have appreciated the joke.

We're flawed because we want so much more.

We're ruined because we get these things, and wish for what we had.

—DON DRAPER, *Mad Men*

CONTENTS

INTRODUCTION

ONE SUMMER DAY in 2010 a Swedish graduate student named Daniel Berg approached me after a talk I gave at Christ's College, Cambridge. During the talk I had casually mentioned internet addiction. Berg told me that I had spoken a truth larger than I knew. Many of his male friends at Stockholm University had dropped out of school and were living in crash pads, compulsively playing *World of Warcraft*. They spoke an argot more English than Swedish. It was all raiding, all the time.

"How do they feel about their circumstances?" I asked.
"They feel *angst*," Berg said.
"But they keep playing?"
"They keep playing."

This sort of behavior does seem like an addiction, in the sense of a compulsive, regret-filled pursuit of transient pleasures that are harmful to both the individual and society. For gaming, the personal cost was highest for Swedish men. "I am," Berg reported, "now the only male in my graduate program in economic history."[1]

Back home in Florida I noticed digital distractions exacting a more impartial academic toll. The smartphones that dotted the lecture halls were as often wielded by women as by men. But when I told Berg's tale to my students, they instantly recognized the type. One admitted that he had lost a year to compulsive gaming. He said that he was in recovery— precariously, to judge by his grades. Another student knew gamers who kept cans by their computers. They used them to avoid having to take bathroom breaks.

The can by the computer became for me a symbol of the shifting meaning of addiction. As late as the 1970s the word seldom referred to anything other than compulsive drug use. Over the next forty years, however, the concept of addiction broadened. Memoirists confessed to addictions to gambling, sex, shopping, and carbs. German sex therapists called internet porn a "gateway drug" that ensnared the young. A *New York Times* op-ed declared sugar to be addictive, "literally, in the same way as drugs." A toothless young New Zealand mother drank up to ten liters of Coke a day, then splashed the headlines when she died of coronary arrhythmia. A nineteen-year-old truant in Jiangsu Province made the news when he hacked off his left hand to cure his internet addiction. Chinese officials judged as many as 14 percent of his peers to be similarly hooked, and set up internet addiction rehabilitation camps. South Korea and Japan followed suit. Taiwanese legislators voted to fine parents who let their children spend too much time online, updating a law forbidding minors' smoking, drinking, drug-taking, and betel-chewing. Only the last habit failed to appeal to Americans, 47 percent of whom showed signs of at least one behavioral or substance addiction disorder in any given year in the early 2000s.[2]

Often they showed signs of more than one. Medical researchers have discovered that substance and behavioral addictions have similar natural histories. They produce similar brain changes; similar patterns of tolerance; and similar experiences of craving, intoxication, and withdrawal. And they reveal similar genetic tendencies toward similar personality disorders and compulsions. The manic gambler and the casino barfly are apt to be one and the same. In 2013 the new edition of the bible of psychiatry, the *Diagnostic and Statistical Manual of Mental Disorders: DSM-5,* described gambling disorders in language indistinguishable from drug addiction. The editors ushered "internet gaming disorder" into the green room of addiction by designating it a "condition for further study." In 2018 the WHO made it official by adding "gaming disorder" to the revised *International Classification of Diseases.*[3]

Not everyone was happy with all the talk of addiction. Clinicians avoided it for fear of discouraging or stigmatizing patients. Libertarians dismissed it as an excuse for lack of discipline. Social scientists attacked it as medical imperialism. Philosophers detected equivocation, the misleading practice of using the same word to describe different things. I mean to give these critics a hearing. For now, though, I will stick to "addiction." The word provides a usefully concise and universally understood way of referring to a pattern of compulsive, conditioned, relapse-prone, and harmful behavior. The important job, and the goal of this book, is to explain why that pattern of harmful behavior has become more conspicuous and varied over time.

A GOOD PLACE TO BEGIN is to review what we know about addictions. They begin as journeys, usually unplanned, toward a harmful endpoint on a spectrum of consumption. The journey can be rapid, or slow, or interrupted. Casual indulgence, even of a drug like heroin, does not always lead to addiction. When it does, the condition is not necessarily permanent. Addicts can and do quit, either permanently or for long stretches of time. Nor is all excessive consumption necessarily addiction. People can gamble too much without being compulsive, just as they can burden their scales without being food addicts. Yet—and this is the crucial point—regular, heavy consumption has a way of shading into addiction, as when a steady drinker's craving intensifies, erupting into full-blown alcoholism. An addiction is a habit that has become a very bad habit, in the sense of being strong, preoccupying, and damaging, both to oneself and to others. The type of damage depends on the substance or behavior. Compulsive gamers may ruin their scholastic and marital prospects. They do not ruin their livers or lungs.

The addiction process is social as well as biological. Conditions like stress and peer behavior help tip individuals into addiction, though the process ultimately manifests itself in their brains. Frequent resort to alcohol, drugs, and drug-like behaviors causes changes in neurons, including altered gene expression. Over time these changes occur in more and larger regions of the central nervous system, like drops of dye spreading on a taut sheet. The changes are long-lasting, particularly in developing brains. The earlier children and adolescents experience an addictive substance or pastime, the likelier they are to retain, even when abstaining, a powerful emotional memory of the behavior that once made them feel so good.[4]

The nature of addiction has implications—more precisely, temptations—for businesses that sell habituating products. One is to encourage early and frequent consumption. Treat the lads, the saloonkeepers used to say, and you'll have their money in the till when they're adults. And the more they drink, the greater the profits. To this day 80 percent of alcohol sales go to the 20 percent of customers who are the heaviest users, a pattern that applies across the business of brain reward. More than half of all marijuana finds its way into the lungs and stomachs of those who spend more than half their waking hours stoned. Insofar as addictions to marijuana, or to anything else, develop most often among the poor, the marginal, and the genetically vulnerable, they are sources of inequality and injustice as well as illness. Yet addiction and its precursor, heavy consumption, remain indispensable profit centers for a range of global businesses.[5]

THESE REALITIES ARE WELL UNDERSTOOD in the addiction research and public health communities. Less well understood is how we got into

OPPOSITE: Manufacturers of addictive products have long sought to attract the young, glamorize suspect behavior, and soft-pedal risks. An advertisement for Junior Partner cigarettes read, "If you want a Cigarette which will not injure your health in any way, smoke the 'JUNIOR PARTNER.' They have a corn shuck mouth-piece, which extracts *the nicotine and the bad effects of the burning paper* . . . [and] have no opium or flavorings in them; are *hand* made, and ¼ of an inch longer than any other Cigarette." What doomed this mid-1880s brand was the tidal wave of cheap, machine-made cigarettes that turned a marginal form of tobacco consumption into a mass addiction.

this fix and why it keeps getting worse, despite the best efforts of those communities. I propose that the main source of the problem has been what I call *limbic capitalism*. Limbic capitalism refers to a technologically advanced but socially regressive business system in which global industries, often with the help of complicit governments and criminal organizations, encourage excessive consumption and addiction. They do so by targeting the limbic system, the part of the brain responsible for feeling and for quick reaction, as distinct from dispassionate thinking. The limbic system's pathways of networked neurons make possible pleasure, motivation, long-term memory, and other emotionally linked functions crucial for survival. Paradoxically, these same neural circuits make possible profits from activities that work *against* survival, businesses having turned evolution's handiwork to their own ends.

Limbic capitalism was itself a product of cultural evolution. It was a late development in a long historical process that saw the accelerating spread of novel pleasures and their twinned companions of vice and addiction. The pleasures, vices, and addictions most conspicuously associated with limbic capitalism were those of intoxication. Considerations of private profit and state revenue encouraged alcohol and drug consumption until rising social costs forced governments to restrict or prohibit at least some drugs. Or so I argued in *Forces of Habit,* a 2001 book on the history of alcohol and drugs. Yet, even as I stated my case, I saw that it applied to more than the usual psychoactive suspects. It applied to all pleasures, vices, and addictions that had become entwined in the emerging system of limbic capitalism.[6]

This idea was not entirely novel. Victorian-era reformers saw alcohol and nonmedical drug use as part of an ill-starred constellation of vice. Granted, vice is a slippery category. Chinese men considered sniffing and sucking the tiny, deformed feet of girls and women to be normal erotic behavior until missionaries and modernizers stigmatized foot binding. Yet, for all the cultural malleability of vices, the Victorians recognized two important things about them. One was that they had become big business.

The other was that they were linked. Rare was the brothel without booze, or the opium den without a gambling house nearby. Victorians also supposed vices to be linked neurologically, with those who had inherited or acquired defective nervous systems being most inclined to them.[7]

The last hunch was a good one. A century later neuroscientists and geneticists were mapping these connections at the cellular and molecular level. They discovered that different substances and activities generate similar types of brain reward and craving. They showed that addicted brains are alike in that reward cues activate the same pathways in drug and behavioral addictions. Researchers began to use the term *pathological learning* for the process that occurs when addictive substances or behaviors augment release of the neurotransmitter dopamine, turning what evolved as a beneficial process into a pathological one. Dopamine does its work of reward and conditioning in pathways originating in or near the limbic midbrain, a key region for regulating mood, pleasure, and pain. The pleasurable effect depends, in part, on the intensity of the signal that dopamine produces after release into the synapses. In neurons as in life, first impressions matter. People keep on doing what their brains tell them is highly rewarding, often past the point where it is still pleasurable, or beneficial. Addicts *want* something after they have ceased *liking* it, even if they realize its harmful effects. "I hate this shit," a Swedish heroin addict told his doctor, "and it doesn't give me much of a high. It is just that somehow, it seems I can't be without it."[8]

Researchers identified common risk factors. Genetic variations and life circumstances—stress, social defeat, neglect or abuse during critical periods of brain development—make some people more susceptible to addiction than others. They feel uncomfortable or depressed until they discover that alcohol, drugs, sugar, gambling, computer games, or some other thrilling behavior temporarily banishes their blues. Frequent resort to these substances and behaviors further damages their neural control systems and, often, other parts of their brains. What the Victorians called vice really is a vicious circle. Self-destructive habits are constitutionally linked, downwardly spiraling, and socially expansive. New stars keep appearing in the vice constellation.[9]

"Addiction is a memory, it's a reflex," summed up the psychiatrist Charles P. O'Brien. "It's training your brain in something which is harmful to yourself." Or *having* your brain trained. The deeper truth is that we live in a world nominally dedicated to progress, health, and longevity but in fact geared toward getting us to consume in ways that are unprogressive, unhealthful, and often deadly. Understanding this paradox—the burden of this book—requires going beyond neuroscience, beyond disordered neurons and defective genes. It requires understanding the history of novel pleasures, commercial vices, mass addiction, and limbic capitalism's ever-growing power to shape our habits and desires.[10]

That history, like the history of technology generally, is one of accelerating change over a long period of time. Limbic capitalism did not spring full-blown onto modern history's stage. On the contrary, it emerged from something primal, the efforts of our species to continuously expand our repertoire of pleasures. The search for pleasure preceded civilization and, I mean to show, contributed to its foundation.

Civilization in turn had disparate consequences for pleasure. It made possible (for some) the higher pleasures of learning, musical artistry, theater, and absorbing games of skill like chess. But it also sickened, immiserated, and subjugated billions of humans by making intoxication more desirable, vice more tempting, and addiction more likely. Civilization also incubated the technologies that quickened the global quest for pleasure. Chief among them were the improvement and spread of agriculture; the expansion and monetization of long-distance trade; the rise of cities, empires, and industry; and, in the recent past, the explosion of digital communication.

Along the way there were smaller breakthroughs that nonetheless had large consequences. Among them were the isolation of plant-drug alkaloids like morphine and cocaine; the application of photography to pornography; the blending of sugar, fat, and salt in processed foods; and the rapid (now virtual) transport of people from one amusement to another. Innovations like these gave entrepreneurs and their state enablers the means to expand and intensify pleasures and to promote vices, increasing the amount of harmful consumption and the variety of addictions.

In brief, civilized inventiveness weaponized pleasurable products and pastimes. The more rapid and intense the brain reward they imparted, the likelier they were to foster pathological learning and craving, particularly among socially and genetically vulnerable consumers. Meanwhile globalization, industrialization, and urbanization made these seductive commodities and services more accessible and affordable, often in anonymous environments conducive to anomie and saturated with advertising. Accessibility, affordability, advertising, anonymity, and anomie, the five cylinders of the engine of mass addiction, ultimately have found their most radical technological expression in the floating world of the internet.[11]

Though the internet supercharged limbic capitalism, it did not invent it. In fact, no one invented it. It emerged from an ancient quest to discover, refine, and blend novel pleasures. New pleasures gave rise to new vices, new vices to new addictions—for some people, anyway. Addictive behavior was, to repeat, seldom majority behavior. But the *risk* of such behavior grew as entrepreneurs rationalized—that is, made more scientific and efficient—the trade in brain-rewarding commodities.

Ultimately this rationalization assumed the aspect of a global economic and political system, in the sense of being organized, interlocking, and strategically active. By the nineteenth century entrepreneurs were doing more than simply selling whatever new pleasures chance discovery and expanded trade made available. They had begun to engineer, produce, and market potentially addictive products in ways calculated to increase demand and maximize profit. They learned to play political hardball. They devoted a share of their profits to buying off opposition. They devised lobbying and public relations tactics to survive the big reform wave of the early twentieth century. They prospered in varying degrees during the mid-twentieth century, when some addictive behaviors were permitted, others winked at, and still others repressed. After the Cold War their enterprises became increasingly varied, legitimate, and global. They created, not merely an age of addiction, but an age of "addiction by design" that is both the hallmark of limbic capitalism and the clearest demonstration of its inversion of the forces of reason and science that made it possible.[12]

1

NEWFOUND PLEASURES

THE HISTORIES OF PLEASURE, vice, and addiction are linked. As the number and intensity of pleasures grew, so did the number of vices and opportunities for addiction. Not all new pleasures were vicious or addictive—most of them were beneficial and socially constructive. Yet vice and addiction flourished in pleasure's lengthening shadow. The expansion of pleasure throughout human history is thus the place to begin the story.

It is one of those stories that starts slowly and then gathers speed. Pleasure's trajectory has been exponential: a long, lumbering takeoff; acceleration in the seventeenth and eighteenth centuries; and a dizzying rise in the nineteenth and twentieth centuries. The process began millennia ago as people discovered, cultivated, exchanged, blended, refined, and commodified pleasures they found in nature, like sugar from cane. They also created and spread pleasures not found in nature, like games of chance. And they built new environments, often anonymous urban environments, in which they could enjoy their new pleasures at low cost and with minimal risk of social sanction.

The revolution in new pleasures, like all revolutions, had an element of contingency. The collective experiment in devising delights and diversions sometimes slowed down and sometimes sped up. No Oliver Cromwell, no closing of the English theaters. No Auguste Escoffier, no Peach Melba. Eventually, however, the revolution became impersonal. It acquired sufficient momentum to overwhelm everything in its path, like an avalanche triggered by loose boulders.

Historians call such boulders "exogenous causes," in that their nature and force were independent of the pleasures they mobilized. This chapter and the next explore these causes, from the migrations of the distant past to the industrial and urban revolutions of more recent centuries. Though many and sometimes conflicting, these causes nonetheless achieved a common effect. They turned what had been a gradual, additive, and often haphazard process of finding new pleasures into a rapid, multiplicative, and increasingly calculated one.

DISCOVERED PLEASURES

World history consists of a long period of migratory divergence and a much shorter period of trade-based convergence. Anthropologists and geneticists debate when bands of *Homo sapiens* began dispersing from Africa; when they arrived at various locations in Eurasia, Oceania, and the Americas; and the extent to which they crossbred with near-human species, such as Neanderthals. New archeological finds, including evidence of earlier-than-expected forays out of Africa, keep these debates simmering. Yet three points seem to be settled. First, *Homo sapiens*'s migrations turned into a global diaspora spanning, at a minimum, some fifty or sixty thousand years. Second, modern humans underwent divergent cultural and biological evolution as bands of hunter-gatherers adapted to new conditions in the lands into which they spread. Third, this global migration triggered an unintended but colossal treasure hunt for plants and animals that were both useful and pleasurable.[1]

Pleasure, the *Oxford English Dictionary* tells us, "is the condition or sensation induced by the experience or anticipation of what is felt to be good or desirable; a feeling of happy satisfaction or enjoyment; delight, gratification; opposed to *pain*." That there were so many new "delights" and "gratifications" to be discovered by itinerant humans was a legacy of the earth's geological history. The gradual breakup of the supercontinent Pangaea, starting around 200 million years ago, had provided ample time

Honey-gathering from a wild bee nest, Mesolithic rock painting in La Araña Shelter near Valencia, Spain. In human hands, honey, like other food-drugs, came to have many uses, from salving wounds to making mead. Beeswax provided fuel for lamps, material for figurines, and, Homer tells us, earplugs to deafen Odysseus's sailors to the Sirens' song.

for flora and fauna to drift apart on separate landmasses and evolve varied properties.[2]

The result was a checkered pattern of natural pleasure resources. Honeybees (*Apis mellifera*) originated in Asia and spread rapidly across Africa and Europe. As groups of *Homo sapiens* expanded throughout Africa and into Asia and Europe, they avidly hunted for honey, celebrating their adventures in rock art found in Spain, South Africa, and India. But when the migrants ventured farther east to the Americas, they had to leave honeybees behind. Those who settled in eastern North America found a substitute in the sap of sugar maples. Those who pushed on to Central and South America found a different prize: colonies of stingless bees (Meliponinae) that provided them with honey and wax.[3]

When the first humans arrived in Australia, about 45,000 to about 65,000 years ago, they took similar advantage of stingless bees. They also feasted on game animals, likely contributing to the extinction of Australia's largest species. The relative lack of biodiversity on the smallest, flattest, driest, and least fertile of the world's inhabitable continents meant that, honey aside, their descendants had to make do with relatively few pleasure resources. An exception was nicotine, which Aboriginal people extracted by chewing the leaves of native tobacco plants mixed with wood ash. Despite their mastery of fire, they seldom smoked the leaves. European diarists described them as habitual chewers, much like East Indians with betel quid. The only other Mesolithic peoples to discover tobacco, American Indians, sniffed and smoked the plant as well as chewing it.[4]

Tobacco (*Nicotiana*) produced a complicated sort of pleasure, including hallucinations and other toxic effects. The same was true of several species of jimsonweed (*Datura*) native to Central America, and *yagé*, or ayahuasca, a drink made from the bark of *Banisteriopsis caapi* vines from the Amazon basin. It may seem odd that the first Americans relished bitter-tasting plants that produced florid hallucinations. But their shamanistic cultures prized altered consciousness as a means of communing with the spirit world, healing bodies and souls, and initiating the young into sacred rites. Unpleasant side effects could be assigned benevolent purposes. To vomit during a peyote ceremony, for instance, was to cleanse the body.[5]

People experienced new pleasures within the context of the stories they told about themselves and the cosmos. The ability to invent and perpetuate such stories, now called "myths," "social constructs," and "imagined realities," was a decisive cognitive breakthrough that made possible *Homo sapiens*'s large-group cooperation and global expansion. That expansion, and the agricultural and industrial revolutions that followed it, continuously created new encounters with psychoactive substances whose effects were shaped by social learning.[6]

The American psychologist Timothy Leary and the psychoanalyst Norman Zinberg gave this learning process the name by which it is now best known: drugs, set, and setting. "Set" is short for mindset, meaning the user's personality, character, and intentions. Set affects the nature of the drug experience, as do the physical and social settings in which consumption occurs. Though Leary and Zinberg were mainly interested in users' reactions to powerful drugs like LSD and heroin, later research showed that the principle applies broadly. Thus Algerians living in France, who associate fresh mint tea with childhood memories and family rituals, display much more neural activity when they smell mint than non-Algerian French who lack the cultural context. The experience of wine drinkers, French or otherwise, depends on background music. *Carmina Burana* makes a glass of cabernet sauvignon seem powerful and heavy, while the "Waltz of the Flowers" from *The Nutcracker* makes the same vintage seem subtle and refined. A pricey label does wonders for the taste of $5 plonk, an effect that can be measured in imaging scans of the tasters' reward circuitry—and in the compliments of dinner-party guests who believe they are sipping high-end Napa cabernet.[7]

Set and setting are also central to the placebo effect. Familiar therapeutic rituals can stimulate the release of neurotransmitters in a patient's brain, affecting mood and improving immune response. Because our brains learn to anticipate, and through anticipation to activate the endorphin, endocannabinoid, dopamine, and other neurotransmitter systems, the process does not require an actual substance that biochemically induces specific pleasurable or therapeutic effects. Assuming that the brains of early humans worked in similar fashion to ours, the early history of pleasure entailed making associations as well as stumbling across plant and animal substances containing molecules that mimicked or stimulated the release of neurotransmitters.[8]

Aphrodisiacs offer a convenient illustration. Humans have long prized spices, foods, and animal parts that enhance fertility, desire, and sexual performance. Some aphrodisiacs, like the sweet swayamgupta-seed biscuits touted by the *Kama Sutra* ("It is possible to sleep with thousands of women who, in the end, will ask for pity"), had a direct physiological effect. Controlled studies of *Mucuna pruriens,* the source of the swayamgupta seeds, have demonstrated positive effects on testosterone and sperm motility. But the aphrodisiac properties of other foods were more likely due to suggestion. Avocados grow in dangling pairs. *Ahuacatl,* the Aztec name for the fruit, means "testicle." Their elliptic heft was enough to make them sought-after aphrodisiacs. Virile appearance likewise enhanced the appeal of narwhal tusks, bananas, asparagus, and ginseng, a popular Chinese medicinal herb whose name, *rén shēn* (人参), means "man root." Ginseng worked through both psychology and biochemistry, being suggestive in shape and also suffused with phytoestrogens, which promote libido and penile vasodilation.[9]

Ginseng shows that the power of suggestion, however potent, is not the only reason humans relish certain substances and behaviors. Biology plays its role. When it comes to filling our stomachs, although we can learn to enjoy a variety of plant foods, our preference for sweet ones is innate. Natural selection favored individuals with a preference for sweet foods that, in nature, are more nutritious and less toxic. It is no coincidence that all plant-eating mammal species have a similar preference, or that chimpanzees are as willing to put up with angry bees to get at the honey in their hives as were early humans.[10]

The hunt for new pleasures was guided by biological clues. Whatever social purposes and cultural scaffolding may have come to surround them, plants that stimulated pleasure-inducing and pain-killing neurotransmitters were more likely to be valued, cultivated, and spread. The stronger the effect, the more likely the plants were to catch on. The intensity of remembered pleasure (or pain), especially if it occurs toward the end of an experience, weighs more heavily in the scales of decision making than the duration of the feelings. The principle that we always remember bursts of pleasure is basic to neuroscience, behavioral economics, ethnobotany, and ethology. Animals gorge on intoxicating substances too, even though they have little in the way of set and setting to guide them. The persistent "crop circles" that once puzzled Tasmanian opium poppy farmers turned out to be the perambulations of self-narcotized wallabies.[11]

Humans exploited new pleasure resources in diverse ways. Early Europeans prized poppies for their edible seeds and oils as well as their potent alkaloids. American Indians used tobacco medicines and rituals to treat convulsions, colic, insect and snake bites, toothaches, sores, and a host of other afflictions, including those of their dogs. Sometimes they ate tobacco leaves, baking them into cornbread. They smoked for pleasure and from compulsion; when no tobacco was available, they gnawed on wooden pipe stems and smoked pulverized pipes.[12]

Multiple uses were the norm. The avocado, valued for stimulating erections, also served to treat ear infections. Honey salved wounds, banished wrinkles, and preserved children's corpses, one of which was discovered when a treasure hunter improvidently dipped his bread into a jar of ancient honey that had been found near the Pyramids. Alexander the Great was reputedly coated with honey as he lay in his coffin—having been done in, scholars speculate, by consuming too much of another preservative, alcohol. Cannabis, a sometime intoxicant, provided fiber, edible seeds and oils, and a complex mix of cannabinoids whose healing properties researchers are still unraveling. The modern notion of separate realms for recreational drugs, nutritious foods, and healing medicines does not fit well with how precivilized and preindustrial peoples understood and used these multipurpose resources.[13]

Whatever one calls them—anthropologists prefer "food-drugs"—these resources were not evenly scattered around the globe. Environmental historian and geographer Jared Diamond's influential observation about the unequal distribution of domesticable flora and fauna, which made possible different types of civilization with different potentials for expansion, applies with equal force to the flora and fauna that made possible different pleasure repertoires. It was better luck for some, worse luck for others, and no clean sweep for anyone.[14]

Chocolate, for example, came from fermented, dried, roasted, and ground cacao beans that had originated in the upper Amazon and spread to Mesoamerica. Though they may not have been the first to do so, the Maya and the Aztecs domesticated the cacao tree and learned to make chocolate, a nutritious and stimulating beverage with a bitter taste. They remedied the bitterness by adding wood ash, chili peppers, vanilla, and other spices. The daily fare of emperors and the final meal of sacrificial victims, chocolate became so valued in their cultures that cacao beans served as booty, status markers, and money. And yet, before the Columbian Exchange of plants and animals between the hemispheres, no one outside the American tropics had access to this food-drug resource.[15]

The early history of pleasure is basically the history of chocolate with regional variations. Sugarcane, rich in the sucrose destined to become chocolate's most important additive, was confined to South and Southeast Asia. So were the red jungle fowl that humans hunted and then domesticated as chickens. Natives used their flesh and eggs for food; their bones for divination, sewing, tattooing, and fashioning musical instruments; and their males for cockfighting, an ancient means of sport and gambling. Kola nuts once grew only in West African forests; opium poppies in Europe; cannabis in Central Asia; tea in southwest China; black pepper in South Asia; and so on. It would take the development of agriculture, civilization, and long-distance trade to make such pleasing and useful substances globally available. And it would take centuries of experiments in refining, blending, and processing to make these substances even more rewarding than when curious human migrants took their first, tentative bites.[16]

CULTIVATED PLEASURES

A partial exception to the rule of scattered natural pleasures is ethanol, the food-drug molecule in alcohol. Any place with ripe, bruised fruit has alcohol. Yeast cells, which float freely through the air, settle on the fruit and produce alcohol through anaerobic fermentation of fruit sugars. Alcohol, as Kurt Vonnegut tartly remarked, is yeast excrement, toxic enough at high concentrations to eventually kill the yeast that produces it.[17]

Fermenting fruit attracts a wide range of animals, from fruit flies to moose. Evolutionary biologists have long puzzled over why animals would eat something that, though it yields calories, nutrients, and pleasure, can also cause illness, erratic thinking, and clumsy behavior. Because these three traits decrease fitness, it would seem that alcohol consumption should be selected against.

The likeliest reason that it persisted anyway is *hormesis,* a biological principle that plays an important role in the history of alcohol and drugs and, more broadly, in the history of pleasure, vice, and addiction. The basic idea is simple. Many chemical compounds are nutritious or beneficial in small doses but harmful or lethal in large ones. (The same is true of behaviors, like gambling, that are harmless pastimes when sporadic but otherwise when habitual.) David Carr, a celebrated journalist, explained alcoholic hormesis in personal terms. "Drink a lot all the time, and your innards will swell up, giving you the look of a pear with legs, and if organ failure doesn't get you, your esophagus might bleed out, or you could just pull a lamebrained move like blacking out and face-planting for good."[18]

The likelihood that Carr or any other drunk will face-plant depends, in part, on the availability of alcohol, a rule that holds for all pleasurable substances whose risks rise with dose. William McGrew, a biological anthropologist, pointed out that hormesis applies to alcohol and alcoholism in the same way that overconsumption of salt applies to hypertension, or sugar to diabetes, or saturated fats to coronary disease. "In all cases," he wrote, "a substance rare in nature has become readily accessible in unnatural conditions, usually as a by-product of the agricultural domestication of plants and animals, or of industrial technology. We humans over-indulge in ethanol ingestion because we have become brewers, vintners, and distillers. Thus, cultural evolution in hominids has taken us from wine to beer to spirits."[19]

It may also have been the other way around—that the quest to consume alcohol inspired cultural evolution. Anthropologists have long disputed the causes of the Neolithic Transition, the piecemeal process of domesticating plants and animals that began more than eleven thousand years ago. The debate comes down to whether convenience or necessity was the mother of invention. Some scholars have stressed pull factors, such as greater food security and more convenience for hunter-gatherers, who had to forage widely for wild foods. Others have stressed push factors, such as mounting population pressure and deteriorating climate. A third possibility, debated since 1953, is that humans cultivated cereal crops less for processing into starchy foods (grits, mush, bread) than for making beer, a beverage at once nutritious, intoxicating, and germ-free. The carbohydrates in the seeds of a grass like barley could be converted to yeast-digestible malt sugar by soaking, germinating, and drying them. Agriculture would have been a way—some think the only way—to ensure a year-round supply of malt for brewing. Domesticating yeast made sense for the same reason. DNA analysis shows that domesticated yeast strains are at least as old as domesticated grain.[20]

The beer-before-bread hypothesis has been complemented by another: competitive feasting. Would-be chieftains used alcohol, according to this theory, to attract people to feasts that created reciprocal debts, reinforced collective beliefs and hierarchies, strengthened social bonds, and, not least, introduced new foods and technologies. Feasts were one part political rally, one part fraternity bash, and one part product launch. They required forethought and advanced preparation. In the Levant and Mesopotamia, where agriculture first emerged, that meant growing and storing sufficient grain for brewing. Festival resources developed elsewhere—rice wine in China, say, or tobacco and cacao in the Americas—would have been subject to the same plan-ahead thinking. As for maize, "Native Americans were drinking corn before they began eating it."[21]

If feasting encouraged agricultural inventiveness, it also altered rank and status. The leader who threw the biggest party called the shots. This social dynamic, according to Greg Wadley, a cognitive scientist, and Brian Hayden, an archeologist, helps to explain why inequality emerged along with agriculture. (Settling in one place does not, by itself, account for social classes. Some hunter-gatherers became sedentary without developing complex hierarchies, while some nomadic pastoralists produced warlords and emperors.) As agricultural societies grew more unequal, alcohol and other food-drugs took on a second but no less vital role as compensation for those who did the onerous work of husbandry. They provided temporary relief from stress, fatigue, anxiety, and the diseases endemic to agricultural societies. They offered, fleetingly, a sense of release, relaxation, solidarity, and pleasure.[22]

Tools for aggrandizers, sops for losers; here again we see the two-sidedness of cultivated pleasures. For all their nutritional, medicinal, and psychic benefits, alcohol and other food-drugs came with snares. In Darwinian terms they signaled, falsely, that they would generate a large fitness benefit: Something this good must be really good for me. They reinforced the importance of, and therefore the need to show deference to, rituals and people associated with the pleasurable experience. That is, they actively *affected* set and setting, as well as being subjectively experienced *through* them. And they fostered a craving for repeated use that induced peasants to keep producing the surpluses that fueled emergent civilizations and allowed rulers the means to stay on top. Biologically, none of this should be surprising. Being always and everywhere linked to motivation, pleasure is always and everywhere prone to exploitation.

That said, beer parties do seem inadequate as an explanation for civilization. Wadley and Hayden readily acknowledged that other motives, like the quest for better nutrition, also played a role in the Neolithic Transition. That transition was, in any event, a ragged affair. It played out at different times and among scattered peoples with varied technologies who faced a range of climates and environments. Barring time travel, reconstructing the motives and tactics of the founders of any early agricultural community must entail an element of speculation.[23]

What happened after agricultural societies became well established is more certain. Plants that contributed to human pleasure were dispersed quickly, often more quickly than staple foods. Thus tobacco, a labor-intensive, soil-depleting crop, competed successfully for arable land with nutritious fare like maize in the Americas or, after the Columbian Exchange, millet in Africa or rice in Asia. Tobacco exemplifies what the archeologist Ian Hodder has called the human entanglement with things, and what the historian Yuval Noah Harari has called, more simply, the luxury trap. "One of history's few iron laws," Harari wrote, "is that luxuries tend to become necessities and to spawn new obligations. Once people get used to a certain luxury, they take it for granted. Then they began to count on it. Then they can't live without it."[24]

From the standpoint of plant species, luxury traps guaranteed their reproductive success. Being unable to live without them, humans propagated desirable plants widely. (They likewise domesticated and propagated animals with succulent meat, sweet milk, soft wool, and plow-pulling muscle—the difference being that sentient creatures paid for their species' success with unnatural confinement, mutilation, and early slaughter.) Desirable plants snared humans with four lures: pleasure, beauty, intoxication, and ease of control. Sweetness and cider, observed the food historian Michael Pollan, spawned the world's apple orchards. Gorgeous flowers inspired manicured tulip fields. A capacity to produce stoned reveries led to the development of new strains of resin-rich cannabis plants. And cheap protein, vitamins, and carbohydrates accounted for the planting of millions of acres of potatoes, a tractable plant that began as food for peasants and ended as French fries. Artificial selection for desirable plant (and animal) traits flattened the world's arable landscapes. The pursuit of pleasure and convenience was the enemy of biodiversity.[25]

Plants whose fruits are rich in sugar—date palms, say, or grape vines—were particularly good candidates for dissemination. They provided sweetness, alcohol, and a reliable source of calories and nutrients. But bitter plants with less nutritional value could still succeed as cultivars if they had the right psychoactive alkaloids. Cocaine, from the leaves of the coca bush, is one such alkaloid. Cocaine increases pleasure by slowing the removal of dopamine from synapses in the brain's reward pathways. It diminishes pain by alleviating sensations of hunger and thirst. When the Incas expanded eastward during the fifteenth century, they found suitable soil and climate for the wider cultivation of coca bushes, which did not grow especially well in the imperial homeland. The new plantations expanded both production and royal patronage, coca consumption requiring imperial sanction. Pleasure, once again, became entangled with the means and perquisites of power.[26]

CIVILIZED PLEASURES

As human societies transformed from small family-based bands into agricultural settlements, they became much larger, more sedentary, and more socially complex. They organized labor to plant and tend crops. They developed skilled specialists, such as potters and smiths, and exclusive groups, such as clans. They acquired elites who presided over the centralized collection and distribution of resources, a portion of which they devoted to communal buildings and to ceremonies and feasts. They bartered with outsiders over considerable distances. Indians at Cahokia, a large Mississippian settlement near present-day East St. Louis, traded several hundred miles south to acquire yaupon holly leaves, which they used to make a caffeinated drink for purification rituals. Indians in northeast Florida who supplied these same leaves acquired copper ornaments from as far away as Appalachia and the Upper Midwest.[27]

Better known to archeologists is the experience of the Sumerian-speaking peoples of Mesopotamia. By five thousand years ago, they had developed large-scale civilizations with walled cities; plow- and irrigation-based agriculture; bronze implements; a system of writing (including the first known word for alcohol and the first beer recipe); and regular trade by cart and watercraft. Overseeing this activity were urban-based scribes, managers, merchants, warriors, and priests, who consumed a growing share of the agricultural surplus and virtually all of the imported luxury goods. The civilizations that subsequently emerged in Eurasia, Africa, and the Americas were similarly stratified. The lower classes paid rents and taxes, either by sharing crops or by their labor. In exchange, they got a measure of protection and the privileges of eating and living—privileges their rulers might revoke at any time. Consensus, the political norm in hunter-gatherer societies, gave way to coercion.[28]

The politics of pleasure were likewise transformed. More than ever, elites, particularly elite males, became the oligarchs of hedonism. The rulers of Near Eastern and Mediterranean civilizations consumed the lion's share of choice meats and wine and aromatic incense. A portion of the luxuries they savored accompanied them to the afterlife. One Phrygian burial mound, discovered in Turkey in 1957, contained the remains of King Gordios. He was the father of King Midas and nearly as rich. His skeleton reclined on dyed textiles in a cedar coffin surrounded by bronze ornaments, inlaid furniture, and ornamental jars and cauldrons. The sediments revealed a lavish funerary banquet: a spicy stew of lentils and sheep or goat meat, deboned and marinated in honey, wine, and olive oil before being barbecued. Gordios's mourners washed it down with a punch made from grape wine, barley beer, and honey mead.[29]

Elite males enjoyed sexual, as well as gustatory, privileges. King Alyattes of Lydia topped his monumental tomb with five phallic columns, one built by prostitutes. Augustus Caesar preferred virgins. His adopted stepson, Tiberius, vented his lust on anyone, including infants. Most rulers preferred courtesans, beautiful women skilled in repartee and the erotic arts.[30]

Although elites enjoyed preferential access to all manner of pleasures, they did not monopolize them. Vineyard expansion put wine within reach of Roman plebeians by 30 AD, if not earlier. Those who lived in cities and towns drank in taverns, where cheap meals and a tryst with a prostitute could also be arranged. In Rome and other imperial cities, taverns provided refuge from the *insulae,* teeming tenements that lined streets filled with clattering wagons and cursing draymen. The din, it was said, killed men for want of sleep. Exhausted workers consoled themselves with tavern food, drink, and dice games. Emperors and aristocrats (the only people in Rome, Juvenal tells us, who got any rest) took exception to tavern dicing on the grounds that it led to drunken brawls and criminal mischief—that it was a destructive vice. The charge was true but hypocritical, as elites themselves loved to gamble. The emperor Claudius fitted his carriage with a board so that he could gamble while traveling. A satirical skit, attributed to Seneca the Younger, had Claudius playing on in the afterlife, where the gods condemned him to an eternity of dicing.[31]

High-born or low-born, men did most of the carousing in Rome and other ancient cities. Drinking enhanced men's stature. In the wrong circumstances, it diminished women's. A nursing woman drinking beer at home was a good mother. An intoxicated woman drinking wine in a tavern was a whore. Gender roles acted as a brake on consumption—for women. So did class—for plebeians. The wine rations of Roman soldiers and slaves were cut with water. Only the wealthy could afford a regular diet of rich food and heavy, sweetened wine, quaffed from silver goblets and foaming conch shells. Small wonder gout became the signature disease of obese, sedentary elites. Podagra, gout of the foot, appeared early in Egyptian and Greek medical texts and proved a reliable source of income for physicians who catered to wealthy patients. Their ministrations demonstrated an enduring principle: The sorrows of excess could be turned to profit.[32]

Another general principle comes to light during this period: Advances in technology, just like advances in husbandry, increased the variety and sophistication of pleasures. Take gambling paraphernalia. Gambling in tribal societies was widespread but rudimentary. American Indians cast binary lots, heads-or-tails devices fashioned from sticks, shells, fruit pits, and animal teeth. The Chinese had more options. One tooth-die found in a 2,300-year-old Qi tomb had fourteen carved sides. Players cast it in a game called liubo, which featured ivory pieces and now-forgotten but evidently complex rules. "They advance together; keenly they threaten each other," wrote the poet Song Yu. "Pieces are kinged, and the scoring doubled. Shouts of 'five white!' arise."[33]

Bronze Age dice games of the Near East were simpler. Players cast four-sided astragals, knuckle bones from sheep and goats that had first done duty in stew pots. It was not until the Iron Age that six-sided dice began to supplant astragals. Herodotus credits their invention, along with coinage, to the Lydians, whose kingdom reached its apogee in western Anatolia in the seventh and sixth centuries BC. The Lydians reportedly devised cubical dice, and games to go with them, during a prolonged famine. They played incessantly on alternate fasting days to distract themselves from hunger. Games, it seems, were about more than idle fun. They provided a means of regulating mood and coping with adversity. In a word, they acted like drugs.[34]

Though the rules of many ancient games have been lost, some of the boards on which they were played have survived. These too became more elaborate. One early example, from the royal tombs of Ur, used animal figures to mark off spaces. Twenty-five hundred years later, Romans raced their markers over three rows of thirty-six carved letters, arranged in elaborate, taunting jokes. INVIDA PUNCTA IUBENT FELICE LUDERE DOCTUM, read one. The words reminded clever players that even they needed luck if they were to prevail against the grudging dice.[35]

The geography of pleasure was, in its own way, the ultimate throw of the dice. Mesoamericans lacked sheep and goats and many other domestic animals good for eating or making astragals. They lacked cocks for fighting and horses for racing. Yet, about 3,500 years ago, they took one of their own resources, rubber, fashioned it into balls, and devised fast-paced team games played in ornate, I-shaped courts. Game days were occasions of ritual, sport, and wagering. Spectators and players alike bet on the outcome, sometimes with their lives. Here again was *Homo sapiens*'s most characteristic pleasure resource: The ability to invent, using whatever materials were at hand, absorbing pastimes governed by abstract rules and rituals that sprang from their fertile imaginations.[36]

DISCIPLINED PLEASURES

When we think about pleasure, we often think about intense, sensuous, and disturbing forms rather than commonplace varieties like conversation, music, and problem-solving. A focus on the origins of commercial vice and mass addiction inevitably aggravates this tendency. To redress the bias, and to broach the question of what counts as socially acceptable pleasure, let me here consider some of civilization's more subtle contributions to the repertoire of human enjoyment.[37]

A good place to begin is "flow." People experience a flow state when they are absorbed in a challenging task. They are serenely oblivious to everyday cares, even to the passage of time. They are clear about what needs to be done and confident in their ability to do it. Freed from anxiety and boredom, they find the flow state intrinsically rewarding. The greater the skill and the more demanding the task, the more intense the reward.

Surgeons find difficult operations "gratifying," "aesthetically pleasing," and "fun." The catch is that achieving flow requires intensive effort, even pain. Beginning with Epicurus (341–271 BC), philosophers have observed that, while pleasure may always be good and pain bad, we should not necessarily prefer the former when considering our long-term interests. Do you want to become a professional musician? That will require the equivalent of four hours of daily effort for seven years, with "deliberate practice" on tricky passages. Those undertaking recreational activities such as chess and rock climbing can also find flow, though here too ability must be developed by lengthy, diligent practice.[38]

The division of labor inherent to civilized life multiplied opportunities for flow. The cities, transportation, and trade networks that agricultural societies made possible gave masons, carpenters, weavers, accountants, and other specialists a chance to hone their skills. The opportunity came at a price. Illness, injury, or idleness could be devastating, causing skilled laborers to lose the psychic rewards of work as well as income and identity. To a privileged few, civilization also afforded the opportunity to excel in learned vocations. The courtroom orator's reward for a carefully prepared speech, Tacitus wrote, was solid satisfaction. But when he worked up his nerve and launched an extemporaneous flourish, he achieved a peculiarly sweet joy—which is to say, the happiness of a peak flow experience.[39]

The formal education necessary to develop oratorical skills provided its own opportunities for pleasure. When information sparked into insight, when "hmm" became "aha," students felt a surge of enjoyment that psychologists have called a cognitive orgasm. Although that may be putting it a bit strongly, neuroscientific studies have shown that people enjoy discovering and assigning value to novel abstractions. Insofar as civilization multiplied abstractions and the means of spreading them, it multiplied occasions for such "idea rewards." Admittedly, some new ideas, such as eternal punishment, brought anxiety and suffering. Against such fears, civilized learning produced new opportunities for the pursuit of beauty and knowledge that offered consolation for the sorrows and anxieties of the human condition.[40]

Paradoxically, disciplined movement *away* from abstract thought offered its own rewards. Many civilized religions devised schools of meditation aimed at a common goal: serene alertness in the present moment. *Dhyana yoga,* one of the most ancient forms, took its name from the Sanskrit words meaning to ponder and to integrate. The yogic sense of spontaneous unity and tranquility came from the learned inhibition of distracting mental activity. Stilling racing thoughts required discipline and practice. The *Svetashvatara Unpanishad* likened it to a wise man restraining a chariot pulled by wild horses. Those who doubt the difficulty of this feat are invited to set this book aside and think of nothing for five minutes.[41]

The satisfaction of flow, the thrill of problem-solving, and the tranquility of meditation are all instances of disciplined pleasures. A different order of preparation is necessary to achieve them than to pop into a tavern or a brothel. Many thinkers, from Aristotle to John Stuart Mill, have ranked disciplined pleasures ahead of the baser sort that we share with animals. Philosophical rankings to one side, disciplined pleasures do require the patient development and maintenance of neural networks that extend, often literally, above and beyond the midbrain limbic system. Enjoying literature in a foreign language can take years to acquire and can be lost quickly without practice. Whether ascending or descending the learning curve of a disciplined pleasure, one thing is certain: The activity is far less likely to arouse criticism than are activities, such as consuming intoxicants, that provide fast brain reward.

It is true that some recreational flow states, like deep play at chess, drew clerical fire as worldly distractions. In the early 1660s Trinity College students, Isaac Newton among them, were warned against the time-consuming snares of the "ingenious" game. Nor was the apprehension purely religious. So worldly a novelist as Stefan Zweig later invented the fate of "chess poisoning" for one of his characters. Work flow states, on the other hand, have passed muster in all cultures, being pleasant to the individual and beneficial to others. Whistling engineer, straight aqueduct; meditating monk, tranquil order. Buddhism, based on the belief that freedom from suffering requires freedom from craving, epitomized disciplined opposition to vice. But even in non-Buddhist cultures, a thing did not generally count as a vice—that is, an immoral practice or habit—unless it was bad for the individual, bad for other people, bad for the social order, or some combination of the three.[42]

Addiction—a concept to be unwrapped later—most often manifested itself as an extreme form of vice. Then as now, an addict was someone who had acquired a ruinously bad habit marked by unusually strong craving and loss of control. The earliest literary record of such behavior appears in a Vedic hymn, "The Gambler's Lament." It describes a gambler so far gone as to become intoxicated by the sight of tumbling dice. He loses everything, leaving his family in despair.[43]

A wealth of other evidence, from Han Chinese historical records to American Indian trickster myths, suggests that gambling had an unsavory reputation throughout the ancient world. In no case, however, did every form and occasion of gambling draw reproach. Overindulgence was the problem, and not just for gambling. The Book of Deuteronomy condemned drunkenness and gluttony in the same breath. Public excess drew the most opprobrium. Marc Antony, a notorious sot, ate and drank so much at a wedding feast that he threw up into his toga during a public speech the next morning. Cicero made sure to memorialize the disgrace in his second philippic; Plutarch, in a passage on impudent luxury.[44]

Morally, ancient societies sorted pleasures into three broad categories. Some, like flow, were always or almost always good. Some, like incestuous intercourse, were always or almost always bad. And some occupied the middle ground of hormesis: good in moderation, bad in excess. Arsenic compounds common to India, China, and Europe served as tonics and aphrodisiacs at low doses, but sickened or killed at high. Social judgments of excess entailed common-sense estimates of harm, as well as considerations of age, gender, marital status, class, health, motive, and ritual context. Casting lots for divination was one thing. Casting them for gambling stakes was another. Then there were taboos, which could trump everything else. Moderation or no, beef was off limits for Hindus, pork for Jews and Muslims.[45]

Historical circumstances also affected appraisals of excess. Drinking alcohol seemed more harmful in 1900 AD, when piped-in water was becoming

safer, than in 1900 BC, when village and city water supplies were often contaminated. Prostitution was unregulated in Lydian Anatolia, where single
women of slender means routinely sold sex to raise dowries. It was heavily
regulated in Turkish Anatolia, where early republican officials regarded prostitutes as sources of syphilitic infection subject to inspection and incar-
ceration. If acquiring new knowledge could bring pleasure, it could also
turn people *against* pleasures when it led to recasting them as dangerous
vices. Not coincidentally, anti-vice activism became a global political force
when civilization's next great turn, toward science and industrialization,
brought the world both more enticing pleasures and more knowledge of
their damaging effects.[46]

EXCHANGED PLEASURES

I am getting ahead of the story. Long before factories began spreading pleasures, caravans and caravels went about the same task. Civilization gave
rise to cities, centers of administration, worship, storage, manufacturing,
and trade. The pattern was set early, in Mesopotamia. By 3000 BC Uruk,
the first true city, home of Gilgamesh and of writing, was a walled and
prosperous commercial center of thirty to fifty thousand people. Artisans
worked imported timber, metals, and lapis lazuli from Afghanistan. In
Uruk as in other city-states, elites increased their power and wealth by
expanding territorial control, expanding trade, or both. This dynamic—
intertwined imperial and mercantile ambitions, often reinforced by missionary aspirations—created, over the next five millennia, a convergent
world. Local political and trade networks became regional, then transcontinental, then transoceanic.[47]

The first and greatest of the transcontinental networks was the Silk Road
or, more properly, Roads. A web of east-west and north-south trading routes
running through cities and oases, the Silk Roads formed the commercial
spine and ribs of Eurasia. They connected the Portuguese to the Cantonese,
the Vikings to the Baghdad Caliphate. The volume of trade along the Silk
Roads waxed and waned, depending on the fortunes of a succession of

kingdoms from the Han Dynasty (206 BC to 220 AD) to the Mongol Empire (1206 to 1368). Then, in the 1490s, the voyages of Christopher Columbus to the Americas and of Vasco da Gama to India gave rise to an epochal shift in global trade. New sea routes and trading ports moved the center of communication and commerce—and, with it, power—to western Europe.

While they prospered, Silk Road merchants trafficked in goods of high value relative to weight, along with trade animals that provided their own locomotion. Chinese warriors and polo players rode horses imported from Central Asia. Roman, Persian, and Byzantine elites displayed their status with Chinese silk so fine as to be translucent. Merchandise traveled astonishing distances. An Indian ivory statuette of Lakshmi, the goddess of fertility, wealth, and auspiciousness, found an inauspicious resting place in the ashy ruins of Pompeii. In 79 AD, when Vesuvius buried the goddess, Roman denarii circulated in the bazaars of India. The smell of Indian spices wafted through the kitchens of wealthy Romans. They seasoned their dormice with pepper, adding honey and poppy seeds when serving the delicacies as appetizers.[48]

Poppy seeds could be planted as well as eaten. Poppy cultivation moved east with Arab traders during the seventh and eighth centuries. Precisely when it became widespread in India is uncertain. The first Indian medical reference to poppies does not appear until about the year 1000 AD. Mughal invaders encouraged its cultivation, as did India's European colonizers. The Dutch and the British realized that opium was an ideal trade good, being at once a source of imperial finance, a device for controlling labor, and a means of paying for spices, silk, porcelain, and tea. "In a neat mirror image," wrote the historian Peter Frankopan, "rising addiction to luxury goods in the west was effectively being traded for—and soon matched by—rising addiction to drugs in China."[49]

Trade introduced pleasure ideas as well as pleasure goods. Chess, invented in northwest India sometime before 600 AD, spread to Persia, Arabia, and finally Europe around 1000. As it traveled, chess evolved, reaching its current form in Europe between the late fifteenth and mid-eighteenth centuries. Europe proved equally fertile ground for the evolution of card games, which originated in Korea and China and filtered west along the trade

Paul Cézanne's *Les joueurs de cartes* (1890–1892) can be read as an allegory of the conflu-
ence of the world's pleasures. The card players of the title were laborers on Cézanne's
father's estate near Aix, and the scene seems quintessentially French. Yet the playing
cards descended from Korean and Chinese inventions, the tobacco in the pipes came
from plants native to the Americas, and the playing board (possibly backgammon)
originated from race games of Ancient Mesopotamia. Even the usual contents of the
olive jar (*upper left corner*) came from trees that once grew only in Asia Minor. The
players' concentration and the tavern-like setting hint at gambling for an undisclosed
stake.

routes. Playing cards, well suited to gambling because they offered more
combinatorial possibilities than dice, became more common in Europe after
the fifteenth-century advent of block printing. They underwent repeated
refinements, notably in France, home of the modern card deck and the earliest forms of piquet, baccarat, and blackjack.[50]

Trade and travel also spread techniques for intensifying pleasure. Concentration and distillation, two key processes, arose from observing that

alcohol and other substances did not freeze or boil at the same temperature as water. In 290, the scholar Zhang Hua reported that China's cold
western regions produced a long-lasting grape wine of unusual potency
("one will not get over one's drunkenness for days"), a likely reference
to a freeze-concentrated brandy. Cold spells led, inevitably, to similar
discoveries. The unfrozen portion of mead or fermented cider was rich
in alcohol, up to 66 proof. Hard cider production was one reason why
European farmers were keen on planting orchards when they migrated
to the temperate zones of North America. Because orchards require pol-
lination, they brought along honeybees to regions where they had not
already swarmed.[51]

These same pioneers knew how to distill fruit wines into brandy. In the
early Middle Ages European alchemists and physicians learned that vapors
from alcohol, which boiled at a lower temperature than water, could be
condensed into spirits, each distilling cycle increasing their strength. Most
distilling was for medical purposes. Spirits were *aqua vitae,* the water of
life. Some clerics also thought them the water of the devil, distilling being
linked to alchemy, and alchemy to magic. Not until the end of the fifteenth
century were apothecaries and physicians generally free to distill and prescribe medicinal spirits. They often combined them with medicinal herbs
and spices. The theory was that, if the essence of one food-drug was good,
the essences of several were better. Insofar as more-is-better acted as a
placebo, they were probably right.

Their problem—in the end, everyone's problem—was the impossibility
of keeping distilled spirits in a therapeutic box. The higher the proof, the
greater the brain reward. Though officials initially tried to restrict consumption to small medicinal doses, the spirits revolution proved irresistible,
particularly in the colder regions of Europe and Russia, where viticulture
was impractical and people preferred whiskey and vodka to the weak *kvass*
fermented from black bread and rancid fruit. Distilling being an idea,
not a thing, it spread quickly through the new technology of printing. Sec-
ondary diffusion occurred when illiterate widows and artisans learned by
watching established distillers, and then entering the trade on the sly. By

the end of the seventeenth century European governments had thrown in the regulatory towel. They taxed spirits regardless of end use, a precedent that gave both the state and the distillers a stake in rising consumption.[52]

And rise consumption did. Brandy exports from Sète, a port in southern France, shot up from 2,250 hectoliters (roughly 60,000 gallons) in 1698 to 65,926 hectoliters (1.74 million gallons) in 1755. As the historian Fernand Braudel put it, the spirits revolution was born in the sixteenth century, consolidated in the seventeenth century, and popularized in the eighteenth century. Nor did this happen only in Europe. Mexicans learned to make mezcal, Pacific Islanders coconut brandy. Whaling crews on liberty partook with enthusiasm.[53]

Knowledge of smoking traveled the other way, from indigenous Americans to Europeans. The idea that one could enjoy inhaling gases from burning drugs was controversial and startling. So startling, in fact, that one of Sir Walter Raleigh's servants doused him with ale, thinking his face ablaze. Smoking conquered Eurasia in the seventeenth and eighteenth centuries, despite clerics who railed against "dry drunkenness" and monarchs who staged exemplary executions. Its attraction is fast, repeated brain reward: inhaled nicotine reaches the pleasure circuits in about fifteen seconds, with one puff soon following another. Smoking is an efficient form of learning, like shaping an animal's behavior with small, frequent treats rather than one large treat at the end of a long training session.[54]

As smoking spread, different cultures devised different equipment, such as water pipes, and different blends, such as tobacco mixed with cannabis, opium, sugar, honey, licorice, cinnamon, or perfume. Well into the twentieth century British sailors sprinkled grog onto tobacco to make the smoke richer and more aromatic. The Maori reversed the process. They added tobacco to their alcohol, which they also flavored with human urine. "Generally speaking Maori home brews are palatable and potent as long as one is oblivious of the content," an Auckland psychiatrist observed. But that was his set and setting talking. For the Maori, knowledge of the customary ingredients would have enhanced the drink's taste and strength. It was just one of a thousand ways that local cultures modified, multiplied, and intensified the new pleasures that merchants and imperialists spread throughout the world.[55]

The culinary revolution triggered by the Columbian Exchange is a classic instance of what has been called glocalization (globalization plus localization). Local cooks took ingredients that had originated on the other side of the world and turned them into dishes and products that suited their tastes and became identified with their own lands. Indian curries contained Mexican chilies, Italian tomato sauce the fruits of native Andean plants. Jamaican punch was laced with rum made from sugarcane transplanted by Europeans. Later, during the nineteenth and twentieth centuries, trade and immigration created a culinary rebound. Glocal creations became global fare. Today it is a dull city where curries, pizzas, and rum punches are not somewhere on offer, often with further refinements reflecting local tastes and ingredients.

The centuries after the Columbian Exchange are sometimes called the Homogenocene, the age of homogenizing. Trade and transplantation blended the world's flora and fauna, making once-distinctive environments more alike. The same fate that befell food-drug crops befell processed goods sold in cafés and confectionaries. The neighborhood apothecary (a word that originally meant "depot," and which came to mean "pharmaceutical dispensary" because of the volume of the drug trade) became increasingly standardized. By the eighteenth century the contents of a physician's medicine chest in Boston differed little from one in Berlin or Belgrade.[56]

Yet the homogenization was never perfect or complete. Experimentation with new pleasures proceeded from bottom up as well as top down. Later, as limbic capitalism assumed a corporate form, top-down innovation dominated or co-opted bottom-up innovation. Steve Jobs, not the local tinkerer, introduced the Next Big Thing. But there was still plenty of room for amateur fiddling. Cannabis growers selected strains for long fibers, oil-rich seeds, or psychoactive resin, depending on local priorities and cultural predispositions. In Afghanistan, cultivators learned how to roll, crush, and sift ripe buds into pure, extremely fine hashish. In Mexico, the innovators were natives who, away from the prying eyes of priests and officials, developed the intoxicating strains of *Cannabis sativa* that we now call marijuana.[57]

People also concocted novel uses for imported goods, which lent themselves to blending as readily as did novel food-drugs. One eighteenth-century samurai sported a *jinbaori,* or armor surcoat, made of Chinese lampas, silk, and gilt-paper strips; European dress fabric brocaded with silver thread; and imported wool dyed scarlet. Dutch and British chemists had devised the mordant that fixed the cochineal dye, which was made by Mexican peasants from the ground carcasses of cactus-eating insects. That samurai carried an interwoven world on his proud shoulders.[58]

MONETIZED PLEASURES

The samurai may also have carried a good deal of debt. By the eighteenth century elites typically acquired luxury goods through credit or cash. Barter was increasingly confined to the fringes of the imperial system. Spirits fetched furs from North American Indians and dog teams from eastern Siberians. Gin and tobacco bought Europeans the rights to fish for trepang in Yolngu waters off northern Australia. But in North Africa and Eurasia the prizes of long-distance trade were more likely to be denominated in *dinars, reals,* and other coins of known value.

Monetized commerce helps to explain several developments, starting with the adulteration of pleasure goods. Merchants often boosted their profits by mixing ordinary food with the likes of chalk or clay. But in the lucrative market for drugs, spices, and aphrodisiacs, which might command their weight in gold, cheating was an overwhelming temptation. In theory, middlemen could have used debased or bogus money to acquire such valuable goods. But that was risky, counterfeiters meeting the same fate as traitors. (In England, they were burned at the stake.) Unless one happened to be a sovereign, it was far safer to cheat the buyer by diluting the merchandise with plaster, alum, or another easily blended adulterant.

The extent to which dilution reduced buyers' pleasure and benefit is an open question, as expectation accounted for at least some of the desired

action. A good medieval cook, "halfe a physycyon," might still work therapeutic magic with adulterated ingredients. Pepper and cinnamon were aphrodisiacs of such repute that confessors asked penitents whether they had
sinned by "spysory." We may suppose that spices were arousing despite a
generous admixture of bone ash and ground nutshells. Suppose, but not
be certain. The only certainty is that the historical record is full of exposés
of good money paid for bad food-drugs.[59]

Adulterated or not, food-drugs became cheaper in money-based economies. Money simplified exchange, multiplied incomes through spending,
made possible banking and credit, and financed the mercantile ventures
and overseas plantations of the early modern European empires. The inter-
twining of capitalism and imperialism, to which were soon added science
and industry, inexorably increased the flow of luxury goods, until they were
no longer luxuries at all. In Shakespeare's England two pounds of sugar-
preserved fruit sold for a sum that would admit a groundling to sixty of
his plays. A century later, in 1700, English men and women consumed an
average of four pounds of sugar a year. By 1800 the figure had increased to
eighteen pounds, much of it spooned into tea that had once been the preserve
of the wealthy. Germans preferred coffee, which, by 1743, could be found in
all but the smallest towns. In Ireland the consumption of spirits, particularly whiskey, rose 750 percent during the eighteenth century, while the
population increased by only 50 percent. No place in Europe was without
tobacco. Chesapeake tobacco exports, around 50,000 pounds in 1620, rose
to 100,000,000 pounds annually in the 1770s. Meanwhile the farm price
declined from more than ten pence to just two pence per pound.[60]

The price declines of tobacco and other commodities did not begin immediately. From the 1540s to the 1640s, Spain's New World mines brought prolonged inflation as a flood of silver coins washed through markets, counting
houses, banks, and tax offices from Amsterdam to Fujian. Landless peasants
starved for want of the price of bread, let alone sugar. Yet the same silver
influx stimulated the trade for Asian luxury goods, especially from China,
where silver, which circulated as currency, was the one Western import in
high demand. (Hence the later expedient of "growing" silver, i.e., using

opium instead of specie to resolve the balance-of-payments problem.) In Europe the inflation finally abated in the second half of the seventeenth century. During the eighteenth century the increased volume of trade, particularly in food-drugs, brought once-exotic goods within reach of ordinary people, with revolutionary consequences for the way they experienced the world.[61]

Finally, money and the enlarged scope of commerce changed the way people thought about social restraints, including those against selling harmful or addictive products. Moral and religious proscriptions had seldom been perfectly enforced. They nevertheless exerted more force in local, face-to-face economies than in monetized, globalizing economies where one could profit by selling unseen goods to unseen people in unseen lands. Money was the ultimate example of the luxury trap. This Lydian invention became increasingly indispensable both as a medium of exchange and as the means of building transactional trust between distant strangers. However, the trust was not invested in those strangers, or in any person. It was instead invested in the money itself and in all that it could acquire, even if the acquisitions came at the cost of the ruin of others. Limbic capitalism— whose outlines began rounding into view during the late seventeenth and eighteenth centuries—was, at bottom, the snapping shut of the jaws of this particular trap.[62]

2

MASS PLEASURES

In 1899 a fashionable French writer named Pierre Louÿs published "A New Pleasure," a story about an Ancient Greek courtesan who haunts Paris after the Louvre acquires her funerary monument. One night Callisto, as the heroine is called, encounters a poet. She complains to him about all the drab houses and all the dull Parisians, none of whom surpass her in learning, beauty, or erotic charms. She proves her point by taking the poet to bed. Two millennia have brought no hedonic refinement, Callisto proclaims. Modern joys pale beside her fondly remembered pleasures.

Then the poet offers Callisto a cigarette. "Art thou also one of those who indulge in this ridiculous exercise?" she asks. "Sixty times a day," he replies. Curious, she inhales the smoke. She falls silent. She cradles the pack in her hand. Then "slowly, with the care one bestows upon the most precious objects," she places it by her recumbent body.[1]

A devotee of nicotine and, in his later years, of morphine, cocaine, and champagne, Louÿs died, at age fifty-five, a few moments after his wife reportedly lit for him one last cigarette. His epitaph might have been "died of new pleasures." Indeed, his story about Callisto, set in the year 1893, could have demonstrated the Belle Époque's new pleasures in any number of ways. Instead of offering her a cigarette, the narrator might have taken Callisto on a tour of the Bon Marché. With lavish displays of Oriental rugs, perfumes, taffeta gowns, and apparel for every leisure outing, the world's premier department store had fashioned itself into a bourgeois consumer paradise. For those who wanted more than shopping, the management offered operatic concerts, buffet dining with wines and sweet treats, and beefsteak roasted in a kitchen that turned out five thousand meals a day.[2]

Had the narrator ventured from pleasure's upper world to its lower, he might have taken Callisto to one of Paris's hundreds of *cafés-concerts,* smoky nightspots where exotic drinks, hot music, high-stepping dancers, brusque comedy, and back-room trysts were all on the menu. He might have taken her to the Moulin Rouge and introduced her to Henri de Toulouse-Lautrec, a regular who gained fame with his lithograph of Louise Weber, the star can-can dancer who performed with transparent knickers. As Weber danced, Toulouse-Lautrec might have offered Callisto a glass of sugared absinthe. Consumption of this mass-produced, mildly hallucinogenic liquor had nearly tripled in a decade. Had the painter chosen to offer her something less commonplace, he might have mixed one of his designer cocktails, concoctions so potent as to lay out fellow artists like Édouard Vuillard and Pierre Bonnard. Had he taken a fancy to Callisto—Toulouse-Lautrec was a lady's man afflicted with syphilis and alcoholism—he might have taken the courtesan to visit his friend Paul Sescau, a photographer adept at sensuous portraiture. By 1893 Paris was the world's center of erotic photography and home to a thriving pornography industry.

Movies debuted in Paris in 1895, courtesy of Auguste and Louis Lumière, who filmed workers leaving their factory in Lyon. Less innocent movies debuted in Paris just one year later, courtesy of Eugène Pirou and Albert Kirchner, who filmed actress Louise Willy disrobing on her fictive wedding night. *Le Coucher de la Mariée* caused such a sensation that Pirou and Kirchner exhibited their film in several locations, including the Casino in Nice. Budding cinema legends Georges Méliès, who pioneered film advertising, and Charles Pathé, who later boasted of industrializing the cinema, clambered aboard the striptease bandwagon. Their efforts launched a new genre of risqué films, *scènes grivoises d'un caractère piquant*—saucy scenes of a spicy character.[3]

Exotic or tame, the pleasures of Belle Époque Paris were promoted and democratized in ways unimaginable a century before. Everywhere Parisians looked they saw ads, from stencils on asphalt to billboards on rooftops. Many billboards offered the services of photographers. Their guild had prospered since midcentury, thanks to the demand for *cartes de visite,* inexpensive albumen prints mounted on small cards. By the 1890s it was the turn of illustrated magazines, which benefited from cheap paper and halftone photographs that cost a fraction of wood engravings. In July 1889 the first color halftones, depicting the recently completed Eiffel Tower, graced *Paris Illustré.* Those wishing to ponder the monument over a glass had not far to turn. By the late 1880s Paris had thirty thousand drink shops, ten times as many as during the 1789 revolution. Many were new American-style bars, complete with zinc counters and an array of alcoholic drinks.[4]

In 1926 one of the denizens of those bars, the expatriate writer Ernest Hemingway, published *The Sun Also Rises.* Among the novel's several alcoholic characters was Mike Campbell, a Scot who explained that he went bankrupt in two ways: "Gradually and then suddenly." The same words describe how humans expanded their pleasure repertoire. Though they had been discovering, inventing, refining, and trading pleasures for millennia, a true mass market did not develop until about 1660 to 1800, the long eighteenth century of pleasure. With further advances in science and industry and related changes in technology and urbanization, the pace of pleasure's democratization quickened again in the nineteenth and twentieth centuries. Even the poorest quarter of Louÿs's or Hemingway's Paris had its morning racing papers and smoky cafés selling plonk by the liter. Those of more substantial means could serve their guests at home, pouring fruit-scented liqueurs from cut-glass decanters.[5]

Social historians have asked when and how people outside the upper classes became consumers committed to "the acquisition, display, and enjoyment of goods and commercial services clearly not necessary to subsistence." Their collective verdict is that, in the West, consumerism developed well before the Industrial Revolution, during the seventeenth and eighteenth centuries. The German provincials who, in 1743, proudly drank their coffee from porcelain cups were already consumers. The subsequent development of factories, cities, department stores, and advertising simply created more of them. Though the history of pleasure is distinct from, and obviously older than, the history of consumerism, it is no coincidence that the pace of both quickened at the same time.[6]

The pace quickened further with the advent of industrialization in the late eighteenth and nineteenth centuries. Beginning in England and soon thereafter in the rest of Europe, North America, and Japan, entrepreneurs and governments exploited breakthroughs in science, technology, energy, and finance to revolutionize manufacturing, transportation, and communication. Fast-growing cities became centers of mass production and consumption as well as migration, administration, and trade. The trouble was that these same cities became hotbeds of vice and addiction, even as the flow of goods from their factories and warehouses homogenized the world's hedonic landscape.

STEAMY PLEASURES

In his autobiography, the American writer Samuel Clemens, better known as Mark Twain, described his uncle's country store in Florida, Missouri, the hamlet where Clemens had been born in 1835. The store was a modest affair. The shelves held a few rolls of calico. The counters displayed salt, mackerel, coffee, gunpowder, shot, and cheese. Behind the counters were barrels of New Orleans sugar and molasses and native corn liquor, conveniently tapped. "If a boy bought five or ten cents' worth of anything," Clemens remembered, "he was entitled to half a handful of sugar from the barrel; if a woman bought a few yards of calico she was entitled to a spool of thread in addition to the usual gratis 'trimmins'; if a man bought a trifle, he was at liberty to draw and swallow as big a drink of whisky as he wanted." If he fancied cigars, he could have those at thirty cents a hundred. "But most people did not try to afford them, since smoking a pipe cost nothing in that tobacco-growing country."[7]

Though eastern Missouri had rich soil and ample rainfall, the bounty in that country store had to do with more than bumper crops. Without the steamboats that young Clemens would one day pilot, the coffee, sugar, and molasses could not have been cheaply shipped against the Mississippi

River's current. Between 1815 and 1860, upriver transportation costs plummeted at least tenfold, downriver costs fourfold. The national market that resulted made it possible for Missouri stores to sell cotton cloth manufactured in Massachusetts.[8]

The lagniappe whiskey was likely of local origin. But its cost had likewise dropped, so much so that whiskey had long since replaced rum as the national tipple. Innovations like the perpetual still, which used heat exchange and continuous mash feeding to save fuel and labor, and steam distilling, which provided rapid, even heating, made better whiskey and more of it. As early as 1823 still makers, who had beaten a path to the U.S. Patent Office, boasted of gallon-per-bushel yields two or three times greater than those possible a generation before. Practically the only thing they had not changed was the use of oak barrels, which improved the flavor of aging whiskey. But even that venerable tradition fell prey to cost-cutters later in the century. So-called rectifiers "aged" their raw spirits with burnt sugar, prune juice, sulfuric acid, cochineal, ammonium sulfate, and other ingredients of deceptive color and taste.[9]

Distillers everywhere found ways to economize. Mexicans traditionally roasted agave, the base material for pulque, mezcal, and tequila, in underground pits. In the late nineteenth century they met the growing demand by building brick kilns, later replaced with locomotive-size steam autoclaves. Elsewhere local innovations, such as charcoal filtering, and imported technologies, such as equipment to heat mash, produced improved beverages at lower cost. The results were especially dramatic in Russia. There indentured peasants harvested base materials for a pittance, then paid one hundred times or more the production cost for the privilege of drinking heavily taxed spirits. It was arguably history's most corrupt and enduring system of intoxication-based exploitation.[10]

During the nineteenth century it became common to speak of "industrial" beverages, like gin or vodka, and "natural" beverages, like wine or beer. The distinction was somewhat artificial, especially after vintners began pasteurizing their wine and brewers began bottling their beer. But we know what contemporaries meant. The big story—and the big worry—was the flood of spirits pouring from mechanized distilleries. Between 1824 and 1874 the English population increased by 88 percent. Beer sales rose by 92 percent, roughly the same pace. But domestic spirits sales rose 237 percent, foreign spirits 152 percent, and wine 250 percent.[11]

The last two statistics, for imported spirits and wine, also reflect the diminished cost of shipping. Commodities that had been local or regional, like beet sugar, became global during the last four decades of the nineteenth century. Steel ships docked in Hamburg, unloaded tropical cash crops, took on mountains of refined beet sugar made with German chemical know-how and Polish labor, and set sail through the Suez Canal for India and China. Among the first civilizations to incorporate cane sugar into their pharmacopeias and cuisines, the Indians and Chinese effectively became the targets of European sucrose dumping.[12]

Between 1830 and 1880 transatlantic shipping costs dropped by half. By 1914 they had dropped by half again. Average steamship size and speed doubled during the second half of the nineteenth century. By the early twentieth century, five-day Atlantic crossings were routine. William Halsted, a dandified American surgeon, sent his dress shirts to Paris for proper laundering. Gossip had it that Pandit Motilal Nehru, father of the future Indian prime minister, used the Suez Canal to do the same. Less fastidious sorts filled steamships with gin and dispatched them to African colonies. Between 1900 and 1910 spirits imports rose over 50 percent in the Gold Coast, over 100 percent in southern Nigeria.[13]

In regions without ports or rivers, steam locomotives sped the flow of goods and passengers, simultaneously tightening the metropolis's control and feeding its growing appetite for luxuries. In 1926 H. G. Wells described Provençal peasants chopping down olive trees and throwing their twisted boughs into crackling fires:

> All these peasants seem to be giving up their olives for jasmin, and they are growing that for the perfume factories in Grasse which serve the transitory, unstable world of luxury in Paris and London and New York. A change of fashion in scent, or some ingenuity of the chemist,

may abolish the profits of this flower-growing, and then these hillsides will know trouble; for olive-trees that are gone are gone for ever. . . . The fate of this countryside, which looks so self-subsisting, is I perceive dependent upon the great consuming centres; those little hidden railways are like suckers from the urban fungi that have drained away all local autonomy. The rural life here has been insidiously and secretly and completely subjugated by Paris.

Though not as subjugated, one might add, as the exhausted Vietnamese who gathered rubber for the fat-tired cars of rich Parisians who motored through Grasse en route to Nice. In a still-colonized world linked by steam, steel, and cable, the tropics remained a vast storehouse to be ransacked for the pleasure of its masters.[14]

In *The Economic Consequences of the Peace* (1919), John Maynard Keynes contrasted the small-continent Europe of 1870, a collection of more-or-less self-subsistent national economies, with the global Europe of August 1914. In the new Europe, Keynes wrote, the middle and upper classes could enjoy "at a low cost and with the least trouble, conveniences, comforts, and amenities beyond the compass of the richest and most powerful monarchs of other ages. The inhabitant of London could order by telephone, sipping his morning tea in bed, the various products of the whole earth, in such quantity as he might see fit, and reasonably expect their early delivery upon his doorstep." Should he wish to travel, he could easily secure "cheap and comfortable means of transit to any country or climate without passport or other formality," or even knowledge of local language or customs, ready cash being sufficient to answer his needs.[15]

Keynes's European golden age of 1870–1914 represented the first stage of modern globalization, which resumed in the late twentieth century after an interregnum of war, revolution, depression, and more war. Both phases of globalization fostered the spread of vice. Borders were permeable, contraband concealable. One French firm advertised that, "in discreet cases," German physicians and druggists might receive by mail that which they could not otherwise obtain. A German doctor inquired whether the

euphemism included morphine. Yes, came the reply. When no order followed, he received a second letter. It offered the drug at half price.[16]

Globalization democratized many less controversial goods. Singapor-
eans shipped canned pineapples; Italians, sardines. Pastimes rode the same
global wave. In 1907 Hawaiian-born George Freeth Jr. gave the visiting
novelist Jack London a lesson in the ancient sport of surfing, which was
reviving as Calvinist missionary influence waned. London, no Calvinist,
was thrilled. He wrote a glowing profile for a popular American magazine
and a letter of introduction for Freeth, who planned to visit California. After
he arrived on the West Coast, Freeth began giving surfing demonstrations
before large crowds, which caught the eye of local reporters. Making a career
as a California waterman and lifeguard, Freeth kept up the shows until 1919,
when another international traveler, the influenza virus, claimed his life.
A bust at Redondo Beach Pier honors this evangelist of water sports.[17]

Surfing, like decorative tattooing and cannabis smoking, was a practice
that spread from the periphery to the core of the emerging global system.
More typical, though, was the diffusion of new pleasures from the industrial core to the periphery. Within two years of showing their first motion
picture in Paris, the Lumière brothers had sent trained operatives to cities
from Uppsala to Sydney, where audiences gawked at such spectacles as
the coronation of Czar Nicholas II. Within four years they were showing
their movies in Beijing and Tokyo. What could not be seen on makeshift
screens could be glimpsed in books and illustrated magazines. "The novelty
of the nineteenth century," wrote the historian Jürgen Osterhammel, "was
the spread of media that allowed people to send news over great distances
and across cultural boundaries and to make themselves familiar with the
ideas and artifacts produced in distant lands."

The process worked asymmetrically. The key ideas and artifacts came
from what sociologists call *reference societies*. China had once been the great
reference society, the source of cultural cues for Japanese, Koreans, and
Vietnamese and of fashionable goods for Middle Easterners and Europeans.
But by the late nineteenth century the most important reference societies
were all Western: Britain and France, followed by Germany and the United

The shock of the new: On April 11, 1925, the botanical explorer Joseph Rock set up his portable phonograph in Qingshui, a Gansu village so isolated that some residents still wore Manchu-style queues. "They had never seen such a thing as a phonograph," Rock wrote in his diary, "and stood in amazement massed around the music box listening to Caruso's 'Celeste Aida,' the Quartet of 'Rigoletto,' etc." Some onlookers seemed more interested in another of Rock's mechanical novelties: his inquiring camera.

States. Non-Western elites who spoke English or French were highly susceptible to their influences. Motilal Nehru may or may not have shipped his shirts to Paris to be laundered. But he did build swimming pools and tennis courts and send his worldly son to Cambridge to study science.[18]

CHANCE PLEASURES

A century later Nehru might have sent his son to attend university in the United States, the dominant reference society during the second phase of globalization and the undisputed leader in pleasure innovation. For most of the modern era, however, that distinction belonged to western Europe. Europeans invented orchestral music, grand opera, public art museums, industrial brewing, gastronomic restaurants, luxury hotels, department stores, electric vibrators, alkaloid and synthetic drugs, hypodermic syringes and ampoules, radio transmitters, cocktail parties, nudist camps, picture postcards, stereographs, motor cars and racing, and the world's most popular sports. Empires, above all the British Empire, spread games like football, cricket, and rugby. Each was a triple-threat pastime: a disciplined pleasure capable of producing flow; a medium for wagering; and a complex spectacle that offered identity, camaraderie, and the satisfaction of bantering in an arcane insider language.[19]

The frequency with which cognates of "lottery" and "casino" (*kajino* in Japanese) appear in the world's languages testifies to the spread of European gambling innovations. Prior to the mid-seventeenth century, gambling was a social activity of enthusiastic amateurs often victimized by swindlers, a favorite subject of Baroque genre painters. To be a professional gambler was to be a cheater: Nobody was lucky enough to make a consistent living from games of pure chance. Disputes over sharp play, aggravated by intoxication and despair over large losses, gave gambling a deserved reputation for violence.

Then mathematicians brought statistical order to gambling. In 1663 Girolamo Cardano's *Liber de Ludo Aleae,* a pioneering study of gambling probabilities, appeared posthumously. Refinements by a *Who's Who* of early modern mathematicians—Blaise Pascal, Pierre de Fermat, Christiaan Huygens, Pierre Rémond de Montmort, Jakob Bernoulli, and Abraham de Moivre—made it possible to precisely estimate the odds for all games of chance. Knowing what the odds were, and how to adjust them (by adding, say, a double zero to a roulette wheel), made it possible for professional gamblers to offer honest games and still make a regular profit. The "house edge" by no means eliminated cheating. It did lessen its temptation.

Governments and entrepreneurs took advantage of the house edge through lotteries and casinos. Lotteries were popular means of financing public and charitable works in Europe and its colonies, including Puritan Massachusetts. In 1756 the colony's General Court authorized Harvard College to fund dormitory construction with lottery tickets, an enterprise begun in 1772 but not completed until well after the Revolutionary War. A prominent economic casualty of that struggle, George Washington's aide-de-camp Peregrine Fitzhugh, floated a private lottery to restore his family fortunes. He put the touch on old comrades, asking them to purchase tickets in what amounted to a genteel form of begging.[20]

By contrast, the casinos that sprouted throughout Europe in the seventeenth and eighteenth centuries were all business. The original, Venice's Ridotto, opened in 1638. It set the basic casino pattern of multiple games, accelerated play, long hours, and a range of culinary diversions, from coffee and chocolate to fine wines and cheeses. Sexual adventure was on offer: Casanova was a Ridotto regular. When he won at the faro table he tipped the servants and showered gifts on the ladies.

Spa towns popular with wealthy pleasure-seekers were natural locations for casinos, typically licensed and taxed by local rulers. Renowned for their gardens and theaters and salons, towns like Baden-Baden also became notorious for the ruin they brought to compulsive gamblers, from roulette fanatics like Fyodor Dostoyevsky to spendthrift rulers like Wilhelm I, the elector of Hesse. Because casinos and other forms of house gambling were so ruinous, especially of aristocratic fortunes, unifying nation-states began restricting or outlawing them in the nineteenth century. First France and then Germany cracked down, which was how the tiny principality of Monaco gained its gambling foothold. When, in 1868, it also gained a railroad connection, it became the principal winter playground for wealthy Europeans, who arrived in first-class railway cars and smart coaches.

When they left Monaco, their purses were considerably lighter. "The gold of the four quarters of the world flows in to enable M. [François] Blanc, the present farmer [concessionaire] of the gaming tables, to fulfill the fabulous promises which he made to the Prince and his subjects upon receiving the concession," a *London Times* correspondent wrote in 1873:

Since that time the Prince has been able to abolish all the taxes, and this fortunate country basks in the sunshine, while folly from all other countries contributes to its wealth. . . . In this fairy scene the visitor who has left almost his last franc upon the green cloth may, before blowing out his brains, obtain at a most moderate price at the hotel built by M. Blanc an exquisite dinner, for the far-sighted speculator expends £8,000 a year that the gambler may not have reason to complain of the dearness of provisions. Nothing is neglected to expose the reason to a thousand seductions. There is an excellent band playing the most charming music; cosmopolitan *cocottes* wander within and without the casino, and their mechanical smiles accompany the jingle of the gold which the croupiers' rakes collect into the treasury of the bank.

And so on. Luxurious, beautiful, enervating, Monte Carlo was a perfumed web that ensnared its "voluntary victims" by overwhelming their reason with a perfect combination of passions.[21]

Down-market gambling, by contrast, became increasingly mechanized. The reel slot machine, invented in 1898, caught on quickly. Mechanical and then electronic "tote boards" permitted racetrack operators to efficiently pool pari-mutuel bets, compute shifting odds, and pay winners—minus, of course, their own commissions. Though the number of tracks declined, betting expanded through telegraphic "race wires" that turned pool halls into bookies' paradises. Regulars became so entranced that they imagined they could see their horses galloping toward finish lines a thousand miles away. "Men and women, boys and girls, yell, call for their horses to win, scream out in their excitement, snap their fingers and jump up and down," wrote an American observer. "They seem to think that they are on the track."[22]

William F. "Bill" Harrah hit upon another sort of excitement to popularize gambling. In 1937 Harrah moved from California to Nevada, where he graduated from bingo parlors to gambling clubs in Reno and Lake Tahoe. Like Blanc, Harrah was a master of set and setting, of making expectation and atmosphere work to enhance customer satisfaction. He saw that gambling houses, then patronized either by upper-class or lower-class men, could increase volume by attracting middle-class couples with an itch for an exotic vacation. But first he had to overcome their scruples. He suppressed cheaters on both sides of the table. He recruited show-business stars and hospitable female staff and advertised nationwide. Dusting off an old synonym, Harrah rechristened gambling as "gaming." And he put on a show where goggle-eyed visitors felt important and spoiled, but never seedy. "Just the fact there's some music—'Ooh, wow! We're somewhere,'" Harrah recalled, slipping into the voice of one his customers. "Maybe the man wants to play, maybe the lady couldn't care less, but there's a little music, she may want to hang around, so it's a good business."[23]

PACKAGED PLEASURES

What Blanc's Monte Carlo casino and Harrah's Nevada clubs had in common, other than the house edge and inhibition-dissolving alcohol, was that they combined unexceptionable with risqué pleasures in singular hedonic environments. The idea was not new. Shakespeare's Bankside had its brothels and bear pits along with thatched playhouses. Visitors to Kyoto's "floating world" dined riverside with sake, tobacco, fresh fish, plucked music, and flirtatious geishas. What was different about Blanc and Harrah was the scale on which they operated and the degree of design, the fanatical attention to detail. Blanc specified that his hotel should surpass "anything that has been built so far, even the Hôtel du Louvre or the Grand Hôtel in Paris. I want people to rave about the Hôtel de Monaco so that it becomes a powerful advertising medium." Harrah pursued the same aim, going so far as to have gold leaf scraped from a bar because he thought it did not look right. He made sure to put two bathrooms in his hotel suites. That would add a touch of class, he thought, and speed arriving couples onto the gambling floors.[24]

Bill Harrah was not shy about joining his own party. When he died of heart disease in 1978, after seven marriages and a life of smoking and drinking, he was sixty-six years old. But he lived long enough to see intricately designed, morally prettified pleasure meccas become the norm in Las Vegas and other gambling towns that vacuumed money from visitors' pockets. The Harrah-style casino-resort epitomized one of the key trends of the late nineteenth and twentieth centuries: the blending of pleasures in seductive, packaged combinations that could be marketed to mass audiences.

The most seductive blends were those that intensified brain reward, whether through environmental design or product enrichment. Ice cream, already hard to resist because of its combination of sugar, fat, and salt, became more so with the addition of crunchy bits of chocolate and fruit. Importers of Turkish water pipes advised customers that a drop or two of perfume would add a pleasant aroma to the smoke. Bartenders added a good deal more. In 1917 Bill Wilson, cofounder of Alcoholics Anonymous, found nothing memorable about his first drink, a glass of plain beer served with a meal. When, at another dinner party, someone handed him a Bronx Cocktail—a scrumptious mix of gin, sweet and dry vermouth, and orange juice—he practically launched into orbit.[25]

Historians can lose sight of the importance of blending because their work often focuses on particular pleasures, vices, and addictions in particular eras and societies. But the people who actually lived in those societies did not experience multiplying pleasures one at a time or in isolation. They experienced them in combinations and in commercial environments. Pub and saloon owners competed for business by offering customers pipes for their tobacco; free or subsidized food, salted to whet their thirst; and silent movies for their amusement. Theater owners drew audiences into their movies with sound. Actors projected dialogue from behind the screens. Accompanists added musical color. Chorus girls sang along. Sound effects men provided the hoof strikes.[26]

Between 1880 and 1910, the world was inundated with what the historians Gary Cross and Robert Proctor call "packaged pleasures." These were technologically innovative, self-contained, blended, mass-marketed products that laid the foundations for a quick-hit consumer culture. Electrified amusement parks blended and packaged fantasies, dazzling the masses with gaudy follies and thrilling rides. Phonographs blended and packaged

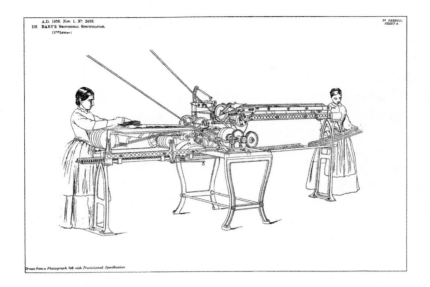

Steam machinery plus cheap ingredients plus cheap labor equaled mass-market pleasures and, in the case of tobacco, mass addiction. This British patent drawing, filed in 1859, shows how processed leaves might be rolled into cigars with the aid of "endless straps" that compressed and wrapped the tobacco. In 1881 the American James Bonsack received a patent for another steam-driven device that extruded an endless paper tube of flue-cured tobacco, which a spinning knife sliced into about 200 individual cigarettes per minute. By 1930 improved German versions of the machine were spitting out 1,800 units per minute.

sound. Cameras packaged sight, and blended it in compelling ways with the help of editing, projection, and music. So powerful was the combination in *Battleship Potemkin* (1925) that Edmund Meisel's score was banned for reinforcing the film's revolutionary theme.[27]

The smallest package, the machine-made cigarette, blended shredded tobacco, flavoring agents, and humectants to create a product that was cheap, addictive, and universal, cutting across class and occupational lines. Writers were as likely to smoke them as royalty. In Cairo, undertakers sold cigarettes as a sideline. Egyptian merchants preferred to give them to customers, as a preliminary to striking a bargain.[28]

Vending machines, packages of packages, debuted on both sides of the Atlantic in the 1880s. In Great Britain they sold postage stamps; in the United States, Tutti Frutti gum. Adaptable to any small object of fixed dimension and price, they soon dispensed everything from chocolate rolls to opera glasses. Called "slot machines" because customers fed coins into a slot, they originally bore no taint of vice. They were conveniences, but anonymous ones—no clerk or grocer witnessed the purchases.[29]

Slot machines lost their innocence in the 1890s, when they were adapted for gambling. "In almost every saloon may be found from one to half a dozen of these machines, which are surrounded by a crowd of players from morning to night," the *Los Angeles Times* reported in 1899:

> Formerly, the machines were arranged to pay cigars and drinks as winnings, but now many of them pay out money, and these are the most popular. . . . The temptation to gamble is placed before a young man every time he enters a saloon, and he can gratify the passion with any small amount of money, from a nickel up. Once the habit is acquired it becomes almost a mania. Young men may be seen working these machines for hours at a time. They are sure to be losers in the end, because, even in the exceptional cases when a winning of money is made from the machine, it is promptly "blown in" in payment of drinks for the gambler and his friends. Thus two bad habits are acquired at the same time.

The new gambling craze was, in every way, a package. The house edge was mechanized, built into a box of cogs and gears and reels. The lever that set them spinning was lubricated with drink. Everything in the saloon was a cue, from the sound of clanking coins to the smell of stale smoke and beer. The anticipation of an uncertain reward, as well as the reward itself, caused intense excitement. Habitual pursuit of that excitement became a "mania," an addiction. Even the gambler's sociability worked against him, his jackpots being liquidated to treat thirsty friends. The only winner was the saloon's owner, a man in an intensely competitive business who had found a surefire way to lure and keep customers.[30]

Vice entrepreneurs were equally quick to make use of communications breakthroughs. Telegraphy made possible race wires; telephones, call girls. By 1891 the leading madams of Melbourne, Australia, had created a telephone service for businessmen who wished to book their favorite prostitutes in advance. New Orleans madams occasionally listed their telephone numbers in the *Blue Book,* a directory of brothels that had ads for restaurants, musicians, cigars, whiskey, drugstores, lawyers, venereal-disease cures, and other accessories and complications that might accompany a visit to one of these establishments.[31]

Advances in pharmacy and medicine cross-fertilized vice. Pharmaceutical manufacturers adapted bakers' mixers, armorers' bullet molds, confectioners' coating pans, and other gadgets, then added steam, diesel, or electric power. Their new machines could crank out two million pills per day, compared to a manual laborer's five thousand. It was a tremendous breakthrough, save that many of these pills and tablets contained narcotics, barbiturates, and other potent and toxic drugs. Compounding the risk, the tablets could be dissolved and injected with hypodermic syringes, which quickened onset of action and intensified brain reward. Invented in the mid-nineteenth century by Charles Pravaz and others, the syringe offered physicians a ready means to inject morphine into their patients and, sometimes, into themselves. In Europe morphine addiction became so closely associated with hypodermic injection that a *Pravaz* referred to either a syringe or a morphine habit.[32]

In the mid-to-late 1880s doctors began injecting another highly touted alkaloid, cocaine, with similar habituating consequences. Some addicts learned to blend cocaine with morphine or, later, with heroin. The practice spread through the early twentieth-century American underworld and then to show business. One performer explained that "in the theatrical world you cannot drink and dance," but a heroin-cocaine speedball worked nicely, if injected fifteen minutes before a cue. "When the band played your introduction . . . you were ready to go on, yes indeedy."[33]

Pleasure innovation remained a bottom-up as well as a top-down affair. But there was a crucial difference. Unlike individual inventors, entrepreneurs with access to research facilities, capital, and mass media did not depend on their own creativity or word of mouth. They could produce and quickly disseminate successful innovations, whether from their own labs or from the discoveries of others. In the 1930s Dutch cigarette factories began copying sweetened U.S. tobacco blends to achieve the popular, milder "American taste." Copyrights and patents offered some protection, but it was never perfect. In the 1940s pharmaceutical copycats ignored or skirted patents on amphetamines, synthetic drugs similar to adrenaline and norepinephrine that had become popular worldwide.[34]

Still, big corporations could always sue pirates, just as they could always scale up their own production and promotion. Capital broadcast new pleasures, literally, in the case of music, from amplified string instruments that had been created by individual engineers and musicians. The most colorful, George Beauchamp ("Bee-chum"), fled central Texas for Los Angeles, where he became a Hawaiian-style steel guitar player, serious drinker, and home tinkerer. Beauchamp had one big idea—that waves from vibrating steel strings could be amplified like radio waves using a magnetic field created by a pickup. He and three collaborators created the first production-model electric guitar. Audiences liked the twangy new sound, which made its live debut at a 1932 Halloween bash in Wichita, Kansas. But it took record companies and radio networks to embed the electric guitar in the modern soundscape by making its distinctive chords as accessible as the nearest jukebox or car radio.[35]

SWEET PLEASURES

The history of chocolate exemplifies how blending, entrepreneurial innovation, cross-fertilization, scaled-up manufacturing, and clever packaging produced more enticing and affordable products. Though populated with remarkable characters, the story begins with an unremarkable fact: Chocolate is bitter. So bitter, in fact, that Dutch and English privateers reportedly dumped precious cargoes of cacao beans from captured ships, swearing that the beans tasted like sheep dung.

The Aztecs solved the problem by mixing in chili peppers and vanilla. Their conquerors, the Spanish, creolized chocolate by adding sugar, cinnamon, and other spices familiar to the European palate. It was in this form that chocolate spread among the European upper and middle classes during the seventeenth and eighteenth centuries. Sold as a solid, chocolate was consumed as a drink, being first dissolved in hot water or milk, to which wine was sometimes added. Samuel Johnson took his with cream or melted butter. But the most popular additive was sugar, which removed the drink's bitterness without altering or overwhelming the taste of other ingredients.[36]

Thus sweetened and spiced, chocolate caught on among European consumers. Between 1770 and 1819 European cacao imports, buoyed by increased production in the Amazon region, rose by 50 percent. Chocolate nonetheless remained pricey, the sort of thing that idle ladies sipped during their toilette. It did not become truly popular until manufacturers in Holland, Britain, Switzerland, and the United States overcame several technical problems.

The first of these problems was what to do about cocoa butter, which makes up more than half of the cacao bean. Cocoa butter's oils rose, unappealingly, to the surface of the drink unless absorbed by starchy additives like potato flour. Cadbury, the British Quaker firm that became a global chocolate dynasty, began by making a blended cocoa gruel. One brand, "Iceland Moss," featured lichen. It flopped. Richard and George Cadbury, the brothers who turned the firm around, decided to gamble. They used their remaining capital to buy a defatting press invented by the Dutch cocoa manufacturers Casparus and Coenraad van Houten. In late 1866, having gotten rid of the excess oils and potato starch, Richard and George began selling Cadbury's Cocoa Essence. They promoted the product as "Absolutely Pure, Therefore Best." It was the perfect pitch. Cocoa was notoriously subject to adulteration, with brick dust for color and who knew what for bulk. Scandal being a form of free advertising, the Cadburys profited from the public's anxiety.

The Cadburys also knew that the separated cocoa butter could be made into edible chocolate products. Mixing in dark brown cocoa paste and sugar, they created a superior form of eating chocolate, marketed in fancy boxes of Richard Cadbury's design. It was surely odd that an austere Quaker should invent the most decadent of packaged pleasures. But business was business, and Richard had an artist's knack for orchestrating delights. To open one of his gaily decorated lids was to release an aroma of chocolate with notes of almond marzipan, orange, and strawberry rising from luscious candies. When the candies were nestled in a heart-shaped Valentine's Day box, another of Richard's inventions, who could resist such a combination of chocolate, set, and setting?[37]

Continental confectioners found a different path to success. In 1875, after several false starts, Swiss chocolatier Daniel Peter learned how to combine condensed milk with chocolate to make a delicious, smooth drink. Peter struck gold a second time when, in 1886, he introduced a milk chocolate bar. By then his countryman Rodolphe Lindt had hit upon conching, a technique that used continuous roller grinding and infusions of cocoa butter to produce a super-fine chocolate that melted in the mouth. The trick was to reduce the bits of cocoa solids and sugar crystals below the point at which the tongue can detect grittiness.[38]

Milton Hershey, a caramel maker, had his epiphany in Chicago when he saw a miniaturized German chocolate factory at the 1893 World's Columbian Exposition. Like steam transportation and illustrated magazines, international expositions spread the gospel of mechanized pleasures. Hershey became a convert to the idea of scaling up the chocolate roasters and rollers. On the last day of the exhibition, he bought the entire miniaturized factory. The closely kept secret of making milk chocolate he found harder to acquire. Failing at industrial espionage, he kept experimenting until he managed to evaporate milk without burning it. Adding sugar, cocoa powder, and cocoa butter, he produced a silky milk chocolate with a tiny, tantalizing note of sourness from fermenting milk fat. All that remained was to price it within reach of the masses.

In December 1904 Hershey opened a large modern factory in Pennsylvania dairy country and began building a company town endowed with
workers' amenities. He kept his costs down by creating a streamlined
manufacturing process and national distribution system for a handful of
standardized products. It was Fordism before Ford, with Hershey churning
out plain and almond chocolate bars instead of cars. The first fiscal year,
1905–1906, Hershey rang up a million dollars in net sales. By 1931 sales had
reached $31 million.

Like other industrialists, Hershey integrated vertically. He already had
access to milk and chocolate. Cacao trees, which the Portuguese first brought
from Brazil to their African possessions in 1824, had become a global tropical crop. Cheap sugar was another matter, particularly when World War
I curtailed European production. In 1916, on a visit to Cuba, Hershey began
buying up prime sugarcane land, starting with ten thousand acres east
of Havana. There he found a congenial second home. Widowed and
childless, he consoled himself in Havana's fleshpots. The small pleasures
he sold to others afforded him extravagant ones: fine cigars, imported
champagne, showgirls, and roulette with croupiers who divined his bets
from a hand gesture. It was a long way to rise—or fall—for a man who began
life as a Mennonite farm boy.

Publicly, his company presented a very different face. Like his European
and American rivals, Hershey created ads that took aim at children and
women, associating chocolate with innocent play, wholesome treats, and
budding romance. Mindful of branding, he labeled his products with
bold silver letters on a chocolaty brown wrapper whose distinctive color
earned the name "Hershey Maroon." Chance favored the prepared chocolatier. When the United States entered World War I, Hershey received a flood
of military orders. He asked for and got three hundred female volunteers
to pack the doughboys' bars. Sales nearly doubled between 1916 and 1918.[39]

America's postwar national experiment with alcohol prohibition proved
another stroke of luck, and not just for Hershey. Alcohol's scarcity, high price,
and poor quality led drinkers to seek alternatives. By 1922 Americans were

consuming 22 percent more sugar per person than they had in 1920. Between 1917 and 1922 ice cream manufacturers more than doubled their sugar purchases. These rates of increase easily topped pre-Prohibition trends, leading observers to infer that "the palate which is denied the stimulating influence of alcohol finds acceptable solace in the more generous use of sugar."[40]

Apart from switching "palate" to "brain," researchers today would agree. Because sugar, like alcohol or morphine or nicotine, activates dopamine and opioid receptors, it can serve as a brain reward substitute for alcohol. Early twentieth-century physicians knew nothing of this neurochemistry, but they did worry about the health implications of sugar substitution. As early as 1919 they saw that people living in states with strong prohibition laws (many enacted years before the national Volstead Act) were consuming much more sugar than those in states where alcohol was legal. Their craving for an alcohol substitute prompted purchases of candy, sweets, and temperance drinks like Coca-Cola. But one eight-ounce bottle of Coke contained five teaspoons of sugar, "a highly artificial concentrated product, in its way quite as artificial as alcohol." And almost as unhealthful, given the risk of diabetes.[41]

When drug policy experts refer to "push-down, pop-up," they mean that suppressing production or trafficking in one place encourages it in another. Fewer poppies in Southeast Asia means more in Central Asia, less smuggling through the Balkans means more through Italy. But if we think in terms of brain reward in general, then push-down, pop-up assumes a larger meaning. In the quick-hit culture of industrialized pleasure, suppressing demand for one product, whether by prohibition, regulation, or punitive taxation, amps up demand for another. Thin out the saloon crowd, pack the ice cream parlor. With so many choices on offer, the world's consumers could substitute one packaged pleasure for another.

So, to some degree, could narcotic addicts. In 1919 New York City's public drug-treatment clinic enrolled street addicts in a gradual detoxification program. The clinic's physician noticed that the addicts showed scant appetite for regular food. But they would devour candy, "particularly nut chocolate bars. For these, addicts all display a fondness, and when offered to them, will never be refused." That sounds like substitutive use—substituting one drug for another, both of which affect opioid receptors. Or it may indicate concurrent use, since many addicts resorted to subterfuges to avoid or delay tapering their doses of narcotics. They relished the sugared chocolate along with morphine or heroin because sweets boosted the effect of the narcotics and vice versa. Nor were sugar-narcotic combinations confined to addicts. In 1910 German health officials complained that certain shopkeepers were selling morphine-laced candies, along with discount morphine injections for "delicate nerves." The candy came in two varieties, bonbons and pralines.[42]

Contemporaries did not equate confectioners with drug and alcohol traffickers. If people had applied a label to the Cadburys or Milton Hershey, it would have been that of enlightened capitalist. But hindsight has a way of highlighting history's ironies. Mass consumption of sugar is one of the grimmer ones. When Hershey's Pennsylvania factory walls began rising, in 1903, U.S. annual consumption of added sweeteners was around 50 pounds per person. By 2003 it was more than twice as much, and two in three American adults were overweight.[43]

URBAN PLEASURES

Packaged pleasures were disproportionately urban pleasures. Turks in Constantinople smoked more cigarettes per day than Turks in small towns, a pattern that held across all modernizing societies. Cities also had higher rates of drunkenness and alcoholism—no surprise for reformers who linked cigarettes to drinking—and more gambling dens and brothels. The brothels were said to be stocked by "white slavers," traffickers who seduced, tricked, or forced women into prostitution. Sensational reporting and fuzzy definitions make it hard to know how common white slavery actually was. But three things are certain. The market centered on cities. The influx of impoverished and naïve immigrants simplified recruitment. And sex trafficking was geographically widespread, with reports from as far afield as Nome and Johannesburg.[44]

Sex traffickers also set up shop in Harbin, a rail hub in northeastern Manchuria that grew explosively at the end of the nineteenth and the beginning of the twentieth century. International migrants, drugs, luxury goods, and French fashions made their way to the "Little Paris of the Orient" via the Chinese Eastern and South Manchuria Railways. In 1939 Harbin acquired its own casino, where patrons chose rooms based on their preference for opium, prostitutes, dining, tea, alcohol, or gambling. Men who wished to spruce up beforehand visited the on-premises barber.

Harbin's unkempt poor took their pleasures elsewhere, in such slums as the inaptly named Garden of Grand Vision. There kidnapped women sold sex for a pittance. Prostitutes took side bets on when their customers would come. Garbage collectors disposed of dead addicts by thrusting fishing spears into their heads and hoisting the bodies from the street into their trucks. They dumped the corpses—often frozen and always naked, the clothes having been sold for drugs or stripped by scavengers—into pits in the potter's field. Prostitutes, some of them as young as thirteen, endured beatings and bouts of syphilis and gonorrhea. These they combated with morphine, or toxic nostrums that turned their urine green.[45]

By the early twentieth century every large city had its equivalent of the Garden of Grand Vision. Commercialized vices were concentrated not only in urban areas, but in particular districts. Barcelona's included a brothel at 44 calle Avinyó, whence Pablo Picasso took the title of his 1907 masterpiece *Les Demoiselles d'Avignon.* The most notorious vice district was in Shanghai's French Concession, where gangsters operated under police protection. By 1920 this area held the city's largest opium and gambling dens, along with tens of thousands of prostitutes. "The dirtiest spot in the Orient," contemporaries called it.[46]

Smaller cities had smudges. Early twentieth-century Nashville, population 78,000, was home to a cluster of saloons, hotels, tobacconists, barbershops, poolrooms, bathhouses, and pawnshops known as the men's quarter. There bachelors enjoyed flings and married men escaped domesticity, smoking, drinking, cussing, and filling cuspidors to their hearts' content. Those caught in one of the infrequent gambling raids were fined $2.01—a penny for the offense, two dollars for the law's trouble. Respectable women shunned the quarter. Prostitutes frequented it at night, trolling for business.[47]

As centers of production, shipment, trade, advertising, and wealth, cities had long collected every sort of pleasure, vices included. But with industrialization, they had become much larger and more densely populated. In 1600, only 9 percent of the world's 560 million people lived in cities. In 1900, 20 percent of its 1.6 billion people did so. Urban populations exploded in the late nineteenth century. In 1900 Berlin held four and a half times as many people as in 1850. Sydney had nine times as many. Growth rates like these were possible only through migration. Urban mortality rates remained high, especially for children.[48]

The immigrants who poured into the industrializing cities were a natural target for vice purveyors. Starting at the bottom of the social ladder, immigrants did the most mind-numbing work; lived in crowded, filthy housing; and endured poverty, predation, and alienation. "The worker is under every possible temptation to drink," Friedrich Engels wrote of Manchester in 1844. "Spirits are virtually his sole form of pleasure and they are very readily available." On Saturday nights he watched demoralized workers swarm into the city's streets, drinking until they collapsed in the gutters. Those who stayed on their feet tottered off to one of Manchester's sixty pawnshops or into the arms of a streetwalker. Treat people like animals, Engels concluded, and they will behave like beasts. That, or revolt.[49]

Temperance advocates knew that one way to attack urban intoxication and its related vices was to reduce the brutal monotony of working-class life. More amenities like parks and playing fields, and more leisure time to enjoy them, would divert workers' wages from drink. One widely discussed European reform scheme, the Gothenburg system, used revenue from strictly regulated public-house monopolies to fund new public and recreational facilities. Nigeria's colonial government, by contrast, charged monopoly prices, kept the money, and surrounded black workers' beerhalls with barbed-wire fences.[50]

But even the honest provision of sober recreation was no panacea. Life in the metropolis, observed the sociologist Georg Simmel in 1903, was psychologically distinct from life in the countryside. In a fast-paced, hyper-stimulating environment where everything was monetized, people of all social classes became hardened and calculating. Saloonkeepers removed tables and chairs to crowd men to the bar, where they drank more and more quickly. Peddlers and candy shop owners sold loose cigarettes to schoolchildren. Newsboys dealt from two literary decks, printable and obscene. Barmen kept nude photos under the counter. Prostitutes were practically metered, with quick "close the door" encounters costing less than lingering sojourns. The exchanges were impersonal and anonymous. People did things in cities they would not have done in small towns, where everyone knew everyone else's business. The liberating effect of urban anonymity was particularly strong for unattached working-class men. Freed from familial controls, and in the company of like-minded compatriots, they took their pleasures secure in the knowledge that they were unlikely to be discovered.[51]

Whether investigating drunkenness, alcoholism, narcotic addiction, or commercialized sex, researchers in late nineteenth- and early twentieth-century Europe and North America reached the same conclusion: the bigger the city, the bigger the problem, particularly in the workers' districts. There was one exception, but it was the exception that proved the sociological rule. Along with big cities, the transportation and industrial revolutions created remote camps for young male workers—canal diggers, track layers, frontier miners—who were unmarried or temporarily single. These settlements attracted freelance vice predators, like the gamblers who roamed the Argentine Pampas. Or they were exploited by vice monopolists, like the company opium stores that pocketed the wages of Chinese tin miners in the Dutch East Indies. Even in the absence of organized corporate predation, there was a marked propensity for vice (and for violence triggered

opposite: To your health: The cover of a liquor price list distributed in a defiantly wet New York City during Prohibition. Inside were eye-catching ads, bulk-order discounts, and a promotional giveaway for nested, pocket-sized tumblers. Prices were steep but delivery prompt, thanks to the telephone service emblazoned on the cover.

by vice-related disputes) in bachelor populations cut off from traditional family and community life.[52]

Not all late nineteenth- and early twentieth-century workers were downtrodden. Nor did they all lack the beneficent fruits of industrialization, the canned foods, electric lights, rail transportation, and other comforts and conveniences that ultimately extended their lives and made them more tolerable. Things were getting better at the same time that they were getting worse. The source of this paradox is that pleasures, vices, and addictions were interconnected. Addictions were most often acquired through exposure to vices. Vices were most often part of a suspect subset of pleasures—suspect, in part, because they could lead to addiction. More pleasures brought more vices, and more vices more addictions. Yet more pleasures brought more happiness, achieved through products and pastimes whose sensible indulgence yielded satisfaction, delight, and gratification.

The revolutions in transportation, communication, industrialization, and urbanization, which were also linked, expanded the linked domains of pleasure, vice, and addiction. Having more of one meant having more of the others. Partly this was a matter of increased accessibility and affordability, which was the economic point of improved transportation and manufacturing. Partly it was a matter of new techniques of refining, blending, packaging, and marketing, which increased products' habituating potentials. And partly it was a matter of greater anonymity and anomie, unintended human consequences of a machine revolution that began in earnest with the improvement of a steam engine designed to pump water from a coal mine.

3

LIBERATING-ENSLAVING PLEASURES

"ALL THINGS TRULY WICKED," Hemingway wrote, "start from an inno-cence." He had in mind a Parisian friendship that grew into an affair that destroyed his first marriage. But the same words might apply to the process of discovering, inventing, and improving the pleasures that unleashed the global rise in vice and addiction.[1]

I say "might" apply because neither historians nor contemporaries have been of one mind about the consequences of the global pleasure revo-lution. No surprise there, as pleasure must ultimately be judged within the context of a particular religious or philosophical conviction. What historians can do, however, is to lay out the different lines of response to the pleasure revolution. We can show how the policy debate was rooted in an underlying conflict between the principle of hormesis (a little is good, a lot is bad) and the logic of free market capitalism. And we can explain why the clash between health and profit finally prompted global attempts to regulate or suppress vice markets.

COMPENSATING PLEASURES

Asked to name the world's worst health catastrophe, most people would pick the Black Death of the fourteenth century, the influenza pandemic of 1918–1919, or perhaps the cigarette manufacturing revolution that began in 1881. But anthropologists and world historians would not pick any of these. They think the world's worst health catastrophe began with an innovation that most of us view in a favorable light. They think it began with agriculture.

The claim may seem perverse. Domesticated plants and animals meant more people, more cities, more trade, and more exchange of useful genes and ideas. Agriculture made possible civilization, which, for nineteenth-century students of cultural evolution, was the highest stage of human progress. But war and genocide took the bloom off civilized progress, and anthropologists began to take a closer look at the benefits of pre-agricultural life. Most civilized people, Marshall Sahlins observed in 1966, assume that human wants are infinite while human means are limited. The gap can be narrowed only through industrialization and economic growth. But there is also "a Zen road to affluence" that assumes that human wants are few and can be satisfied by simple technologies requiring minimal labor. "Adopting the Zen strategy," Sahlins wrote, "a people can enjoy an unparalleled material plenty—with a low standard of living." That was how humans had lived before agriculture. That was how hunter-gatherers like the San people of the Kalahari region were still living, to the growing interest of anthropologists rethinking the history of the human condition.[2]

How much leisure and security hunter-gatherers enjoyed is debatable. What is not debatable is that the vast majority of those who abandoned hunting and gathering for agriculture initially paid a steep price in diminished stature, health, status, and, longevity. Human misery grew with human population. Twelve thousand years ago our species numbered five to eight million people, all hunter-gatherers. Two thousand years ago only one or two million hunter-gatherers remained, compared with 250 million agriculturalists. Yet these sedentary farmers suffered afflictions that rarely troubled wandering bands—a monotonous and vulnerable food supply; rapacious elites; accumulated filth; infectious and parasitic diseases; rat, flea, and fly infestations; toxic molds; and tooth decay. The evidence is in the bones. Paleolithic men lived more than two years longer and were six inches taller than their Late Neolithic counterparts. Privileged classes, another legacy of the agricultural revolution, fared better, but still they suffered from tuberculosis, malaria, diarrheal diseases, chronic inflammation, and other common ills of early civilizations.[3]

Civilization did have some significant offsetting advantages. States quelled anarchic violence. Roofs and walls provided shelter. Endemic infections like measles afflicted infants and children but generally spared adults, who had acquired immunity, and who, being sedentary, could more easily nurse ailing offspring. The vulnerability of tribal peoples to these same infections accelerated the expansion of agricultural settlements, as in the European conquest of North America. More generally, civilization encouraged future orientation, the division of labor, literacy, and the exchange of knowledge, including such knowledge as smallpox inoculation. It made possible the cumulative advances in science, agriculture, industry, public health, education, and medicine that underlay the health gains of late modernity, particularly those that have occurred since the late nineteenth century. Putting it all together, someone born in 1950 could expect to grow nearly a foot taller, weigh 50 percent more, and live more than 2.5 times longer than someone born in 1700.[4]

The unevenness of the tradeoff—eleven millennia of misery and early death for a quarter millennium of rapid material progress and an eighth millennium of better health and longer lives—has led anthropologists and historians to call agriculture-based civilization one of history's biggest mistakes. A better analogy would be history's longest mortgage. The costs of civilization, like the interest on borrowed money, were frontloaded. It was pay, pay, and pay some more. Then one day humans owned the house, and could afford to relax a little.[5]

But how did they relax during civilization's long grind? They took advantage of newly discovered and more widely available pleasures. The communal jug during the harvest crisis, the wad of fresh coca before a long trek, the festive day of gaming and dancing—all of these were means of compensation and escape. In Hindu, Islamic, African, and Latin American societies, cannabis smoking was the poor man's out. "Ganja is three cent," an Indian laborer in Trinidad explained to an interviewer, while half a bottle of rum cost forty cents.[6]

It was, however, tobacco that became the universal solace. In the early seventeenth century rulers from England to China tried in vain to suppress the alien but fast-spreading vice of tobacco smoking. During an expedition against Baghdad in 1625–1626, Sultan Murad IV caught a score of his officers in the forbidden act. When they "were put to death with the severest torture in the imperial presence," wrote scholar and geographer Kātib Chelebi, "some of the soldiers carried short pipes in their sleeves, some in their pockets, and they found the opportunity to smoke even during the executions." Back in Istanbul, soldiers persisted in smoking, often in the barracks latrines. No matter how rigorous the prohibition, there were more smokers than nonsmokers.[7]

It was much the same in China. In 1639 the Chongzhen emperor, alarmed that peasants were cultivating tobacco instead of grain, decreed decapitation for those who sold the plant in the capital. The first known victim, beheaded in 1640, was the servant of a student from Fujian who had traveled to Beijing for the imperial civil service examination. But no amount of judicial killing could alter two essential facts. Peasants earned more, as much as ten times more, by growing tobacco instead of other crops. And everyone took to the new pleasure. "I laugh to think that in days of yore people had only ordinary leaves," wrote one Qing poet, "as I watch a world of smoke and cloud pour out of you."[8]

Tobacco smoking grew explosively in China in the 1640s. By 1656, Chelebi reported, it had spread to every habitable place on the planet. Granted, smoking offered an unusually rapid and repeatable form of brain reward. Yet the timing is also significant. The 1640s and 1650s were arguably the two worst decades of what was inarguably the worst period in early modern global history: the chaotic horror show of plague, famine, frigid temperatures, inflation, riot, rebellion, war, pillage, and rape that historians call the general crisis of the seventeenth century. In China things got so bad that tigers padded into cities to feed on human carrion. Rats joined in, nesting in the bodies they picked clean. Tobacco and other novel food-drugs launched their careers as global commodities at this nadir of human affairs. Misery wanted surcease, not company.[9]

The sociologist Sidney Gamble, who took this photograph in China between 1917 and 1919, offered no description beyond "Peking Congee Distribution. 2 Boys—1 Smoking." It is likely that the boys were orphans and that the older boy derived as much satisfaction from his tobacco as from the rice gruel he was about to receive. Smoking was a comfort anyone could afford.

Aldous Huxley held the misery-reduction principle to be universal. In 1958 he observed that, throughout history, alcohol and narcotics had addicted and killed millions. The persistent carnage ran counter to every Darwinian rule in the book. Why would people risk "death preceded by enslavement" by continuing to take psychoactive drugs? His answer was that drugs provided an irresistible means of self-transcendence and mystical experience in an otherwise harsh and monotonous existence. While hermits and monks had achieved escape through asceticism and spiritual discipline, the masses had glimpsed nirvana with chemical assistance. How often they achieved temporary transcendence, as opposed to fleeting moments of pleasure or analgesia, we do not know. We do know that, from antiquity, people assigned divine attributes to poppies, wine, coca, chocolate, peyote, and other substances whose psychoactive effects were intensified by ritual. Food-drugs were many things, but one of them was a complicated form of grace.[10]

LIBERATING PLEASURES

The historian Daniel Lord Smail, a close reader of Huxley, also sees pleasure and escape as central to history. But he goes beyond Huxley in arguing that cultural traits and practices, as well as drugs, have psychotropic effects. Historians who think (or fear) that biology determines culture have it backward. Culture determines biology, or at any rate the biology that matters most, the flow of the neurotransmitters that govern consciousness and feelings. Every society has a distinctive set of cultural practices that move neurotransmitters as efficiently as placebos or nocebos do. These practices are, in fact, the placebos and nocebos of politics. The historian's job is to explain how they have changed over time.

The two great turning points for Smail are the Neolithic Transition and modernity's long eighteenth century. Prior to agriculture, humans, like other higher primates, had evolved an acute sensitivity to social obligations, alliances, and status. Status differences were present in hunter-gatherer societies, yet social differentiation was minimal because of the typical band's small size, mutual dependence, itinerancy, and lack of a storable surplus for elites to control. Agriculture changed every one of those egalitarian circumstances, permitting the emergence of class distinctions which, for the poor, amounted to institutionalized stress.

To keep the commoners under control, elites used what Smail calls "teletropic" practices, emotional carrots and sticks that enabled them to maintain and enhance power by manipulating consciousness. Feasting was a carrot. So were religious rituals, monumental architecture, chariot races, theatrical displays, and, to quote the political philosopher Étienne de la Boétie, "other such drugs [that] were for the Ancients the allurements of serfdom, the price for their freedom, the tools of tyranny." Should those means fail, the powerful could always unleash violence. The point of an act like crucifixion was not just to kill, but to kill in a hideous way that inspired terror and emphasized the futility of resisting state power. Smail uses the prefix "tele-" to describe this emotional effect because it occurs over a distance, say, the distance from Golgotha to an onlooker's amygdala, the center of the neural circuitry of learned fear. Teletropic practices, common to all civilizations, provided the emotional shock and awe that kept the masses subordinate.[11]

Yet civilization meant more than the immiseration of the many for the benefit of the few. It also entailed the discovery, dissemination, improvement, and commodification of new pleasures. Though many of these new pleasures were food-drugs, others were cultural innovations, such as reading novels or trading gossip in cafés. Setting mattered too. "Such an uproar!" remembered Jimmie Charters, a legendary barman who presided over Montparnasse watering holes in the 1920s. He poured drinks for a crowd of "excited women, amorous couples, jittering fairies, gay dogs, overserious young men expounding theories, and a few quiet, observing souls who took it all in and appreciated it." The collective intoxication came from the libations, but also from "the spirit of freedom from all the conventions and ties that bound these people at home." Smail calls such liberating activities "autotropic," referring to things that people can do for or to themselves to alter their own feelings. Insofar as autotropic pleasures empowered rather than cowed individuals, they were of growing concern to authorities.[12]

Masturbation, the classic autotropic pleasure, had not been a particularly great worry in Western antiquity or Christian Europe. Confessors assumed the practice to be widespread but did not single it out for special attention. They concentrated on interpersonal sexual acts like sodomy, incest, and adultery. That situation changed during the eighteenth century. Authorities held masturbation to be harmful because it degraded a social act into a subversively private one based on fantasies liable to lead to compulsive self-abuse. "Masturbation seemed more and more to look like what we would call addiction," wrote historian Thomas Laqueur. "It enslaved just like alcohol, drugs, or some other object of unquenchable desire."[13]

Whether masturbation was enslaving or not, three of the five "As" described in the Introduction—anonymity, accessibility, and affordability—had by then come into play, at least among the educated classes. (The other two, advertising and anomie, would come later.) The houses of the well-off had more privacy, with hallways and separate bedrooms. Their libraries held more books, which continued to grow in popularity and decline in price. The books included novels and romances widely supposed to arouse erotic thoughts. Risqué illustrations featured *déshabillées* ladies in post-masturbatory repose with an open book dropped nearby, its purpose achieved. It was not that these books were necessarily pornographic. Simply reading novels, even the high-minded sort, produced "a certain kind of absorption, a deep engagement of the imagination, a bodily intensity that could, it was feared, veer with terrifying ease toward the dangerous excesses of self-pleasure."[14]

To which most will reply, "So what." If the Enlightenment finally delivered the goods to an expanding portion of long-suffering humanity, giving people compensating and liberating pleasures like reading, then it ought to be counted a blessing. And as autotropic practices replaced teletropic ones, life became more peaceful. People who spent their time drinking chocolate and reading epistolary novels thought and acted more civilly than those who spent their time watching blood sports and public executions, both of which waned in Europe during the eighteenth and early nineteenth centuries. The humanitarian and consumer revolutions overlapped with and reinforced one another. If some consumers embarrassed themselves or strayed into the realms of compulsion, they were unfortunate but necessary casualties. If unscrupulous sorts exploited consumers' vulnerabilities by building empires of vice, that was a regrettable necessity. Better to live in a world with printing presses and pornographers than a world that had neither. All victories have a price. All battlefields have scavengers.[15]

THE WAGES OF PLEASURE

Thus modernity gave us tools—sharp tools—that allowed us to manipulate our own moods, rather than have the ermined and crimsoned do it for us. We did not, as it were, have to wait for the last king to be strangled with the entrails of the last priest. We were free, emotionally free, if we had a good book and a pipe and a mug for company. We could even relish the follies of kings by picking up a newspaper or tuning in to the BBC. "The Simpson crisis has been a great delight to everyone," Evelyn Waugh wrote in 1936, referring to Edward VIII's abdication of the British throne in order to marry the divorcée Wallis Simpson. "At Maidie's nursing home they report a pronounced turn for the better in all adult patients. There can seldom have been an event that has caused so much general delight and so little pain."[16]

The notion of democratized fun dovetails with other attributes of modernity, including secularization, individualism, egalitarianism, and consumerism, recast as the new dispensation of an autotropically reformed faith. "Where individuals once relied on religion and ritual as sources of dopamine and other chemical messengers," Smail wrote, "they turned increasingly to items of consumption, giving up God in favor of mammon." And yet, as Smail acknowledged, modernity was not exclusively autotropic. Throwback regimes kept popping up, along with spectacles like Kristallnacht. Adolf Hitler, remarked George Orwell in 1940, had grasped one great truth, the vacuity of a hedonistic view of progress. He knew that the masses could still be induced to sacrifice for collective dreams, and he was right.[17]

Regimes no less ruthless than Hitler's managed to turn supposedly auto-tropic pleasures into means of psychotropic control as well as gushers of revenue. In 1930 Joseph Stalin, who needed soldiers and planes, and who had rationalized away Bolshevism's primal suspicion of alcohol, ordered his underlings to "get rid of a false sense of shame and directly and openly promote the greatest expansion of vodka production possible." In China, Mao Zedong and his successors promoted state-monopoly cigarettes. These took the place of opium in the national smoking culture, so much so that the People's Republic was the world's largest cigarette market by the end of the twentieth century.[18]

Despite these episodes, the shift toward autotropic pleasures, the lush, late-maturing fruit on civilization's thorny vine, may seem like a net gain from the vantage of a secular society accustomed to consumer luxuries and utilitarian thinking. But that is not how earlier historical actors always understood the discovery of pleasurable but potentially addictive practices. Having heard academic experts like Smail testify for the defense, let us summon voices from the past as witnesses for the prosecution. At bottom, their case is simple. The flood of new pleasures encouraged vice and fostered enslavement.

The perceived danger and offensiveness of vices varies with cultural and historical circumstances. Prior to the nineteenth century vices were largely understood as personal failures. The word derives from the Latin *vitium*, meaning moral weakness or failing. Individuals manifested vices, just as they manifested virtues. Historians and authors personified vices through notorious celebrities and characters: Nero's ruthless cruelty, Satan's rebellious pride, Tartuffe's religious hypocrisy. The worst offenders were said to be "vicious," from *vitiosus*, full of vices. Blackbeard the pirate was vicious. He dressed the part.

However many vices individuals embodied, they were personally accountable for them and liable to divine sanctions. The New Testament tells us that the impious Herod Agrippa was eaten alive by worms. In the ancient texts of Hinduism, worms fed on the wicked in *krimibhojana*, one of that religion's many hells. George Whitefield, the eighteenth-century British evangelist, made do with just one hell. But it had ample room for drunkards, whose "heinous sin" of habitual overindulgence had turned alcohol, one of God's "good Creatures," into a "deadly Poison" that destroyed their bodies and corrupted their souls. Their one hope was to seek redemption in Christ, shun wicked company, and enter a life of mortification and self-denial.[19]

In 1628 the English Puritan polemicist William Prynne offered similar advice to those who sported lovelocks. These were the long strands of crisped, braided, and beribboned hair favored by modish courtiers who lived "in perpetual bondage to their curling irons." Vanities like these, Prynne warned, would lead to larger vices, and larger vices to hell. In 1648 another Puritan, Essex vicar Ralph Josselin, confided to his diary that the death of his infant son was due to his own vanity, lusts, and excessive playing at chess. The last detail is the telling one. Early modern clerics, Jewish and Islamic as well as Christian, often denounced chess as a time-wasting vice that fostered scriptural neglect and gambling. In theological terms, chess was an occasion of sin. Like sin itself, its consequences might be visited on idlers' children. And woe to those foolish enough to head straight for the gambling tables. In the eyes of Protestant moralists, a profligate gambler like Marie Antoinette got her just deserts when her executioners dumped her corpse and severed head in a quicklimed grave.[20]

Beyond clerical anger over the flagrant violation of taboos, and the fear of collective punishment that they might bring, lay a thinly veiled contempt for the likes of Stuart fops and spendthrift Catholic queens. As a rule, novel pleasures and pastimes were more likely to be suppressed, minor vices elevated to major, and potentially addictive substances subjected to strict prohibitions if they were associated with disliked, deviant, or foreign groups. It mattered that Chinese immigrant laborers were associated with opium smoking; diaspora Jews with distilling and tavern keeping; and, in the United States, German immigrants with beer gardens devoted to Sabbath drinking. The great joke during Prohibition was that, when the Chicago police raided a restaurant serving liquor, the only person they arrested was an anarchist. Revelry was one thing. Contempt for the laws of God and man was another.[21]

Viewing controversies over pleasure, vice, and addiction through the lenses of religion and religious deviance makes sense. Self-indulgence was at odds with the world's major faith traditions, which sought altered consciousness through daily spiritual practices embedded in communal life. While human cognitive and social development spawned many means of pleasure and transcendence, religions typically favored those predicated on inner and outer discipline. Vices like gambling and tippling, by contrast, fostered indiscipline and blasphemy. Alien vices associated with corrupt faiths were worse yet. An Englishman sporting a lovelock, Prynne fumed, looked like a Frenchman or a Virginian, which was to say like a Papist or a degenerate Anglican. It is hard to know which he hated most. But hate he surely did.[22]

Vice opposition also had a secular aspect, which became more pronounced during the nineteenth and twentieth centuries. The sorest points for anti-vice activists were personal and familial harms, collective costs, and threats to the future of the group, be it tribal, racial, or national. Suicidal gamblers who left destitute wives and children epitomized the first problem, accidental fires set by smokers the second. The third, concern for the future, centered on the health and motivation of the young. In mid-twentieth-century Kenya, elderly people could smoke cannabis without scandal. Those under forty who lit up risked becoming pariahs. Kenyan society—any society—required fit parents, providers, and defenders.[23]

War or its prospect heightened fears of youthful dissipation. Better to die fighting for liberty than to die drinking bad whiskey—words spoken at the 1778 funeral of a Continental soldier who had done precisely that. War correspondent Frederick McCormick, who watched drunken Russian soldiers and sailors blunder into defeat in 1904 and 1905, spelled out the strategic lesson: "The chief enemy of an army is the nation's moral diseases. A great people with a great army, who could not defeat the Japanese in one single battle, must first have been the victim not of the enemy, but of themselves."[24]

A decade later the Russian government, among others, imposed wartime prohibition. World War I was a watershed, a catastrophic natural experiment in public policy that prompted numerous anti-vice measures. In 1914 France issued an emergency decree against absinthe sales. In 1915 Britain reduced its beer supply, and in 1916 it tightened drug regulations. In December 1916, well before America's entry into the war, the U.S. Public Health Service banned heroin at military relief stations. In 1917 American officials shuttered red-light districts near military camps for fear of venereal infections. That same year General Philippe Pétain issued orders making it more difficult to purchase alcohol in French army zones. More than three quarters of his mutinies involved intoxicated *poilus*.[25]

In war and in peace different types of anti-vice arguments often collided, with consequences considered in the next chapter. Here it is enough to say that, whatever their motives and backgrounds, nineteenth- and early twentieth-century reformers agreed on three important things about vice. The first was that technology had upped the stakes. Not only was intoxication more dangerous in an industrialized landscape, but industrialization itself was more productive of vice. Pornography had been a luxury good until steam presses and photography slashed production costs. By 1872 the London-based Society for the Suppression of Vice confronted a flood of nude photographs, cheap to make and easy to mail. Choicer erotica lined the lids of snuff boxes. These the society seized, along with more than five tons of printed matter and hundreds of engraved plates, lithographic stones, wood blocks, and metal stereotypes. Neither the seizures nor the convictions of forty pornographers, some sentenced to hard labor, put a stop to the mechanized trade.[26]

The second realization was that those engaged in commercial vice were organized and politically active. If their trade was illegal, as in unlicensed gambling houses, they hired lookouts, doorkeepers, guards, and card sharps and paid off landlords and police. If their trade was legal, as in the case of licensed brewing and distilling, they used the government's thirst for revenue and their financial clout to shape policy to their liking. "Any serious interference with the [alcohol] traffic," a Canadian royal commission admitted in 1895, "must necessarily depreciate the value of a large amount of property . . . in excess of the whole of the chartered banks of the Dominion." Tactics like falsely registering anti-prohibition voters or blacklisting businesses that refused to hire drinking men were commonplace. So was bribery. Nor were clergy immune. Those who acquiesced to the local liquor barons could expect generous contributions in their collection plates. "The liquor trade was always lawless," Presbyterian minister Harry Fosdick said in 1928. He denied the charge that Prohibition invented graft and organized crime. British temperance advocates made the same point. The drink trade menaced the public as much as its product did.[27]

More broadly, vice no longer simply meant bad traits in weak persons. During the nineteenth and early twentieth centuries vice also came to mean the systematic *encouragement* of those traits, as when kimonoed cigarette girls dished out free samples. Opponents began to speak of vice as commercial and organized. Fosdick condemned "the organized liquor traffic," substituting the pejorative "traffic" for "trade." The same linguistic shift occurred in other Western languages.[28]

The third realization was that vices could be personally harmful and socially nefarious in ways that had not been fully appreciated in the past. Physicians had long warned of the ill effects of habitual tobacco use. In the nineteenth century, they began linking it to such socially alarming conditions as declining fertility. This was a particular concern in France, where many blamed the Prussian victory of 1870–1871 on demographic stagnation, and some doctors fingered nicotine as an infertility suspect. Other French physicians stressed the links between growing alcohol consumption and rising rates of insanity, which purportedly doubled between 1868 and 1888. Auguste Forel, an influential Swiss psychiatrist, neuroanatomist, and eugenicist, also singled out alcohol for attack. *Blastotoxie,* fetal damage, could result if one or both parents were intoxicated during conception. "If you get drunk, expect an idiot!" proclaimed a Bulgarian temperance journal. The fact that poverty, malnutrition, or poor prenatal and neonatal care might also explain "hereditary" defects did not stop critics from blaming alcohol, or extending the indictment to cocaine and other drugs.[29]

Drinkers ran a greater risk of contracting a venereal disease, saloons and taverns being the most common gateways to the Victorian sexual under-

Failing eyesight brought on by syphilis plagued John Danenhower, a U.S. Navy officer who committed suicide in 1887. Blindness was only one consequence of the protean disease physicians called "the great imitator." In the half century after 1875, the growing understanding of syphilis's origins and complex symptoms inspired campaigns to control prostitution, universally recognized as a reservoir of syphilis and other venereal infections.

world. Hygienists warned that prostitutes ("treponema machine-guns") were prolific sources of *Treponema pallidum*, the bacterium that causes syphilis, and that the disease could blind, cripple, and kill. As diagnostic tests improved, it became obvious that syphilis was shockingly widespread. By the mid-1920s, 10 percent of the French population and 10–15 percent of the Chinese urban population showed signs of the infection.[30]

Behind the statistics lay ruined lives, including lives of promise and power. Syphilis robbed Jean-Andoche Junot, one of Napoleon's longest-serving generals, of his military prowess and then his mind. Syphilitic iritis spoiled the eyesight of Lt. John Danenhower, an Annapolis graduate and Arctic explorer who, in 1887, shot himself after accidentally grounding a ship. He left behind a wife, two children, and a farewell note tied to his lapel. Vincent Van Gogh, who in 1890 shot himself more clumsily and died in a coma, may have suffered from syphilis (among other ailments) during his last, tormented years. The man in whose arms he died, his brother and artistic champion Theo Van Gogh, was certainly infected. He succumbed to syphilis the following year, in 1891, in the form of paralytic dementia. Locomotor ataxia, another of syphilis's calling cards, crippled and numbed Catherine Hershey, philanthropist and wife of chocolate magnate Milton Hershey. As she lay dying in 1915, Catherine dispatched her husband from the room for a glass of champagne so that he would not have to witness her end. Nine years later Lenin, similarly afflicted, died in a manner suggesting neurosyphilis, possibly acquired from a prostitute during his European exile. If true—the diagnosis has been disputed—that casual encounter arguably changed the course of Russian, Soviet, and world history.[31]

ENSLAVING PLEASURES

Junot, Danenhower, the Van Gogh brothers, Hershey, and Lenin all died in middle age. So did countless diabetics, smokers, and ruined gamblers who took years off their lives. Folk wisdom, seasoned with medical reports of dubious origin, reserved the most lurid end for sots, said to spontaneously combust in a lambent blue flame. Advocates of temperance stood on firmer ground when they cited statistics of heightened disease and mortality rates among alcoholics. To death they added the charge of slavery, an epithet that connoted more than addiction. In the seventeenth, eighteenth, and nineteenth centuries the accelerating global pleasure revolution produced not just millions of slaves of consumption, but millions of slaves of production, many condemned to the living death of plantation agriculture.[32]

Food-drug cultivation took off because it offered profits for planters and merchants; high value to weight for shippers; cheap energy and pleasure for the masses; and steady revenue for governments once they began imposing taxes or state monopolies, the norm by the late seventeenth century. Mercantilists fretted over the loss of specie to pay for consumer imports like sugar. But that defect had an obvious remedy, which is why, between 1630 and 1660, the English, French, Dutch, and Danes joined the Spanish and Portuguese in establishing New World sugarcane colonies. These required gang labor to level forests and tend the cane. Vanishing natives and indentured servants not answering to the demand, planters resorted to the transatlantic slave trade. Between six and eight million Africans, over half of those enslaved in all, ended up on sugar plantations. As many as three in seven died during passage or in the first two years after they arrived.[33]

The survivors' labor helped to secure their own replacements. Between 1700 and 1830 cane-derived rum exports paid for one in four slaves imported from Angola to Brazil. Rhode Islanders who entered the African slave trade favored "Guinea rum," a potent local distillate whose high proof reduced shipping costs. Rum secured Indian labor, too. Thirteen years of bondage could be had for as little as thirteen gallons of rum and four cloth coats. In Jamaica, where trapping eliminated cane-eating rats, alcohol bought overtime. Slaves who killed the furry nuisances got a rum bonus in proportion to the number of tails they produced.[34]

If pleasure, vice, and addiction were implicated in involuntary *production* (so much so that anti-slavery Quakers on both sides of the Atlantic boycotted West Indian sugar), they were also becoming more conspicuously tied to involuntary *consumption*. Observers from the seventeenth through

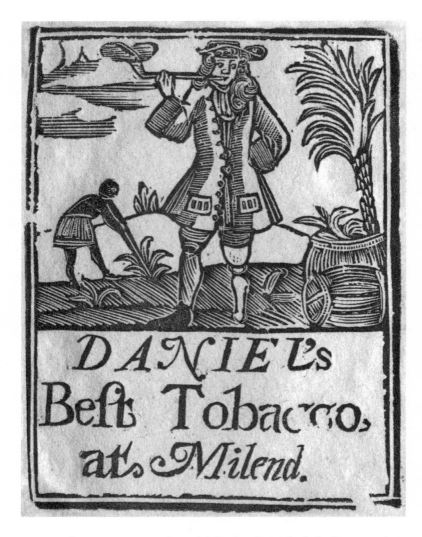

Seventeenth-century Virginia tobacco labels often depicted rakish planters smoking pipes while Africans toiled in their fields. Meant to ensure quality and build brand loyalty, these eye-catching woodblock labels could not help but convey another message too, that tobacco enslaved its producers as well as its consumers.

the nineteenth centuries instinctively reached for the language of servility
to describe those who could not abjure bad habits:

Tobacco has such a hook in their hearts that they return to it after a while,
as if seeking pardon. (1620)

These are fellows which talk of freedom, but no affrican is so great a Slave,
as such are [they] to their Passion for gaming. (1774)

The unhappy dram-drinkers are so absolutely bound in slavery to these
infernal spirits, that they seem to have lost the power of delivering themselves from this worst of bondage. (1778)

It is not the man who eats Opium, but it is Opium that eats the man.
(1850)[35]

"Addiction," from the Latin term for assigning a debtor to a creditor,
likewise connoted servility. By the eighteenth century it also meant being
in thrall to a behavior or substance. Explorer John Lawson called Carolina
Indians "much addicted" to drunkenness and to smoking tobacco. "It is
commonly taken in a bad sense," lexicographer Samuel Johnson explained
in 1756, "as, *he addicted himself to vice.*"[36]

The reflexive verb catches the eye: Johnson's guilty party had landed himself in the soup. But by the late eighteenth and early nineteenth centuries,
reform-minded physicians, the best known of whom were the American
Benjamin Rush and the Englishman Thomas Trotter, were shifting the onus
from the addict to the habituating substances, particularly to spirits. The
idea was not new. European observers had been describing pathological
loss of control over alcohol since at least the early seventeenth century, Asian
observers over opium since at least the sixteenth. Murad III, sultan of the
Ottoman Empire from 1574 to 1595, once kept a prospective grand vizier in
his presence for four hours to make sure that he was not an opium addict.
(The man stayed calm and got the job.) Rush and Trotter did, however,

put this familiar picture in a psychiatric frame. Rush described habitual spirit-drinking as both a prolific source of mental illness and a mental illness in itself. It might begin as free agency, he observed in 1812, but through habit it developed into a "necessity" impervious to considerations of health and morality. "*The habit of drunkenness is a disease of the mind,*" declared Trotter in 1804, using italics for emphasis. Repetition strengthened the habit and gradually altered the mind. He described a family that regularly drank spirits at one o'clock, before the midday meal. "If the time passed, or if they were from home, and did not get the usual dram, it was attended by a considerable *sense of consciousness,*" Trotter wrote. "In plain English, they had got into a very bad habit, and found themselves low spirited for want of their cordial."[37]

It sounds quite modern: one o'clock—the cue; "sense of consciousness"— the conditioned response; "low spirited"—the onset of withdrawal. Scholarly fashion once glossed such insights as the discovery of addiction. They are better understood as early, halting steps on a long, contested journey toward a medical model that regards addiction as a form of "pathological learning" grounded in specific neurotoxic changes whose damage varies according to social and developmental context. Trotter, Rush, and their nineteenth-century successors never settled on a common etiology, treatment regimen, or language for alcoholism and other addictions. In 1819 the German-Russian physician C. von Brühl-Cramer, another pioneer of the disease concept, settled on *Trunksucht,* "addiction to drink." He modeled the term on the *Lesesucht,* the "addiction to reading" that had swept Germany in the late eighteenth century. Von Brühl-Cramer's translator, Christoph W. Hufeland, was struck by another parallel, to nymphomania. He rendered *Trunksucht* as "dipsomania." "Alcoholism" did not appear until 1849, when the Swedish physician Magnus Huss coined it. The suffix "-ism" denoted toxic diseases, such as ergotism, poisoning caused by the common fungus ergot. In due course other physicians attached the ending to virtually every addictive substance. Anglophones wrote of opiumism and heroinism, Slavophones of *morfinizm* and *kokainizm,* Francophones of *caféisme.* Yet, with the partial exception of alcoholism, none of the isms achieved anything like universal currency. Many writers continued to prefer variations on words like "habit" or "mania."[38]

Whatever terminology they used, early authorities on alcoholism hailed from countries where spirits-drinking was common. This at least made sense. Potent, fast-acting forms of brain reward are most likely to cause cases of poisoning and addiction, and so most likely to stimulate medical thinking about pathological consumption. The same thing happened with morphine injection. The diffusion of hypodermic medication in the 1870s and 1880s provoked a response among Western physicians, who cautioned against the liberal injection of morphine and noted the similarities between alcoholism and morphine addiction. Yet they too failed to settle on a common clinical language.

Given the divided state of nineteenth-century medicine, the Babel of addiction was inevitable. Physicians operated across deep cultural and, often, sectarian divides. They had no international bodies (or insurers or epidemiologists) to tidy up their diagnostic categories and no universal language of scientific communication. Nor were doctors concerned with the same types of addictive behaviors, which varied from region to region. Western and northern European physicians focused on the toxic, hereditary, and habituating effects of spirits. These figured less prominently in Qing China. Though the Chinese certainly recognized alcoholism, called *shi jiu* in medieval texts, they were increasingly concerned about opium *yin,* or craving, during the nineteenth century.[39]

History's first run at the medicalization of addiction was terminologically, conceptually, and geographically messy. All the same it was a real trend with real consequences for how contemporaries understood vices and who, or what, bore responsibility for them. If repeated exposure to certain substances damaged the body, deranged the mind, and destroyed the will, causing grievous harm to self and others, not excepting the unborn, then steps to minimize or eliminate the exposure were in order. Individual harms, social costs, risks to the future: Medical authorities reinforced all three lines of argument. Their findings bolstered rather than displaced religious and cultural objections to vice. In fact, many Victorian physicians, most

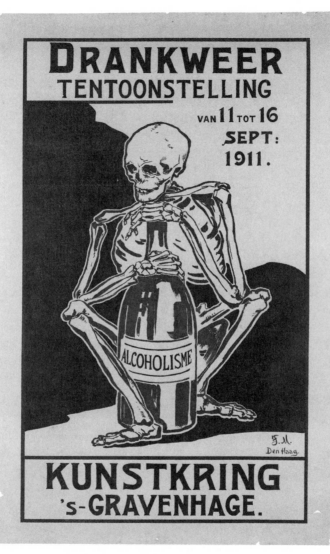

conspicuously those serving as Protestant missionaries, shared these moral objections. They yoked science and faith to the plow of reform.

LINKS IN A CHAIN

Medical commentary bolstered something else—the idea that pleasures, vices, and addictions were linked. Beginning in the 1870s, several American and British physicians took the position that alcoholics and drug addicts suffered not from distinct vices but from a single, treatable nervous disease called *inebriety*. Thomas D. Crothers, an outspoken proponent of this idea, advertised treatment for "alcoholic, opium, and other inebriates" and treated patients from three continents at his Connecticut asylum. Opinion was divided over inebriety's predisposing factors, which might include stress, nervous exhaustion, hereditary degeneration, early exposure (as when parents quieted infants with opium), or none or all of the above. But whatever pleasure and relief narcotics and alcohol initially provided, they had cumulative toxic effects, including tolerance and an "education of the nerve centres in the experience of poisoning" that accounted for craving and relapse. Denied one form of stimulation, inebriates often switched to another. Crothers wrote of a businessman who collapsed and died in midlife, despite having renounced his heavy youthful drinking. The undertaker resolved the mystery when he found morphine secreted in a small bag covering a crucifix suspended from the man's neck.[40]

OPPOSITE: Poster for an exhibition in conjunction with the Thirteenth International Congress against Alcoholism, The Hague, 1911. Early twentieth-century medical opinion accepted the link between alcoholism and early death and, more tentatively, the idea that alcoholism was a mental disease—a disease with social and hereditary causes and consequences. "Every inebriate," the British alcoholism expert R. Welsh Branthwaite informed delegates to the 1909 congress, "is either a potential criminal, a burden upon public funds, a danger to himself or others, or a cause of distress, terror, scandal, or nuisance to his family and to those with whom he associates." He perpetuated his ilk through example, precept, parental neglect, and perhaps "direct procreation."

Though a prescient idea, inebriety lacked experimental proof. It did not catch on outside Anglo-American specialist circles and fell into disuse during and after World War I. By then most authorities had also restricted "addiction" to compulsive narcotic use. Alcoholism spun off into its own universe, with many mid-twentieth-century researchers taking the industry-supported line that it was a specific disease afflicting only a minority of users of what was otherwise a "social condiment." This state of affairs persisted until the late twentieth and early twenty-first centuries, when neuroscientists fashioned a new brain disease paradigm, far more detailed and compelling than the old inebriety theory. They brought into the addictive fold alcohol, tobacco, and other drugs, and added behaviors like compulsive gambling, eating, and social media use that involve many of the same neural pathways. This time the lumping impulse was international. To *yin* (瘾), Mandarin speakers added characters for drugs, smoking, sex, and the internet. Researchers even resurrected Lamarckian ideas, recast in the language of epigenetics, arguing that acquired addictive traits could be passed on to offspring.[41]

The inebriety theorists, then, had missed the brass ring by about a century. But if the case for the underlying pathological unity of addictive behavior was not yet persuasive, medicine was more successful in establishing and reinforcing other vice linkages, such as the widely noticed predilection of smokers for strong drink. Physicians warned that boys who took up tobacco risked poor grades, bad jobs, alcohol and drug habits, and an early death. Alarmed mothers dragged "cigarette fiend" sons to the local courthouse to have their throats painted with silver nitrate, a supposed preventative. Though the advertising-savvy tobacco industry managed to partially neutralize such fears after World War I, smoking never entirely escaped its sinister associations. Heroin addicts were invariably cigarette smokers, often tattooed with a rosette of thoracic burns from nodding off with lit cigarettes dangling from their mouths. In Nazi Germany, where personal and state health were theoretically indivisible, doctors denounced smoking as "lung masturbation" and cataloged its unhealthful properties, a project assisted by the Reich Committee for the Struggle against Addictive Drugs.[42]

Both secular and clerical authorities stressed vice linkages. Qing officials associated opium smoking with gambling and crime among the lower orders and with demoralization and cowardice among soldiers. Rabbis illustrated *Haggadot,* texts setting forth the order of the Seder, with sketches of cigarette smokers as petty thieves and impious youths. Protestant ministers warned of the wicked city, where no watchful eye restrained curious country boys. "They visit the theatre; the circus; the puppet-show; the restorative; the gaming house; the brothel," a Baptist minister warned in 1842. "They become familiar with scenes of vice; and with vicious men. They are at first disgusted; then amused; afterwards pleased; and finally enlisted in the service of vice. . . . The remonstrances of conscience are soon drowned in the tumult of passion."[43]

Nowhere was passion more ruinous, or vice more strategically conjoined, than in gambling houses. Gamblers flattered and fleeced gullible young men, and implanted in them an appetite for the sporting life. When they grew to manhood they returned to the tables, this time in charge of their estates. Plied with food, drink, and cigars, and inclined to chase their losses, they fell to skinning-house pros who read the backs of their cards as easily as the dismayed looks on their faces. Their family's fortunes ruined, the gamblers became mired in debt, debauchery, and drink. Because gambling was so destructive, some Protestant reformers called it the vice God hated most. Weeping readers of *The Old Curiosity Shop* (1841) would have agreed. It was compulsive gambling by Little Nell's guardian-grandfather that sent Charles Dickens's saintly heroine to her early grave.[44]

Aristocrats took the deepest plunge. "The stakes are enormously high," wrote Elisabeth Charlotte, Duchess of Orléans and sister-in-law of Louis XIV, in May 1695. "People behave like lunatics when they play. One will bawl, another bang the table so that the room shakes, a third blaspheme to make your hair stand on end." These histrionics were not the norm, however. The usual posture of aristocratic gamblers was one of studied nonchalance. Win or lose, they were not to show emotion. Gentlemen were expected to have the nerve to face a crisis calmly—as in a duel, which high-stakes gambling closely resembled—and to have pockets deep enough to cover their losses.

But that was not always the case. Crockford's, a West End gambling club run by a former fishmonger, specialized in wining, dining, and bleeding the aristocracy. William Molyneux, "Lord Dashalong," forked over the equivalent of $33 million. When he died, in 1838, he owed the proprietor another $5 million. His son, the 3rd Earl of Sefton, dutifully discharged the debt.[45]

If gambling and other vices brought down the wealthy, they also kept those of small means in their stations. As we have seen, contemporaries associated ruinous intoxication with laborers in work camps and slums, and with floozies who claimed whatever was left in their pockets after they settled their bar tabs. Missionaries puzzled over Chinese workers who smoked opium intermittently for years, with no ill effects, only to fall into a ruinous daily habit. Scandinavian clergy noted, in their meticulous church records, how drunkenness cursed the same families for generations—and then preached sermons of self-reformation. Lay observers in many cultures remarked on heavy smoking and drinking by soldiers coping with fear and boredom and by bingeing peasants who would sell, or do, anything for alcohol. "You often saw children drunk as well," a Russian translator recalled of his village in the 1880s. "Many of the mothers put vodka into their babies' milk. 'It's good for my baby,' one woman told me. 'See how well it makes him sleep.'"[46]

Enlightened opinion held that such practices bred generations of idiots and inebriates. While researchers today no longer speak of *blastotoxie* or degeneration, they have confirmed that early exposure to intoxicants can have dire consequences, particularly in poor populations. Poverty, stress, intoxication, and addiction interact to sustain caste. The brains of poor children raised in stressful environments show structural differences, notably in the prefrontal cortex, the region of executive control. As they grow older, they are likelier to suffer mental illnesses, to struggle to govern negative emotions, and to discount future rewards in favor of immediate gratification. These conditions all predict risky behavior, the odds rising for those born in cultures or neighborhoods where multigenerational poverty, powerlessness, familial instability, and open vice are the rule. Among the risky behaviors are drug use, which can cause further executive and cognitive impairment, especially during adolescence. Should drug use or any other compulsive behavior, including overeating, reach the point of preoccupation, the person will become socially isolated, unemployable, and stigmatized. Isolation, joblessness, and stigma being potent stressors, their addictive behavior will increase, along with the likelihood of relapse following abstention, voluntary or otherwise. Anomie completes addiction's vicious circle.[47]

By contrast, people with status, meaningful work, spouses, and futures are less likely to become or to stay addicted. Physicist Richard Feynman, walking past a Copacabana Beach bar, suddenly found himself craving a midafternoon drink. He wondered why, got the willies, and quit on the spot. Told by his doctor to give up smoking or die, the Pulitzer Prize–winning biographer Douglas Southall Freeman reached over, stubbed out his cigarette, and never took another drag. Told the same in his hospital bed, then senator Lyndon Johnson opened a pack, pulled a cigarette halfway out, and left it untouched on his nightstand—a talisman that worked for fifteen years, until he left the presidency. International surveys consistently show professionals quitting at higher rates than manual workers, who spend proportionately more of their smaller incomes on smoking. The same is true of alcohol and narcotic addictions: Airline pilots and doctors do much better in treatment than those with lower status and fewer resources. Having something to lose matters.[48]

Losing everything matters too, which accounts for the catastrophically high rates of addiction among conquered native peoples from the Arctic to the Outback. Dispossessed, dislocated, demoralized, and diseased, they were easy prey for traders glad to demonstrate how to swill the spirits in which they trafficked. Because they lacked cultural norms for restrained drinking—or, conversely, because they retained cultural preferences for spiritual quest through intoxication—native people developed a reputation for drunkenness, nowhere more so than in North America. "Whole Indian tribes have been destroyed by it," Rush observed in 1798. Adding insult to injury, an 1850 California law permitted officials to treat Indians who frequented "public places where liquors are sold" as vagrants and to auction off their labor to the highest bidders—slavery by another name. More enlightened legislatures tried to restrain the liquor trade, though profits of up to 400 percent assured widespread violation of the laws. Some frontiersmen sold from flasks secreted inside stovepipe boots, hence "bootleggers." The term stuck.[49]

So did the acquired knowledge of how to make alcohol. Long after the government got serious about suppressing liquor sales to Native Americans, the survivors fell back on home brewing. A public health nurse who visited Alaska in the 1950s noted that the Aleuts made theirs in barrels, throwing in scraps of anything that would ferment, including food from their malnourished children's plates. Not that the parents were ungenerous with the booze. When their children arrived at school, teachers reported, they were obviously hung over.[50]

Such conditions were, by any reckoning, appalling. Perhaps they seem more so today, because of the accumulated evidence of developmental harm from childhood and adolescent exposure to toxins. But Victorian reformers already harbored suspicions on that score, and they were determined to stop the flood of intoxicants and vices that threatened both their own and native societies. How they and their twentieth-century successors fared in that undertaking is the subject to which we now turn.

4

ANTI-VICE ACTIVISM

We know about the hungover Aleut children because a visiting nurse happened to make an indignant report about their condition. Had the context of their alcohol consumption been different, she might well have adopted a kindlier tone. Had the parents been doling out a spoonful of brandy to treat head cold symptoms, she would not have condemned their behavior. She might even have commended it.

This duality runs through the history of pleasure, vice, and addiction. The world is full of toxic things—often, though not always, enjoyable things—that can benefit humans and other organisms in low doses but harm or kill them in high doses, with the exact amounts varying from individual to individual. From alcohol to zinc, it is the dose that makes the poison, an idea often expressed in cautionary rules of thumb. Dilute wine to avoid drunkenness. Mind the patient's dose of opium, unless euthanasia be intended. Drink beer at meals and brandy only in moderation, "rather from Necessity than Pleasure." Hold back on sugar, lest you suffer unquenchable thirst.[1]

Cultures evolve rules to limit, however imperfectly, the harmful effects of potentially toxic and habituating pleasures. People adapt, like the Kenyans who judged cannabis smokers by their age. But such folk homeostasis has two flaws that limit its effectiveness. It is absent in "virgin soil" contexts, as when American Indians first encountered alcohol. And it is no match for modernity's rapid technological and commercial advances. Prudential rules are well and good. But how to get people, particularly those whom circumstance or heredity has made vulnerable, to follow them in a world filled with cheap, potent, heavily promoted pleasures?

THE LOGIC OF REFORM

The most common answer has been stricter control of vice, the key objective of a reform movement that reached its peak in the late nineteenth and early twentieth centuries. The movement was both international and transnational. It was international in that it led to formal negotiations among nation-states for suppressing sex trafficking, limiting narcotic manufacturing, and forbidding liquor sales to Africans in colonial possessions. It was transnational in that it inspired individuals to create nongovernmental networks and organizations that advocated reforms across national boundaries. The largest of these, the World's Woman's Christian Temperance Union (WWCTU), had three-quarters of a million dues-paying members by the 1920s, and branches from Australia to Sweden.[2]

Historians have not been especially kind to anti-vice activists, whom they have accused of cultural imperialism, moral hysteria, nest-feathering, and prejudice against workers and minority groups. Even those who were innocent of fanaticism, scaremongering, careerism, and class or racial bias acted from motives that were often at odds with those of their nominal allies. The danger is that, in admitting these flaws, we forget that the reformers were confronting a real crisis, often in imaginative and progressive ways. They were early adopters of a key principle of behavioral economics, that free markets incentivize deception and manipulation, particularly in industries that derive the bulk of their profits from excessive consumption. Reformers excoriated individuals, companies, governments, and empires that preyed on human weaknesses. Some singled out particular ethnic groups, especially Jews. Thoughtful critics, though, understood that the problem was systemic. Arrest a Jewish saloon-keeper, return to find a German or an Irishman polishing the bar and nodding the boys into the back room. Without industry-wide policing, competitive pressures would always render those who abided by responsible norms vulnerable to those who disregarded them for maximum profit.[3]

Some prominent anti-vice activists rejected capitalism. Auguste Forel was a socialist, Lenin a communist, Hitler a national socialist. The majority, however, accepted private competition in ordinary commerce. Famines occurred under feudalism and communism, as one put it. They did not occur under capitalism. The solution was to restrict access to commercial vices, which were anything but ordinary commodities. Restriction did not necessarily mean prohibition, the endpoint of a spectrum that ran from light regulation to prison with hard labor. Prohibition could also be achieved indirectly, by raising sin taxes to the point where the vice was financially out of reach. Or mostly out of reach, given that heavy taxes created black markets almost as reliably as outright bans did.[4]

Internally, the reformers' challenge was to agree upon which legal measures should apply to which vices and with what sanctions. Externally, the challenge was to persuade governments to adopt and enforce these measures despite cultural and political opposition. The best rationale for state action, and the place where reformers found common ground, was the argument that some products and practices were so baneful that governments had to step in. Here anti-vice activism aligned closely with Progressivism, then also emerging as a transnational force. Markets had limits. Child labor should not be freely bought and sold. Neither should whiskey, cocaine, pornography, and slot machines. Progressives and prohibitionists also believed in improving lives by improving environments, particularly urban environments. Social engineering had a two-front logic. Misery fostered vice. Vice fostered misery. So attack both simultaneously. That is why activists like Frances Willard denounced the oppression of women and workers as well as the abuse of intoxicants. Pay shop girls decent wages, argued suffragist Mary Lease, and perhaps they would not sell their virtue on the streets.[5]

The reformers' timing was impeccable. The spread of literacy in industrializing nations—by 1880 three-quarters of English men and women could read—encouraged sympathetic understanding of the plight of others. The temperance literature that the reading public devoured stressed the menace of drink, as did novels like Émile Zola's *L'Assommoir* (1877) and

Nana (1880). The first portrayed a working-class Paris couple's descent into alcoholism, the second the short, meretricious life of their *femme fatale* daughter. Meanwhile the Victorian and Edwardian middle classes were having second thoughts about the unbridled capitalism that their own values and industry had fostered. No aspect of the unregulated market was morally uglier, or more threatening to the wellbeing of women and children, than commercial vice.[6]

The prospect of collective ruin moved the levers of power. The era from the 1860s through the 1960s was one of intensive state-building, in which governments funded both internal improvements and hygienic reforms to foster healthier populations. The means at hand were carrots—one French mayor paid a bounty to every nursing mother whose child survived its first year—and sticks. The sticks included sanctions against toxic and infectious threats, commercial vice among them. "Men must live straight if they would shoot straight," said U.S. Navy secretary Josephus Daniels. "Prostitution and its twin brother, drunkenness, must be fought vigorously and unceasingly until they have become anachronisms."[7]

Hygienic reform created a virtuous circle. The healthier people became, and the purer their food and water, the less need they had of the analgesic and antidiarrheal properties of narcotics and the antimicrobial properties of alcohol. Temperance activists built public water fountains to compete with saloons. Municipal governments had their own reasons for providing potable water, starting with cholera prevention. Yet the effect was the same, in that safe water demoted beer and other alcoholic drinks to recreational beverages that consumers could forgo.[8]

Public health's international success inspired emulation. Even governments that lacked the resources and stability necessary for effective sanitary reform felt compelled to make a stab at hygienic policing, as in the Chinese Republic's campaigns to regulate prostitution and reduce opium and cigarette consumption. None made significant headway. Cigarettes were so common among Chinese laborers that chair bearers and carters gauged distance by the number smoked along the route. Yet the attempts held meaning. By the 1930s hygienic policing was a hallmark of all modern states,

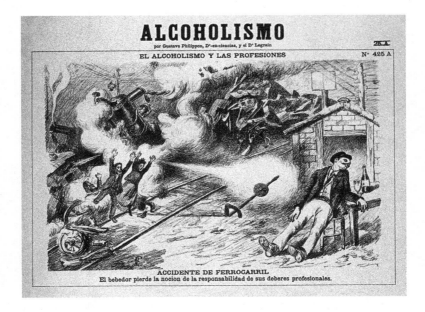

El bebedor, the heavy drinker asleep at the switch, loses all sense of professional responsibility, resulting in the loss of innocent lives and state property. Other panels in the Spanish poster series showed inebriated sailors rowing a boat into the path of a steamship, an unsteady workman falling from a roof, and an epileptic schoolchild sired by a drunkard.

and an obsession of fascist ones. Citizens did not have the right to destroy their bodies with poisons, a German addiction authority observed in 1938. The belief that "your body belongs to you" was Jewish Marxist claptrap. Real Germans bore the torch of Teutonic ancestry. They kept their bodies fit for their clan and people. Alcoholics who thought otherwise risked sterilization, the fate of perhaps thirty thousand heavy drinkers, mostly lower-class men. Others wound up in the camps.[9]

Though few anti-vice activists were overtly fascist, all were anti-libertarian. "Civilization spells restriction," wrote one of them in 1926. And the restrictions kept mounting, thanks to a century-long anti-libertarian wave against unfettered commerce and unchecked social costs. At its core, the social welfare case for coercive anti-vice measures was the same as that for mandatory smallpox vaccinations, an argument made by the U.S. Bureau of Prohibition.[10]

Anti-vice activism was well timed in other respects. If modernization had multiplied and cheapened vices, it had done the same for healthy and disciplined pleasures. Reformers like Mohandas Gandhi called these "counter-attractions." Spend your money on books, not on liquor, President Emilio Portes Gil told Mexican workers. Progressive Swedish laborers who joined temperance lodges thought reading and political discussion were as essential to the autonomous life as abstinence. British temperance societies nudged laborers toward sobriety by stocking street carts and stalls with ginger beer, sarsaparilla, and cocoa. In the 1870s, when billiards caught on as a working-class recreation, temperance reformers built billiard halls serving nonalcoholic drinks. In Philadelphia, the Quaker Joshua Baily countered another barroom attraction, the free lunch, by offering cheap temperance meals. In 1874 he established the Workingman's Central Coffee-House in a nest of groggeries. Each day two thousand workers dined on wholesome soups and sweet buns, washed down with coffee. Well-heeled visitors paid with large-denomination bills and asked for no change. Here was a philanthropic enterprise that begged for expansion.[11]

Vice itself could be made to pay for these counter-attractions. Fabians and other secular progressives championed variations of the Gothenburg system, the Swedish-born municipal dispensary scheme that channeled alcohol monopoly profits into public recreational and educational projects. The system featured stern publicans—police officers, really—on fixed salaries. They forbade treating, gambling, prostitution, and sales to minors or the intoxicated. One disappointed English sailor returned to ship after just two hours of liberty in Gothenburg. "I never was in such a place," he complained. "It is impossible to get drunk." Had he managed anyway, his liquefied wages would have gone to a park or library.[12]

Anti-vice activists seized on new communication and transportation technologies. The steam presses that printed obscene stories also cranked out penny reform tracts. Photoengraving cut muckraking periodicals' costs by more than half. Missionaries deluged government offices with telegraphed petitions against colonial opium sales. Temperance lecturers used stereopticon projectors to display fatty livers and alcoholic hearts. Fast ships carried missionaries looking for converts, and reformers looking for audiences and ideas. William Stead, an English journalist who crusaded against child prostitution, had the misfortune of booking his passage on the *Titanic*. Most reformers, however, arrived safely at their destinations. If vice became steam-propelled during the nineteenth century, so did anti-vice activism.[13]

One of the most tactically modern of the reformers, the Maine-born Presbyterian minister Wilbur Crafts, was also one of the most puritanical. In 1895 Crafts founded the International Reform Bureau, a Washington, D.C., lobby and clearinghouse. The bureau orchestrated campaigns against everything from liberalized divorce to opium sales. Craft saw vices as threats to salvation and public order and demanded the suppression of drink, drugs, gambling, obscenity, cigarettes, vampire movies, and Sabbath breaking. Better to err on the side of the Puritan Sunday than the godless Continental Sunday of bullfighting, beer idolatry, and horse racing. If new social conditions required the curtailment of individual liberty in economic and moral conduct, then so be it.

Crafts gave five lectures a week and wrote a book a year, including multiedition bestsellers like *World Book of Temperance* and *Protection of Native Races against Intoxicants and Opium*. Together with his wife and coauthor, WWCTU officer Sara Jane Timanus Crafts, he learned Esperanto. He promoted the language as a key to universal reform, a project shared by secular reformers. International travel, commerce, and reading, Crafts declared in 1906, were creating a phalanx of "international men." He spoke those words on the deck of an ocean liner. Before his death, in 1922, he took his anti-vice crusade to twenty-nine lands.[14]

Transnational purity reformers came from a variety of religious and political backgrounds. Wilbur and Sara Crafts epitomized the Western, more particularly American, anti-vice activists who combined evangelical zeal with white-man's-burden imperialism and a woman's rights agenda. The

temperance leader Frances Willard was cut from the same cloth as Kate
Bushnell, a medical missionary who spent thirty years as a "peripatetic puritan" crusading against forced prostitution. Yet Gandhi, the most famously
puritanical reformer of them all, combined *Vaishnava* Hinduism and Jain-
ism, a dash of Theosophy and utopianism, and staunch opposition to Western imperialism and commerce. Though Gandhi would enter history as
the father of Indian independence, he believed that true self-rule required
Indians to rid themselves of their vices as well as their English overlords.

Gandhi saw vices as linked and hierarchical. He particularly despised
cheap European liquor, which steamships had allowed hypocritical Christian imperialists to foist on the world. He was hardly alone in this com-
plaint, echoed by indigenous leaders and missionaries from Botswana to
New Zealand. But for Gandhi, drink was just the first domino in a line of
morally and physically ruinous vices. He wished to bury them all as deeply
as the pestiferous filth (another preoccupation) that befouled his beloved
nation. If it were within his persuasive power, he wrote in 1925, he would
prevent "women of ill-fame" from appearing on stage, abolish drinking and
smoking, and keep "degrading" ads, stories, and images out of the press.
Alas, he sighed, "I have not the persuasive power I would gladly possess."

The last remark was so modest as to be disingenuous. Gandhi organized pickets and boycotts of liquor stores. He made prohibition part of the
Congress Party platform. He campaigned against opium in poppy-growing
districts and supported international anti-narcotic organizations. He cor-
responded with temperance activists, Christian missionaries, and social
hygienists. He published his own health advice and that of others, reprint-
ing entire articles in his mouthpiece journals. He attacked vice in lectures,
warning college students to avoid the snares of tobacco. Gandhi knew
perfectly well how to use his celebrity to sway youthful audiences.[15]

So did his opponents. In 1921 one of them, a tobacco manufacturer, marketed "Mahatma Gandhi Cigarettes." The label bore the Great Soul's por-
trait. "Of all the abuses to which my name has been put," Gandhi wrote after
a friend sent him the label, "I know nothing so humiliating to me as the
deliberate association of my name with cigarettes." The demoralizing vice

enslaved the smoker, drained his purse, fouled his breath, and "sometimes even causes cancer." He called for the manufacturer to withdraw the brand and for the public to boycott its sale.[16]

THE LIMITS OF REFORM

Gandhi won that skirmish. The offending brand vanished. But he and his allies lost other battles. However briskly the progressive, statist, religious, medical, nationalistic, and propaganda winds blew at their backs, and however great their personal fame, activists like Gandhi and Crafts failed to prevail over commercial vice. Their reform record was checkered, their legacy fragile. That was literally so for Gandhi, whose eldest son, Harilal, died in alcoholic obscurity in 1948, less than six months after his father's assassination. In the century after World War I, entrepreneurs managed, slowly but surely, to legitimize, glamorize, and expand the empire of vice and multiply its forms of addiction. How and why anti-libertarian reformism, which once seemed so formidable, lost to commercial libertinism is the puzzle at the heart of this book.

It is a puzzle because many other international reform efforts succeeded. They produced enduring agreements against privateering, the transatlantic slave trade, the military use of expanding bullets and poison gas, the unlimited killing of whales and migratory birds, and the atmospheric testing of nuclear weapons, to name but a few. None worked perfectly, but all worked well enough to make a difference for the better, and without rancorous second-guessing. No one could say the same of anti-vice activism.

Of course, issuing letters of marque or releasing mustard gas did not produce pleasure in the same way as sipping whiskey or rolling dice. Repeatable brain reward puts vice in a unique category. Within that category was a lucrative subcategory, that of regular consumers. The relative inflexibility of their demand, especially in the short run, meant that any pronounced reduction in supply would cause upward pressure on prices. Sometimes shortages were circumstantial. In 1917 tobacco shortages sent the price of blended American cigarettes to a record high in remote corners of Europe.

"Prophecy of the Tea-Leaves" appeared in 1918, just as global prohibition was cresting. Eight countries had imposed statutory prohibition on alcoholic beverages. Several others, including France, had banned absinthe. But the prophecy that more prohibition would follow, or that governments would suppress the vices to which alcohol was linked, was not borne out. "John Barleycorn," the personification of booze, pivoted, grabbed the goat of global prohibition by the horns, and wrestled him over the cliff.

More often the shortages were the product of restrictions, punitive taxes, and prohibitions. Those who reaped profits from legally induced shortages added a surcharge for the higher risk and overhead, including bribes, that their illegal enterprises entailed.[17]

American markets for pornography and nonmedical narcotic use, both illegal by the 1920s, demonstrate prohibition's effects on supply and price. Books like *Ladies of the Parlor* were trafficked by smugglers or run off at local printing shops, which pornographers rented by night and manned with their own crews. Secrecy was of the essence, competitors being quick to inform on rivals. Pornographers improvised under-the-counter retail outlets, from camera shops to drugstores. Legitimate bookstores ran, as a sideline, rental libraries offering books at two cents a day. These offered cover for obscene book rentals that could fetch a dollar a day.

Those who purchased pornography outright paid through the nose. Hardcover literary fiction sold for $2 a copy. Garden-variety erotic books sold for $5 to $10, "quality" titles for much more. The advent of 16 mm film technology in the 1920s and 1930s brought new opportunities for inflated profits. With little more than a camera, a chorus girl, and a tub to wash the processed film, decentralized producers made pornographic movies for about $25 a reel. Traveling salesmen rented them for $50 for one-off showings at fraternity houses or American Legion posts. Car dealers rented them to get the backlot boys to attend sales rallies. Others bought the films, booked a hotel meeting room, and charged anywhere from $2 to $25 a ticket. One middle-level distributor took over a Times Square hotel suite, showed his films to potential customers, and closed the sale if they liked what they saw. By 1956 he had amassed cash worth a third of a million in today's dollars. He did this despite an addiction to Dilaudid, a drug derived from morphine.

The market for narcotics worked in much the same way as the market for pornography. The Times Square pornographer got his Dilaudid from a German refugee doctor who charged him $25 for the prescription and a pharmacist who charged him another $25 to fill it. Things were worse for street addicts, who hustled to scrounge $5 to buy a 5-grain (aspirin-sized) dose of powdered "heroin" that was 95 percent adulterated. That worked out to about 30 cents, the price of a half-dozen candy bars, for a single milligram of pure heroin.[18]

Looked at one way, numbers like these simply mean that prohibition was working. High prices reduced consumption, particularly among urban workers, who were the main object of prohibition legislation. Just as important, suppliers could not operate openly. They were forced underground or, in one case, underwater. Algot Niska, a legendary Finnish smuggler, towed a homemade booze torpedo behind his boat.[19]

That was fine by the reformers. They knew that vice could never be eliminated. They meant to banish it from public view, where it tempted the uninitiated and shocked the respectable. A stag film at a late-night fraternity smoker was well outside the bounds of commercial normality. Granted, this segregation of vice did not last. Its permeation of global visual and commercial culture later in the twentieth century was the surest sign that traditional anti-vice activists had lost their fight, culture wars notwithstanding. In the 1920s, however, reform activists could still hold their heads high. They had the satisfaction of knowing that many vices (cigarettes being an increasingly conspicuous exception) remained expensive, marginalized, stigmatized, and, if not illegal, then more or less tightly regulated. And they believed, reasonably, that their propagandizing stood a better chance against that which was illegal or dodgy than that which was openly advertised and commercially mainstream.

These victories came at a cost. Inflated prices attracted traffickers who, because they operated completely outside the law, were more inclined to corruption, adulteration, and violence than their legal forebears. Addicts, particularly those who used narcotics, supported their habits with more and riskier crimes, including drugstore burglaries. Luxuries that became necessities that became addictions had their own iron law: Strict bans produced fewer consumers, but they were on average worse off and more disruptive. For those who were not addicted, the dangers and inconveniences of the black market prompted deep resentment. Familiar pleasures in familiar settings offered the potential of liberation as well as enslavement. Shuttered taverns and saloons cost working men comradeship, relaxation, newspapers, credit, political favors, job leads, and mail drops as well as alcohol. They resented these deprivations, and the class bias at the heart of prohibition.[20]

The virtues and defects of prohibition were most apparent in the United States, which conducted a long national experiment in curtailing the manufacture, distribution, and sale of alcoholic beverages. National Prohibition began in early 1920, when the Volstead Act implemented enforcement of the Eighteenth Amendment's ban on "intoxicating liquors." It lasted until 1933, when the Twenty-First Amendment repealed the Eighteenth, returning alcohol control to state and local governments. In that interval Hollywood movies and global press coverage turned Prohibition into an object lesson in what could go wrong when alcohol restriction became too ambitious. The Volstead Act imposed a less-than-total ban, allowing for medicinal and sacramental use and limited home brewing. However, several rural states, which already had prohibition laws, tightened their statutes to outlaw personal purchase, possession, and consumption. Local authorities and vigilantes made sure that enforcement fell most heavily on poor whites and racial minorities, who worked off their fines on construction gangs. Crime bosses with protection money had an easier go. Versed in the art of bribing police to ignore their brothels and gambling dens, they were set to cash in on bootlegging, provided that they could fend off rivals with similar intentions.

For all its loopholes and hypocrisies—whiskey's enemies were more numerous on the floor of Congress than in its cloakroom—Prohibition did have a substantial impact on consumption and prices. Per capita consumption initially fell to 30 percent of pre-Prohibition levels, before gradually increasing to 60 or 70 percent by 1933. The drink most affected was beer. Pre-Prohibition improvements in brewing, preservation, and shipping had made draft beer plentiful and cheap. A nickel brought an oversize schooner sliding down the bar. Between 1900 and 1913 per capita alcohol consumption rose nearly a third on this tide of beer. But when the nation's 1,300 breweries could no longer legally produce full-strength beer, urban prices rose between five- and tenfold.[21]

Bootleg spirits took up some of the slack, though a quart could exhaust half a laborer's weekly wages. Asked why her husband, a shipyard worker, was drinking less, a New Jersey housewife replied simply that it was due to liquor's poorer quality and higher cost. Across the Hudson River, in Manhattan, the number of patients treated in Bellevue Hospital's alcohol wards dropped from fifteen thousand a year before Prohibition to under six thousand in 1924. Nationally, cirrhosis deaths fell by more than a third between 1916 and 1929. In Detroit, arrests for drunkenness declined 90 percent during Prohibition's first year. Domestic violence complaints fell by half.[22]

But the silver cloud of Prohibition in Detroit had a black lining. Located near Windsor, Ontario, where much of Canada's legally distilled booze was illegally funneled into the United States, Detroit soon became a center of organized crime and headline-grabbing violence. In 1929 the city logged the nation's highest homicide rate. More than anything else, problems generated by enforcement—gangs and corruption, ethnic and class resentments, poisoned liquor and full jails—rocked Prohibition's political boat. Rocked, but did not sink. In 1928 the dry Republican presidential candidate, Herbert Hoover, trounced his wet Democratic and Catholic rival, Al Smith. Protestant prohibitionists fought on. Henry Ford, who declared that liquor and the industrial age could not coexist, threatened to close down his factories if prohibition laws were repealed.[23]

It took the crisis of the Great Depression to end the Noble Experiment. Hard times mocked the promise of Prohibition-based prosperity, created an urgent need for revenue, and cost Republicans control of Congress and the White House. The Democrats' 1932 landslide paved the way for the return of legal beer and the fast repeal of the Eighteenth Amendment. What killed Prohibition was a drastic change in context. Set and setting mattered for vice laws, as well as vices themselves.[24]

The level of taxation was another important variable in vice policy. Bootlegging persisted in states that restored legal alcohol sales. Criminals "redistilled" industrial alcohol in big-city warehouses, out of sight of the Internal Revenue Service. Country moonshiners kept holler stills gurgling and hissing. But the overall level of bootlegging declined after 1933, as

Peck & Peck, an upscale women's clothier, designed this anti-Prohibition scarf. The drum and fife players evoked the libertarian revolution against overbearing authority on which the United States was founded. The clothes identified them with modernity, though not with license: The chicly dressed woman is no flapper. The top-hatted drummer's clumsiness—he has just banged the other drummer on his bandaged head—slyly alluded to Prohibition's failure to keep toffs from drinking. The lower-taxes claim is dubious. Excises on alcohol could increase the government's total take, or shift the tax burden away from the wealthy, but they did not guarantee lower overall taxation, as events in the revenue-hungry 1930s and 1940s would prove.

licensed distilling and import firms came back on line. Then, in the crisis of World War II—another abrupt change in context—the federal government tripled liquor excise taxes. Illegal distilling surged as base materials again became available. By 1950 governments, tax-paying businesses, and illicit traffickers were competing for a share of the liquor pie, just as they had always done. Those unable to pay liquor-store prices were the bootleggers' best customers, a pattern that held, and still holds, worldwide.[25]

The vicissitudes of American alcohol control in the first half of the twentieth century illustrate a problem that plagued anti-vice activists everywhere. Modernizing nation-states were unreliable, or at best inconsistent, reform partners. They had the power and motivation to address the social and health consequences of commercial vice, but also a thirst for revenue and ambivalence about suppressing the habits of their own elites. Stalin reopened the floodgates of taxed vodka, Mao nationalized the Chinese cigarette industry. Indian politicians, who drank champagne and taxed the arrack of the poor, never got around to national prohibition, despite Gandhi's insistence that they do so. In 1937 Gandhi observed that, in America, a right-thinking minority had failed to make Prohibition stick because drinking was insufficiently shameful for the majority. In India, where drinking was stigmatized and only a minority indulged, prohibition would be "easy to carry out." Lost revenue would pale beside the virtue of national sobriety. His prophecy failed spectacularly. By 2014, India accounted for half of the world's whiskey sales.[26]

Smaller nations proved equally shaky reform partners. The smallest of them all, Vatican City, invested in the fledgling Italian motion picture industry despite the censorious decrees of Pope Pius X, who forbade his own priests from viewing movies. After 1904 Transvaal disallowed opium sales to laborers, but temporarily relaxed the prohibition when more than sixty-three thousand Chinese immigrant workers arrived to restart gold-mining operations disrupted by the South African War. In Siam, which also had a growing Chinese presence, neither the country's Buddhist heritage nor the protests of Christian missionaries prevented the monarchy from farming out concessions for liquor distilling, opium sales, and gambling. By 1895 the three vices provided 51 percent of Siam's revenues. Most tempting of all were tobacco taxes. Eliminate them, a cynic wrote in 1902, and half the world's governments would go under.[27]

That was certainly true of Bulgaria, which became increasingly dependent on tobacco production and revenue during the twentieth century. Before World War II Bulgarian farmers and exporters prospered by supplying German tobacco giants like Reemtsma. Lung masturbation proved ineradicably popular in Nazi Germany, where per capita cigarette consumption doubled between 1935 and 1940. Bigwigs Hermann Göring, Adolf Eichmann, Martin Bormann, Eva Braun, and Joseph and Magda Goebbels puffed away, hypocrisy being no stranger to revolutionary movements swollen with opportunists. After the Reich's demise, Bulgaria supplied Eastern European and Soviet smokers. By 1966 the small nation was the world's largest cigarette exporter. By the early 1980s Bulgarians themselves were among the world's heaviest smokers. Half of the country's men and women smoked cigarettes, one of the few affordable and abundant luxuries.[28]

None of this occurred without opposition. In Bulgaria the first to protest were Protestant missionaries and churchgoers who linked smoking with drinking and prostitution. Forel-influenced leftists viewed smoking as a bourgeois indulgence and font of degeneration. Communists agreed in principle. In practice they listened to Radio Moscow through a haze of tobacco smoke. "Bulgarian gold" paid the nation's bills. In 1947 the People's Republic of Bulgaria created an integrated tobacco monopoly, Bulgartabak, and used the proceeds to finance the country's modernization. Public health took a back seat. Philip Morris was paying attention. In 1973 the monopoly's director, Dimitŭr Iadkov, paid a courtesy call on the Philip Morris CEO, Hugh Cullman. Iadkov was surprised to see a map on Cullman's wall with BULGARTABAK plastered over the expanse from East Germany to Vladivostok. "I really envy you," the capitalist told the communist. "I always dream of those markets. I say this with sincere envy, because for our company the market rules."[29]

THE DIVISIONS OF REFORM

Anti-vice activists also understood the importance of markets, which is why they wanted to suppress, marginalize, or tightly regulate those for commercial vice. The "or" is important. In addition to the problems of consumer resistance and state ambivalence, reformers had to deal with their own disputes over tactics, rationales, and priorities. Disagreements within the reform coalition were fully apparent by the early nineteenth century. They have persisted to this day.

What happened in Richmond, Virginia, in the fall of 1833 illustrates the problem. Faced with a sudden increase in illegal gambling houses, Richmond citizens convened a meeting. So many people turned up at the capitol building that onlookers perched on window sills. They elected an investigative committee that promptly identified at least fourteen secret gambling houses, some a block or two from the capitol grounds. In these haunts professional gamblers tempted the young and excited the passions, robbing men of character, reason, and earnings. They got away with it, the committee reported, because laws against gambling were inadequate and inadequately enforced. Professional gambling had been illegal in Virginia since 1727. Yet indictments were few and successful prosecutions fewer. Witnesses were reluctant to testify. When professional gamblers were found guilty, they received light punishments, these sometimes pardoned. The committee recommended more tightly drawn laws, stricter enforcement, and harsher sentences. Fines and imprisonment would do for white men. Slaves, free Negroes, and mulattos should be whipped.

More punishment was a classic reaction to defiance, and a plainer demonstration of race's role in intensifying such punishment can scarce be imagined. Even so, the committee's report was neither unthinking nor unanimous. Its members considered, and rejected, two alternatives. One was to put the players on the same legal footing as those who organized and exhibited the games. But that action would punish the victims as well as the victimizers. The other was to try to diminish the harm by limiting gambling to a few licensed houses. But legalization might make gambling fashionable, luring ten moths to the flame for every one burned at present. One had only to look at Paris, where gambling was "taxed as an amusement." The yearly revenue of 5.5 million francs (roughly $27 million today) came at the cost of gambling mania and suicides who plunged into the Seine or shot themselves on the spot. Most European nations, and all but one American state, had chosen not to legalize this pernicious vice.[30]

Three of the committee's more cosmopolitan members published a minority report that dissented on the point of legalization. Gambling, the minority observed, still flourished outside the law, notoriously so in London. The Commonwealth of Virginia, which had increased gambling sanctions since the 1727 ban, had fared little better. No amount of punishment could eliminate the passion for gain without work. Of late "a certain class of moralists and their followers," meaning evangelical Protestants, had made matters worse by lumping faro and roulette with more innocent pastimes like dancing and theater. By arousing skepticism about puritanical meddling, they had blinded citizens to what was baneful and what was not.

The best way to minimize gambling would be to license it in bonded houses, while suppressing it elsewhere. The spies of legal proprietors, anxious to protect their monopoly, would abet law enforcement. Patrons who clung to the anonymity of the secret houses would risk arrest. Those who moved to the licensed houses would be safe from the law, but not from the eyes of neighbors and creditors. Their disapproval would discourage extravagant wagering, or perhaps any wagering at all. As for visibility making gambling fashionable, that was hardly a concern. The illegal houses were already patronized by gentlemen of standing, not excepting legislators and judges, who could often be seen discussing their wins and losses with studied nonchalance.[31]

The dissenters failed to carry the day. Operating a gambling house remained illegal. By the early 1900s conviction could bring sixty days in jail and a stiff fine. If these measures had any effect, it was not discernible. Richmonders from all walks of life, including lads scarce sixteen, continued to crowd the green tables, pressing their unequal fight against the cool professionals on the other side. As the dissenters foresaw, the punters were more concerned about being discovered by their employers and creditors than by the police, who winked as they passed by.[32]

Gambling was neither the only nor necessarily the highest reform priority. Activists in spirits-drinking societies most often named alcohol the kingpin of vice. Others attached greater opprobrium to prostitution, narcotics, or tobacco, particularly cigarettes, the "little white slaver" that led to all other evils. And yet, whatever their primary target, anti-vice activists would have instantly recognized the tension between the Richmond majority and minority reports. The suppression versus regulation dilemma applied across the anti-vice spectrum. Should the state ban alcohol, or should it content itself with rules to keep drunks, bettors, and boys outside the tavern doors? Should prostitutes be arrested and punished, or should they be segregated and inspected to prevent the spread of venereal disease? Should addicts be denied drugs, or should they be allowed legal prescriptions from doctors and public clinics?

These controversies were long-running, divisive, and bitter. Inebriety specialists—physicians who advocated a unified disease model of addiction—were denounced from pulpits as tools of Satan who dignified vice. The most ardent prohibitionists, Crafts among them, questioned even the medicinal use of alcohol, a stance that alarmed physicians who defended their professional judgment in prescribing alcohol like any other regulated drug.[33]

Anti-vice activists who were secular or religiously liberal were more inclined toward regulatory approaches. Those who were religiously conservative were more inclined toward suppression. Root-and-branch solutions were especially popular among evangelical Protestants, the backbone of the global missionary enterprise. By temperament and theology, evangelicals were suspicious of self-indulgence and believed that sin and scandal were themselves grounds for vice suppression. Vice might ruin health, but what mattered in the end was salvation. Abstinence was a sign of salvation, intoxication a fatal impediment. The Gospel, wrote a Hangzhou missionary, was the one sure remedy for China's woes. But England's demoralizing opium trade crippled his ability to apply it.[34]

The more evangelicals in a given place, the greater the likelihood of prohibition. The growing number and influence of Methodists and Baptists in the American South helps explain why 825 of the region's 994 counties were dry by 1907, a decade before wartime prohibition. (Louisiana's holdout Catholic parishes were the exceptions that prove the rule.) Things were otherwise in South America, where *evangélicos* had yet to gain a foothold, though some governments did adopt specific alcohol controls. Bolivia forbade the sale of liquor on weekends, Chile regulated where and when alcohol retailers could operate. But U.S.-style prohibition never caught on.[35]

In Catholic countries, the perennially touchy subject of fornication brought out similar differences of religious temperament. Traditionalists favored suppression and punishment, modernists regulation and medicalization. In World War I soldiers from rural Slovenia, where old-school Catholic prudery ruled, got lectures on the importance of sexual continence and threats of strict punishment if they acquired venereal infections. Soldiers from Italy, which was also Catholic but more urban and cosmopolitan, got sex education and medical advice about using condoms.[36]

Anti-vice activism attracted people with fundamentally different ways of knowing truth and acting in the world. It was a coalition of opposites. In Western nations, the leading figures included scientific experts like Forel, who cared about health and efficiency but dismissed anti-vice moralizing as an impediment to sound policy and effective treatment. Opposed to them were transnational activists like Crafts, whose demands for social and political reform sprang from religious convictions of right and wrong. Compromise with evil being unacceptable, or at best a stopgap, these moral crusaders gravitated toward prohibition, damning schemes like controlled liquor sales. Wealthy industrialists and employers had yet different motives. They had little interest in blanket prohibitions and less in personal abstinence. They nevertheless favored restricting workers' access to alcohol and other vices—in brief, class legislation. There was also a predominantly non-Western group, including nationalists like Ho Chi Minh, who regarded European vice commerce and taxation as imperialist tools. That all four of these positions (and hybrid variations like Gandhi's) gained credibility and adherents in the early twentieth century, and that their rise coincided with growing concern about the excesses of industrial capitalism and the crisis of World War I, goes a long way toward explaining the wave of anti-vice activism that characterized the 1910s and 1920s.[37]

Anti-vice activism persisted after the 1920s, though its rhetoric and rationale became increasingly secular and scientific. In Romania, traditional Orthodox arguments against tobacco were a mixture of religious injunction—smoking was sinful—and nativism—smoking was what Gypsies and Turks did. Religious arguments began to assume a hybrid medical character: As a form of slow suicide, smoking was a sin against God. By the late twentieth century, the religious aspect had dropped out, leaving a catalog of health afflictions linked to what had once been called *iarba dracului*, the devil's herb.[38]

Though the timing differed, the drift toward secular rationales occurred in all societies, theocracies excepted. Not only did medical evidence become more credible, or at least more specific, but it could be made to dovetail with nationalist fears and aspirations. When, in 1899, Nemoto Shō, a Christian and temperance advocate, introduced a ban on tobacco use by minors in the Japanese Diet, he emphasized that smoking undermined the health of the young and the vitality of the nation. Let adolescents keep smoking, he warned, and they could "bring our country down to the miserable conditions of countries like China and India." Icing the cake, Nemoto pointed out that "civilized" nations like Germany had enacted bans on underage smoking. Japan must follow suit. In 1900 it did, even though the same government established a revenue-generating monopoly over all tobacco products four years later. The proceeds financed internal development and imperial expansion. Once again, modernizing ambition pulled the state in two directions.[39]

Richmond P. Hobson, a dashing American prohibitionist turned transnational anti-narcotics crusader, wanted his nation to go in just one direction. When, in 1924, he backed pending congressional anti-heroin legislation, he too named China and India as the next stops on the degeneration express. But heroin was far worse than tobacco, because it addicted teenage dabblers in a week and turned them into criminal zombies bent on spreading the habit to others. "So ghastly is the plight of the narcotic addict, and so hopeless his chances of permanent recovery," Hobson declared, "that in scientific circles addicts are called 'The Living Dead.'" Medically trained addiction experts called them no such thing, and they despised Hobson's falsehoods. Yet he managed to strike both public-safety and national-security nerves. When, in 1928, Hobson approached John D. Rockefeller and other philanthropists for funding, he went a bold step further, claiming that narcotics threatened the foundation of civilization itself. By the 1920s and 1930s, sickness and safety were surer rhetorical bets for anti-vice causes than sin and salvation.[40]

One reason for the rhetorical shift, apart from the secular and scientific drift of Western societies, was that a whiff of fanaticism had attached itself to moral crusades. The historian Jack Miles's observation—"Religion makes people do things that make no sense, and this constitutes both its worst weakness and its greatest strength"—seems nowhere truer than with respect to vices. Crusaders struck frappé glasses from the lips of astonished drinkers. They smashed drugstore windows. They defaced movie posters judged indecent. Count Leo Tolstoy, who influenced Gandhi and other religious utopians, attacked his own imagined vices. In 1884 he gave up smoking, wine, meat, tea, card-playing, and hunting. He tried to give up sex with his long-suffering wife, Sophia, but failed. "It was so disgusting," he wrote postcoitally, "I felt I'd committed a crime."[41]

Fanatical enemies made useful foils. Few people openly defended vices. But many ridiculed bluenoses, grim puritans whose obsession with denying others' pleasures belied the claim that anti-libertarian laws were reasonable and justified. Nor was the stereotype of the fanatic confined to the devout. Anti-vice activism had a secular wing rooted in *Lebensreform,* a German lifestyle-reform movement that also assumed a transnational character in the early twentieth century. Its adherents' disdain for alcohol and tobacco and enthusiasm for rural simplicity, organic food, nudism, and common-law relationships ("vegetarian marriages" in Germany) struck many onlookers as crankery or, worse, sexual license flying the colors of radical reform. From another angle, the same practices amounted to a principled rejection of an industrial order whose mass-produced poisons immiserated generations of workers; whose hang-up about nakedness intensified carnality; and whose gorging on meat inspired bloodlust and war. Plausible or not, none of these suppositions could overcome sensationalist reports of nude gymnastics, promiscuity, and occultism in "godless Edens" popping up across Western Europe and North America.[42]

Even those reformers who were neither eccentric nor godless felt conflicted over anti-vice priorities. Some broke with their allies. One was Bishop Charles Henry Brent, Episcopal Missionary Bishop to the Philippines. In 1909 and again in 1911–1912, Brent chaired international opium conferences. These laid the foundation for a treaty system to limit narcotic production to medical and scientific needs. Any other use, including state revenue, Brent deplored as a vice and a crime. So great was his moral authority on the issue that he continued to attend League of Nations opium conferences long after failing health made such journeys unwise. "That damned opium mess has started up again," he confided to his diary in August 1923, referring to an upcoming round of international negotiations. But the president wanted him in Geneva. So off he went.[43]

Diplomatic historians have depicted Brent as a classic moral crusader, religious admirers as a "saint upon earth." He was both and he was neither. Born in Ontario and ordained an Episcopal priest in 1887, Brent began his pastoral work in the United States, where he served in Boston's most vice-ridden parish. There he found sinners in abundance, including a reformed alcoholic who dared not drink from the communion chalice. Yet Brent understood his parishioners' sins broadly, as anything that blocked the search for completeness in God that was the core of Christian life. He did not suppose that the merely recreational qualified as an impediment. Brent himself found time for chess, the odd hand of bridge, bowling, hockey, tennis, and golf. He enjoyed music and theater, save George Bernard Shaw's *Major Barbara,* "too full of disbelief in human ideals to be effective." His own ideals elevated the Social Gospel and Christian unity over emotive proselytizing and enforced abstemiousness. By 1926 he had parted company with more conservative Protestants on the wisdom of the Volstead Act. Brent questioned both the principle and the effectiveness of America's experiment with alcohol prohibition. Some reforms, he thought, were a bridge too far.[44]

THE HASH OF REFORM

In 1929 Brent succumbed to heart disease in the course of yet another overseas trip. He was buried where he died, in a simple oak casket in a Lausanne cemetery. The funeral service, like the moral activism he had embraced, was multilingual. And yet, if one were to ask what Brent and his generation of reformers had accomplished, the frank answer would be that they had created, in the bishop's words, a damned mess.[45]

The mess was not entirely their fault. During the last three decades of the nineteenth century and the first three decades of the twentieth, two rising global forces collided. One was commercial vice. This force was the lucrative, potentially addictive side of an accelerating pleasure revolution that had acquired tremendous inertial force, owing to the (sometimes strategically conflicted) interests of business and government. The other was anti-vice activism. This force was the vehement (though tactically conflicted) opposition of reformers who condemned commercial vice as a threat to moral, material, national, and racial progress. These same reformers gained strength and credibility from the larger progressive reaction against free-market abuses.

The collision produced a policy hodgepodge. National alcohol prohibition was on its last legs when Brent died in 1929. Finland threw in the towel in 1932, the United States in 1933. In Helsinki the repeal carnival lasted two days. Waiters filled beer mugs from pitchers of vodka. Bootleggers dumped their stock at fifteen cents a quart. Police doubled their patrols.[46]

Prohibition gave way to national or state control, often with local prohibition options. The situation in Latvia was typical. Wartime prohibition reduced drunkenness. Postwar repeal increased it. In 1921 the parliament created a government monopoly over alcohol production and distribution. In 1925 it limited retail sales by place and time. The law forbade sales from noon Saturday until Monday morning, more evidence of how worries over working-class drinking shaped alcohol control. The government also diverted 1.5 percent of alcohol revenues to temperance propaganda and allowed municipal and county councils to ban sales altogether. Those that did so were mostly in Latvia's rural districts. Taverns and restaurants serving alcohol clustered in cities and larger towns.[47]

Despite rural holdouts, the drift of the 1920s was toward regulated alcohol sales. Every Canadian province except tiny Prince Edward Island had abandoned optional prohibition by the end of 1930. "The world is going dry," the head of the Canadian WCTU had boasted in 1925. It was not, either in Canada or in the new League of Nations. Wine-producing countries, particularly France, blocked international inquiry into intoxicants other than narcotics. The cultural habits of Europeans were not to be questioned, though opiate use by Asians was fair game.[48]

Europeans did question the habit of gambling—up to a point. The larger continental states had outlawed commercial gambling in the nineteenth century, which opened the door for Monaco and other casino principalities. Macau similarly benefited when British officials cracked down on gambling in Hong Kong, prompting local gamblers to flee to the nearby Portuguese colony. Yet these same British colonial officials tolerated horse racing and high-stakes card games in private homes and clubs. Austrian police ignored poker games in the ski resorts, especially when the public prosecutor and the police captain happened to be playing. Rank had its privileges.[49]

So did money. In 1837 the French Chamber of Deputies outlawed gam-

OPPOSITE: Nazis were ambivalent about lotteries, but not so ambivalent as to outlaw them. Instead, in 1938 and 1939, the Reich consolidated state lotteries into a single national lottery, sanitized the marketing methods, advertised the benefit to Nazi charities (here the Winter Relief campaign), and banned Jews from buying tickets. For gambling to be seemly it could have nothing to do with an officially despised race. War was another matter. By 1941 rumors circulated in Berlin that Winter Relief proceeds were going to the military.

121

bling houses. But then, in 1907, the French government decided to again permit some casino games, eventually cutting itself in on 60 percent of the action. Local governments took another 20 percent. Revenue was a constant temptation, and the main reason why outposts of legal casinos and pari-mutuel wagering survived. In 1933 even the Nazis, not known for their toleration of public vice, agreed to reopen the casino at Baden-Baden, Dostoyevsky's old stomping grounds. After all, there were tourist dollars to be had.[50]

In places where organized gambling remained illegal, it persisted sub rosa in vice districts. Criminal syndicates ran keno and faro parlors, greased palms from the take, and pocketed the rest. Al Capone took a million-dollar cut from his floating casino and sports book in Cicero, Illinois, a Chicago suburb with railway connections and an easily subverted town government. It was the failure to report this gambling income, not his bootlegging profits, that finally tripped up Capone, who was indicted and convicted of tax evasion in 1931. He furnished his prison cell with an Oriental carpet, cabinet radio, wingchair, and fringed lamp.[51]

Similar conflicts and temptations surrounded the control of prostitution. In the nineteenth and early twentieth centuries prostitution fell into one of three categories: legal and regulated, illegal, or illegal but regulated anyway. After the Revolution, France evolved a system of state-regulated prostitution intended to minimize the spread of venereal disease through registration, regular medical inspection, confinement of infected women, and restriction of sexual transactions to designated places. Nineteenth-century European states experimented with French-style *réglementation,* which spread globally on the tide of empire. After 1898, when Spain ceded the Philippines to the United States, Filipina madams redecorated their brothels with the stars and stripes to advertise their licensed status and attract American troops. Draw they did. Prevent they did not. A sixth of the soldiers treated at Manila's military hospital had contracted venereal disease.[52]

Independent governments such as China and Argentina established their own registration schemes. None proved particularly effective. Clandestine prostitutes, mostly poor women in fast-growing cities, continued to sell or barter sex. In 1900, when Russian officials had registered thirty-four thousand prostitutes, informed observers judged the true number ten times higher. The situation was little better in other Continental cities. European officials consistently traced half or more of venereal infections back to clandestine or part-time prostitutes.[53]

Many Anglo-American Protestants opposed regulation. England's leading proponent of abolition, Josephine Butler, waged a seventeen-year campaign against the Contagious Diseases Acts, which permitted the compulsory inspection and commitment of infected prostitutes to "lock hospitals." Though Parliament finally repealed the laws in 1886, Butler's domestic and transnational allies divided over other issues. Was it enough to be rid of the scandal of licensed brothels and venereal hospitals where women were confined against their will, or should prostitution itself be outlawed? Should there be, as William Stead argued, toleration of consensual prostitution but prosecution of the trade's coercive aspects, such as child trafficking?[54]

North American purity crusaders rejected such fine distinctions. They regarded prostitution as a ruinous social evil, the more vicious for its connection to intoxicants and pornography and its embodiment of the sexual double standard. Though Canada briefly experimented with regulation, as did several American municipalities, reformers managed to formally outlaw prostitution in all but a few places, New Orleans's Storyville being the most notorious. Yet selective prosecution quickly emerged as an alternative form of regulation. In St. Paul, Minnesota, madams made monthly appearances in police court to pay fines for "keeping a disorderly house." What they were actually doing was paying taxes and renewing a contract to keep an orderly disorderly house. If they tolerated robberies or assaults, or procured women through kidnapping and fraud, they could be put out of business. If they kept the lid on they could count on stability and jovial support, the police being happy to toast the détente at the madams' open-house Christmas parties.[55]

DRUG EXCEPTIONALISM

No single cause explains the variation in anti-vice policies. Differences in rigor and timing reflect cultural, political, religious, and developmental differences, as well as military contingencies. Napoleon doubled tobacco taxes after his defeat at Leipzig; belligerents banned distilling during World War I. Some anti-vice activists were more skilled and tenacious than others. It mattered that Bishop Brent championed the cause of international narcotic control and that Josephine Butler took on Britain's Contagious Diseases Acts. And yet, viewed globally, there was more to anti-vice activism than a victory here and a defeat there. The broader pattern of 1870–1930 was toward secular and utilitarian justifications for anti-vice measures, and toward formal or tacit regulation of vice, rather than moralizing prohibition. Over the following six decades, the normalizing trend would intensify, with skeptics and opportunists in consumer societies questioning whether many traditional "vices"—their scare quotes said it all—were objectionable in any respect.[56]

There is an important exception to the trend, though the exception is so consistent across cultures that it too seems part of a general pattern. The exception is the global campaign against the nonmedical use of psychoactive drugs, which in the early twentieth century meant chiefly those derived from opium poppies, coca, and cannabis. The premise behind a series of international treaties was that if drug supply could be limited to medical and scientific needs, nonmedical use and addiction would dry up, like a weed withering from lack of water. That did not happen. What did happen between the 1912 Hague Opium Convention and the 1953 Opium Protocol was a gradual tightening of international production controls, coupled with increasingly strict domestic drug laws in countries as different as Canada, Mexico, Jamaica, France, Egypt, and the Soviet Union. A point often made about the United States, that Prohibition did not so much disappear as resolve itself into a rump war on drugs, applies broadly to the mid-century world. That includes colonies and ex-colonies. As late as 1974 drug offenders in Francophone Africa faced prison terms of up to five years because the French Public Health Code was still in force.[57]

This war against nonmedical drug use was the most enduring legacy of anti-vice activism. Mid-century improvements in venereal disease prophylaxis and treatment, the decline of the sexual double standard, improved contraception, and more opportunities for consensual extramarital intercourse reduced the number of prostitutes and the anxiety surrounding them. Smoking, drinking, and gambling also became less contentious in the mid-twentieth century. But opium, coca, and cannabis remained out of bounds. Nonmedical use, sometimes called pleasure use, was said to lead to slavery, as manifested in addiction, and to ruin, as manifested in disease, pauperism, and depravity. Drug addiction was the last stop for sociopaths and weaklings who were content "feeding on the dunghill of life."[58]

The prejudice was international. A Russian psychiatrist called cocaine and crime "blood brothers." An Egyptian physician said that years of hashish smoking accounted for the beggars sleeping in Alexandria's doorways. A Brazilian professor of legal medicine blamed *maconha* smoking for strange criminal behaviors. A Peruvian psychiatrist described *cocaístas* as apathetic illiterates, frequently homeless and delinquent. A Japanese documentary photographer depicted narcotic addicts as "living corpses."[59]

It fell to Mao Zedong to add an exclamation point to drug intolerance—or perhaps, given his fondness for cigarettes and sleeping pills, to the mid-century drug double standard. Despite the official campaigns against it, narcotic trafficking flourished in China in the 1920s, 1930s, and 1940s. A kaleidoscopic cast of warlords, gangsters, military officials, and freelancers wrung money from what was, in effect, the world's largest narcotic market in the world's largest failed state. But then, in 1949, Mao won control of the mainland. He immediately began building a modern nation along Stalinist lines. That nation exercised absolute control over its territory and people, including their vices. Backsliding addicts and narcotic dealers wound up in re-education camps or at the local execution grounds. "It is easier to get people's sympathy by killing drug offenders than killing counter-revolutionaries," the Central Committee explained in late 1952. Local authorities were told to execute at least 2 percent of those arrested on drug charges. Nor did the regime spare gangsters, madams, pimps, bar and nightclub owners, and other parasites of the decadent past. Mao even suppressed golf, which wags took to calling "green opium." Courses were dug up or repurposed; in 1954 the venerable Hung-Jao Golf Club became the Shanghai Zoo. In a story rich in ironies, this was perhaps the richest of them all. Puritanism did not die. It lived on in Maoism, which, however belatedly and transiently, developed the revolutionary will to launch its own radical brand of anti-vice activism.[60]

Like much else in Mao's China, the campaign was at once eccentric, extreme, and one-off. Few postwar leaders cared to emulate the Great Helmsman's crusade against commercial vices and luxuries. They and their citizens were headed in the opposite direction.

5

PRO-VICE ACTIVISM

IN 1993 JOHN BURNHAM, a historian of medicine and psychiatry, published *Bad Habits,* a study of drinking, smoking, nonmedical drug use, gambling, extramarital and taboo sexual behavior, and swearing in American history. The gist of the book is that these vices, which respectable people had once associated with the male underworld, and which Victorian and Progressive reformers had marginalized if not suppressed, trotted back into the commercial and cultural mainstream after the repeal of Prohibition. In the 1940s and 1950s the trot turned into a canter; in the 1960s through the 1980s, a full gallop.

The United States became an affluent version of the Victorian underworld for many reasons. The Depression brought temptations other than alcohol revenue. Cash-strapped studios sexed up movie content, until checked in 1934 by stricter enforcement of the Motion Picture Production Code. Hard-up pastors surrendered the parish hall to bingo players, who fingered good-luck charms and smoked like fiends as the tension built. World War II exposed millions to unfamiliar vices, as did innovations in marketing, transportation, and technology. Selling beer was simple when consumers had televisions to watch the ads and refrigerators to chill the newfangled six packs. Consumers had more leisure time, too. Postwar partying commenced on Friday night, not Saturday.

Libertarians and libertines grew bolder. Hugh Hefner, who launched *Playboy* in 1953, sandwiched nudes between editorials denouncing puritanism and advertisements for high-end cars, stereos, hip clothes, cologne, liquor, and cigarettes. Tobacco advertisers loved *Playboy,* whose readers skewed young and smoked heavily. Hefner's formula, widely copied, linked the fantasy of unrestrained sexuality with the fantasy of upward mobility in a liberated consumer culture of anything goes. Anything included illicit drugs, or at least the softer, aphrodisiacal variety. In the 1970s Hefner supported NORML, the National Organization for the Reform of Marijuana Laws. NORML hewed to the well-worn rhetorical path of the anti-prohibitionists: "personal liberty, cost, crime, forbidden fruit, the failure of legal restrictions, and everybody does it."[1]

In fact, everybody did not do it. Hefner and his allies provoked indignant opposition among moral traditionalists and helped rekindle culture wars that bore more than a passing resemblance to the purity crusades of a hundred years before. Though Republicans rode reactionary moral politics into office, they and their corporate backers in no way reversed the mainstreaming of vice that had provoked moral conservatives in the first place. By the 1990s convenience stores were as well stocked with beer, tobacco, rolling papers, lottery tickets, condoms, and pornography as any dive in America in the 1890s. U.S. military service clubs featured slots, which annually extracted $150 million of beery servicemen's change. That which had been countercultural and disreputable had become commercially normal and socially ubiquitous.[2]

That vice should have become mainstream in a prohibition-minded society that, as late as the 1920s, supplied half the world's Protestant missionaries was a remarkable development. That it should have occurred in a culturally dynamic society that, in the 1940s, became the world's leading superpower and cultural reference point, was a globally significant development. "When I heard rock 'n' roll for the first time," remembered the Czech musician Petr Janda, "it was better than when I lost my virginity." For others the epiphany was America's uncorseted consumerism, broadcast in a simplified, supranational English to French youth who welcomed *le weekend* and Germans who voiced approval with *cool.* In 1979 the United States, with about 5 percent of the world's population, accounted for nearly half the world's advertising expenditures and three-quarters of its large transnational advertising agencies. An executive at the largest, J. Walter Thompson, voiced a common sentiment when he wrote that young people in countries like Spain thought that everything good came from America. They might not care for American politics, but they loved American music, movies, cars, cash, and freedom. Link those traits to a brand (he had in mind Winston cigarettes) and watch sales take off.[3]

WARTIME

There was more to Victorianism's global retreat than follow-the-cultural-leader. Many of the same forces that shifted the moral balance in the United States operated independently and simultaneously elsewhere, particularly in Western societies unencumbered by planned economies or Islamic religious strictures. One such force was World War II. Some 70 million individuals, mostly conscription-age men, served in the world's armed forces. From training camp on they were exposed to barracks life, where piety was a social liability and street-smart men set the tone. "The society of soldiers is not polite," the *Infantry Journal* conceded in 1943. "It is a society of men, frequently unwashed, who have been dedicated to the rugged task of killing other men, and whose training has emphasized that a certain reversion to the primitive is not undesirable." As if to underscore the point the U.S. Army supplied soldiers with cheap beer, pin-up girls, 50 million condoms a month, and free cigarettes, often bartered for sex when the men were overseas.[4]

More refined pleasures also boosted morale. The Wehrmacht sponsored radio-request programs and variety shows for its troops. German soldiers, trapped in Stalingrad, improvised their own when they found a grand piano in a ruined street. A hundred men, shivering beneath blankets draped over their helmets, listened raptly as a comrade played Beethoven's *Appassionata*, oblivious to Soviet artillery fire. In other respects, though, German servicemen behaved as swinishly as those of any other nation. Surreptitious recordings of German POWs revealed what amounted to sexual tourism. Bordeaux was "one big brothel," Paris a place where a soldier had only to visit "a bar where there's a girl sitting at a table, and you may be quite sure that you can go home with her."[5]

That would not do. German officials disapproved of fraternization and its attendant risk of venereal disease. But they knew that their soldiers were unlikely to pass up the sexual opportunities of conquest and occupation. So they established more than five hundred brothels in which non-German women were forced to work under strict hygienic discipline. Soldiers underwent sanitary inspection, got a stamped and dated pass, picked up a packaged condom and small can of disinfectant, and joined the queue. Seventeen-year-old Martin Eichenseer soon found himself in the company of a dark-haired Slovakian girl about his age. "Sex with her was great even though I didn't know what she was saying," he remembered. "The worst part was when she spread her legs and I had to spray her with the can of disinfectant. Only then would she sign my card. You had to bring back the empty can with the pass. If you didn't spray or bring it back you got two weeks extra labor and guard for punishment."[6]

What runs through all of these stories is the normalization of vices. Cigarettes came with rations, prostitutes with a pass and a packaged condom. Wartime also fostered practices that, though not yet considered vices, turned out to be habituating. The classic case was taking methamphetamine tablets, which the Germans called Pervitin. At the beginning of the war the drug had no particular military association. In the late 1930s German confectioners even added it to boxed chocolates marketed to housewives. (*Hildebrand-Pralinen erfreuen immer*—"Hildebrand chocolates always delight"—lays fair claim to the truest advertising slogan ever written.) Once the army recognized Pervitin's fear- and sleep-suppressing properties, it became a key component of *Blitzkrieg* and a high-priority military drug. The Germans shared it with ski-mounted Finnish troops, punching above their weight against the Red Army. The British and Americans soon caught on and began supplying their own aviators and soldiers with quantities of amphetamine. Researchers noticed improvements in mood. So did Germans on leave. They called Pervitin "the holiday pill" and relished its effect on their libidos.[7]

The other holiday drug was alcohol. The German military tolerated stress-release drinking, Nazi ideology be damned. Commissaries sold schnapps, an arrangement that also recycled soldiers' pay. Soldiers recuperating in hospitals drank. A sympathetic doctor told the German infantryman Heinrich Böll, wounded on the Eastern Front, to drink a lot so that his wound would heal more slowly and delay his return to combat. Soldiers on active duty drank, too. "We had terrific drinking bouts before each sortie," said a bomber pilot, who topped off his booze with Pervitin to make sure he remained alert. Officers gave out liquor as a reward for extra work, execution duty included. Fully a third of the unexplained deaths that Wehrmacht pathologists investigated between 1939 and 1944 turned out to be alcohol- or narcotic-related. Even so, wrote Peter Steinkampf, a historian who studied wartime drinking, "the military command turned a blind eye to alcohol consumption, as long as it didn't lead to public drunkenness among the troops."[8]

Cycles of chemically enhanced alertness and relaxation under the pressures of war got a moral pass. Sometimes more than a pass: Instructions for abandoning ship warned sailors to raid the slop chest for cigarettes, essential for lifeboat morale. The problem was that veterans did not necessarily forgo wartime habits. Böll, who gulped Pervitin during the war, kept taking the tablets after the war as he worked on novels late into the night. He had plenty of civilian company. Amphetamine and methamphetamine, adrenaline-like drugs that increase energy, lessen depression, and suppress appetite, had been gaining popularity before 1939. The war acted as an accelerant, creating more users, greater hardship, and bigger stockpiles, which often found their way into postwar black markets. Homeless Japanese orphans exchanged stolen goods for methamphetamine, which gave them energy and kept hunger at bay. Japanese of all ages recycled butts and cadged cigarettes, lit with magnifying glasses when matches were in short supply. Officious streetcar conductors who pointed to no-smoking signs were told, with irony, "Do we have a democracy, or don't we?" The most harmful escape was cheap drink spiked with methyl alcohol. Several hundred imbibers of these concoctions died in the year after surrender. No one knows how many Japanese, disabled veterans among them, went blind.[9]

"Don't startle 'im, Joe. It's almost full."

For Willie and Joe, cartoonist Bill Mauldin's everyman GIs, capturing the bottle was as important as capturing the German. Soldiers in every army drank during World War II, the amount varying by availability, unit discipline, and cultural tradition. When conscription funneled young men into Cold War armies, comradely drinking persisted. "Even if you are not an alcoholic when you go into the Red Army," admitted a former Soviet soldier, "you are when you come out."

POSTWAR PLEASURE MECCAS

If the history of pleasure, vice, and addiction was bound up in attempts to escape boredom, misery, and stress, it was just as closely tied to shifts in migration, transportation, and communication. The war affected these, too. Despite the cratered marshalling yards and torpedoed ships, the mass production of merchant vessels, transport planes, and airport facilities improved the flow of goods and people over long distances. Between 1939 and 1950 the inflation-adjusted cost of sea shipment fell 46 percent, and airfares fell 38 percent. DC-4s, civilian versions of military transport planes, dotted the skies from Argentina to Scandinavia.[10]

Affordable marine and air transport boosted migration. The United Kingdom, which in 1948 liberalized its immigration policy, took in more than half a million immigrants by the early 1960s. Among them were ganja and hashish smokers. They made the domestic cannabis market—a minor nuisance before the war—larger and less transient. In the late 1950s and early 1960s, cannabis smoking spread from "unemployed coloured men," as the head of the Drugs Branch called them, to native Britons. White youth lighting up prompted adverse publicity, stricter laws, and headline arrests. Rolling Stone Keith Richards's 1967 bust was the most notorious.[11]

Less controversial was vacation travel to remote locales. The most favored of these destinations became pleasure meccas, places of keenly anticipated tourist pilgrimage outfitted to accommodate crowds of visitors. Like any other economic activity, pleasure meccas flourished in locations of comparative advantage. The most successful enjoyed a mix of scenic views, historical and architectural landmarks, cultural and countercultural venues (the motor coach touring the hippie ghetto), restaurants, sporting events, amusement parks, shopping, and, of course, vice. But not just vice. The joke about Amsterdam, that it was an airport surrounded by cannabis shops, hardly did justice to the home of the Rijksmuseum, the Anne Frank House, and the Ajax football club. The optimal formula for tourism was a mix of pleasures, disciplined and otherwise, that attracted diverse clienteles with different tastes and price points.

Save for a handful of world cities like Paris, London, and New York, with their high-rent tourist districts such as the 7th Arrondissement, the West End, and Midtown Manhattan, few postwar pleasure meccas could offer the full menu of attractions. But there were other ways of cracking the market. Germans in heavily bombed cities like Munich and Würzburg painstakingly rebuilt the medieval quarters, making sure the glockenspiel towers chimed on time. The Dutch excelled at repurposing. Nieuwe Kirk, in Amsterdam's Dam Square, became a recital and exhibition hall. A former Breda nunnery, tucked away near the Belgian border, emerged from its ecclesiastical chrysalis as an international casino. Other entrepreneurs sliced and diced, taking whatever attractions were available locally—beaches, safaris, skiing, unusual cuisine—and combining them in distinctive ways. The sum of the multisensory pleasures was greater than the parts. One did not simply dine in Santorini. One dined alfresco on a terrace overlooking its spectacular volcanic harbor.

Starting in the 1970s, Santorini and other scenic harbors were increasingly filled with cruise ships, floating pleasure meccas stacked hull to bridge with cabarets, casinos, dining rooms, shops, spas, and sugary poolside drinks topped with maraschino cherries. Passengers gained, on average, a pound a day as they sailed, unhurriedly, from one tourist destination to another. For those of a more cultural bent, there were European river cruises. The 1992 opening of the Rhine-Main-Danube Canal made possible transcontinental excursions that strung together Rhenish castles, half-timbered towns, and Baroque palaces like so many pearls on a riverine chain. Viking Cruises, the industry leader, took the tour-by-day, party-by-night model global, offering similar packages on the Nile, Yangtze, and Mekong Rivers. The lounge bar stayed open during the postprandial history lectures.[12]

Airlines, the means by which most cruise passengers arrived at their embarkation ports, had different origins. Their primary selling point was speed, not luxury. Even so, in the 1930s and 1940s airlines began providing tobacco and alcohol as amenities and tranquilizers, especially on interna-

Cocktail-hour rush, *Viking Skirnir,* Nuremberg, 2017. Pleasure meccas, and the pleasure ships that link them, combine many different attractions. The one constant is alcohol, a liquid as indispensable to the modern tourism industry as diesel or jet fuel.

tional flights. Boeing built a cocktail lounge into the belly of its capacious 377 Stratocruiser. When the seat belt sign blinked off, the rush was on. By the 1950s and 1960s the coach-class norm was beverage-cart booze, another airline profit center. Air crews partied too, sucking oxygen and popping Dexedrine to recover from bar-and-bed-hopping layovers. "You were supposed to have fun, play as much as possible," a Pan Am flight attendant remembered. "This was the sixties, so besides liquor there was also plenty of marijuana, hash, and other substances available. . . . Shocking, maybe, but that was the way it was."[13]

Past tense noted. Drug tests put a damper on crew orgies. Smoking bans cleared the cabin air. But the aviation industry was by no means done with recreational vices. In 1997 Swissair and Singapore Airlines added seatback casino games on long-haul flights: Just swipe and play. Passengers changing planes in Amsterdam gambled between flights, trying their luck at blackjack or roulette if they tired of slots. "This kills time for sure," explained a Greek passenger with a five-hour layover. The same could be said for the sex shop at Frankfurt International. More conventional airport diversions included alcohol, coffee, and sushi bars; massage spas; restaurants; boutiques; and duty-free shops. Lacking an airport, Vatican City used an old train station and the 1929 Lateran Treaty to set up its own three-story, duty-free store complete with Gordon's Gin and Cuban cigars.[14]

Postwar tourism and travel normalized what had once been considered vice. Vacationers might personally avoid the topless sunbathing deck or the ubiquitous bars and slots, but they could not avoid the message that these things were now part of the modern leisure landscape. The luxuries and temptations to which Europe's aristocratic Grand Tourists had long been exposed had filtered down to the middle and prosperous working classes. Tourism expanded thirtyfold in the half century after 1960, accounting for between 5 and 10 percent of global GDP. With the rise of destination cities like Bangkok, Macau, and Dubai, it became an Eastern as well as a Western phenomenon.[15]

What Bangkok, Macau, and Dubai had in common, other than ever-expanding airport terminals, were officially permissive policies toward foreign visitors and unofficially permissive policies toward vice. Dubai, for example, could never have assumed its modern form—boom town, tax haven, money laundromat, air hub, architectural fantasia, and global brothel—unless the local sheiks had welcomed non-Muslim investors, residents, tourists, and migrant laborers, virtually all of whom came from outside the United Arab Emirates. Luxury hotels offered freshly arrived sex workers free lodging, with the understanding that they would offer their services to hotel guests. Though Dubai authorities staged occasional crackdowns for the sake of appearances, they mostly turned a blind eye to the discos, champagne brunches, and Ukrainian prostitutes, who found themselves in a price war with Chinese newcomers.[16]

Vice was almost as open in Manama, the capital of nearby Bahrain. There young men in Bedouin attire tossed down rounds and eyed the exotic dancers. "You need a drink to be able to enjoy other things," explained a Saudi visitor, a weekend regular. Saudi drinking, like Arab drinking generally, increased with the oil boom. Western advertisers slyly encouraged the trend, penetrating the kingdom by air-shipping thousands of magazines and newspapers printed in Lebanon, a regional entrepôt that tolerated alcohol advertising. Saudi censors tore out what they could. But advertisers knew that they prioritized scantily clad women, and that many of their whiskey ads would get through. Then, in 1986, the King Fahd Causeway opened, linking Saudi Arabia directly to Bahrain, making possible an influx of thirsty mainland visitors. By 2009 four million Saudis a year made the pilgrimage. Their spending accounted for a tenth of the Bahraini economy.[17]

South Africa's workaround disproportionately benefited one man, Sol Kerzner. The "Donald Trump of South Africa" got his big break when, in 1977, the apartheid government granted nominal independence to Bophuthatswana, a tribal homeland within driving distance of Johannesburg and Pretoria. Kerzner began building Sun City, a gambling and golf resort with name entertainers, porn theaters, and topless showgirls of varying hue. "What excited me," Kerzner later said, "was that in a country where the races had been kept apart by law, we'd created a place where people of all colours could eat together, gamble together, watch international shows together, even sleep together." No conservative Afrikaner, he thought, could visit the place and return home unchanged. Whether the change was in fact the progressive one implied by his liberal spin on exploiting racial gerrymandering was another matter.[18]

DISNEY WORLD, VEGAS RULES

Pleasure meccas are more than places. They are evolving hedonic formulas whose ingredients entrepreneurs experimentally change, improve, and copy to maximize profits. Vice is never the only ingredient. Dubai sports a giant mall with an indoor ski run. But some amount of vice is indispensable to the recipe, so much so that even the Walt Disney Company could not entirely forgo it.

Walt Disney was a driven, detail-oriented businessman with a genius for merchandising and a knack, concealed behind an affable façade, for browbeating associates into bending technology to his visionary ends. Having invented the animated feature film in the late 1930s and early 1940s, Disney devoted the 1950s and early 1960s to conquering a new entertainment medium, television, and a seedy old one, the amusement park. Disney wanted to get rid of the hawkers and tunnels of love, add childhood nostalgia and futuristic fantasy, and provide lots of parking and wholesome entertainment.

It was the perfect formula, perfectly timed. And yet Disney never quite expelled the snake of vice from his Edens. The original Disneyland, which opened in Anaheim, California, in 1955, featured a tobacconist on Main Street. Disney himself smoked heavily, a habit acquired as an ambulance driver in World War I. He also drank, though he tried to keep booze out of his parks. In this he—more precisely, his corporate successors—failed. Disney's Magic Kingdom in Orlando, Florida (which Disney envisioned but did not live to see open), was nominally dry. But it served alcohol at catered events and, in 2012, offered beer and wine at a French restaurant tied to *Beauty and the Beast*. "This really isn't about the alcohol," explained a Disney executive. "This was about the restaurant and having a great thematic experience." So great, apparently, that the park opened four more such restaurants in 2016. Thematic imbibing was by then well established at other Disney properties, including Orlando's techno-utopian Epcot Center, which had served alcohol from the time it opened in 1982. Disney's fleet of cruise ships featured bars as well stocked as those of its competitors. Only gambling remained off-limits.[19]

The trick the Disney Company worked was to edge up to the expanding limits of the permissible without compromising the family-friendly brand. Though the company did not initiate the Gay Days that began in Orlando in 1991, when three thousand gays and lesbians visited the theme park on one Saturday, it did not discourage them either. It was wise not to do so, as gay people spent heavily on travel. In 1996 Disney also became one of the first large corporations to offer benefits to same-sex couples, to whom, in 2007, it extended its Fairy Tale Wedding package, average price $28,000. Orlando's leading Baptist clergy registered disappointment, though not surprise. "At the end of the day," said one, "they're in business to make money." The same was true of Walt Disney Studios. Executives there released family movies under the Disney imprimatur and adult-themed fare through other studios that were part of their growing media empire. Multiplex audiences were none the wiser.[20]

Las Vegas worked the trick in reverse, evolving from an outpost of gamblers and showgirls to an international entertainment, convention, and family vacation destination that managed to keep its Sin City reputation intact. Like other pleasure meccas, Las Vegas depended on public infrastructure and a favorable legal climate. The desert city enjoyed cheap power and a reliable supply of water, thanks to the federal Boulder Canyon Project and federal highway connections to fast-growing California, its natural market. Even then, Las Vegas would have remained no more than a regional destination had it not been for the jet revolution, also federally subsidized. Jet travel slashed ticket prices and put gamblers on six continents within a long day's flight. One casino operator, Sam Boyd, routinely advertised in Honolulu. Airlines offered nonstop flights from big cities and bonus coupons for drinks, meals, and slots. High rollers, known from house records and customer referrals, had their airfares comped. Travel packagers took care of the rest, putting together inexpensive junkets that enabled casino-resort operators to grind out profits throughout the year. That they could do so legally was another legacy of the Depression. In 1931 Nevada's state government had authorized adult gambling and, for good measure, expedited divorces. It took the legislators and governor five weeks to undo what it had taken anti-vice activists five decades to accomplish.[21]

If Bill Harrah planted the seed of the modern gaming industry by creating an atmosphere suited to middle-class tourists, it was Harrah's favorite architect, Martin Stern Jr., who realized the vision on a colossal scale. Stern raised the Las Vegas skyline, created the self-contained resort hotel, and changed the face of the world's pleasure meccas. When it came to architecture and design, what happened in Vegas did not stay in Vegas.

Stern studied art and architectural engineering, worked as a set designer on *Gone with the Wind* (1939), and led a platoon of combat engineers during the war. He built bridges for his troops and blew up the Germans'. Then he began to put things back together again. He became a military governor, which gave him a crash course in coordinating food distribution, power, transportation, financial services, and construction. Returning to Los Angeles, Stern used his logistical know-how to design everything from army bases to car-friendly coffee shops. In 1953 he broke into the Las Vegas market with a commission for room additions to the Sahara Hotel, to which he later added a high-rise tower and convention facilities. Stern earned a reputation as a hotel and casino designer with a nose for the bottom line. Were cheaters a problem? Stern added an "eye in the sky" to his Mint Hotel casino addition that enabled professional spotters to monitor the action through a one-way glass in the ceiling.

Stern's greatest talent lay in designing integrated casino-resorts. His seminal building, the International Hotel, was the world's largest when it opened in 1969. A towering megaresort with a distinctive Y shape (rooms in the branches, elevators in the service core), the International offered 1,510 air-conditioned hotel rooms; almost as many slot machines and gambling

OPPOSITE: The view (1969) from the top at the Mint, a downtown Las Vegas hotel and casino that Martin Stern refurbished before surveillance cameras were the norm. The Mint hired former professional gamblers as spotters to detect cheating. The casino advertised their presence "for security purposes" and offered guests a free behind-the-scenes tour. The watchers' real job was to make sure that the sheep-shearing proceeded in an orderly fashion.

tables; ornate bars and restaurants; fur, clothing, and jewelry stores; child-care; convention facilities; and a cavernous showroom opened by Barbra Streisand. The casino, then also the world's largest, beckoned visitors as they checked in at the front desk.[22]

Stern himself shunned gambling, refusing even to play poker. The house edge was another matter. Stern waived part of his architectural fee to take percentages in his hotels and their gambling revenue. He became enormously wealthy, with homes in Deauville and Malibu, a second wife half his age, and a thriving architectural practice. And he became enormously influential, with adaptations of his International Hotel and his still larger MGM Grand (opened in 1973, now Bally's Las Vegas) rising in Las Vegas and other resort cities around the world. Several were designed by Stern himself, or by architects who had worked in his firm.[23]

Tempting as it is to cast Stern as the Howard Roark of Las Vegas, the success of the casino megaresorts also required legislative maneuvering and canny marketing. Nevada amended its gambling laws in 1967 and 1969 to make it easier for publicly traded corporations to enter the casino business. The move simplified financing for large-scale projects and accelerated the displacement of aging ex-bootleggers and syndicate skimmers who had sullied the mid-century Las Vegas scene. Companies like MGM, Hyatt, and Del E. Webb bought up existing properties and built new ones in Las Vegas and other Nevada cities. Accommodating journalists, public relations professionals, and filmmakers burnished the safe-edge entertainment brand and broadcast it through news stories, gossip and travel columns, and movies like *Ocean's Eleven* (1960) and *Viva Las Vegas* (1964). "An exciting place," reassured comedian Bob Hope. "You don't think of it only as a gambling place." Though culturati reliably dumped on the city's diversions—"so bad it's not good," said Andy Warhol—their scruples were drowned out by entertainment and travel columnists who liked Las Vegas and its hoteliers' willingness to provide them with complimentary rooms, meals, and show tickets.[24]

Las Vegas promoters had it both ways. They took the traditional lost-weekend ecosystem with its core of tainted and risky pleasures—gambling, booze, cigarettes, boxing, and prostitutes—and built around it a respectable entertainment package. They marketed this package as a liberating experience, a glamorous getaway vacation to an adult playground that promised temporary escape from the workaday world. So successful was the rebranding that the number of Las Vegas tourists leapt from 800,000 in 1941 to 38.6 million in 2005. In that year alone the number of visitors to the city was greater than the populations of Poland or Canada.[25]

Tourism on that scale could generate steady profits by means other than gambling. The innovator who best grasped the logic of diversification was Steve Wynn, the non-gambling son of a compulsive gambler who had left his family mired in debt. Like Harrah and Stern, Wynn found his calling in integrated hedonic design. In 1989 he opened his breakthrough property, a South Seas–themed and junk bond–financed resort called the Mirage. There was nothing junky about the property, though. The tower design alone went through fifty different study models before it met with Wynn's approval. He treated his guests to celebrity chefs, a rain forest in the lobby, and white tigers with Siegfried and Roy to keep them in line. The Mirage was more a self-contained entertainment resort that happened to have a casino than a casino that happened to provide entertainment. What his Las Vegas was about, Wynn observed, was giving visitors "a rich and deep emotional experience. They want to do things they are familiar with, but they want to do it bigger and better when they go on vacation."[26]

Walt Disney might have uttered the same words. Old gambling hands grumbled that Wynn's success had turned Las Vegas into an "adult Disneyland." Rat Pack casinos had given way to gargantuan themed resorts. Gone were the days when the pit bosses and dealers knew the regulars by name. Gone, in fact, were most of the gambling tables. Casino designers had replaced them with serpentine banks of digital slots into which players wandered, with the assistance of color-coded carpets. The endless stream of conventioneers and vacationers who opted for other forms of entertainment paid sky-high prices, from $60 for a Kobe beef burger to more than $600 for a bottle of premium vodka. The vodka was featured at packed dance clubs with celebrity DJs and long lines at the door. One club, Wynn's XS, raked in a million dollars on a good night. Gambling, as a proportion of total Strip revenue, fell from over half in 1996 to about one third in 2016. Gone were the discounted rooms, cheap food, cigars, and free drinks that had once served as casino bait. "The hotels look to make money off all their amenities now," said one pit manager. "It's a lot more commercial than it ever has been."[27]

Technologically rationalized would be a better term than commercial. Computers tracked the players at the video poker bar, flashing colored lights when they had gambled enough to qualify for a free drink. (Hit "max bet" four times, a sympathetic bartender told one of his customers.) "The number-crunchers, the bean-counters have ruined Las Vegas," complained a long-time visitor. "There's no value to it; there's no benefit." Marc Cooper, a journalist and old-school blackjack player who hated the new regime, read the scene as a parable of neoliberalism. "Vegas is often described as a city of dreams and fantasy, of tinselish make-believe," he wrote. "But this is getting it backward. Vegas is instead the American market ethic stripped completely bare, a mini-world free of the pretenses and protocols of modern consumer capitalism."[28]

When Cooper composed his jeremiad, in 2004, the word "American" was superfluous. For more than a decade a multinational and increasingly consolidated casino-resort industry had been prospering by taking Las Vegas global. By 1994 a subsidiary of Hilton Hotels, which had also acquired Stern's International prototype, was running or planning casino-resorts in Canada, Turkey, Australia, Uruguay, and Egypt. The last drew a thousand Israelis daily, gamblers content to let bygones be bygones. Hilton's rivals were eyeing sites in eastern Europe, the Caribbean, and South America; Wynn thought the Iguazu Falls, in northern Argentina, would be ideal. "Perhaps with the exception of the Asian countries," said the economist Bill Eadington, who invented the field of gambling studies, policy attitudes had swung "from viewing gambling as a vice to treating it as an opportunity to be exploited."[29]

Wynn and other casino-resort developers, notably Sheldon Adelson, doubted whether Asia was an exception. Macau, a Portuguese colony that in late 1999 became a semi-autonomous territory under Chinese control, seemed a particularly good candidate. Situated on the western side of the booming Pearl River Delta, Macau was a five hours' plane ride from three billion people. Disney, intent on establishing its own brand of resort meccas in the rising East, had been expanding in Tokyo since 1983 and was about to open in nearby Hong Kong. Adelson thought Macau held similar potential for gambling. The catch was that the city had a reputation as a down-at-the-heels, crime-infested, regional vice center. It was like the bad old Las Vegas, save that Macau's chain-smoking, day-tripping gamblers preferred baccarat to craps.[30]

Adelson had a solution. In 1999 he had launched his own Las Vegas mega-resort, the Venetian, complete with shopping malls, gondolas, and singing gondoliers. All that remained was to glocalize the model. In 2004 he opened the Sands Macao featuring Eastern and Western table games; slots adapted to Asian tastes; a fifty-ton chandelier; cigar bars and in-room saunas; and international menus that ranged from marinated female crab to crème brûlée. Customers practically beat down the doors. Adelson retired his construction debt ($265 million) in nine months, began expanding, and became a multibillionaire and big shot in American and Israeli politics. By 2014 he had three more Macau properties and had helped turn the city into a true pleasure mecca. With posh shopping and dining, historical and architectural tours, handbills for hookers, and local gambling addiction rates at 6 percent and climbing, Macau became "the Vegas of the East." Nearly 44 percent of its GDP derived from travel and tourism. With casinos still officially banned on the mainland, Macau also became the world leader in gambling volume, despite the 2007–2012 global financial crisis and recession, fears that corruption-sensitive authorities would crack down on junkets, and growing competition from other would-be Asian casino tigers. By 2014 Macau's gambling revenues were seven times those of Las Vegas, which by then was a mature market that faced competition from casino-resorts in other American states.[31]

The pattern was not hard to find. Casino entrepreneurs and designers like Harrah, Stern, Wynn, and Adelson discovered gushers of revenue.

Revenue spurred emulation. Emulation encouraged normalization. Normalization enhanced revenue, creating a virtuous circle of sanitized vice. The principal threats to this spiraling growth came not from the crusaders of old, but from competitive overbuilding and the prospect of brick-and-mortar obsolescence as a new generation of digital entrepreneurs discovered other ways of mainstreaming vice.

MARKETING VICE

The central insight of behavioral economics is that market transactions are often irrational. No parties to these transactions, including experts, can escape the cognitive biases and emotional vulnerabilities that are legacies of human evolution. One of the most important of these legacies is that we understand the world through stories, including attractive and justificatory stories designed to persuade us to consume products that pose financial, physical, and moral risks. The economists George Akerlof and Robert Shiller have called such stories "phishing for phools." Phishing occurred in both financial services and consumer products markets, and for the same reason. If one firm did not do it, another would. When, in 1993, Bank of America decided that it would no longer handle the credit card business of Nevada's brothels—legal in the state's rural counties—a rival bank stepped forward to provide the necessary services. "They were thrilled to death to have us, and they had no qualms," explained the owner of Mustang Ranch, which billed several thousand dollars a night. "We are a legitimate business, you know."[32]

"Legitimate business" was a story that depended on a specific change in context, a Nevada law enacted in 1971. Such shifts had long shaped attitudes toward vice, as when war, military hygiene, and racial ideology prompted Germany and Japan to set up regulated brothels in which women from conquered lands were forced to work. But these and other instances were *reactions* to altered circumstances, bad or good. What changed during the last century was the growing ability of corporate actors to *design* contexts that would reduce or eliminate qualms about vices to pave the way for their commodification and growing sales.

Their primary tool was advertising, which could spin stories about anything, including the birth control pill. Though it came to enjoy widespread acceptance and recognition as a tool of sexual emancipation, it is easy to forget how controversial the pill was when introduced commercially in 1960. Unlike the condom, oral contraception lacked a disease-prevention rationale. It raised social concerns about promiscuity; religious objections about separating sex from procreation; and nativist hackles about declining fertility among the right sort of people. Even progressives did not all fall into line. Alice Schwarzer, the Gloria Steinem of German feminism, blasted the pill as a patriarchal plot to ensure women's constant sexual availability.

Against these scruples stood a raw commercial fact: In 1960 over a fifth of the planet's population, some 630 million people, were women of childbearing age. It would be easier to crack this vast market if manufacturers, in addition to playing on growing fears of overpopulation, reframed the pill as a morally acceptable medication. Thus Schering AG, a pharmaceutical multinational, targeted German physician-gatekeepers with ads showing a neatly attired *hausfrau* with a toddler and babe-in-arms gazing up at an older physician and pleading, "Two children so shortly after each other was simply too much for me." With Anovlar 21 available, what responsible practitioner could refuse her request? Young, unmarried women were another matter. So advertisers stressed the need to prevent too-early pregnancies, playing on physicians' paternal sympathies. In Spain, where natalist views were more entrenched and where Francisco Franco's authoritarian government banned contraceptive ads, Schering and its competitors resorted to stealth marketing. They promoted their new drugs as "anti-ovulatories," useful for treating irregular or painful menstruation. While the euphemism did not end the controversy, it did get their foot in the door. Then the door swung wide open in the 1970s, when Spain's democratic transition and pent-up demand for family planning transformed the market.[33]

Lottery tickets were an easier sell, especially when tied to a big jackpot and a good cause. Education and senior services worked well. So did the promise of restoring the York Minster or completing the Sydney Opera House. Cash cows for governments, nonprofits, and advertising agencies alike, lotteries expanded rapidly in the late twentieth century. Between 1970 and 1988 U.S. ticket sales grew an average of 31 percent per year, as state after state jumped on the Lotto bandwagon. The Protestant South, where Klansmen had once thrashed gamblers and bootleggers, held out the longest. But it surrendered when mainstream politicians and business leaders, who preferred to keep other taxes low, endorsed the cause. Rural residents, innocent of the illegal numbers games familiar to the urban poor, learned to play through brochures and television ads, which recast the formerly criminal vice of gambling as a civic virtue.[34]

Alcohol posed a harder challenge, though one to which postwar American advertisers proved more than equal. Beer was the low-hanging fruit. So, target ambivalent homemakers with "beer belongs" campaigns: belongs at the picnic, belongs at the barbecue, belongs in the new fridge. Target young consumers, whose moral views and habits were plastic, whose brand loyalties could last a lifetime, and who were already drinking on the sly. Blanket college newspapers with ads and campuses with marketing reps. Offer emotional identity. Cue the buddy music. Cut to the raised-beer salute. Make the average guy feel proud. And manly and athletic. Run ads during sporting events. Pay top dollar for extravaganzas like the Super Bowl, reaching enormous audiences in festive environments. Insert public service spots to remind revelers to find someone else to drive. Add drinking triggers—amber lighting, foaming heads—and "pulse" the spots to maximize consumption. Saturate the market for two months, shut off the ads, and turn them back on. Recall would be instant, repetition having burned the message into the audience's neural circuits—and reinforced the acceptability of drinking to enhance mood and express identity. Should mood enhancement become compulsive, ascribe the problem to a small, mysterious minority. Their plight merits research—here is our check to fund it—but no reason to suspend business as usual.[35]

Consume our brand, goes a classic phishing story, and you will be like fashionable people. Thus Amstel Brewery commissioned the artist Nola Hatterman to paint a nicely turned-out gentleman enjoying a glass of its beer on an Amsterdam terrace. Hatterman, who completed the work in 1930, chose as her model Jimmy van der Lak, a Surinamese who settled in Amsterdam in 1926 and won celebrity as a boxer, bartender, and cabaret performer. (The paper behind him is open to nightclub ads.) Right idea, wrong skin color. Amstel, fearing lost sales and preferring white images of beauty and prosperity, declined to purchase the painting. No matter. *On the Terrace* now hangs in Amsterdam's Stedelijk Museum.

Tactics like these could be adapted to emerging markets. Malaysia was a majority-Muslim country with a bibulous minority, a vibrant urban night-life, and a biddable government. It was therefore in the alcohol multinationals' sights. In 1995 the distributor of Jose Cuervo tequila hired "freelance promoters," outfitted them in sombreros, décolleté blouses, and denim shorts, and dispatched them to Penang pubs. In the name of "brand awareness" the promoters invited cheering patrons to lick salt from their breasts, take a shot of Jose Cuervo 1800, and have a go at the limes wedged in their mouths. Carlsberg played a subtler game. Its ads featured a blond woman—the "long cool Dane"—and a "Carlsberg man"—a bloke with pan-Asian features. The Norse goddess might be unattainable, but the beer, personified as a friendly fellow, would always be available—for those of legal drinking age, of course. Those under eighteen could attend Carlsberg-sponsored rock concerts or visit its logo-plastered music and comic book stores. Diageo, which marketed Johnnie Walker Scotch, keyed its Malaysian campaign to "inspiring personal progress." The company launched a Johnnie Walker–branded campaign that asked Malaysians to choose their favorite role model from a list of global figures. Among the candidates were Nelson Mandela, Mother Teresa, and—wait for it—Mohandas Gandhi.[36]

Carlsberg and Diageo had much else in common. They were consolidated, integrated firms that, by the late 1990s and early 2000s, were engaged in global oligopolistic competition. Their managers knew that the future lay in developing nations with growing economies, youthful populations, and low alcohol consumption relative to mature Western markets. They also knew that advertising worked best where consumers were naïve or at least not jaded. You can only watch so many beer commercials, as one American television writer put it, before you start rethinking the wisdom of Prohibition. Less saturated markets lent themselves to high–low marketing. Multinationals introduced premium brands for prestige sales while acquiring, creating, and promoting local brands for volume. They cut out bootleggers by offering some lines at rock-bottom prices. They advertised on hyperlocal radio stations, which broadcast in regional dialects aimed at a single ethnic group or even a single town. They put up billboards near schools.

They embedded their brands in popular leisure activities. What could be wrong with drinking if everyone at the local café or stadium was knocking back a few? They used retailers as agents of normalization, allies against burdensome regulations and taxes, and a means of diversion to underage drinkers. They covered their tracks with responsible drinking campaigns and charity programs.[37]

The results were as expected. From 2006 to 2010 countries in regions targeted by the alcohol multinationals (western and southwestern Africa; South, Southeast, and East Asia; and the central Andes) were the likeliest to report gains in per capita consumption. Ground zero, Nigeria, suffered a 38 percent increase in alcohol-related traffic deaths over the seven years from 2006 to 2013. Brewers ignored labeling requirements; retailers, licensing and age restrictions. The government took its cut and looked the other way.[38]

In 2011 Sally Casswell, a New Zealand researcher surveying the shambles of alcohol control, wrote that "we face a global production and supply machine, global producer-funded organizations actively promoting ineffective policies and global consumer marketing using global media to interact with an increasingly global youth culture." The point of this chapter—of this book, really—is that the same commercial juggernaut boosted the fortunes of all vices, not just boozing. By the late twentieth century global anti-vice activism had been routed on a broad front by what can fairly be called global pro-vice activism. Multinational distribution and marketing machines had built a scaffolding of persuasion, camouflaged with strategic bits of public relations dissuasion, around a range of products that carried a serious risk of habituation and harm.[39]

Making matters worse, the risks posed by different vice products were multiplied by patterns of sequential or overlapping consumption. Though researchers disputed the causes of the vice linkages, no one doubted their statistical reality. Baby boomers, for example, were more likely to try marijuana if they first smoked tobacco or drank alcohol, and they were more likely to try other illicit drugs if they first smoked marijuana—a finding that has been replicated in North American, European, Middle Eastern, Asian, and Australasian societies. There was no accounting for Australia's mid-1970s marijuana and heroin surge, concluded the criminologist Malcolm Hall, without reference to his compatriots' "enormous" and increasing consumption of alcohol, nicotine, and diazepam. The rising tide of commercial vice lifted all boats.[40]

TOBACCO IN TROUBLE?

The recent history of the cigarette raises the question of whether some licit products are so risky that, sooner or later, marketing efforts are bound to fail, despite many decades of success. Employing classic phishing tactics—cigarette smoking is modern, sophisticated, sexy, slimming, appropriate for women, and *de rigueur* for movie stars and their fans—the tobacco industry, with the assistance of two world wars, had created for its addictive product an international market, centered on North America and Europe. What had been a vice in the 1910s, when strangers snatched lit cigarettes from the mouths of young men loitering on street corners, became, by the 1940s, an indispensable commodity. On the chaotic first night of Paris's liberation, August 25, 1944, Charles de Gaulle told his American liaison that he required three things to get the French government running: cigarettes, C-rations, and Coleman lanterns. Smoking was virtually a right of postwar citizenship. Buenos Aires advertisers added a Peronist touch, telling the city's cigarette-mad residents that "everyone" was entitled to smoke brands with "the right Argentine flavor." In 1949 eight in ten British men smoked, and four in ten women. James Bond, the dashing British spy who made his fictional debut in 1953 (and who once shot a heroin trafficker), smoked and drank nonstop through thirteen of Ian Fleming's books, until their similarly inclined author succumbed to heart disease at age fifty-six.[41]

By 1964, the year Fleming died, much evidence linked cigarettes and other tobacco products to the early onset of lethal diseases, including cancers of the respiratory system. If the public was fooled by industry hokum—we are funding research, causality is uncertain, relax and carry on smoking—epidemiologists were not. Over the next three decades they compiled a formidable list of smoking-related harms, including, crucially, those suffered by nonsmokers exposed to tobacco smoke. Told that he needed bypass surgery, an athletically inclined Maryland bartender protested that he had never smoked. Oh yes you have, his doctor told him. Your customers did it for you. So, he realized, had his parents, his classmates, his teammates, and even his coaches. His blocked arteries were collateral damage, his story a rebuke to the industry's argument that adults freely chose the risks of smoking.[42]

Worse yet were revelations about the industry's true business model: promoting adolescent addiction through campaigns designed to recruit new smokers to replace those who died or finally managed to quit. Leaked documents and exposés made it clear that the industry dissembled about its marketing practices while enhancing the seductiveness of its product. If tobacco had been a hook in the human heart, the modern cigarette was a harpoon. Manufacturers added menthol to soothe and anesthetize; ammonia, to enhance the flavor and boost the nicotine's kick. They engineered cigarettes to be addictive, and in so doing created an unparalleled menace to public health.[43]

The policy pushback, which began modestly in the mid-1960s, acquired real momentum by the century's end. Western governments mandated increasingly explicit and graphic warning labels; imposed advertising restrictions and higher taxes; funded anti-tobacco messages; sued to recover medical costs; and enacted bans on indoor smoking in public buildings, restaurants, and bars. Disneyland, which also banned indoor smoking, closed its tobacco store in 1991 and ended all cigarette sales in 1999. That same year the U.S. Justice Department brought suit against cigarette manufacturers and their trade organizations for four decades of fraud that had purportedly netted them $280 billion in illegal profits. The largest civil racketeering suit in history was premised on a law originally intended to combat organized crime—which was the government's point. The tobacco industry operated lawlessly as a matter of course. And now it was going to answer for it.[44]

In one way, it did. Business fell sharply in Western nations that pursued serious anti-smoking campaigns. In 1993 British adults smoked, on average,

40 percent fewer cigarettes per day than they had in 1973. Even James Bond quit smoking cigarettes on screen. There was a problem, though: diminishing returns. In Britain and elsewhere those who took up or persisted in the habit were less educated and less future-oriented. That or they were mentally ill. "Dear Salem People," wrote a Massachusetts woman in a letter to the R. J. Reynolds Tobacco Company. "I am manic depressive and we hear voices. In 1990 I heard a Voice and he asked me to smoke. If He is asking me to smoke, I'm gonna smoke." Money was tight, though. Could the company help her obtain her seven monthly cartons of Salem cigarettes? "They are desperately needed for my sanity."[45]

The shift in smokers' class and mental health status may have slowed the rate of quitting, but it helped health officials in another way. Products associated with the downwardly mobile and the deviant are harder to market. In France the habit became sufficiently odious that, by 2010, a majority of nonsmokers said that they could not date a smoker. American smokers who kept lighting up found themselves with fewer and less-well-connected friends. Smoking was as bad for your social health as your physical health, observed Nicholas Christakis, a sociologist and a physician. But was loserdom part of the addictive trap, or a motivation to escape it, or both? Here opinion was divided. Many anti-smoking advocates spoke of "denormalization," a few bolder souls of the health benefits of stigmatization. Though the latter struck critics as piling on, particularly in cases like that of the bipolar woman, it might still do to give other sorts of smokers a psychological boot in the pants.[46]

In the 1980s and 1990s, tobacco companies responded to the growing crisis by executing a global pivot. They took advantage of trade liberalization and overseas investment opportunities to expand into lower- and middle-income markets that had fewer tobacco controls. They acquired, renovated, and built factories in places like Serbia and the Philippines. Teens in Asia, Africa, and Latin America, they discovered, were also susceptible to their blandishments.

Health activists fought to head off a looming pandemic. In 2003 they launched the Framework Convention on Tobacco Control (FCTC), a WHO treaty that called for participating countries to implement a range of domestic tobacco control measures. Though 180 nations eventually became party to the treaty, many of these were relatively poor nations like Kenya, where smoking remained widespread and trafficking in cigarettes commonplace. As late as 2008, 90 percent of the world's population still had no protection from tobacco marketing.[47]

The upshot was that, while global per capita consumption flattened, the total number of smokers and cigarettes kept rising through the early 2010s. In 1980, 721 million smokers consumed 5 trillion cigarettes. In 2012, 967 million smokers consumed 6.25 trillion cigarettes. Consumption dipped to 5.7 trillion in 2016, though how much slippage was due to tobacco control and how much to switching from tobacco to other products is uncertain. What is certain is that in 1900 global consumption had been around 4 billion manufactured cigarettes. In a century and change, when the population had grown 4.5 times, cigarette sales had grown more than a thousand times. Not all of these sales were legal. Tobacco multinationals flooded low-tax markets with popular brands in expectation that they would be smuggled into high-tax markets and sold on the street or in shops and bars. The practice was so widespread that, in 2004, Philip Morris finally agreed to pay the European Union a $1.25 billion fine—basically, the price of doing business.[48]

Global tobacco marketing also had a demographic tailwind. In 1990, 44 percent of the world's people lived in cities. In 2018, 55 percent did so, with every sign that the trend was accelerating. As in the case of other vices, city life was more conducive to smoking. There was more pressure, more anonymity, and more exposure by way of more retailers and more promotions. Better yet, from the industry's point of view, the world's young, urbanizing populations were growing fastest in emerging nations that had the weakest tobacco controls.[49]

China's story was different, in that the state exercised a durable tobacco monopoly. Its main competition came from counterfeiters, not multinational rivals. The counterfeiters sold their cigarettes at home and abroad, trying not to flub the packaging or misspell the warning labels. But, counterfeit or otherwise, cigarette sales boomed in the new China, thanks to expanding incomes and the traditional Chinese association of tobacco with prosperity. By 2013, the average Chinese smoker consumed 22 cigarettes a day, 50 percent more than in 1980.[50]

None of this is to say that transnational tobacco control efforts have been a failure. Progress was bound to be incremental, just as it had been with narcotic control a century before. When governments did finally embrace FCTC marketing regulations and tax hikes, they got results—an 8 percent per year decline in youth tobacco smoking in Uruguay, for example. On the other hand, tobacco multinationals had weathered the end-of-century crisis. They had expanded abroad and fought a profitable rear-guard action in domestic markets, where they cultivated racial and other minorities, gays among them. Consolidated and high-tech, the industry kept prices high and costs low, using robot-equipped factories to churn out cigarettes and squirt liquid into e-cigarette cartridges. A new product with endless flavoring and blending possibilities, e-cigarettes came with a strategic advantage. They divided the industry's opponents, as they represented both real health advantages over combustible cigarettes and a real threat to reignite youthful nicotine addiction.[51]

Investors rewarded the industry's persistence and ingenuity. Price-to-earnings ratios for multinational tobacco stocks, beaten down in the late 1990s, rebounded smartly in the early twenty-first century. The largest companies enjoyed stable demand, global scope, high margins, and high barriers to entry. A plant capable of competing efficiently in the global cigarette market cost upwards of $300 million. And that did not include the time and money necessary to develop premium brands, or the payroll for a small army of lawyers, lobbyists, expert witnesses, researchers, and public relations advisers to defend what was, judging by long-term stock gains, the most successful corporate endeavor of the past century.[52]

GLOBAL CAPITALISM, TRANSNATIONAL CRIME

In short, what Casswell said of the alcohol industry, that it had become a global supply machine with a bottomless bag of marketing tricks, also applied to tobacco. It applied as well to gambling and to emerging vices like digital games and food loaded with sugar, fat, and salt. The first representation of the Statue of Liberty to appear in Beijing's Tiananmen Square was not the Goddess of Liberty created by protestors and destroyed by soldiers in 1989. It was a picture of the actual statue, displayed in the Kentucky Fried Chicken store that opened in 1987. Lady Liberty appeared alongside a poster proclaiming "America—Catch the Spirit" and a quotation from Chairman Sanders, *haodao shun shouzhi*, "so good you suck your fingers."[53]

Such spectacles were possible because China's leadership had deviated from the Maoist path and liberalized the economy in the 1980s and 1990s. Chinese morals were loosening, too. The percentage of Beijing residents who reported having premarital sex rose from 5.5 percent in 1989 to 70 percent in 2005. That same year Guangzhou City hosted a Sex and Culture Festival. Fifty thousand visitors browsed sex toys, most made in the surrounding Guangdong Province. By 2010 the *People's Daily* was reporting, a little ambivalently, that most of the world's "vibrators, dildos and lingerie carry the 'made in China' label." More worrisome was the domestic revival of pornography, prostitution, venereal disease, and narcotics, especially visible in booming Special Enterprise Zones along the eastern and southeastern coasts. The young and the strung-out found their Boswell in Mian Mian, a recovering heroin addict who published *Candy* (2000), a racy novel set in the fleshpots of Shenzhen and Shanghai. Chinese authorities banned the book. It became an international bestseller.[54]

"If you open the window for fresh air," Premier Deng Xiaoping was fond of saying, "you have to expect some flies to blow in." Chinese authorities swatted the most noxious ones. Newspapers told of drug traffickers dispatched by "righteous gunfire" and urged the closure of illegal casinos and brothels not conforming to "our socialist system." But as socialism became a flexible premise and corruption widespread, prostitution and drugs returned. "You know, customer is God," said one Shanghai businessman. "You get his heart, and then you get his project." The fastest way to some men's hearts, he discovered, was through their noses. Give crystal methamphetamine and, for form's sake, take a sniff too. Forget the boring dinner, agreed a Shanghai businesswoman. What you needed was a private room for skating ice (snorting meth), a sauna, and a bar girl to share the fun.[55]

Members of the new elite, enriched by *guanxi* capitalism, rediscovered old luxuries. Golf courses sprouted in the Chinese landscape, like dandelions after a hard winter. Beijing and Shanghai hosted golf shows, along with specialized beauty pageants for contestants with and without plastic surgery. Diageo opened "whiskey embassies" featuring bespoke blends and deluxe brands. The pricey bottles made excellent gifts for greasing the intermeshed wheels of business and government, save during the intermittent anti-corruption campaigns. Then it was best not to be seen on the links or toasting with a glass of single malt Scotch.[56]

As always, the biggest worry was the young. The challenge confronting secular officials in China—a rising, restless, wired generation inclined toward Western freedoms and vices—mirrored the challenge confronting religious officials in conservative Islamic nations. Young men, particularly affluent ones in Saudi Arabia and other Gulf states, had a discreet safety valve in nearby pleasure meccas like Dubai and Manama. Others ran greater risks, as in Iran, where the morality police punished vice with the lash and the noose. Substitute nooses for guns, and the bulletins from the Islamic Republic News Agency ("68 Drug Traffickers Hanged Nationwide") might have run in a Chinese daily. The difference was that Chinese officials adopted a bend-don't-break policy. They tolerated discos and bars, but not mainland casinos and drug trafficking.[57]

Revolutionary Iran's puritanical repression re-created the conditions of the Prohibition era. Bootleggers delivered black-plastic-wrapped bottles to Tehran apartments and homes, some daringly equipped with back-lit bars. If the police put in an ill-timed appearance, there was always a chance of negotiating a bribe. Otherwise offenders risked flogging, stiff fines, prison, and, for a third offense, death. Yet even these threats did not stop the traffic. "The demand is high and the income is excellent," said one bootlegger. "It is hard to quit." So was drinking. One Tehran translator, who put in fourteen-hour work days and organized weekend parties in her two-bedroom flat, raised her glass of bootleg liquor and said, "If I didn't have this, what kind of life would I have?"[58]

The answer is, a life that would be both more and less miserable, that would be without the liberating-enslaving pleasure by which two hundred thousand Iranians had become alcoholics, and through which thousands more made a dicey living. Bootleggers sold homebrew and, for those who could afford it, smuggled French wine and Russian vodka. Traffickers provided, at greater risk, opiates and methamphetamine for the nation's estimated 2 million drug addicts, most of whom had switched from the traditional opium to more easily concealed and adulterated heroin. The opiates came from Afghanistan. The meth came from illegally converting pseudoephedrine, a legal precursor chemical of which Iran improbably became the world's fourth leading importer.[59]

The diverse origins of Iran's alcohol and drugs, and the permeability of its borders despite fierce repression, say something important about the world in the late twentieth and early twenty-first centuries. China's opening and the disintegration of the moribund Soviet empire in 1989–1991 marked a second coming of global capitalism. The first, an outgrowth of European imperialism, had collapsed in the crises of the mid-twentieth century, only to reemerge at the end of the Cold War as a system of sovereign states committed to private ownership, market economies, and global commerce supervised by intergovernmental agencies like the World Trade Organization. By 2010 imports and exports, increasingly produced by cheap labor and efficiently shipped as containerized cargo, accounted for over half of the world's economic output. That compares to less than a quarter in 1900 and less than a tenth in 1800.[60]

If global trade was big trade, it was not necessarily licit trade. Transnational criminal organizations, coalitions of local or regional groups that cooperated to move products and people illegally over long distances and to launder the profits, seized new opportunities. Lebanese counterfeiters cranked out fake Viagra, selling it to both Palestinians and Israelis. Colombian drug traffickers hid cocaine in plastic toys and banana stalks and sent them on their containerized way to Florida and Antwerp. Eurasian traffickers exploited the band of corrupt and failed states that ran from China's western border through the Middle East and the Balkans to the European Union. Along this "New Silk Route" they shipped drugs, weapons, trafficked humans, poached caviar, pillaged hardwood, endangered species, and stacks of $100 bills, the world's preferred criminal currency. Much of the cash ended up in Dubai, where anyone could open a bank account. From there funds could be transferred to trafficker sanctuaries like Pakistan, where factories turned out heroin for export and fixes for the country's 1.5 million addicts. Barter was another option. Itinerant Mexican traffickers swapped black-tar heroin for shoplifted Levi's 501 jeans, all the rage back in Xalisco. South African gangs traded poached Cape Town abalone for Chinese methamphetamine, sold locally or transshipped to North America by direct air or sea routes.[61]

Whatever their product or means of shipment, criminal organizations took advantage of mobile phones and the internet to simplify communication and logistics. Informal economies provided cheap, disposable labor. By 2007 over half of the world's workers were scraping by with self- or off-the-books employment. In Rio's favelas they often joined drug gangs. They hunkered down during sweeps, watched the police and soldiers depart, and lit firecrackers to signal the reopening of business. Elsewhere in Latin America idle youth called *los nini* (from *ni estudia ni trabaja,* those who neither study nor work) became drug processors, mules, soldiers, and dealers. They earned steady pay and a measure of status. Yes, a Michoacán methamphetamine cook admitted to a documentary interviewer, we are hurting people in the United States. "But what are we going to do? We come from poverty." A compatriot, who wore the uniform of the Michoacán rural police, agreed. "It's never going to stop, period." If the meth was not cooked in his state, it would be in Sinaloa or Guerrero.[62]

The desperate and the indebted themselves became a form of contraband, as human trafficking revived after the Cold War. From 2013 to 2017, there were, on any given day, between 23 and 27 million people worldwide who had been tricked or coerced into forced labor. United

Border wall, Imperial Sand Dunes, California, October 2012. The smugglers abandoned their hung-up Jeep Cherokee and homemade ramp, fleeing back to Mexico when U.S. Border Patrol agents approached. They had been transporting drugs, or people, or both. The Jeep was no great loss. Some smugglers bought used tractor-trailers and then simply abandoned them after delivering the contraband. The real cost of doing business was outfitting private armies and buying off the Mexican police, armed forces, and government. After the Cold War, Mexico's paramilitary trafficking organizations globalized. They extended their supply chains west to China and south to the Andes, and their distribution networks east to Africa and Europe and north throughout the United States, their primary market.

Nations investigators found that the most common fate of women and girls, who made up the majority of trafficking victims, was prostitution. Some arrived at their destinations by plane with false passports and visas; others in cargo containers with bread, water, and a blanket. Thugs kept them in line with threats, beatings, drugs, and tattoos. The Zetas, a Mexican crime syndicate, marked their property with a "Z." Romanian pimps, who pandered poor migrant women in downtown Madrid, tattooed bar codes on the wrists of those who tried to escape.

Nigerian traffickers dispensed with markings. They threatened sorcery if their terrified victims contemplated flight.[63]

Global vice crisscrossed the boundaries of licit and illicit commerce. By the late twentieth century, when tobacco taxes were high and rising, an estimated one-third of internationally traded cigarettes were sold illegally. Smokers in European port cities like Hamburg walked into their favorite dive, asked for "blue-seal" cigarettes, and walked out with big savings. The seals were bits of blue paper that legal manufacturers glued to the package where tax stamps were to be affixed. But the stamps were not affixed, owing to the connivance of tobacco companies and smugglers. Every country had a cigarette hustle. In Angola cigarettes of all types—legally manufactured, counterfeited, smuggled—wound up in the hands of storekeepers, who fronted them to war orphans to peddle on the streets. What, exactly, was the status of this trade?[64]

Cannabis use and trafficking was another gray area. In Spain cannabis became so common that, by 2007, it had assumed the status of a legal illegal drug, not unlike the alcohol that underage teenagers indulged in with the help of older friends. "Because so many people smoke joints," a student told researchers, "it's like you're less afraid to try it." If nothing happened to other smokers, said another, nothing was going to happen to you. Several of Spain's autonomous governments coped with the situation by permitting personal cultivation and consumption at home or in private clubs while forbidding trafficking and public smoking. Yet smugglers continued to import cannabis from Morocco, and a whiff of the air in Barcelona on a Friday night was enough to realize that the public ban was not a police priority.[65]

Then there were Russia's casinos, 2,700 of which opened during the 1990s. Though nominally legal, they were often run by the *Mafiya,* which took advantage of lax licensing and owner screening. After 2007, when the government tried to restrict where the casinos could operate legally, criminal operators shrugged and went back to running the establishments illegally, along with their overseas bookmaking, internet gambling, and money-laundering operations. Transnational corporations had managed to hold state sovereignty at bay, observed the political scientist Phil Williams.

But transnational criminal organizations had managed to bring it under something like permanent siege.[66]

That siege marked the culmination of a long reversal of fortune in which modernizing states moved from an ambivalently offensive stance against commercial vice to an unambiguously defensive one. In the late nineteenth and early twentieth centuries, when governments decided to rein in at least some vices, they effectively became gamekeepers. They confronted two sorts of poachers, usually rivals but sometimes allies: businesses that skirted regulations and dodged taxes, and criminal enterprises that defied prohibitions and paid no taxes whatsoever, save bribes. Governments also had to contend with warring reform factions. The factions insisted that their preferred mix of prohibitions, regulations, taxes, and punishments best served public health, safety, morality, order, revenue, prosperity, and preparedness. (And not necessarily in that order: The curse of reform is that different values mean different priorities.) The result was a perpetual policy debate in which the clearest trend, nonmedical narcotic use excepted, was disenchantment with strict prohibition.

That was where things stood in the early 1930s. What happened next was that the reform project of minimizing, segregating, and stigmatizing vice became ever more elusive. Commercial vice reemerged from the shadows as a result of depression and war, sophisticated advertising and marketing campaigns, advances in hedonic engineering and environmental design, and the rise of a leisure and tourism industry tied to improvements in long-distance transportation. These improvements, together with the growth of informal economies, multinational industries, transnational criminal networks, and borderless trade, created a global superhighway of vice that made Burnham's bad habits commonplace and their suppression increasingly futile.

6

FOOD ADDICTIONS

BURNHAM'S LIST OF BAD HABITS—drinking, smoking, drug-taking, gambling, sexual misbehavior, and swearing—is the traditional one. Respectable Victorians would have recognized all of them as vices, and would have been appalled by their normalization in the twentieth century. What would have truly astonished them, though, would have been the proliferation of so many novel pleasures, vices, and addictions.

Here again the key is the accelerating pace of hedonic change—the Moore's Law, as it were, of brain reward. In prehistory the process was gradual and often serendipitous. Hunter-gatherers discovered novel food-drugs. Peasants eventually cultivated them, in part to alleviate the burdens of civilization. Long-distance trade spread novelties like card-playing, smoking, and distilling, intensifying the joys and sorrows of gambling, tobacco, opium, and alcohol. European empires and plantations made food-drugs cheaper and more widely available. Industrialization and urbanization made them more potent and socially contested, prompting the prohibition battles of the late nineteenth and early twentieth centuries. But when the reform cannon fell silent, vice entrepreneurs emerged from their foxholes. At first they advanced cautiously, then rapidly and in tight formation.

They met fragmented opposition. Public health advocates fought back, though selectively and on safe ground with initiatives like regulating cigarette marketing, protecting nonsmokers from secondhand smoke, or cracking down on intoxicated driving. They managed nothing like the transnational (and often religious or utopian) activism against all species of commercial vice that had inspired their Victorian and Progressive Era fore-bears. "Vice" itself largely disappeared from the language of public health, for fear of stigmatizing patients and interfering with harm-reduction efforts. Even so, few in the addiction field were oblivious to the multiplying threats. Foremost among them were addiction to food, the subject of this chapter, and addictions to or through digital devices, the subject of the next.

Not everyone agreed that these behaviors constituted addictive disorders, as opposed to the actions of improvident individuals who simply ate or texted too much. But the skeptics found themselves confronting something new: a confident and high-tech addiction research establishment that had recast a variety of addictions as a set of related brain diseases. Inebriety, the forgotten hypothesis that different intoxicants produced a common syndrome based on disordered nerve cells, returned with a vengeance. Only this time it was more than alcohol, tobacco, and narcotic drugs that medical researchers sought to incorporate in their grand unified theory of addiction.

THE BRAIN DISEASE MODEL

The best known of the beyond-drugs researchers is Nora Volkow. Born and educated in Mexico City in cosmopolitan circumstances—her father was a chemist and a grandson of the revolutionary Leon Trotsky, her mother a Madrid fashion designer who had fled the Spanish Civil War—Volkow was an academic prodigy. She read everything, mastered four languages, swam competitively, trained in medicine, and did her psychiatric residency in the United States. There she built a research career using neuroimaging to study psychiatric disorders. Among them was addiction. Her favorite uncle and her maternal grandfather, who had killed himself, were alcoholics. Why, she wondered, had so many people sacrificed themselves on the altar of a destructive habit that they had tried and failed to control? Why was addiction so robust?

During the 1990s Volkow had a chance to find out. She and her colleagues did research on the neuropathic effects of every major psychoactive substance, work that accelerated an ongoing shift toward the brain disease model of addiction. So pronounced was the shift that the model acquired its own acronym, BDM, and its own manifesto, "Addiction Is a Brain Disease, and It Matters." Written by Alan Leshner, director of the National Institute on Drug Abuse (NIDA), the call to arms appeared in 1997 under the imprimatur of the journal *Science*. "We now need to see the addict," Leshner wrote, "as someone whose mind (read: brain) has been altered fundamentally by drugs." Because the alteration was permanent, addiction having thrown "a metaphorical switch" that affected every realm and level of brain activity, the tendency to relapse had been baked in. Yet there was cause for hope. Medical science should pursue anti-addiction medications to reverse or compensate for neural changes whose nature was daily becoming clearer. Focusing solely on criminal or social aspects skirted the issue. "If the brain is the core of the problem," Leshner concluded, "attending to the brain needs to be a core part of the solution."[1]

Whatever the merits of his claims, Leshner's timing was impeccable. NIDA's embrace of neuroimaging, neuroscience, and the trope of a drug-hijacked brain that might yet be rescued by medical research brought prestige, focus, and optimism to a field that had long been deficient in all three. When, in 2003, President George W. Bush named Volkow director of NIDA, the field got something else, a charismatic leader with energy to burn. Not content to administer an agency with a budget of nearly a billion dollars (purportedly accounting for over 85 percent of the world's funded addiction research), Volkow turned the job into a media pulpit from which to preach the gospel of addiction neuroscience.[2]

Addiction neuroscience extended to compulsive overeating, a point Volkow emphasized in a 2014 TEDMED talk, "Why Do Our Brains Get Addicted?" She began her talk with the usual suspects: booze, dope, and bad character. Most people, Volkow said, dismissed alcoholics and drug addicts as weak-willed individuals who sacrificed everything for intense but transient pleasures. Yet addicted patients often admitted that drug use was no longer pleasurable. Scientists knew from animal studies why it had brought pleasure at first: A drug or another stimulus had released a burst of dopamine that activated their brain's reward pathways. But human brain imaging added crucial details. Repeating the stimulus reduced, often on a long-term basis, the availability of certain neural receptors, particularly dopamine D2 receptors. The loss of D2 receptors desensitized the brain and increased both tolerance to and dependence on the outside stimulus. The receptor loss occurred in the brain's mood-affecting limbic structures, but also the frontal regions that were connected to them, and that regulated judgment and self-control. Addiction was like a workout in reverse. Instead of adding self-discipline, it inexorably reduced it, along with the pleasure to be had from the activity.

Then why persist in something that is bad for you? Because evolution favored humans who were motivated to engage in activities that enhanced fitness, like eating and sex. So our brains had evolved more than one way to release dopamine to signal reward for these activities. They released the neurotransmitter not just when we engaged in these activities, but when we encountered cues associated with them. We responded to conditioned stimuli, a process, detectable in imaging studies, that explained the persistence of habits both good and bad. Anything that increased dopamine in the brain's motivational circuitry sustained the drive to perform the behaviors necessary to procure the reward, even though the intensity of the reward itself was often diminishing. Desire escalated independently of the pleasure it produced, which was why addictions were both hard to shake and apt to return. Wanting was a keener and more persistent feeling than liking.

Volkow thought dopamine double-tracking was an ingenious evolutionary solution to the problem of motivation. Unfortunately, another process, culture, had disrupted the arrangement. Civilization had disassociated reward from fitness, a trap evident in the mass cultivation of food-drugs like cacao and sugar cane, which humans had blended into irresistible treats. Down went the PowerPoint slide of a PET scan of a cocaine abuser's brain. Up went a similar slide of a morbidly obese patient's brain, followed by a picture of chocolate to die for. "The visual of this great-looking chocolate is making me want to eat it now," Volkow admitted. Her dopamine was already flowing, predicting reward.[3]

Much evidence supported Volkow's claim that pleasure is about anticipation as well as sensation, suggestion as well as ingestion. Placebos release neurotransmitters, dopamine among them. People experience pleasure in their imaginations, enjoying the "reality lite" of daydreams as well as reality itself. Set and setting, which shape their drug experiences and behaviors, depend on conditioning and cues. Addicts are particularly sensitive to the latter. Dostoyevsky's gambling alter ego required only the faint clink of coins on a roulette table two rooms distant to go "almost into convulsions," his brain racing ahead before his hand could plunk down a bet. Tobacco advertisers performed marketing judo with warning labels, inadvertent cues that, on the evidence of brain scans, stimulated smokers' cravings. In some conditioned subjects, cues alone could forestall withdrawal symptoms. Physicians stabilized institutionalized narcotic addicts with nothing more than sterile hypodermic injections. The journalist Peter Gzowski, in rehab for smoking and drinking, fell for the same trick in the case of caffeine. He needed a jolt to start the day and recalled the relief he felt when he quit shaking long enough to hold the first blissful cup of coffee to his lips. He fortified himself with coffee until his discharge, when he learned that the staff had been giving him decaf all along.[4]

Conditioning could not, however, account for the fact that most people exposed to pleasurable stimuli did not develop fully addicted brains. These brains Volkow likened to cars that had lost their brakes. Plainly, some brains come with better behavioral brakes than others. Genes play a role, as do development and social circumstance. Effective prevention, however, requires more than identifying genetic mutations and redressing individual misfortunes. We have to confront the social changes that bombard us, from an early age, with brain-weakening stimuli. Humans excel at changing environments, Volkow pointed out. Why not reengineer our environments to strengthen, rather than weaken, our biology? If demonstration projects reduce obesity in small communities by providing healthy food choices or encouraging exercise, then scale them up. Practically and morally, the course was clear. Match resources to humanitarian projects of scientifically proven value.[5]

Which was fine, save that it left a crucial question hanging. Could such enlightened actions succeed without first dismantling enterprises that encourage unhealthful activities? Trotsky, an ardent prohibitionist who once court-martialed a regimental commander for serving wine at a banquet to honor the revolution's anniversary, would surely have reminded his great-granddaughter that Progress requires a wrecking ball. Anti-vice activism (to which the stigma-wary Volkow is an ambivalent heir) held that commercial vice, which paid for business and imperial gain in the coin of toxic habit, had to be checked before progressive social engineering could succeed. Why create regulated pubs, from which workers would soberly depart to enjoy drink-financed parks and libraries, unless a monopoly backed by force of law had first shuttered privately run dives?[6]

If Volkow's politics had some gaps, so did her history of the brain disease model. Though she stressed the role of brain imaging, the shift in scientific understanding had begun earlier, in the 1940s and 1950s. The key figure in alcohol studies was E. M. Jellinek, a polymath who recast alcoholism as a chronic disease of a minority of drinkers who had progressed from periodic relief drinking to prolonged intoxication over which they had lost control. His drug-research counterpart was the neuropsychiatrist Abraham Wikler, the presiding genius at NIDA's forerunner, the Addiction Research Center. Wikler showed that narcotics produce physiological changes throughout the central nervous system and that sensitivity to socially embedded cues causes relapse long after withdrawal. In the mid-1950s, experiments on rats by the psychologists James Olds and Peter Milner demonstrated that self-stimulation of reward pathways in the brain's septal region produces compulsive behavior. Investigators replicated their work in creatures from snails to humans, and proved that drug infusions work in like fashion. In 1957 the neuropharmacologist Arvid Carlsson showed that dopamine, also shared across species, functions as a crucial neurotransmitter. The work eventually earned him a Nobel Prize.[7]

The pace of discovery quickened in the 1970s. Researchers mapped the receptor sites for most important addictive drugs and proved the existence of an endogenous opioid system with multiple functions, including an

Victor Juhasz's 2014 drawing of Nora Volkow captures the NIDA director's energy and confidence. So effective was Volkow in popularizing the brain disease model that even those who flatly rejected the concept, such as the psychologist Stanton Peele, conceded her global leadership in the field. The real problem, Peele argued in 2015, was how to "stop Nora Volkow from taking over the world."

excitatory effect on dopamine. In 1975 NIDA held its first workshop on brain reward, with James Olds in attendance. In the late 1970s and early 1980s NIDA researchers pieced together brain reward pathways, which they described as distinct from the anatomical pathways for withdrawal symptoms. The criteria for diagnosing addiction shifted from physical dependence toward compulsion, craving, and anhedonia caused by long-term brain changes. Researchers began investigating whether different substances and behaviors activated the same reward pathways, a hypothesis confirmed and vividly illustrated by a rising generation of neuroimagers. "It was as if we had made the body transparent," marveled researcher Michael Kuhar. "It was an absolute fairy tale come true."[8]

Volkow may have confined the brain disease model's history to the recent past, but she took an expansive view of its future. Bodies that could be made transparent could yield secrets beyond the effects of a few potent drugs. In fact, Volkow all but ignored drug addicts in her TEDMED talk. She focused instead on morbidly obese individuals who could not quit eating. One of them was a young woman who had been bullied to the point of contemplating suicide. Like Volkow's grandfather, she was an anguished victim with an altered brain lost in a sea of stimuli that promised relief and reward. The difference was that her trigger was food.

FOOD AS DRUG

It may seem odd that the director of a vast drug-research agency, funded by a government that subsidizes cattle feed and high-fructose corn syrup, should choose to focus on food addiction. But Volkow was hunting bigger game than drugs. She was after a scientific explanation of pathological learning across a range of behaviors known to be risk factors for diseases that cause most of the world's chronic illness and early death. To know what was destroying the brain's appetite-control mechanisms was to know what was destroying lives. Nor was she alone in this quest. Just think, Kuhar mused, how many diseases could be traced back to defective reward-control systems. Medicine needed to start thinking of the brain's reward and conditioning pathways as a central biological system that underlay pathologies "way, way beyond drug abuse." That included habitual overeating, by any reckoning one of the most important of the reward-based pathologies.[9]

This too was an idea with a history. Since the late 1950s physicians had been discussing, quietly and tentatively, the concept of food addiction and the closely related syndrome of binge eating. It was also in the 1950s that a Harvard undergraduate named Bart Hoebel became curious about obesity. A psychology major with an original mind and unusual breadth of interests, Hoebel doggedly pursued controversial research on sugar addiction in rats, finally winning a professorship and research lab at Princeton and pioneer status in the food addiction community. In 2007 Hoebel joined Kelly Brownell, another storied professor of psychology and neuroscience; Mark Gold, a psychiatrist-neuroscientist and addiction *avant-gardiste;* and nearly forty experts from two dozen disciplines at a landmark international conference on food and addiction. The venue (Yale), the keynote speaker (Volkow), and the proceedings publisher (Oxford) testified to the institutional support and academic prestige of food addiction research and the brain disease model it corroborated and extended. In hindsight, it was just such support and prestige that had been wanting in earlier attempts to integrate the addiction field.[10]

Food addiction also had good press, and lots of it. Authors such as David Kessler, former head of the U.S. Food and Drug Administration (FDA), and Michael Moss, a Pulitzer Prize–winning journalist, published bestsellers indicting food companies for hooking customers with foods rich in sugar, salt, and fat. "If it quacks like a duck, it is a duck," wrote Gold, who also had a popular touch. "Food, highly palatable and energy dense, has become a substance of abuse." Women's magazines jumped on the story. "Are you 'addicted' to sugar?" asked *Figaro Madame,* which likened sugar to cocaine. Celebrities chimed in. "My drug of choice is food," wrote Oprah Winfrey. "I use food for the same reasons an addict uses drugs: to comfort, to soothe, to ease stress."[11]

Ordinary people learned to speak the same language. Canadians in Food Addicts in Recovery Anonymous said that they thought of meals all day long, that they binged while feeling helpless and hopeless, that they fought through "hard days" to resist their cravings, and that they depended on sponsors, like those in Alcoholics Anonymous, to control a "lifelong addiction." Margaret Bullitt-Jonas, an Episcopal priest who stared at empty pie plates with a sick, self-loathing feeling, thought food addiction was like any other overwhelming impulse that could suddenly crack your resolve:

> You might be driving down the street on a Saturday morning, minding your own business, when suddenly the urge comes over you to stop at the bakery, pick up a banana cream pie, drive home and eat the whole thing right away, very fast. Because you're a compulsive overeater, this idea doesn't sound ridiculous or bizarre. It sounds eminently sensible and reasonable. And urgent. You can't talk yourself out of this sudden craving, and you're not even sure that you want to. It doesn't matter if you're not hungry—what does physical hunger have to do it? It doesn't matter if you made all sorts of promises to yourself just that very morning that you wouldn't do something crazy with food today. The urge to eat is upon you, and there's only one thing you can do. Eat.

The key, agreed the writer Caitlin Moran, was preoccupation. Ordinary overeaters pigged out on holidays. Compulsive overeaters thought about food constantly. Then they walked into their kitchens in a panicky state and ate themselves into a trancelike calm. They kept at it until bursting stomachs and overwhelming regrets made them stop "in the same way you finally pass out on whiskey or dope."[12]

Skeptics dismissed analogies between food and drug addiction as fashionable medical rationalizations. Addiction researchers countered that the behaviors showed objective and measurable similarities. Compulsive overeating, like drug addiction, causes sickness and early death. It contributes to rising rates of obesity, a key risk factor in heart disease and at least thirteen types of malignancy. (Which is why bariatric surgery lowers cancer risk by one-third over ten years.) Obesity is closely linked to diabetes, a leading cause of adult mortality in rich countries like the Gulf States and in middle-income countries like Mexico. The trend is indisputably global. Between 1980 and 2015 rates of obesity doubled in seventy-three countries and rose steadily in most others.[13]

Not all obese patients are food addicts. But the one-quarter or more who are satisfy a basic medical criterion of addiction. Their habitual, craving-driven behavior is bad for themselves and burdensome for society. Americans have paid an especially high price. By 2006 more than a third of U.S. adults, twice as many as in 1980, were obese. That same year medical payers forked over $1,429 per person more for obese patients than for patients of normal weight, a 42 percent difference in average annual cost.[14]

Brain imaging revealed another resemblance between food and drug addiction. Food addict scans looked like those of other addicts, with reduction in the number of dopamine D2 receptors and activation of the same neural pathways by reward cues. Showing a female food addict a milk-shake produced the same imaging results as showing an alcoholic liquor. Naltrexone studies suggested that the visual similarities were more than coincidental. An antagonist (receptor blocker) administered for narcotic overdoses, naltrexone is also used to treat alcoholism and compulsive overeating, gambling, and sexual activity. By binding to opioid receptors, naltrexone suppressed dopamine activity in experiments in humans and animals, including rats, which ate less of their beloved chocolate. That the same antagonist should have the same suppressive effect in different addictive behaviors indicated a common neurochemical basis.[15]

Then there was substitutive behavior. The greater the body mass index (BMI) of obese patients, the less likely they were to use alcohol or illegal drugs. Conversely, when smokers and other drug users became abstinent, they gained weight, often by eating sweets. Ronald Reagan's jelly bean habit (favorite flavor, licorice) was a consequence of his having quit pipe smoking when he went into politics. Tobacco, alcohol, and other drugs compete with food, especially sweet food, for brain reward sites. As they say in Alcoholics Anonymous, if you want to stay sober, don't get too hungry. The journalist David Carr, in treatment for cocaine and alcohol, heeded the advice too well. His substitute doughnut habit reduced him to wearing sweatpants from the communal swag pile.[16]

George Koob, a behavioral physiologist who later became director of the National Institute on Alcohol Abuse and Alcoholism (NIAAA), liked to say that humans have limited reserves of pleasure. To spend them improvidently is to invite a reckoning. Koob called this reckoning "biological Calvinism" and described it as a Darwinian tragedy. Pleasure is essential for survival and procreation, but only to the point where it becomes disruptive and toxic. That is why a hedonic control system evolved. Alas, we discovered the means to wreck the control system through the likes of cocaine binges. Intense pleasures made us vulnerable to cue-triggered craving and, worse yet, lingering ennui, persistent depression, and heightened stress after the high had passed.[17]

Persistent withdrawal effects explain both relapse and substitution. Addicts to food, or to anything else, learn to cope with withdrawal and abstinence symptoms by resorting to other substances or behaviors when their accustomed reward is unavailable. Bariatric surgery, it turns out, entails a surprising risk. Alcohol abuse rises significantly during the second postoperative year, particularly among younger male patients already familiar with alternative brain rewards of smoking, drinking, or drugs. They have other ways of getting off. So do narcotic addicts. In February 1978, a winter storm struck New Haven, Connecticut. Snowbound methadone patients had no access to clinics for three days. Most drank. Some gorged themselves "as if it were Thanksgiving," until withdrawal brought on nausea. Others melted sugar cubes in their bent-spoon cookers, drew up the contents into their syringes, and then drank or skin popped the solution. Whatever it took, in other words, to get them through the night.[18]

Food, drug, and behavioral addictions have common risk factors. They tend to move together, as Volkow put it. One theory stressed "reward deficiency syndrome." Defective genes and difficult life circumstances, such as constant stress or social defeat, had deprived some people and animals of the normal quota of dopamine D2 receptors. When they found that Cokes and fries—or drugs or gambling or another stimulating behavior—could lift their low spirits, they wound up on a self-medicating treadmill, with junk food one of several fixes. The longer they stayed on the treadmill, the more they damaged their hedonic regulatory systems and other parts of their brains and bodies. In a controlled study of obese patients, Volkow and her associates discovered a strong inverse correlation (−0.84) between dopamine D_2 receptor availability and BMI. They could not determine whether low receptor availability was a preexisting risk factor or a consequence of habitual overeating, though it was entirely possible—given the larger pattern of evidence, probable—that it was both.[19]

Another possibility, and another parallel between food and drug addiction, is that risk extends across generations. Several studies suggested that pregnant food addicts could harm their unborn children. In animals, high-fat consumption during pregnancy altered dopamine and opioid gene expression in offspring, enhancing their preference for highly palatable foods. In humans, the children of obese women whose diets were rich in fat and sugar were at higher risk of insulin resistance, obesity, and ADHD (attention deficit hyperactivity disorder). The last trait, ADHD, was linked to a higher risk of other addictive behaviors, from smoking to compulsive internet use.[20]

This line of research recalls, in a disheartening way, the puzzle of inter-generational poverty. I argued in Chapter 3 that stress, intoxication, and addiction have historically interacted to sustain low caste. Others have emphasized discrimination based on race, ethnicity, class, education, gender, and place of residence; the socialization of poor children into self-defeating attitudes; and the genetic effects of "assortative mating" on children's educational prospects. (Meaning that parents' report cards cast long shadows.) To this list of explanations, none mutually exclusive, we must now add the possibility that class-specific maternal diets rich in sugary drinks and other unhealthful foods cause or reinforce traits that further diminish the life chances of poor children. One researcher, Caroline Davis, proposes warning pregnant women that sweet foods can produce "'fetal sugar spectrum disorder,' with symptoms that are not dissimilar to those seen in the off-spring of women who drank during pregnancy."[21]

FOOD FIGHT

Putting aside the question of whether habitual overconsumption of rich food harmed offspring, did it really constitute an addiction analogous to alcoholism, as neuroscientists now insisted? Their critics said no, and challenged the broader claim that addiction to food or anything else was a chronic, relapsing brain disease. This debate has become so sprawling and contentious that I have recast it as a dialogue between the pro–food addiction camp and the anti–food addiction camp, taking one contention at a time. The antagonists are composites. The arguments are real.[22]

CON: You can't compare drugs and food. We don't have to take drugs. We do have to eat.

PRO: Eat food, yes. Eat engineered food, no. People don't overconsume corn. They overconsume corn processed into Cheetos, Doritos, and other mass-marketed, synthetically flavored products designed to maximize brain reward.

C: So take junk food off the grocery list.

P: Not so easy if you're hooked.

C: Get unhooked. This is a bad habit, not a real brain disease like schizophrenia or multiple sclerosis. People quit bad habits all the time.

P: People don't quit cravings or forget cues. They don't restore lost receptors with a snap of their fingers.

C: But they can overcome bad habits by adopting other, healthier habits. They can change their routines. Start going to Weight Watchers, stop going to McDonald's. What you call addiction has an element of choice and a developmental trajectory. People wise up as they get older. They outgrow addictions, often quitting on their own. Ex-tobacco smokers outnumber current smokers in several developed nations.

P: Yet people have to eat, as you say. And shop for groceries. Talk about cues. But, yes, there are workarounds like learning to prepare meals with fresh, carefully measured, low-fat ingredients. And avoiding fructose, which is nothing but a brain-pleasing additive.

c: The vast majority of people eat and drink fructose at least occasionally. Ditto other feel-good additives. Yet they don't all become addicts.

p: You could say the same thing of drugs. Fewer than 20 percent of the people who ever try crack or heroin wind up as addicts. More people than that have trouble controlling food intake, ruining their health in the process.

c: You're saying that sugary, salty, and fatty foods are more addictive than hard drugs?

p: No. But even if they were, addictive potential would not determine addiction prevalence. Availability, price, and susceptibility are critical. Processed foods are cheaper and more widely available than processed drugs. Then there are the "food deserts" in poor neighborhoods, where processed food is practically the only sustenance available and where people have more addiction risk factors anyway. Cost and social distribution explain why, overall, we have more control problems with food than with drugs, even though most people experience smaller dopamine spikes from eating rich food than from taking drugs like heroin.

c: A "control problem" is not the same thing as an addiction. You keep confusing eating too much with addiction.

p: And you keep ignoring the fact that addictive behavior develops along a spectrum. People can gamble or drink too much without being compulsive. In the United States there are more alcoholics in the top 10 percent of alcohol consumers, who average more than four drinks a day, than in the next 10 percent, who average between two and four drinks a day. But the second 10 percent are far likelier to *become* alcoholics than those who drink little or nothing. That's why we call them at-risk drinkers. The same goes for rich, sugary foods. Heavy and binge consumers may be subclinical, in the sense that they don't yet have all the addiction symptoms. They may not even be obese, because of bulimia and other purging disorders. Yet they are still at risk.

c: Subclinical is a synonym for "in the majority." Suppose a few morbidly obese bingers do have uncontrollable cravings. They are *outliers*. The only thing they explain is NIDA's sick-brain model, which is based on extreme cases. That goes for drugs as well as food. The study subjects have more psychiatric problems than the general population. Labeling all people who are addicted to something at some point in their lives—which would be most of us—with a brain disease tag that was derived from a relapse-prone subpopulation with mental illness is worse than a mistake. It's a hex on ordinary addicts who would otherwise quit or cut back as they mature and their life circumstances change.

P: If they live long enough to reform, and not before they have racked up significant personal and social costs.

C: Which could be caused by social and situational factors, not some brain switch stuck on "feed me." Over half the world's adult population is overweight or obese. They can't all be food addicts. If the real causes of obesity are things like food deserts, food-industry subsidies, people driving instead of walking, bigger portions and more calories, advertising, and tacit cultural approval of overindulgence—hey, the game's on, call the pizza guy—then establishing more chapters of Food Addicts in Recovery Anonymous isn't the answer.

P: No one thinks a global trend like obesity has a single cause. The medical literature makes it clear that the majority of obese patients do not meet clinical criteria for food addiction. The case that highly palatable food acts like an addictive drug doesn't require that all obese people be addicts, just as the case for gun control doesn't require that all homicide victims die from gunshot wounds. Even a brain disease critic like Stanton Peele concedes that some people have become so dependent on overeating for emotional gratification, and have paid such a steep price for it, that they "fulfill more or less closely the criteria for addiction." A thing can be real and yet not the most common type.

C: A thing can also be a Trojan horse. Food processors have a stake in the brain disease model, especially the genetic angle. The industry can say, oh, let's identify and warn a few unusually susceptible individuals to watch what they eat and then carry on business as usual with the masses. The alcohol and gambling industries have been running that scam for years.

P: What disease doesn't have an element of social construction? Or constituencies that gain or lose from shifts in social meaning, official definition, and medical opinion about its extent and causes? That's no reason to ignore its pathophysiology or dismiss genetic factors, which may be socially influenced though not socially fabricated. Think of autism. Is it overdiagnosed? Probably. Is it a source of revenue for activists, researchers, and clinicians? Yes. Is it a neurodevelopmental disorder, or spectrum of disorders, of genetic and possibly environmental origin that disrupts the lives of children and their families? You bet it is. To ignore that fact would be unsympathetic and unscientific.

C: You don't choose autism.

P: Nor do you choose compulsive overeating, a life-threatening biobehavioral disorder accompanied by observable, predictable, and lasting brain changes at the cellular and molecular level, including altered gene expression. That's a disease. And it fits the American Society of Addiction Medicine's definition of addiction as "a primary, chronic disease of brain reward, motivation, and related circuitry . . . reflected in an individual pathologically pursuing reward and / or relief by substance use *and other behaviors*."

C: Tell the Society that real diseases have specific biological markers that you can detect and diagnose with something like a blood assay. What it calls a disease is just a dependence syndrome. Or syndromes, plural, with many pathways and triggers, some cultural and some biological.

P: What's cultural about genes? Family, adoption, and twin studies have consistently shown that half or more of addiction liability can be attributed to heredity.

C: "Can be attributed to heredity" is the mother of all fallacies. Predisposing genes are neither a sufficient source nor a necessary condition for addiction. Heredity affects behavior in specific environmental contexts. Take kids with the suspect genes, keep them free from early trauma and exposure, give them a stable neighborhood and vigilant, sober parents, and watch what happens to their projected addiction rates.

P: But hold the environmental factors constant, and more of the genetically predisposed will become addicted.

C: So what if they do? NIDA's worldview won't save them. Lumping disparate syndromes under a generalized disease model has accomplished nothing therapeutically. Name one breakthrough treatment that has come out of food addiction neuroscience. For all the brain disease talk the world keeps getting fatter. As for alcohol, tobacco, and other drugs, why pursue high-tech brain interventions when we have proven, population-based prevention strategies like higher taxes and advertising bans? The brain disease model misallocates effort and resources.

P: Scientific understanding often precedes effective treatment by many decades. The germ theory matured in the nineteenth century, antibiotic therapy in the twentieth. Medical researchers may yet discover treatments that would decrease the likelihood of developing food and other addictions, reduce harms, diminish stigma, and improve prognosis. Think of opioids. We already have drugs to curb craving, ease withdrawal symptoms, and reverse overdoses—

C: —every one of which was known to medical science before NIDA fell in love with brain scanners—

P: —and researchers are working on vaccines to block the euphoric effects of drugs like cocaine. These could prevent new cases of addiction and relapse among existing ones.

C: Drill down into the literature and you'll find that enthusiasts for anti-addiction vaccines admit that any such "breakthrough" would be complicated, expensive, fraught with technical and ethical problems, and less than 100 percent effective. Keep drilling and you'll find that neuroscientists disagree on key issues. Is dopamine more about wanting or liking? Is it stress hormones that trigger withdrawal and relapse? Is there one pattern of brain adaptation or are there many, each keyed to a different addictive stimulus? Plenty of fistfights go on behind the scenes.

P: How is that different from cancer chemotherapy and immunotherapy? This isn't about magic bullets and lockstep science. This is about using hard-won knowledge to make sustained progress against deadly, biologically related diseases. The brain disease model is not perfect. It *is* plausible and coherent, and it has addiction investigators all over the world speaking, for the first time, the same neuroanatomical and neurochemical language. That fact alone justifies patience and further research.[23]

Or it may *not* justify further research, depending on how one judges this ongoing debate. Making judgment even more difficult is the presence, beyond the practical and empirical questions just sketched, of a second set of philosophical and political issues. Critics, especially social scientists, have accused advocates of the brain disease model of reductionism, biological essentialism, and naïve positivism. They have detected sympathy for the drug war, insofar as brain vulnerability implicitly warrants a strict police approach to controlling drug supply. And they have complained of visual sleight of hand, manifest in the use of sharp color contrasts to make subtle neural differences pop from the scans of the supposedly hijacked brains of addicts.[24]

Reductionism, the most common charge, has the distinction of being both accurate and beside the point. Science advances through focused research on narrow questions. Bench researchers want to know how the absence of, say, a particular presynaptic receptor disrupts inhibitory feedback, or how DNA variations create receptor subunits that increase addiction vulnerability. Sociology and economics will not help them find answers. In a 2015 reply to their critics, Volkow and Koob argued that patiently resolving these sorts of technical questions within the brain disease model offered the best hope of realizing further therapeutic gains, destigmatizing addiction, and effectively targeting prevention programs. The experimental work might seem humdrum, but the promising new paradigm that guided it was anything but. So stay focused, stay funded, and stay tuned.[25]

But tuned to what? To only one channel? The real problem was the collateral and collective reductionism that came about because Volkow and her scientific allies absorbed so much of the available publicity and resources. Not least of their big-ticket endeavors was NIDA's International

Program, which had trained no fewer than 496 fellows from 96 countries by mid-2014. NIDA has had a global effect, an effect intensified by NIAAA's embrace of the brain disease model for alcoholism research. Yet NIDA has also had a narrowing effect, in that it has taken attention away from social drivers like poverty, sophisticated marketing, and addictive product design. When Leshner affixed the brain label, in 1997, he stipulated that addiction was "a brain disease for which the social contexts in which it has both developed and is expressed are critically important." The nub of the case against addiction neuroscience is that subsequent research largely ignored all but the first three words. Disordered neurons and faulty genes got attention. Everything else got lip service.

The neglect reached the point that leaders of the addiction research field began to dissent. Griffith Edwards, a psychiatrist and editor of the journal *Addiction,* wrote that drugs are much more than chemicals that act on the brain. They are also potent symbols freighted with social meanings. Those meanings have real and sometimes toxic consequences for drug users and for drug policies, which function within specific social "ecologies" that change over time. To pretend otherwise is to fly blind. Another luminary, the pharmacologist Harold Kalant, called the NIDA-NIAAA brain model a "reversion to a strictly medical basis that really ignores all of the work that has been done for a century now in the social field, in the behavioral fields, in the economic field. . . . I think it's a serious mistake, and I'm sure there will come a point when the importance of all these other fields will again be recognized."[26]

FOOD ADDICTION BY DESIGN

No time like the present. To render my own verdict on the food addiction fight: the neuroscientific case is less wrong than incomplete. One could make just as compelling a case for the analogy between addictive food and addictive drugs by studying the behavior of food multinationals and their advertisers, as by studying PET scans and naltrexone trials. Their behavior is plainly part of limbic capitalism, the term I use for the design, production, marketing, and worldwide distribution of mostly nondurable goods and services that create (initially) intense brain reward and foster destructive habits in consumers. Big Food has come to resemble Big Tobacco, down to off-the-record meetings of executives anxious that they would be sued over the health effects of their products, as indeed they were.

In the courts of law and public opinion, the key issue has been convenience food loaded with sugar, fat, and salt. If you want to know why people overeat, said the celebrity chef Wolfgang Puck, look no further than those three ingredients. Sugar is the most obvious enhancer, because it is the most drug-like in its effects. Hoebel learned as much when he told a research assistant to give naloxone, a drug that blocks the action of opioids, to his sugar-happy rats. They promptly went into shaking, teeth-chattering withdrawal. More, the human preference for sweets is inborn, arguably augmented by maternal diets, and inarguably reinforced by early exposure to sugary products, every bite or sip of which imprints the lesson that all food and drink should be sweet. Fat, which provides a delicious "mouthfeel," perfectly complements the taste of sugar. Sugar in turn helps to conceal the large quantities of fat. Salt enhances the product's sweetness and masks less desirable tastes like bitterness. A natural preservative, sodium crystals can also be fashioned into unnatural shapes that cling to every morsel of snack foods, the better to deliver the maximum burst of flavor. Artificial ingredients complete the package by improving freshness, texture, color, and taste. One Illinois firm listed eighty thousand artificial flavor formulas, a thousand for banana alone. Looking for an exotic touch? Add "banana foster."[27]

Human pleasure has always entailed blending goodies. What the food companies did was to elevate blending to the level of corporate science, just as they had with the methods of food production, manufacturing, distribution, and marketing that ensured their quick-hit products would remain cheap and accessible. Though critics like David Kessler fingered these practices as the causes of global obesity, industry insiders knew they were essential for growing market share and fighting for corporate survival. Even that was no sure thing, as behemoths like Nestlé and Kraft swallowed venerable confectioners like Rowntree and Cadbury. Darwinian logic applied to food and equities markets with as much force as it did to the neurobiology of motivation.

The problem, then, has been the system—oligopolistic limbic capitalism, division of hyper-palatable food—and not simply the men and women who did the engineering. They were technicians versed in chemistry, biology, and mathematics whose job it was to improve products and solve problems. Did microwaved cake batter smell like scrambled eggs and taste like cardboard? Then try encapsulating the yummy aromas in yeast cells, which would vibrate and burst in the microwave oven. The ultimate goal was to achieve the "bliss point" of maximum palatability at minimum cost. The process was algorithmic. Food engineers applied mathematical models to calculate the likeliest combination of ingredients and then validated the results with large-scale testing. Food became Pharma. New food products, like new drugs, emerged through data-driven winnowing. By the 1980s only one in ten experimental food products made it to national or global markets. The rest washed out in focus groups or regional sales trials. The selective pressures were relentless, and they ran in only one direction. "Ninety percent of it is about making you *feel* good," said Frito-Lay food scientist Robert Lin, "and feeling good means tasting good."[28]

Food scientists strove to make the tasty tastier, the cheap cheaper, and the fast faster. They accomplished all three with the potato. Chefs had long known how to turn the humble staple into a treat by thin-slicing potatoes into chips or sticks, frying them in fat, and then coating them with sugar and salt. The problem was that homemade chips and French fries were relatively pricey, much like cigarettes before mechanical production. But the labor and cost constraints vanished with the postwar automation of chip- and fry-production lines; the mass cultivation of machine-friendly potatoes on large industrial farms; and time-saving conveniences like vending machines, fast-food franchises, and bagged chips ready to buy, open, and enjoy. Convenience, General Foods CEO Charles Mortimer said in 1955, was a food ingredient that ought to be spelled with a capital "C." The same could be said of Cost. Countries like the United States that industrialized and subsidized agricultural output saw food prices, measured in hours of work required to purchase the same amount of food, drop ten-fold in the century after World War I. Chips were cheap—and irresistible. "No one can eat just one" became the centerpiece of a Lay's potato chip campaign that turned loss of control into a virtue.[29]

Then there was the Pringle, a uniformly shaped and neatly stackable "potato chip" that was really nothing more than a starchy matrix for sugar, salt, fat, MSG, and other flavors. In one experiment researchers discovered that the louder the crunching sound transmitted through headphones, the likelier Pringles-munching subjects were to taste the chips as crisp and fresh. Extra crunchy was born as a selling point.[30]

Set and setting affect all food-drugs, not just chips. Coffee tastes more intense in white mugs than in clear ones. Sodas are sweeter when drunk from a red can, popcorn when eaten from a red bowl. (Check the colors on the popcorn boxes the next time you are in a theater.) Set and setting also figure in product-line extensions, which can be tailored to specific cultures. North Americans like potato chips with sour-cream and barbecued-meat flavors. Russians like red caviar flavor chips, Thais hot-chili-squid flavor, and Chinese ketchup flavor. If you are not Thai or Chinese and you just went "yuk," it simply demonstrates the point.[31]

Finding the right food formula does not guarantee success. Feel-good products face continuous competition for shelf and menu space (and, ultimately, brain space) from similarly designed and continuously upgraded rivals. Enter the advertisers, whose first job is to catch the customer's eye. Product placement—the practice of paying to have a brand featured in a television show or movie—is one method. Coca-Cola, an early adopter, was managing at least one televised appearance a day by the mid-1950s. But most food companies relied on paid commercials, which inexorably evolved into food porn. Storyboard artists sketched light-flared egg yolks dissolving under a beating whisk while sliced cheese melted in a mouth-watering cascade, the effect enhanced by strobe lighting. "You're using the same part of your brain—porn, food," a commercial director explained.

"What we're trying to do is be the modern-day Pavlovs and ring your bell with these images."[32]

Multiplying screens made the imagery inescapable. Charles Spence, an Oxford experimental psychologist and food industry consultant, described stepping onto a London Tube escalator lined with video ads. "All I could see, out of the corner of my eye, was a steaming slice of lasagne being lifted slowly from a dish, dripping with hot melted cheese, on screen after screen." Spence judged the effect irresistible. Our brains have evolved to detect, track, and lock onto protein in motion. For commuters not otherwise distracted, it was ding, ding, and ding.[33]

Advertisers reinforced sight with sound. Fast-food commercial sound-tracks ("the music that works best is a powerful, driving, highly rhythmic beat that builds energy thru percussion") could be dialed up or down. Settings could also be varied, so long as they evoked good times. "It's always about being happy," said an Australian marketing expert. "Just do a favor for yourself, come to this fun place. Eat happy." By 2009 happy eating had migrated online. *Mukbang* or *meokbang* (Korean for "eat broadcast") became part of the webcasting repertoire, garnering millions of followers and thousands of dollars in revenue for young, cute, pattering, and gluttonous "broadcasting jockeys," who streamed amateur food porn—eating huge plates of food while talking to their online audience.[34]

Professional food porn aimed at kids was the most controversial aspect of food advertising. Internal industry studies, independent medical research, and brain imaging pointed to the same conclusion: Logo recognition and brand loyalties formed early and stuck. Advertisers had known as much since the early twentieth century, but the principle assumed new urgency in the age of fast food. Some companies, such as breakfast cereal makers, spent twice as much money on advertising, mostly aimed at children, as they did on the actual ingredients. These included generous helpings of sugar, salt, and fat.[35]

Cigarettes and alcohol were promoted in the same way. For each of these products, teams of public relations, marketing, and advertising professionals

normalized, sold, and built brand loyalty for habit-forming products targeted, implicitly or explicitly, at mostly young consumers—consumers they rewarded with "a lift," "full satisfaction," "gustatory pleasure," or some other euphemism for a hit. These marketing campaigns cut across product lines and sometimes combined them. Displaying anchovies, cheeses, and potted meats next to Budweiser beer, for example, yielded higher sales for both the beer and the snacks, a win-win for grocers. Their stores became proving grounds for "planogramming," modeling merchandise placement and displays to maximize sales. Put sugary cereals at kids' eye-level and let mommy, please, do the rest. American advertisers also commissioned psychological profiles and consumer surveys—including focused, emotionally tuned surveys of heavy users—to perfect their campaigns for pancake syrup, candy bars, beer, and similar quick-hit products. By the 1950s and 1960s such sophisticated tactics were routine in the big advertising agencies.[36]

More importantly, American products and advertising tactics were exportable. Snack bars and televisions sprang up in postwar Europe. Eateries defied traditionalists and communists alike by serving Coca-Cola and hamburgers. By 1964 Kraft was using satellite technology to beam cheese ads from the United States to Europe. Advertising guru Albert Stridsberg grasped that the processed product mattered less than the communication process, which made it possible "to reach vastly increased numbers of people simultaneously." Where Marshall McLuhan saw the emergence of a global electronic village, Stridsberg and other advertisers saw a global electronic market shaped by their hands. The shape of that market had an unmistakably limbic form. By the late 1970s and early 1980s, six categories of branded products absorbed 80 to 90 percent of the money multinational

OPPOSITE: Though nominally dedicated to progress and health, modern life is increasingly dominated by corporations dedicated to getting us to consume in ways that are unprogressive and unhealthful—one of many possible readings of Banksy's 2009 parody, *Angel of the North*. Footsore after a night of clubbing, this cigarette-smoking Venus stumbles through the detritus of vice, including fast food and sugary drink containers.

firms devoted to international advertising. They were processed foods, soft drinks, alcoholic beverages, cigarettes, drugs, and toiletries.[37]

As had brewers, distillers, and tobacco companies before them, multinational food companies invested advertising and promotional money in developing countries on which their future growth depended. Nestlé hired Brazilian slum vendors to market products to poor neighbors, authorizing them to extend up to a month of credit for the purchases. The two dozen bestselling items were all loaded with sugar. In 2010 a supermarket barge named *Nestlé Até Você a Bordo*—Nestlé Takes You Onboard—began ferrying powdered milk, chocolate, ice cream, and juice to eight hundred thousand prospective customers in isolated Amazon towns. Nestlé's critics reacted as if the British East India Company had resumed shipping opium to the Pearl River Delta—which, in historical and neurochemical terms, was uncomfortably close to the truth. In July 2017, when Nestlé finally ended the controversial service, private boat owners filled the vacuum. The hook had been well and firmly planted.[38]

Global food marketers also finessed religious differences and dietary taboos. By 2012 McDonald's had opened 271 stores in the Indian market, where cattle were sacred to Hindus and roughly a third of the population avoided meat. Solution: Replace the beefy Big Macs with chicken Maharaja Macs and, for vegetarians, McAloo Tikki burgers, made with spicy fried potato patties. The décor was as adjustable as the menu. McDonald's crowned its Jakarta flagship store with a forty-foot inflated Ronald McDonald in a lotus position. *Ronald Bertapa,* the meditating Ronald, was a masterpiece of corporate ambiguity. He could be taken either for a Sufi saint or a smiling Buddha, though the customers inside were hardly bent on eradicating desire.[39]

The paradox in all this was that business rationality begat social irrationality. It spun off collective harms and costs that were initially unanticipated and mostly borne by others than those who had produced them. The sociologist Daniel Bell would have called these externalities the cultural contradictions of limbic capitalism. Other sociologists preferred "McDonaldization," a concept they applied to everything from theme parks to sex work, which was increasingly scripted, deskilled, and online. Like anything else, vice could be rationalized. The most disturbing aspect of McDonaldization, though, was its ability to take seemingly ordinary goods and services and turn them into unhealthful habits. The obvious case was McDonaldization in its primal form: the production, franchising, and sale of fast food and sugary drink.[40]

Governments have been as apt to abet the process as to interfere with it. By 2011 the average Mexican was consuming 45.5 U.S. gallons (172 liters) of Coca-Cola products per year, not counting other sources of sugar. Mexicans at the time being roughly seven times as likely to succumb to diabetes as to homicide, such consumption was preposterous. The Mexican government belatedly recognized as much and overcame industry opposition to impose a tax on sugar-sweetened drinks. The tax, which took effect at the beginning of 2014, reduced sales 5.5 percent during the first year and 9.7 during the second. What often gets left out of this story, however, is that the Mexican government had granted Coca-Cola bottlers generous tax breaks when they expanded into the country's interior in the early 2000s. The 2014 sales tax was an attempt to close the door on a horse that the government had helped lure out of the barn.[41]

The inconstancy and co-optation that happened in Mexico happened, in one form or another, throughout the world. Activists might trash the odd McDonald's, like the half-built store wrecked in Millau, France, in the heart of Roquefort country. But McDonald's rolled on, launching stores in Rome and Mecca, Moscow and Beijing. By 2000 the company had established thirty thousand outlets and inspired numberless copycats. The world was eating happy—and fat. The lines of diabetics at local health clinics stretched out the door. Fast-food pleasure and profit came at the price of lethal disease, premature senescence, tooth decay, and environmental degradation through deforestation, runoff, aquifer depletion, and climate change. One pound of hamburger generated, on average, twenty-five pounds of carbon dioxide emissions. Then there was the suffering of billions of penned, caged, antibiotic-stuffed animals bound for grill and oven, not to say the misery and self-loathing of compulsive overeaters who gobbled their salted, sweetened flesh.[42]

How widespread is this compulsive overeating? Studies using validated research instruments, such as the Yale Food Addiction Scale, consistently find that at least one in four obese adults meet the criteria. Applying WHO obesity data, there would have been 150 million adult food addicts in the world in 2014, or more people than lived in Russia. Applying the more guarded prevalence rates of Steve Sussman, an expert on substance and behavioral addictions, the global total would have been closer to 100 million. But neither the higher nor the lower estimate included children and adolescents, who run a higher lifetime risk of compulsive overeating than their elders. And neither contradicted the new reality, which is that engineered food addiction has become a nine-digit aspect of the human condition.[43]

7

DIGITAL ADDICTIONS

THOUGH CRITICS DISPUTED Volkow's claim that food addiction is a brain disease, all but doctrinaire libertarians agreed with her on one point: Overeating has an element of conscious commercial design. Volkow's worries about hyperstimulating environments were widely shared, and not just by those concerned with compulsive overeating. Students of the casino industry, including the journalist Marc Cooper and the cultural anthropologist Natasha Dow Schüll, found an uncanny resemblance between engineered gambling and engineered food. The similarities were most obvious in Las Vegas, a place where, as Cooper put it, the market ethic had been laid completely bare. So had the impulse to fine-tune and then standardize the exploitation of consumer weaknesses, a trend critics called "McGambling."

MACHINE GAMBLING

For all the diversification into glitzy entertainment, casino operators never gave up on gambling. But they preferred the automated variety, installing as many slot and video poker machines as they could cram onto their casino floors. The machines took no coffee breaks, demanded no maternity leaves, required no skill to play, and ensnared customers with maximum efficiency. "There's no decision—it's all done for you," explained one slots manager. "You just stand there and get excited." Or very excited. "For some people, something like the Fourth of July is going off in their brains as they gamble," the sociologist Bo Bernhard told Cooper. "It's trendy to say gambling is sweeping America. But mostly it's machine gambling that's sweeping America. And these machines are a convergence of so many factors: the logic of capitalism, technology, and increasing comfort with machines."[1]

Compulsive gamblers are mostly escape gamblers, as distinguished from action gamblers who favor the craps and blackjack tables. James Bond did not play slots. But women do, and not all are retirees in tennis shoes. "Today the problem gambler is likely to be a thirty-four-year-old woman with two kids and two years of college," said Robert Hunter, a Las Vegas addiction therapist. "And a video game addiction. We're not seeing many of the dinosaur action gamblers who play to feel a rush. We're seeing people who say they want to feel numb, want to blank out, want to lose track." The point was to disappear, said one of his patients, a woman in her late thirties who moved to Las Vegas after she married. The disappearing act cost her $200,000 over three years.[2]

If her losses were unusual, her status as a Las Vegas resident was not. Between 1960 and 2015 the resident population of Clark County, home to Las Vegas, grew by two million. The gambling industry cashed in. By 1991 gambling ranked as the locals' fourth most popular commercial recreation, trailing only eating out, movies, and shopping. By 1999 some 6 percent of the county's residents were compulsive gamblers, a rate over four times the national average. Exposure mattered, as did novelty and social class. Most prone to frequent gambling were recent arrivals and those with a poor education, many of whom toiled in the resorts. When they went off duty they patronized neighborhood casinos or McGambled at one of the ubiquitous machines in restaurants, bars, and grocery stores. Some "locals' casinos" sweetened the pot, awarding frequent play with credits that could be swapped for cigarettes and liquor.[3]

Schüll wanted to know why machine gambling was so addictive and why so many addicts were women. The answer was an updated digital version of the hunter–prey story of commercial vice. Using Las Vegas as their proving ground, the hunters perfected computerized gambling machines that doubled as marketing and tracking devices. The machines' television themes and resemblance to consumer gadgets gave them an aura of entertainment innocence and attracted a new generation of prey. Many of the younger players were anxious, depressed women seeking respite from burdensome lives in a high-pressure society whose expectations they could not meet. They played less for a big win that would let them escape than to escape, period. The goal, said one, was "to stay in that machine zone where nothing else matters."[4]

Casino architects obligingly created machine-lined labyrinths in which gamblers lost themselves, satisfying their desire to escape until their stamina or money ran out. Solitary, continuous, and rapid wagering created a trancelike state that rendered players oblivious to anxiety, depression, and boredom. Digitized machine gambling was as reliable as Valium and faster acting. Regular players of video gambling devices became addicted three to four times more quickly than those who gambled in other ways. They also played more rapidly, whipping through a new video poker hand every three to four seconds. Their fingers flew over the controls. The most compulsive players became transfixed, unable to leave their machines despite growling stomachs and bursting bladders. One retired firefighter, who played fourteen hours at a stretch, said the place could burn down and he would stay put as long as he had gambling credits. "Forget it—I'm not leaving unless I can take the machine with me, I'll die of smoke inhalation first."[5]

Game designers, who knew the risks of addiction and the odds against winning, avoided playing. Asked if he indulged, an artist at Reno's International Game Technology replied, incredulously, "Slots are for losers." The director of a department called Responsible Gambling at the company said that her designers did not think about addiction. They thought about beating the competition. "They're creative folks who want machines to create the most revenue." Others were more candid about the price of victory. "I don't feel great preying on psychological weaknesses of little old ladies," a game developer told Schüll. "I can't sit here and say, *I only put the screws in the bomb, I only assemble the warhead,* because I'm sure that products I've made have destroyed people's lives somewhere."[6]

The slot machine had indeed been weaponized. The weapon's power first became apparent in 1984, when Las Vegas's Four Queens Casino installed "virtual reel" slots armed with microprocessors. Each machine could produce ten times more reel stops than standard electromechanical models, hence larger potential jackpots. When casino staff compared the performance of the old and new devices, they found that digitized slots doubled revenues. Trade magazines spread the good news.[7]

Over the next two decades digitized gambling swept the casino industry. With 10 percent of the gamblers providing 80 to 90 percent of the take, anything that speeded up and extended play among regulars was bound to grow revenues. Labor costs shrank, too. Player identification cards and barcoded cash tickets replaced antediluvian change attendants pushing coin carts and tellers selling rolls of quarters from cages. Even cocktail waitresses' jobs were not wholly safe. By 2008 Harrah's Entertainment was experimenting with automated bars in casino lounges. Patrons could play touch-screen games, watch YouTube, and design and order their own customized drinks with a click.[8]

As with resort architecture, what happened in Vegas did not stay in Vegas. Digitized machine gambling expanded rapidly in revenue-hungry nations from Scandinavia to South Africa. Designers adapted to local conditions and traditions. Pachinko parlors, Japan's de facto casinos, got a digital makeover. But everywhere the strategy was the same—to establish and reinforce player habits. The result has been a familiar spectrum of heightened risk tailing off into compulsion and ruin. By 2012 Hungary, a nation of ten million that allowed digitized gambling in pubs and bars as well as casinos, was home to an estimated one hundred thousand gambling addicts and another half million regulars in danger of losing control over their play. In Britain betting shops proliferated along the main streets. The big draw was FOBTs, fixed-odds betting terminals that offered virtual games from roulette to slots. Punters could burn through £500 in a minute. Counting only those sessions in which gamblers lost £1,000 or more, FOBTs brought in £2.3 billion per year. May as well put heroin on a cheese trolley, a professional poker player wrote disapprovingly, and leave it twixt the chemist and the bus stop.[9]

It was in Australia, however, that digital gambling became a national obsession. By the late 1990s the country had one "pokie" for every eighty adults. Local clubs and pubs installed the machines, as well as hotels and casinos. Eight in ten Australians gambled, four in ten regularly. Casinos encouraged them with loyalty cards offering bonuses and discounts and easy-to-use debit cards that silently tracked their habits and acquired marketing leads about the addicted minority who provided most of the revenue. In one Australian casino, just 2.3 percent of the loyalty card holders accounted for 76 percent of the slot take. The gambling lobby protected and widened the take. In 2015 the government of New South Wales, the country's most populous state, raised the maximum amount that casino gamblers could store on their smartcards from $1,000 AUD to $5,000 AUD. The move, which stunned hardened industry observers, was clearly designed to keep problem gamblers glued to their custom-designed seats.[10]

For confirmed machine-gambling addicts, there was no leaving the perch anyway, regardless of the credit line. It had become part of their mental furniture, their blues ejection seat. "It starts while I'm on my way to the casino," an addicted gambler told Schüll:

I'm in the car driving, but in my mind I'm already inside, walking around to find my machine. In the parking lot, the feeling gets even stronger.

By the time I get inside, I'm halfway into that zone.

It has everything to do with the sounds, the lights, the atmosphere, walking through the aisles. Then when I'm finally sitting in front of the machine playing, it's like I'm not even really there anymore—everything fades away.[11]

CAUGHT IN THE WEB

The machine-gambling language of preoccupation, anticipation, cue-arousal, and oblivion-seeking is strikingly similar to that of drug and food addicts. The principal difference is that food addicts have to eat. Drug and gambling addicts at least have a shot at a clean break. But their digital cousins, internet addicts, are more like food addicts. Online temptation is well nigh inescapable, internet access having become an assumed feature of life in developed societies. Addiction therapists know the score. They aim for "abstinence from problematic applications and a controlled and balanced internet usage," just as food addiction recovery groups promote measured and balanced eating.[12]

The similarities do not end there. Both food and internet addicts become obsessed, lose control, display tolerance (bigger gulps, more time online), manifest associated disorders like anxiety and impulsivity, and experience depression during withdrawal. They often relapse and persist despite family badgering and social opprobrium. And their numbers have been growing. Surveys undertaken in the United States and Europe between 2000 and 2009 (before widespread smartphone use aggravated the situation) reported internet addiction prevalence rates between 1.5 and 8.2 percent. Chinese studies found values ranging from 2.4 to 6.4 percent, though some subgroups, such as Taiwanese university freshmen, approached an 18 percent addiction rate. In developed nations, internet addiction has become at least as common as food addiction. Among adolescents it is much more so.[13]

Addiction to the internet and other electronic pastimes reveals itself most clearly in the harsh light of abstinence. In 2010 an international team of researchers asked one thousand college students from ten countries to go without electronic media for twenty-four hours and to record how they felt. The typical response involved a combination of surprise, restlessness, boredom, isolation, anxiety, and depression, often prefaced with a frank admission of excessive use and addiction that cut across cultures:

> CHINA: As matter of fact, I'm quite addicted to the computer and the Internet. In the wake of this experiment, I realized that media is spread like a web that binds me.
> UGANDA: It will not do any good if I do not begin on the note of acknowledging that I am actually very tied to the media.
> ARGENTINA: I realized that, out of every 24 hours, I'm connected to a machine 15 hours a day.

MEXICO: It was quite late and the only thing going through my mind was (voice of a psychopath): "I want Facebook." "I want Twitter." "I want YouTube." "I want TV."

UNITED KINGDOM: As soon as my 24 hours were up, I grabbed my beloved Blackberry and turned on my laptop. I felt almost like a drug addict getting a fix after a long stint of going cold turkey.[14]

As with alcohol, drugs, processed food, and gambling, electronic media consumption is subject to the principle of hormesis. Consumption runs along a spectrum from occasional, beneficial use to relieve boredom and boost morale—the digital equivalent of a coffee break—to heavy, escapist use that harms self and others. Clinicians differ over whether to call the latter condition internet addiction, internet addiction disorder, internet use disorder, pathological internet use disorder, or something else entirely. They do, however, discern a common denominator. The heaviest users are those who have come to strongly prefer recreational life online as a way of tuning out IRL (in real life) hassles. They behave much like machine gamblers slipping into the zone, save that most of their activities, such as massively multiplayer online role-playing games (MMORPGs), have a social aspect that reinforces the virtual seduction. No self-respecting *World of Warcraft* DPS (a character who inflicts a large amount of damage per second) would want to miss their guild's next big raid. IRL types take a dim view of such pursuits. Teachers issue failing grades, parents threats, employers pink slips, spouses papers for divorce, and judges treatment orders for internet boot camps.[15]

Libertarians and medicalization skeptics think forced treatment is absurd. The arguments over food addiction—Is it really an addiction like drugs? Is it an acquired brain disease to which some individuals are more susceptible than others?—have cropped up again over internet addiction. Only this time the debate has been messier, because internet addiction includes a much wider range of activities than compulsive eating. Among them are addiction to digital pornography, online gambling, video and role-playing games, adult-fantasy chatrooms, shopping on sites like eBay, social media platforms, and websurfing. Different groups of people display different types of addiction. Boys and men are more inclined to online video games and pornography, girls and women to visually oriented social media and compulsive buying. Some psychiatrists class the latter as an addiction, others as a type of obsessive compulsive disorder. If comparing food and drug addiction is like comparing apples and oranges, comparing food, drug, and internet addiction is like comparing apples, oranges, and several varieties of grapes.[16]

THE WORSE ANGELS OF OUR NATURE

Another thing that makes internet addiction difficult to assess is its relative novelty, especially habitual social media use via camera-equipped, internet-accessible mobile devices. History wants perspective. Little is available here. In countries like India, cheap voice-activated devices with intuitive video-oriented apps have only just begun to bring the social media revolution to poorer and less literate consumers. Yet some account is necessary, as there is no denying digital technology's accelerating role in the history of pleasure, vice, and addiction. Briefly, three developments stand out.[17]

First, digital connectivity and mobility have spawned genuinely new patterns of addictive behavior. Putting aside academic disputes over categories and causes, the behaviors themselves have become social facts. When I told people that I was writing an updated history of addiction, the near-universal response was that I should include kids glued to their smartphones. What had once been a peripheral nuisance has become a real worry, given

OPPOSITE: Gijsbert van der Wal's November 2014 photograph of students ignoring *The Night Watch,* Rembrandt's most famous painting, went viral as an indictment of a lost virtual generation, addicted to social media. Some protested that the young scholars were simply gathering art-historical information from the Rijksmuseum's excellent app, but that seemed unlikely. In June 2017 I stood at the same spot and glanced over the shoulders of fourteen students of the same age and posture. With one exception, it was social media all the way down. The contrast with students across the room, who were being drawn into the masterpiece by means of live instruction, was striking.

the rising toll of accidents caused by distracted drivers, not to say reports of increased bullying, anxiety, and academic failure. Compulsively studying social media posts leaves less time for studying everything else.

Second, the development of the internet created new, global opportunities for the dissemination of old vices and addictions, including gambling, psychoactive drugs, prostitution, and pornography. Indeed, porn has accounted for a significant portion of internet traffic from the time of its commercial inception. Swearing, the last of the bad habits that John Burnham profiled in his book, also gained a new outlet. Swearing never had much of a commercial aspect, which is why I have said little of it. Yet traditional vice it is. An emotionally charged form of speech processed through the limbic system, rather than the cortical language regions, swearing is a taboo, aggressive act of a cue-triggered nature. Like the other masculine and lower-class vices with which it is associated, swearing offends and demeans others. It flourished among soldiers during the world wars and then became increasingly common public behavior. From the vantage of 1993, when *Bad Habits* was published, normalized swearing struck Burnham as another defeat for American opponents of vice. In the ensuing quarter century that defeat has turned into a global rout. Online libertinism and anonymity encourage profanity, flaming, and other forms of verbal aggression such as trolling, succinctly defined in the online Urban Dictionary as "being a prick on the internet because you can."[18]

Third, both developments, new bad habits and new outlets for old ones, have been engineered to maximize revenue, data on consumers, and time spent on the device or app. No less than for gambling machines, attention is the key corporate asset and behavioral science the means to claim it. For every individual attempting to exercise self-control over computer use, pointed out the ethicist Tristran Harris, there are a thousand experts on the other side of the screen whose job it is to break it down. Game makers study young players and analyze their mouse clicks to devise reinforcement schedules that prolong play and stimulate purchase of products tied to the game. Some are limited-time offers: You had better keep playing or you will miss out. Others are virtual gold pieces "farmed" by Chinese proles playing MMORPGs in twelve-hour factory shifts to supply impatient gamers in South Korea and other affluent countries with the virtual assets necessary to advance quickly in rank. One Fuzhou gold farmer earned $250 a month—good pay, he said, in comparison to other jobs. Most of his wages, and the middlemen's profits, came from free-spending "whales" whom the computer-game industry had cultivated and caught.[19]

All three aspects of digital vice and addiction—new, old, designed— figured in journalist Nancy Jo Sales's *American Girls: Social Media and the Secret Lives of Teenagers* (2016). Sales interviewed more than two hundred smartphone–equipped girls aged thirteen to nineteen, asking how social media had affected their lives. The gist was that they had displaced reality into a digital realm of celebrity idolatry, genital exhibitionism, drunken hookups, pornographic sex, constant distraction, collective insomnia, malicious gossip, cyberbullying, desensitization, and anxiety about appearance and popularity. The chief beneficiaries were makeup manufacturers and Silicon Valley honchos who equated teen time with advertising revenue. They were, Sales wrote, as prone to objectify women as the schoolboys who sexted female classmates and expected nude photographs in return.

Sales's subjects volunteered that they were addicted to or obsessed with their phones, internet videos, and social media, to which the heaviest users devoted from nine to eleven hours a day. As with other addictions, reinforcement had a positive and negative dimension. Every like on a post or photo, every retweeted message, was a small psychic jackpot that could arrive at any moment. The continual flow of information, especially information about where one stood in the hotness pecking order, was a potent form of reward. Not having access to that information was a source of gnawing anxiety. Like much else online, it acquired its own name, FOMO. Fear of Missing Out.

Missing the big weekend party was fear one for the older, sexually active girls. "People get drunk, hook up," explained Madison, a Boca Raton high school student whom Sales interviewed together with three of her friends, Billie, Sally, and Michelle. "Seniors are like, Let's live it up. We're all going off to different colleges, I'm never going to see you again, so let's just, you know, do it." Sales asked if porn had anything to do with the sexual carousel:

> They all said, "*Yes.*"
>   "Boys look at porn all day," said Billie.
>   "They watch it during class," said Madison.
>   "Whenever you text a guy and ask, What are you doing?, they say they're watching porn," said Sally. "Some guys in my class were actually watching it while someone was doing a presentation. This girl Jennifer was giving a presentation and these guys put their phones like that"—she held her phone up to show the screen. "They were like, Oh, Jennifer, I have a question, and they raised their phones and it was a porn video. She couldn't even concentrate. It was so sad. I felt so bad for her."

Their teacher, sitting in the back of the classroom, saw nothing. Why didn't they tell her? Sales asked. The girls looked around at one another. "If you tell on them, they'll never let you forget it." When Sales asked another group of girls, in Los Angeles, why they didn't just walk away from social media if it was making their lives miserable, the answer was "because then we would have no life." It is the classic addict answer, with a twist. Anxiety and dysphoria have acquired a new partner in the list of withdrawal symptoms—fear of social death.[20]

Wired kids in other cultures have found themselves similarly entangled with smartphones, the stickiest of the world's sticky things. They say they cannot imagine life without them. Phones are their lives. They would freak out if they lost them. They need apps for confidence. They long for perfect selfies. Everything revolves around social media. They cannot abandon online friends and late-night chat sessions for fear of ostracism. No less than their American peers, they have fallen into the ultimate luxury trap.[21]

The trap became more insidious after 2007, when smartphones and tablets conquered the consumer electronics market and social media went mobile. By 2015, 92 percent of American teenage girls were online daily, 24 percent "almost constantly." It is easy to see why. A smartphone in a personalized case seems like the ultimate in teenage liberation, a portable vending machine full of mood-brightening apps. But in this instance, as in so many others, the sheepskin of consumer autonomy conceals the wolf of emotional manipulation from a distance.[22]

The most obnoxious manipulators are boys who badger girls for nude photos and hookups and who harass and slander them should they fail to deliver. Yet boys too pay a price for easy, uncensored internet access. They become ensnared in a loutish bro culture and a world of pornographic fantasy that can result in sexual dysfunction. The reason college men are having trouble getting erections, a male Ivy League student told Sales, is excessive porn use. Masturbating to online pornography is like drinking ten cups of coffee a day. The prospect of "random non-intimate sex" with a real person rather than a porn star sculpted to trigger arousal cues is like drinking just two cups of coffee, "not that stimulating in comparison." Biological Calvinism applies to online pornography as well as to alcohol and drugs. A reckoning there has been, manifest in hookups turned into letdowns or outright failures to launch.[23]

It is as if, in the span of a century, there have been three revolutions of technology and sex. The first, artificial contraception, separated sex from procreation. The second, digital pornography, separated sex from physical contact between persons. And the third, online remoteness and impersonality, separated sex from courtship and its customary object, marriage. When sex is cheap, quick, and always available, why bother with corsages, dinner dates, and engagement rings?

More than tradition is at stake. Since the pioneering work of Norbert Elias, historians and social scientists have come to appreciate that acquiring and displaying good manners has greatly strengthened the faculty of impulse control on which social order depends. Sales's informants did not need a dead German sociologist to know that something had gone wrong. If these guys said to our faces what they say to us online, one of them told her, we would probably kick them in the balls.[24]

Critics accused Sales of pushing a feminist agenda and ignoring the other uses of social media, such as sharing family news or networking with activists. No smartphones, no Arab Spring. No social media, no Black Lives Matter. New consumer technologies have their liberating side. In his magnum opus on the historical decline of violence and intolerance, *The Better Angels of Our Nature* (2011), the psychologist Steven Pinker proposed that the acceleration of human and animal rights revolutions since the 1960s was a byproduct of the consumer electronics revolutions. The annual doubling of transistors on integrated circuits put the Enlightenment's Republic of Letters on steroids. It connected a literate mass audience and broadcast the methods and ideals of the scientific and humanitarian revolutions. Against Wikipedia, pernicious beliefs stand less chance of survival. Prejudices about the innate criminality of certain races, or women's enjoyment of rape, or the necessity of beating children, or the moral irrelevance of animal suffering stand a mouse click from debunking. The internet is bad news for those who, paraphrasing Voltaire, would have us commit atrocities because they can make us believe absurdities.[25]

This is a plausible theory, though not a watertight one. The Republic of Flamers and its legions of bots have proven equally adept at filling cyberspace with absurdities and invective, as comment chains and Twitter feeds attest. Nor has the Republic of Tempters been idle. In the mid-1990s the internet Jekyll, which began life as an academic email and file-sharing network, assumed a second, Hyde-like character as a global libertarian commons of untaxed commerce, seductive pastimes, and vice. As late as the 1960s, observed the psychologist Adam Alter, people swam in waters in which there were relatively few addictive hooks. Chief among them were cigarettes, alcohol, and drugs. The last were expensive, risky, and often hard to obtain. But by the 2010s consumer waters had become filled with hooks. They had names like Facebook, Instagram, porn, email, and online shopping. Fishing had become phishing.[26]

Alter neglected to mention food addiction, a real-life phenomenon with online triggers like *mukbang* and fast-food-delivery apps. But adding compulsive overeating and its digital prompts only strengthens the point. In the early twenty-first century—the same period that Pinker identified as a golden age of statistically declining physical violence and expanding rights—people face more, and more cunningly fashioned, inducements to harmful habits than at any point in history.

Though the harms vary from country to country, the global pattern is clear. The average adult living in the world of 2014 was thirty times less likely to die from war or homicide than from a condition linked to bad health habits. These include familiar killers like smoking, drinking, drug use, and unprotected extramarital sex as well as relative newcomers like overeating, salt- and sugar-rich diets, techno-sloth, and distracted driving. It is as if the worst angels of our nature emerged at the same moment as our best. Even if Pinker is right about the pacifying and humanitarian implications of electronic communication, the same underlying technological revolution has brought grave risk as well as great opportunity in its wake.[27]

As they multiplied, the digital hooks became sharper. In September 2006 Facebook was just another "fun" site, a novelty open to anyone who was thirteen years old and in possession of a valid email address. Ten years later it was an obsession, with more than a billion daily active users, a claim on the attention of nearly 40 percent of the global online population, and the foundation of the world's fifth most valuable corporation. None of this was accidental. Like food engineers, designers of social media platforms and video games rely on pleasure's traditional art of combination. The difference is that, instead of sugar, salt, and fat, they select from a menu of psychological ingredients. The big six are compelling goals just beyond the user's immediate reach; unpredictable but stimulating feedback; a sense of incremental progress and hard-won mastery; tasks or levels that gradually become more challenging; tensions that demand resolution; and social connections to like-minded users. Insiders call the social aspect the "rewards of the tribe." Tribes punish, too. "You've got to keep up with the virtual Joneses," explained Ryan Van Cleave, an English professor who lost his job at Clemson because he was playing *World of Warcraft* sixty hours a week. When he finally quit, to avoid losing his family, he suffered drenching sweats, nausea, and headaches.[28]

A product does not have to be a game to have game-like effects. Instagram, a photo-sharing app that ballooned from 1 million users in 2010 to

700 million in 2017, offers a textbook example of variable reinforcement. Some posts bomb. Others get lots of likes. Users chase likes by continuously posting photos and constantly returning to the site to support their friends. Instagram is simple, quick, and universal, being visual, linked to platforms like Twitter and Facebook, and requiring no language fluency. And it is, like, addictive. "I wake up in the morning and my heart is racing out of my chest," said one user. "How many new followers did I get? How many people did I lose? What am I going to post today?"[29]

Nir Eyal, an applied psychologist and former video game designer, has called Instagram a meticulously designed, habituating product unleashed— his word—on consumers who make it part of their daily routine. They do so because Instagram and similar apps exploit small stressors like boredom, frustration, or FOMO by turning them into internal triggers, prompting "an almost instantaneous and often mindless action to quell the negative sensation." Successful product designers know how to combine psychology and technology to scratch these itches, forming bonds of positive associa-tion and strong habits good for their bottom line.[30]

Just how good became apparent in 2012, when Facebook paid $1 billion to acquire Instagram, yet to reach its second birthday. The investment proved a bargain. Most of Facebook's activity involves looking at other people's photos, and Instagram is ideally suited for targeting ads. Foodies snapped three-star meals, quilters quilting bees, skiers their favorite resorts. "This data is WORTH S***LOADS!" tech enthusiast Robert Scoble told *Forbes,* referring to information about user preferences. It became worth even more when Instagram added video capacity in 2013. Facebook had a window into its shutterbugs' souls—and into their vices, when they broke the rules by sharing illicit drug ads and pornographic video clips using hard-to-detect Arabic hashtags.[31]

Whether it was forbidden content that drew users to the internet and social media platforms, or mini-hits of stress-relieving information, or both, critics began to detect ill effects of heavy use. With the exception of trauma caused by distracted driving and walking, few of these effects are acute and none toxic in the manner of alcohol or drugs. Internet addicts are not overdose candidates. Their heavy use is instead a slow poison, one whose cumulative toll is cognitive and moral.

The primary danger, particularly with smartphones, is constant distraction from personal conversation, sleep, driving, study, reflection, practice, and work, which translates into difficulty achieving or maintaining intimacy, health, safety, knowledge, creativity, expertise, and socially constructive flow states. Like gambling machines, social media and other digital diversions offer alternative flow states through virtual shortcuts that exact their price in money, time, and diminished real-life accomplishments, satisfactions, and tolerance for electronically unvarnished life itself. "It was an unpleasant surprise," wrote a Mexican student who participated in the abstinence experiment, "to realize that I am in a state of constant distraction, as if my real life and my virtual life were coexisting in different planes, but in equal time."[32]

Or unequal time, given that there are only so many hours in a day. "Facebook remains the greatest distraction from work I've ever had," the writer Zadie Smith confessed, "and I loved it for that." With a literary career at stake, she broke off the affair after two months. She was wise to do so. The novelist Jonathan Franzen, who wrote portions of *The Corrections* wearing a blindfold and earplugs, doubted whether anyone working with an internet connection was capable of writing good fiction. Professors doubted whether students so equipped could sustain original arguments, fears borne out by research showing social media use inversely correlated with grades. Psychologists showed that mere proximity to a silenced smartphone diminishes cognitive ability, particularly in habitual users. Lit up or vibrating, the devices are guaranteed to divert attention, as is any form of regular online access.[33]

The condition acquired a name, "time suck," defined in the Urban Dictionary as something "engrossing and addictive, but that keeps you from doing things that are actually important, like earning a living, or eating meals, or caring for your children." Like other forms of addictive behavior, time suck is self-perpetuating. If dereliction from real-life duties creates stress, or immersion in the virtual world creates loneliness, anxiety, and depression, then escapism is just the thing. A remark George Koob made about the spiraling distress of alcoholism—"People often drink because they don't feel good, but drinking makes them feel worse, so they drink more"— applies equally to digital addictions.[34]

To the extent that they undermine self-control, the internet and linked mobile devices have become part of what Pinker, in another context, called the decivilizing process. It is a label that can be applied to all forms of limbic capitalism, though not to capitalism per se. The production and exchange of unexceptionable goods and services has generally acted as a progressive force. Market competition benefited ordinary people, few of whom cared to live in a town with one store run by a state monopoly. Mercantile and industrial capitalism fostered traits of self-discipline, future orientation, and efficient time management. And capitalism produced the wealth that funded institutions of public health, safety, and education that let people lead more salubrious, secure, and rational lives. These conditions Pinker associated with the long-term decline in violence and brutality. And yet these same characteristics and circumstances would also seem to be antithetical to vice and addiction.[35]

So we have a mystery. Why did violence and cruelty decline while commercial vices and novel addictions proliferated? One answer is that technologies of violence—weapons—and technologies of addiction—weaponized pleasures—are psychologically distinctive. The pulses of missile-launch officers going on watch remain steady as they seat themselves at their computer consoles. The pulses of video poker addicts race as they seat themselves at their beeping machines. "Human behavior is goal-directed, not stimulus-driven," Pinker wrote, "and what matters most to the incidence of violence is whether one person wants another dead." Actually, behavior is both goal-directed and stimulus-driven. Yet his point stands. Technology made weapons much more lethal, but the lethality failed to translate into higher sustained rates of violent deaths because other historical developments made people less inclined to kill one another. Those developments amount to a checklist of modernity, starting with personal security under the rule of law and the expansion of mutually beneficial trade. Pinker called trade "gentle commerce"; his ally Robert Wright, a non-zero-sum game. "If you ask me why I am not in favor of bombing Japan," Wright observed, "I'm only half-joking when I say that they built my car. . . . To the extent that you think someone's welfare is positively correlated with yours, you're more likely to cut them a break."[36]

But what if, instead of cars, the trading partner made junk food or addictive drugs and apps? Limbic capitalism is capitalism's evil twin. It is stimulus-based, ungentle, and zero sum. It produces large and sustained profits (and with them the means of stymying opposition) through commerce in exceptionable products like pornography and cigarettes or, in the case of food and phones, quotidian products made exceptionable by addictive engineering. The good twin and the evil twin are joined, not at the hip, but at the historically contingent point where science and technology made it possible to turn a commodity into a vice. Sometimes the process was inadvert. Hypodermic medication was a medical breakthrough that carried, unexpectedly, a greater risk of addiction to narcotic drugs. But from the late nineteenth century on, vice-product invention, refinement, and marketing became deliberate processes. These processes undercut the Enlightenment hope that gentle commerce would lift all boats. What actually happened was that conjoined-twin capitalism raised some boats and sank others. That is why mainstream anti-vice activists and their public health descendants preferred regulation and selective prohibitions to outright socialism. Reform was about killing the evil twin.

DOUBLESPEAK

The moral justification for elimination of vice is straightforward: Destroy predacious products before they destroy us and our communities. To which the predators reply, it is not about the products. It is about individuals. No matter how tempting our lures, people can still resist them. They have made some variant of this argument for every addictive product and pastime, digital or otherwise. All that is necessary is facility in doublespeak. Nir Eyal gave a textbook demonstration in two lectures before the Habit Summit behavioral design conference, the annual gathering (for up to $1,700 a seat) of limbic capitalism's digital clan.

Eyal devoted his first talk, in 2014, to the four cardinal virtues of habituating product designs. They increase "customer lifetime value," the total sum of money that can be extracted from a user. They allow greater leeway to increase prices, because of less flexible demand. They super-charge growth with "short viral-cycle time," meaning that engaged users will quickly recruit others. Finally, they increase consumer "defensibility" against rivals. Up went a slide of a bomber bristling with machine guns. The message was unmistakable. We have you, and we will keep running you through our wringer.[37]

Three years later, in 2017, Eyal again addressed the Habit Summit. He began with a walk-back of the head-fake variety. Yes, there had been abuses. Distraction was a problem. But it could be dealt with by gentle social pres-sure. Try saying "Is everything OK?" to the smartphone boors at your restaurant table. Encourage the consumer to download attention-retention apps that block online triggers and limit time spent on the device. Why, he used the apps himself. The social-media-as-drug crowd had it wrong. "We're not freebasing Facebook and injecting Instagram here," Eyal said. "We can't believe we're powerless. We're only powerless if we think we are." All but thumbing his nose at Volkow, he put up a slide of bakery shelves groaning with carbs. "Just as we wouldn't blame the baker for making such delicious treats, we can't blame tech makers for making their products so good we want to use them," he said. "*Of course* that's what tech companies will do. And, frankly, do we want it any other way?"[38]

The managers of Shenzhen-based Tencent, a leading Chinese internet services provider, shared the sentiment. In 2016, a year in which the com-pany reported a 38 percent increase in operating profit, the annual report identified online gaming as an important growth engine. The gains had come through data mining, used to tweak the performance of existing games and gain "deeper insights" into players' behavior, meaning what kept them online and spending to improve their characters. The big winner was *Honor of Kings,* a fantasy role-playing game that (this detail omitted from the report) the state-run *People's Daily* denounced as a "poison" and a "drug." Rather than dispute the analogy, Tencent's managers spun it, telling investors that their strategy for promoting smartphone games was to "engage a large pool of casual gamers and gradually advance them to mid-core and hard-core categories." Already hard-core players of games like *League of Legends* could be placated with "attractive new content" prepared with the help of "insights gained from data mining."[39]

Some insiders lost their stomach for euphemism and equivocation. In 2017 Loren Brichter, who created the pull-to-refresh mechanism by which users of Twitter and other apps could update their feeds by swiping down on the touchscreen, said he regretted his invention. He called it addictive, a lever on a slot machine. Justin Rosenstein, who coded the like-button prototype, wished he had not bestowed "bright dings of pseudo-pleasure" on a distracted world. Chamath Palihapitiya, Facebook's former vice president for user growth, hated that "the short-term, dopamine-driven feedback loops that we have created are destroying how society works. No civil discourse. No cooperation. Misinformation. Mistruth." It was not, he emphasized, an American problem. It was a global problem, and stubborn in the bargain. Capturing and monetizing eyeballs had become an irresistible game.[40]

Repentant or not, Silicon Valley elites watched out for the eyeballs of their own families. "We limit how much technology our kids use at home," Apple's Steve Jobs told an incredulous reporter, who had imagined his dining table tiled with iPads. "Not even close," Jobs said. He wanted his children to discuss books and history at family meals. The five children of Chris Anderson, former editor of *Wired,* complained of their parents' tech-denying rules. "That's because we have seen the dangers of technology firsthand," Anderson told the same reporter. "I've seen it in myself, I don't want to see that happen to my kids." Palihapitiya was more explicit. He didn't use "this shit" and wouldn't let his kids, either. Other tech executives and engineers dealt with the problem by imposing time limits, refusing phones to their children before their mid-teens, and never, ever allowing screens in their bedrooms. Extending the low-tech writ beyond their homes, they enrolled their children in prep schools where iPhones, iPads, and even standard laptops were forbidden.[41]

No one doubts that, functionally and aesthetically, iPhones and iPads are remarkable technological achievements. But so were the clipper ships that carried opium to China. Creativity and parasitism, splendor and hypocrisy run through the history of limbic capitalism like bright, intertwined threads. Those who count the money understand this reality. They deal with the unseemly conflict as most of us do, by compartmentalization.

The champion in this regard was Martin Stern, the architect who conceived the high-rise casino megaresort. One day in 1969 Stern was driving toward the International Hotel, his Las Vegas prototype. Approaching an intersection, he gazed up at his creation, oblivious to the red light he was about to run. He was transfixed. "This is a goddamned good-looking building," he told his startled teenage son. "This is a *really* goddamned beautiful building." It was, too, and it would be copied all over the world. But what Stern did not admire was his building's principal attraction, gambling. He thought the table games and slot machines he had cunningly laid out were "stupid" pastimes for tourists and losers. He was neither.[42]

THE POST-SPATIAL UNDERWORLD

Though Stern's glittering mousetrap had three physical dimensions, it also operated in the fourth dimension of time—more precisely, in the nighttime. Historians and sociologists think of the nighttime as a temporal frontier whose colonization was made possible by artificial lighting, electrification, and motor vehicles. Victorian pub crawlers and prostitutes were early nighttime pioneers, in that they used gas and electric lights to expand their scope of operations. In postwar Japan gamblers and bar and cabaret workers extended the night with the help of amphetamine "awakening drugs." Stern took the next logical step, creating a self-contained, air-conditioned, parking-equipped, nonstop pleasure palace. Inside it day and night were as irrelevant as wall clocks, omitted to keep gamblers lost in play.[43]

The mice still had to reach Stern's cheese. That is why transportation speed and price mattered so much to Las Vegas and other pleasure meccas. In the 1950s Chicago to Las Vegas by car was two days, six meals, and a motel bill. A $75 tourist ticket on a TWA Constellation reduced the trip to five hours, with plenty of time left for an evening of play. Over the next three decades large, fuel-efficient jets and deregulated fares dramatically increased tourist volume. In 1958 about 60 commercial flights landed daily at Las Vegas. By 1988 well over 500 did so.[44]

It follows that, before the internet, the history of pleasure, vice, and addiction was largely a history of spatial and temporal expansion. There were places, at first isolated places, where people discovered, cultivated, processed, blended, and traded food-drugs, until eventually psychoactive commodity chains spanned the world. There were urban districts, like Harbin's Garden of Grand Vision, where people sought or tolerated commercial vices and where addiction-centered subcultures took root. And there were late-night hours, after the streetlights flickered on, when rouged streetwalkers emerged from the shadows to troll for customers.

Anti-vice activists made it their mission to shrink these domains to a minimum. They won some victories. Yet, despite their sustained campaign against illicit drug use and cigarettes, they lost the larger war to contain and marginalize commercial vice. By the 1990s, one had only to switch on cable television, stroll the aisles of the local video store, or glance at the magazine rack to understand that, in the Protestant nations that had been its cradle, anti-vice activism was on the ropes.[45]

The internet delivered the knockout blow, launching anti-vice activism out of the ring and landing it somewhere in the third row of seats. A restrictive strategy predicated on physical supply chokepoints (open your trunk), human checkpoints (show me your ID), and regulation of space and time (no ads near schools, no selling after hours) had scant chance against a technology operating in the virtual fifth dimension of a globally connected, post-spatial environment. Anti-vice activism did not compute. Digital commerce did, and in ways that transformed the availability, affordability, anonymity, and advertising of vice.

The obvious example is sex. Before the internet children received informal instruction on sex from peers and media, formal instruction from teachers and parents. After the internet children had only to enter a string in a search engine. An analysis of the top thousand "how to" searches in the United States in late 2007 revealed that 17.3 percent involved sex, including four of the top ten. The wording of these four—how to have sex, how to kiss, how to get pregnant, how to make out—suggested that young fingers were doing the typing. Porn videos offered advanced erotic instruction, or what passed for it in the objectifying world of internet sex. Those seeking guidance for illegal activities accounted for another 9.5 percent of the top how-to searches. Growing marijuana led the pack. Though readily accessible, do-it-yourself vice was not entirely anonymous or free. Tracking cookies, viruses, and malware exacted their toll, and pornographic websites often charged for regular access. But it was easier than dealing with strangers in dicey neighborhoods, or running the risk of being seen there. Silicon Valley executives knew what they were doing when they forbade computer screens in their children's bedrooms.[46]

Constructive knowledge is also on offer. How to write a résumé came in at number five in the 2007 study, how to write a book at sixty-two. A few keystrokes allow internet users to immerse themselves in the works of Caravaggio or Callas. The question, though, is relative traffic. In 2018, a search for "how to grow marijuana" yielded fifteen times as many hits as "Callas arias." The headline lesson of the content surveys is that the internet provides a mostly frictionless entry into what used to be called "the life." The life was the underworld, an exciting but precarious place where outlaw players hustled, pimped, gambled, got high, and did anything to scrounge a buck. The life was a term of class, subculture, and place, more often heard in poor neighborhoods than in rich ones. But with the advent of the internet and social media, everyone was virtually in the life, no matter where they lived.[47]

Alcohol marketers, who knew that up to 20 percent of sales went to underage users, quickly spotted the internet's potential. By 1995 liquor companies had begun sponsoring sites offering giveaways, promotions, and information about how to play drinking games. When social media arrived, alcohol multinationals tied their brands to pop-culture "influencers." Most of the ads are accessible to underage viewers, who upload their favorites to YouTube. Tweeters sing alcohol's praises. Facebook and Myspace users post photos and videos of themselves and other kids getting drunk or high. Just as American Indians had learned to drink from the worst possible tutors, fur trappers and backwoods traders prone to riotous binges, wired teenagers learn to drink from peers who swill booze, hug toilets, and pass out on the floor. Pathological learning is social as well as chemical and commercial.[48]

The cybervice portal operates in closed societies as well as in open ones. As early as 1995, Chinese communist officials denounced the threat of "pornographic and reactionary" internet material. Over the next two decades, China's business deeds often spoke louder than its official words. Chinese manufacturers supplied most of the sex toys sold (and demonstrated) on the internet. Chinese software companies like Tencent prospered by designing addictive online games. And Chinese firms supplied precursor chemicals, advertised on the internet and exported in bulk, used to make deadly synthetic drugs. Money had no ideological color.[49]

The Chinese were consistent in one regard. Their main worry was young people, a concern echoed in every national survey of internet vice exposure. Studies of pornography consistently find that neophytes enter the digital underworld at an early age. In 2003 Australian researchers learned that 84 percent of boys and 60 percent of girls aged sixteen and seventeen had accidentally or deliberately viewed internet pornography, including "images of virtually any sexual practice imaginable." These figures, likely underestimates, were compiled at a time when only one Australian home in three was connected to the internet. Kids found a way. In Iceland they tapped in with game consoles. In Kenya students used internet cafes and university dorm rooms, where they downloaded pornography and staged blue-movie nights. One undergraduate was turned on by a friend who sent him a porn link. "Since then I have craved for more sites like that," he said. "It is very addictive."[50]

The internet provides a means of accessing commercial sex, as well as experiencing it virtually. By the late 1990s New York City prostitutes were

Internet ads appear both on- and offline, as in this 2010 billboard outside a liquor store in Lincoln, England. Framed with Doric pilasters and floodlit for the convenience of nighttime motorists and passersby, the pitch combines availability, affordability, and anonymity with an advertising catchphrase and URL. Another trait associated with heavy consumption, anomie, is implicit. If you are lonely and blue, we have a cheap, internet-accessible booze date for you.

advertising escort services online. Booking dates by computer was easier and safer than dodging police and street predators. Classified advertising websites like Craigslist and Backpage (which was shut down in 2018) ran ads for prostitutes and pimps, including those who trafficked in minors. Back-page, a Minnesota prosecutor charged in 2016, was "the platform by which children are bought and sold." Another prosecutor called it a "dystopian hell." But hell has its defenders, including internet trade associations and tech companies that resist crackdowns and censorship for fear of adverse precedents. Vice wants to be, if not free, at least readily available.[51]

Vice also wants to be mobile. "I can say to my phone, 'Siri, where are the hookers?'" observed Robert Weiss, a therapist who specializes in sex addictions. "And it will geo-locate escort services within a half-mile, a mile, two miles, three miles, with phone numbers and maps and reviews of the different prostitutes." In India, where prostitution was traditionally confined to red-light districts, prostitutes abandoned brothels, bought cheap mobile phones, took an assumed name, and visited clients who called or texted. Hello, I'm Neelan, and my terms are cash before disrobing. The business being flexible and anonymous, part-timers ventured into the market. Men liked the convenience of mobile sex. AIDS workers took a dimmer view. Safe-sex counseling worked better when prostitution was physically concentrated than when it was digitally dispersed.[52]

Websites, dark or otherwise, began to traffic in drugs and drug paraphernalia. Online shoppers bought everything from powdered caffeine, more dangerous than it sounded, to fentanyl, every bit as lethal as its reputation. By 2014 an estimated forty to sixty thousand websites offered drugs without a prescription. Those with names like buyoxycontinonline.com left no doubt as to their intention. Other sites provided information on how to con doctors for narcotics. Faking fibromyalgia was a good bet. Just be sure to pick a doctor on the wrong side of the tracks and pay cash for your appointment.[53]

Rights to choice drug URLs command top dollar. In 2011 pot entrepreneur Justin Hartfield paid $4.2 million for marijuana.com. When governments dispensed with the pretense of prescription cannabis, he reasoned, he could cut out the local pot shop and sell directly. Marijuana.com would be the new wine.com. Meanwhile help was at hand for male customers worried about drug screening tests. They could order a Screeny Weeny, a fake penis connected to a bag of synthetic urine that could be strapped on and squeezed to emit a stream of clean urine. The manufacturer offered circumcised and uncircumcised versions in a variety of skin tones. Headshops provided refills. They took orders online.[54]

Just as important is information about drugs: what dose to take, how to inject, how to produce your own. Digital know-how helped transform European and North American cannabis markets. With the help of information, seeds, and specialized equipment acquired through the internet, domestic cultivators began growing potent strains of marijuana such as sinsemilla and *nederwiet*. High-THC domestic pot competed well with, and often replaced, traditional smokes like Moroccan hashish or commercial-grade Mexican marijuana. Legitimate nurseries and hardware stores got in on the action, selling growing media, cloning trays, high-intensity lighting, generators, fans, and dehumidifiers for indoor cultivation. The largest and most sophisticated operations added computers and other automated equipment that relieved growers of monitoring chores and cut labor costs. Growing pot became as rationalized, and as digitized, as anything else.[55]

Automated pot farming can also be read as a dystopian augury. Futurologists (and one historian-turned-futurologist, Yuval Noah Harari) have argued that the big story of the recent past is the uncoupling of consciousness from intelligence. Kludgy human brains have failed to keep up with digital algorithms. The gap keeps widening as information-processing power keeps doubling. *Homo sapiens* is bound for the evolutionary scrap heap. People will be replaced by smart machines that—or who—dispense with most or all of their economically useless forerunners. We face extinction by design.[56]

That prospect should prompt skepticism. Library shelves and video bins are littered with dystopias that failed to materialize. Yet the brief history of digital addictions suggests that there are other ways that digital devices can parasitize their creators. They not only excel at data processing, they excel at recognizing, predicting, and manipulating human feelings. "Hey, Siri, where are the hookers?" teaches the iPhone something, not just the iPhone's owner. If information and the ability to process it are what really count, who is the owner and who the owned in such circumstances? With machine intelligence divorced from conscience as well as consciousness, and with algorithms deployed in the service of habituation as well as profit, who is to say that the singularity will not be an addictive one, with a fading species' penultimate act seeking succor in digital opiates? Of course, the skepticism rule applies to this scenario, too. With one footnote.

Some of us are already there.

8

AGAINST EXCESS

What Google and virtual assistants like Siri must have learned about someone who spent a decade researching the history of pleasure, vice, and addiction can only be imagined. And yet I could not have written this book without tools to search the internet. Who knew that designer sex toys could connect wirelessly for music synchronization, allowing users to arrange the playlist for optimal pulse patterns? The ancients had carved phalluses, the millennials vibrating Bluetooth phalluses. Here was the technologically eclectic history of pleasure in one rechargeable package. Better yet, it was molded from the same bright, sturdy plastic as Lego blocks.[1]

Toward the end of my research I used the internet in a more conventional way, to share drafts and gather comments. The most heartfelt criticisms were of two sorts. Either I had been too quick to accept the idea of novel addictions and their neural commonalities, or I had understated the menace of limbic capitalism and failed to explain how to counter its onslaught. The book I had written, one historian told me, was about who controls our brains. Naming the system was not enough.[2]

When lines of criticism diverge, it is tempting to treat them as canceling each other out. I resisted the urge. I took the charges of credulity and political quietism seriously and used them to refine, extend, and summarize my argument. Lest that summary be dry, I have imagined another dialogue, this time a subreddit on limbic capitalism that distills the questions posed by my critical readers. Once again I have invited an addiction skeptic to kick off the discussion:

Everyone agrees that vice has gone viral. Online, there's a porn of every-
thing. The question is whether these products and services lead to actual
addiction. You use that word in a lot of different contexts.

And the contexts keep changing, along with the terminology. The medical historian Charles Rosenberg wrote that "in some ways, disease does not
exist until we have agreed that it does—by perceiving, naming, and responding to it." That goes double for addiction. Whether or not you think it is
a disease, we are in a bull market for perceiving, naming, and responding
to it. We live in an age of addiction, socially constructed or otherwise.[3]

Take tanning. Google "tanning addiction" and you will find millions of hits,
many to refereed medical literature. You will find references to physical and
psychological dependency; tolerance, craving, and withdrawal; the release of
"opioid-like endorphins" that can be blocked by naltrexone administration;
and studies showing that 95 percent of frequent tanners prefer tanning beds
that emit ultraviolet light to otherwise identical beds that do not. Even the
placebo effect has limits when it comes to the drug-like power of UV rays.

Tanning addiction, says a pediatric dermatologist, is "the new form of
substance abuse disorder." Better to call it an emergent form of addiction,
one of several. Like the others, it is a mix of ideas peculiar to a time and
culture. No medical researcher could have cobbled together "tanning addiction" without a neurotransmitter model of pathological learning, the development of experimental tests like naltrexone blockade, and a battery of
questionnaires. Have you tried to cut down on your tanning? Felt annoyed
by others criticizing it? Felt guilty about it? Felt the need to tan when you
get up in the morning? Check enough boxes, and you are a tanning addict.[4]

Critics of diagnosis creep would roll their eyes.

They would indeed. They view tanning addiction—worse, "tanorexia"—
as of a piece with shopping addiction and plastic surgery addiction and
other faddish afflictions invented by medical imperialists and their co-
conspirators, unhappy consumers who blame new products and services for

their troubles. Given enough time, every excess will wind up in the *Diagnostic and Statistical Manual of Mental Disorders.* The addiction establishment is addicted to hype. The hype is not entirely benign. Words matter when they sort, stigmatize, and coerce.

The catch is that cells and molecules matter too. Recall Rosenberg's exact words, "*in some ways,* disease does not exist until we have agreed that it does." Those other ways include the cumulative damage feel-good tanning does to DNA. Twenty-something tanners post revenge selfies of their skin cancers. Yet the industry campaigns against laws barring children and teenagers from tanning salons. Its official scientific adviser says it is absurd to call "our natural and intended attraction to sunlight as addictive." On the contrary, we get less exposure than ever before. The tanning industry is just doing the world a favor.[5]

Now *that* is malevolent hype. If it is hard to imagine tanning addiction without the brain disease model, it is equally hard to imagine it without an industry armed with advanced technology, marketing and public relations experts, and a target demographic: young white women with a history of depression. Whatever you think of tanning addiction, the business itself is an archetype of limbic capitalism. Fights over addiction nomenclature distract from the real problem, the harm caused by engineered excess.

This is why the concept of hormesis is useful. The word comes from the Greek for rapid motion or eagerness—"stimulation" in English. Stimulants often provide beneficial effects at low doses, harmful ones at high doses. The net benefit or harm of a dose varies by genetic endowment, historical circumstance, and social setting. Other things being equal, higher doses entail both higher risks and higher profits for suppliers. Small doses of ultraviolet radiation are in fact good for you. But tanning salons do not make money by irradiating occasional customers with minuscule doses. Their bread is buttered, so to speak, on the wrong side of hormesis. That is true of all limbic-capitalist enterprises.

Enterprises can be regulated. Why allow children to toast themselves into a cancerous state? Or limbic capitalists to seduce, sicken, and kill tens of millions of people every year? Why are their enterprises so resilient? Sorry, but I wrote on the title page of your manuscript, "NO SOLUTIONS."

Tragedies do not have ready solutions.

Why is limbic capitalism tragic instead of simply evil?

Limbic capitalism is tragic because human nature creates a malign exception to a generally benign rule of commerce. The rule is that social progress follows the adoption of innovations that survive the test of the marketplace. History justifies the assumption for most durable goods. The more durable, the better.

In 1861 Britain's biggest railway, the London and Northwestern, was spending a fortune replacing worn iron rails. So the directors tried an experiment. They bought recently invented Bessemer steel rails and laid them alongside their best iron rails on a heavily trafficked route. The steel rails lasted at least seventeen times as long as the iron. Jackpots like these launched the steel age, with lower cost, greater safety, and higher quality for thousands of products, from cars to washing machines. Goodbye scrub boards. That is why I said the costs of civilization were front-loaded. The benefits came later, in the industrial age, when science, technology, and capitalism finally—in this case literally—delivered the goods.[6]

Not for the wage slaves who toiled at the mine faces or shoveled coal into the furnaces.

Like any enterprise involving money, capitalism shared a border with criminality. Companies abused and discarded workers. They conspired to restrain trade and create monopoly profits. They dodged taxes and adulterated products. They polluted and despoiled the environment. The great question from the 1860s on was what to do about these abuses. Much of the history of the next century flowed from the clash of two contending answers. One was communism, based on state ownership and dictatorial—at times, murderous—economic planning. The other was progressivism, based on bureaucratic management to minimize abuses and state initiatives to improve workers' lives. In social terms, progressivism succeeded where communism failed. Workers in mixed industrial economies became healthier and wealthier. A Swede born in the late twentieth century lived twice as long on average as one born in the mid-nineteenth century, and got to shop at Ikea in the bargain.[7]

So, add sewers and schools and minimum wages and antitrust laws and furniture stores and civilization's yoke becomes light. Fair competition advances all.

Fair competition to find a better iron alloy, yes. Or to make cheaper textiles, proceeds from which, by the way, supported the writings of Friedrich Engels and Karl Marx. Neither man despised the *products* of factories and mills. They despised the *conditions* of their manufacture. What to do about them propelled the Victorian debate over political economy. But limbic capitalism differs in one crucial way. Innovation and competition, however fair and orderly, tend to make the social consequences of improved production worse, not better.

That is why drink figured so prominently in Chapters 1 and 2. The primal but precious civilized pleasure, alcohol, flowed freely throughout the world of steam and steel—too freely. In the 1950s and 1960s a French demographer, Sully Ledermann, showed that many diseases and social problems closely tracked national alcohol consumption. Tuberculosis, cancers of the digestive tract, psychiatric admissions, accidents, crimes, vandalism: Their rates rose when French alcohol consumption rose, and not just among the heaviest drinkers. Hormesis applied to the group as well as to the individual. This was a powerful idea, and it laid bare the contradictions of French policy. Successful efforts by alcohol producers, retailers, and the French treasury to boost consumption, Ledermann said, amounted to an investment in alcoholism and alcohol-related mortality.

The French largely ignored Ledermann. But his ideas caught on among Scandinavian, British, and North American alcohol researchers. By the mid-1970s they had made reduction in overall consumption a central goal of alcohol control policy. Naturally, this put them on a collision course with alcohol multinationals promoting affordable, standardized beverages to consumers who took more, better, and cheaper products as a birthright.[8]

Some version of this wealth-versus-health conflict is built into every business that sells habituating products offering rapid brain reward and relief from boredom and depression. The costs, from emphysema to school failure, vary with the products. What the costs have in common is that they are mostly borne by others than those who produce and market the merchandise. The heaviest costs are borne by those who lose control over their consumption, who also happen to be those who are most socially and genetically vulnerable. If capitalism is often socially progressive, limbic capitalism is often socially regressive. Sometimes it is savagely so.

The evil twin again. But not every poor person becomes an addict.

Nor does every disaster befall the addicted. The just-this-once texter who crashes. The weekend opioid user who overdoses. The nonalcoholic drinker with throat cancer. Dead is dead.

And living is living. The accident victim texting for help. The surgical patient recovering with the help of narcotics. The couple celebrating their anniversary with a champagne toast.

Just so. Pleasures are liberating. Pleasures are enslaving. Which one is a matter of circumstances: dose, age, means of administration, length of use, expectations, social conditions, and genetic predispositions—predispositions that our ancestors' social conditions also shaped.

Fate.

Once, perhaps. Today the fate of addicts is more likely to be engineered, in a statistical sense. Corporations are not gods. They go after numbers, not specific individuals. They create heavy, habitual consumers in target-rich groups. College sports clubs are popular in Brazil. Most of the clubs have corporate alcohol sponsors that discount booze in exchange for advertising rights and exclusive brand use. So the clubs throw open-bar parties. A cheap admission ticket buys all the booze the students can drink. Result: overdose deaths, sexual assaults, and undergraduates who develop a taste for bingeing. The bingers effectively become corporate-owned human annuities, bought cheaply and with minimal regard for collateral damage.[9]

The coin of persuasion has two sides.

Behavioral economists call the flip side "nudging." Set up choices in the right way and you can get our brains' tendency to make quick, intuitive, follow-the-herd decisions to work for us instead of against us. Place the carrot sticks rather than the French fries at eye level in the school cafeteria line. Advertise the fact that most people do not drink heavily or smoke at all. Tactics like these promote healthier behavior. Nora Volkow was right. We can change environments to strengthen rather than weaken human biology.[10]

But you said there was a hole in Volkow's argument.

Even as we are steered toward good choices, entrepreneurs in competitive markets devise ways to steer us toward bad ones. The academics who popularized the concept of nudging, Richard Thaler and Cass Sunstein, gave the example of food shops competing across a crowded airport corridor. One sold fruit and yogurt. The other sold Cinnabons, frosting-lathered cinnamon rolls with 730 calories and 24 grams of fat. Each. The staff baked the buns in ovens equipped with inefficient exhaust hoods, situated in the front of the store, so that the aroma lingered in the walkway. No prize for guessing who did the most business.[11]

Cinnabon epitomizes the modern consumer dilemma. A century ago, if you had told people that one day they could snack in air-conditioned comfort while waiting to be whisked away in a winged tube to any destination they desired, they could scarce imagine such a scenario as anything but utopian. If you had told them that such snacking would make them so fat they could barely squeeze into their seats, or that it would increase their risk of diabetes and cancer, they might view it otherwise.

Thaler and Sunstein thought Cinnabon an amusing counterexample. What happened next was not so amusing. Cinnabon went global, opening stores in more than fifty countries. The company took in more than a billion dollars a year.

Every business wants to be the next Cinnabon, selling an irresistibly tempting product. The products can be legal, illegal, or a bit of both. Restaurant chains pitch bacon milkshakes, bacon sundaes, bacon everything. Bakers sell caffeinated donuts. Hotel minibars stock house-blended cocktails. Electronic bingo machines work like slots. Mobile gambling apps encourage betting during games. Pot shops offer marijuana edibles; studios, ganja yoga. Durban street dealers sell *whoonga,* heroin combined with cannabis and antiretroviral drugs. Chemists crank out NPS, new psychoactive substances continuously tweaked to avoid drug laws. Users buy "legal highs" online, along with flavored e-cigarette cartridges—a nice complement for their hash oil. Or they shop for augmented or virtual reality headgear, good for enhancing gaming and porn.

Though these are recent examples, they have historical parallels. Looking back, what made limbic capitalism so formidable was that its underlying technologies were so flexible. Opportunities for refinement and blending, often with seemingly unrelated inventions and products, kept multiplying. Things got entangled with things as well as with people. History's bottle was full of genies. When they escaped, they mated. Or they acquired matchmakers. Competition prompted experimentation and emulation.

Marlboro was once an obscure cigarette brand. In the early 1960s it became a world-beater when Philip Morris added ammonia compounds as binding agents. The chemicals also provided notes of chocolate and, more importantly, boosted the "satisfaction" of the smoke by increasing free nicotine molecules. Rivals lost market share. Then their spies and engineers discovered Marlboro's secret and copied it. It was like doping in sports. Either you cheat too, or you lose. By 1989 the tobacco industry was mixing in more than ten million pounds of ammonia powders every year. Industry lawyers called the ingredients "processing aids and flavorants." They occurred "naturally"—there's that word again—in the human body. They were harmless. Why, even food manufacturers used them as additives.[12]

You see the pattern, past and present. It amounts to a stealthy phishing contest. Multiply and sharpen the hooks, then make getting caught seem routine. That is another reason why these enterprises are so resilient. They create the impression that normal use of their products is either beneficial or harmless. And vice versa, that beneficial and harmless use is normal.

Addiction is not normal.

Yet addiction itself can be turned to advantage, if its frequency is low enough. The gambling industry freely admits that some of its customers lose control. So it pledges millions of dollars to subsidize hotlines, treatment centers, and doctors who study the genetic and neurochemical basis of gambling addiction. Cue the public relations ritual. Summon the photographers. Smile for the cameras. Hand over the poster-sized checks. Let's find out what's wrong with this addicted minority suffering from a psychological disorder. You normal types carry on gambling, while we learn how to keep the problem types out of trouble. Of course, the industry will do this only in a token way, because it has invested for more money in creating the problem minority that sustains its profits.[13]

If the goal is maximum profit, why invest even token sums in addiction research?

To foster a climate of plausible denial around images of safe recreational gambling. Or of drinking, drug-taking, snacking, soda-drinking, or catching some rays. You can draw a line from the deceptive science promoted by tanning industry flacks back to the mid-1950s, when the tobacco industry laid down a research smokescreen to counter the first big cancer scare. Science, including corrupted science, is a public relations trump card that other industries have learned to use. The copying is another reason why limbic capitalism should be understood as an evolving system, not just a random collection of businesses that happen to sell habituating products and services.

Yet these businesses also compete with one another.

Of course they do. Smoke more tobacco, eat less sugar. One mid-century brand, Lucky Strike, advertised itself as a slimming substitute for sweets. Nor was Big Sugar shy about pointing the dietary finger. In the 1960s and 1970s its trade association quietly funded heart disease research that downplayed sugar's role, casting fat and cholesterol as the villains. Industry leaders knew that if people cut back on fat they would add more sugar to their diets.[14]

Me-not-them remains a popular game. Try vaping instead of smoking. Try cannabis for pain instead of opioids. Shun the House, visit the Mouse. Disney lobbied to keep casinos from competing for tourist dollars in its Florida backyard. Yet it hired sommeliers to recommend wines in its restaurants.

There is a team-of-rivals aspect to limbic capitalism. In its way, it resembles the fractious anti-vice coalition of a century ago. Competition does not prevent cooperation, such as common opposition to advertising bans, which create unwanted precedents. Nor does it prevent emulation. Cannabis dispensaries offer fast-food-style drive-thru service. Casinos urge gamblers to "play responsibly." It is the same gambit as "drink responsibly," the classic public relations ploy by the alcohol industry to divert attention and shift blame.[15]

Gambits require small sacrifices. Between 1982 and 1996 Anheuser-Busch, then the world's largest brewer, spent over $11 million a year on responsible-drinking messages. That seems like a lot until you realize that, for every one of those dollars, it spent $50 promoting its products. The company report that broke down the numbers promised that management's every action was "guided by one overriding objective—enhancing shareholder value." It was true. That 2 percent was money well spent to polish the corporate image and deflect political heat.[16]

There are many ways to buy protection. They are obvious in high-risk, high-profit illegal enterprises, where bribes and violence are routine. *Plata o plomo,* silver or lead, as the narcos like to say. Easier to miss are the legal forms of inducement in limbic capitalism's licit branches.

The best example is charity, the oldest form of money laundering. Remember the Garden of Grand Vision, the Harbin vice district where garbage men collected dead addicts with a fishing spear? One of the Garden's most notorious slumlords, Zou Xisan, also directed the Harbin Morals Society, to which he contributed monthly. When the police chief asked him if he did not think it wrong to simultaneously profit from his den of iniquity, Zou replied, "I give alms to people of the world, so I am not concerned."[17]

Charitable recycling sanitizes vice. Even China's communist government, which rounded up and shot the Zous of the world, eventually authorized lotteries for sports and welfare programs. Lotteries were cleaner than casinos, and gave the punters a chance to scratch their gambling itch. Lesser-evil thinking spread. In 1994 the British government set up the Heritage Lottery Fund. It kept museums, cathedrals, and parks open and the tourist economy humming. A disguised regressive tax became a social win.[18]

What about the Quaker chocolatiers? The Cadburys may have rotted the imperial teeth. But they were true philanthropists.

So were Victorian-era brewers like J. C. and Carl Jacobsen. J. C. made a fortune producing high-quality lager in a brewery outside of Copenhagen. He preached moderation and promoted good beer as a salubrious alternative to spirits. He established the Carlsberg Foundation, which later merged with his son and rival Carl's Ny Carlsberg Foundation. Neither man was duplicitous in his giving. Neither promoted vice, judged by prevailing

Danish standards. Yet their philanthropic legacy remained a public relations temptation, the more so as the company prospered internationally. The Carlsberg Foundation was not shy about linking its world-class art and research programs to the Carlsberg Group's world-class sales.[19]

Carlsberg, though, was a model of propriety compared with Purdue Pharma. Purdue's modern history began in 1952, when three New York City physician brothers, Arthur, Mortimer, and Raymond Sackler, acquired Purdue Frederick, a small pharmaceutical company. The Sacklers and their successors built sales in the United States and later overseas through a network of companies called Mundipharma—literally, "drug world." The formula was simple: Push the product and spread the wealth. They hired lobbyists, paid medical opinion leaders, and marketed drugs to likely physician-prescribers whom they showered with meals and conference trips and company-backed research for new drugs. Among these were narcotics for chronic pain patients.

The label "patient" is important. Street addicts were not sympathetic. Patients suffering from chronic diseases were. Helping them, or purporting to help them, was the surest way to avoid strict regulation or prohibition. The same thing was happening, at the same time, with medical marijuana. Why outlaw a therapy that could benefit AIDS and cancer patients battling weight loss and nausea? Few could object to such humanitarian ends, though cannabis distributors coveted more than sales to the terminally ill.

Purdue's executives faced a similar temptation. During the 1980s and 1990s, they increasingly focused on selling narcotics for pain relief. They marketed MS Contin, a timed-release morphine pill, and then OxyContin, a timed-release oxycodone pill that packed a heroin-like punch. Most of the MS Contin went to cancer patients. But Purdue coveted the much larger noncancer pain market. In late 1995 the FDA, lobbied by Purdue, granted approval to prescribe OxyContin for moderate-to-severe pain lasting for more than a few days. The company immediately went prospecting for receptive practitioners and, through them, the pay dirt of opioid-naïve patients suffering from common complaints like arthritis and back pain. Most side effects, Purdue promised, would quickly diminish. Its pills would provide "smooth and continuous" pain relief. There was no need to worry about "iatrogenic 'addiction' to opioids legitimately used in the management of pain," as the condition was "very rare."[20]

Except that it was not rare. During the early 2000s the overprescribing of OxyContin triggered a sharp rise in opioid abuse and addiction and an increased demand for narcotics. Other suppliers, legal and illegal, jumped in. Pharmaceutical manufacturers and distributors kept the pill mills stocked, turning them into regional distribution hubs. Patients learned to work the system. They shopped doctors, filled prescriptions, sold pills for many times their copays. When the pills got pricey, Mexican traffickers, who had been organizing their own distribution network, competed with high-quality heroin. They later added fentanyl, a powerful opioid that could be synthesized anywhere and smuggled with ease. But Purdue got the ball rolling, and the ensuing epidemic of addiction and overdose was catastrophic. By 2016 and 2017 overdose deaths were causing a decline in U.S. life expectancy. It was the first two-year drop since the lethal flu epidemics of 1962 and 1963.[21]

Meanwhile the Sacklers and their heirs made sure to spread the profits. They founded research institutes, professorships, and lecture series at name-brand universities. They built new museums from Harvard to Beijing. They expanded old ones from New York to Paris. The donations won the family decades of prestige and good will, until the opioid addiction debacle became too big to conceal. Allen Frances, a psychiatry professor, told a reporter that he had spent a career making presentations in Sackler-this and Sackler-that lecture halls. He thought the name a synonym for good works tithed from capitalist bounty. Then it dawned on him that the family had earned its fortune through mass addiction. "It's shocking," he said, "how they have gotten away with it."[22]

Shocking, but also part of a pattern. The tobacco tycoon who endowed a university: James Duke. The narco who built soccer fields for poor kids: Pablo Escobar. The casino magnate who funded Zionist causes and cancer research: Sheldon Adelson. The Pharma family who added wings to museums: the Sacklers. Licit or illicit—not a hard-and-fast distinction—limbic capitalists created community stakeholders as well as community losers. When you catch whales—the gambling term Purdue executives used for their heaviest-prescribing doctors—lots of people get a cut of the oil and blubber.[23]

Limbic capitalism's beneficiaries are not always the intended ones. Private equity firms, for example, had nothing to do with the opioid addiction epidemic. Yet from 2011 through 2016 they invested over $5 billion in private drug treatment facilities in order to capitalize on all the new addicts. That is another reason limbic capitalism is a self-sustaining system, rather than a loose alliance of plotters. Engineered excess creates stakeholders by creating externalities, side effects not reflected in the actual price of the product or the balance sheet of the supplier. In the United States, nearly two thirds of drivers aged eighteen to twenty-nine have admitted to texting while driving. After 2011 the total number of crashes, which had been declining for years, began rising. Auto insurance bills rose too. Drivers lost money, though not smartphone makers.[24]

Suckerfish ride the sharks of limbic capitalism. Many suckerfish, in many shapes and sizes. Think of hiring officers. For them any type of excessive consumption or addiction is a useful marker. Useful in the sense that it offers clues to class, character, and stress—and to intelligence, which is positively associated with impulse control. It simplifies their decision making and avoids future losses. Statistically, smokers, compulsive snackers, insomniac gamers, and positive drug-testers are poor hiring bets.

Maybe in the abstract. But how much do employers actually save by shunning casualties of limbic capitalism?

It is hard to say in the aggregate, though individual studies point to considerable savings. Counting smoking breaks, added health-care costs, missed days, and reduced productivity, minus the "benefit" of smaller retirement outlays due to early death, each smoker costs private employers in the United States an average of about $6,000 a year. Each screened-out smoker therefore saves $6,000 a year. That figure is lower for countries with less costly health care. But nobody makes money for the boss when they are smoking on the loading dock or home sick with bronchitis.[25]

We have better estimates for externalities in the form of "problem prof-its." Medical technology firms sell over $3 billion of drug-testing equip-ment and services annually, with yearly sales growing by 4.5 percent. On the other end, billions of consumers and workers, would-be or otherwise, purchase products to quit smoking or lose weight. The global diet industry hit $215 billion in 2016, with an 8.3 percent annual growth rate. One day the suckerfish will be as big as the shark.[26]

There are second- and third-level problem profits, too—suckerfish riding suckerfish. More immunotherapy for lung-cancer patients (at $100,000 a year) means more work for pulmonologists if the unleashed immune sys-tem also attacks the patient's healthy lung tissue. More opioid deaths mean more donor organs and busier transplant units. More bariatric surgeries mean more follow-on operations to remove excess skin. Bariatric surgery patients who abuse alcohol or drugs instead of food face additional treatment costs. Rehab is no charity, especially not in the United States, where repeated admissions exhaust the savings of desperate families. More broadly, the lack of medical cost control makes the United States the world's most lucrative market for the repair of engineered excess. Pharma loves limbic capitalism, and not just because of the market for its own addictive products. Lipitor, a drug that lowers "bad" cholesterol often linked to bad diets, can sell for twenty times as much in the United States as in socialized medical systems.[27]

So, on closer inspection, your global tragedy turns out to be just another Yankee farce.

Not really. It is true that unusual freedom, wealth, and power gave Amer-icans a leading role in the globalization of limbic capitalism, particularly after World War II. And it is true that they paid an unusually large toll for its excesses. Yet other nations with rising incomes followed suit. Saudis, for example, are among the world's most obese people. If you seek bariatric surgery, you will be as well served in Riyadh as in New York.

More importantly, nothing foreordained that Americans would create the world's "reference society" for limbic capitalism. The history of pleasure, vice, and addiction in eighteenth- and nineteenth-century Europe had little to do with the United States. It had everything to do with trade, empires, cities, industries, and an outpouring of hedonic creativity enlivened by the arts. Belle Époque Paris is as natural a launching point for this story as Silicon Valley. If the United States had never existed, the globalization of limbic capitalism would have run its triumphant course, though perhaps with a more refined accent.

But you would not say that the globalization of slavery or genocide would have continued to run its triumphant course. Reformers, governments, and international organizations checked other predatory systems that spun off loot-rich externalities. Why not this one?

First, because it never enslaved or killed everybody in a given population. Many people found potent new pleasures liberating, if in a risky way. Chapter 3. Second, late nineteenth- and early twentieth-century reformers and governments *did* impede the progress of limbic capitalism, especially when it posed a threat to national security and public order. Chapter 4. Third, for every obstacle the reformers managed to create, they encountered one of their own. The revenue hunger of governments facing economic depression and rearmament. Military vice during World War II. The explosion of tourism afterward. Globalizing opponents with deep pockets, weaponized products, and an expanding bag of marketing tricks. Chapter 5.

The upshot was that anti-vice progressives gradually, unevenly lost ground. So, for that matter, did other progressives. The free market revival of the late twentieth century backfooted reformers of many stripes. Anti-vice activists enjoyed their greatest influence when governing elites in modernizing states were convinced that laissez-faire did not yield the best social outcomes, particularly for the health of the citizenry upon which state security depended. When vice was equated with hereditary degeneration, market interference was mandatory. At the beginning of the twentieth century, anti-vice activists had statist winds, sometimes nasty statist winds, filling their sails. When the winds shifted at century's end, they had to tack into the gusty rhetoric of market maximization: maximization of utility, international trade, shareholder value, and freedom itself.

Admittedly, libertarianism in practice meant libertarianism with benefits. The benefits were corporate welfare and subsidies for key interest groups, who passed the bill to posterity through government bonds. Still, free market fundamentalism was indisputably part of the late-century Zeitgeist. Just as indisputably, it opposed vice control. It is no accident that Milton Friedman, the leading libertarian economist, was also the intellectual godfather of drug legalization. He remains one of its patron saints.[28]

Progressive critics of neoliberalism, to use their term for the free market revival, argued that there was a social link between global capitalism and mass addiction that went beyond simple opposition to regulation. The demand for addictive products rose with the widening inequality and growing misery that came from axing the welfare state, eliminating consumer and environmental protections, exploiting cheap and part-time labor, privileging investors, and crying devil-take-the-rest. No jobs or rotten jobs, both exacted a toll. By the 1990s most of Mumbai's rag pickers were using brown-sugar heroin. When completely broke they sniffed glue or gasoline. More startling was the epidemic of opioid addiction among working-class white Americans, a once-prosperous group little troubled by narcotics. Untroubled, that is, until their employment prospects, morale, and family stability eroded in a nation also becoming, under the political cover of a culture war, the global reference society for neoliberalism.[29]

The progressive social critique found its champion in the experimental psychologist Bruce Alexander. Early in his career Alexander studied morphine addiction in rats. He discovered that it was harder to addict contented rats housed in spacious, park-like conditions than psychologically abused rats consigned to lab cages and Skinner boxes. For ethical reasons Alexander could not run this type of addiction-proneness experiment on humans. So he mined the historical, sociological, and anthropological record. In 2008 he published his findings in *The Globalisation of Addiction: A Study in Poverty of the Spirit.*

Alexander's premise, like mine, was that we live in an age of addiction. This he defined as a spectrum of overindulgence in a growing variety of harmful drugs, pursuits, and beliefs. Alexander went so far as to call belief in free market orthodoxy an "addictive faith." Better to say a faith partially and implicitly based on addiction, though that is a quibble. The real issue is causation. Alexander zeroed in on demand. For him, the basic problem was the dislocation, competitiveness, alienation, and anxiety caused by a relentlessly globalizing market economy. Addiction was, at bottom, a worldwide social problem, not an individual disorder.[30]

Anyone who thinks that the inequities and disease burdens of early civilizations drove people to seek release in alcohol and other drugs can hardly discount such an explanation. The question is whether it is the whole story. Those Mumbai rag pickers lived in a city with lots of cheap heroin. The strung-out Americans lived in the land of Purdue Pharma and Mexican dealers in beater cars who delivered smack like pizza. Just hit speed dial and score.[31]

Alexander accents demand. You accent supply. He says anomie explains mass addiction. You add accessibility, affordability, advertising, and anonymity.

And addiction neuroscience. However well the psychological soil may be prepared by stress and inheritance, the weeds of ruinous habits will not grow unless someone sows the seeds of brain reward and alteration. Even granting the criticisms of the brain disease model, there remains this insight: Without oh-wow moments and memories, without intense liking that morphs into craving, addiction is unlikely to take hold. Chapter 6.

The theory that neural exposure and conditioning are fundamental to addiction has a paradoxical implication. Like it or not, the brain disease advocates who sought to medicalize addiction shared common ground with the vice police. No addiction-reduction strategy was feasible that was not also a supply-limitation strategy. Ironically, the same problem applied to Alexander's critique. If advanced capitalism had rendered billions of people psychologically vulnerable to proliferating addictions, then all the more reason to reduce exposure to a minimum.

Or to dispense with advanced capitalism.

Not happening anytime soon.

What about religion? If free market ideology acquired new life in the late twentieth century, so did conservative religious beliefs. Why didn't ministers and mullahs apply the brakes to limbic capitalism?

They wanted to. As the Catholic *Catechism* puts it, the virtue of temperance requires the faithful to avoid every kind of excess. Limbic capitalism is about encouraging excess. Yet the religious animus against commercial temptation failed to spark a transnational reform movement similar to that of a century ago. The late twentieth century had no equivalent of the WWCTU in its prime, no religious anti-vice crusader with the global stature of Mohandas Gandhi or Bishop Brent. Missionaries exerted far less political influence in a postcolonial world.[32]

Religious leaders still mounted campaigns against vice, of course. But the campaigns were more inward-looking, more concerned with keeping the faithful in the fold. Evangelical Protestants, for example, had long confronted commercial and secular cultures promoting materialism, relativism, individualism, and sexual freedom. Now they had also to contend with the internet and social media, which they regarded as rivers of filth and idols for destruction. But the wired young—the future—were ever more inclined to habitually worship these idols, even when doing so made them miserable. It was the ultimate in set and setting: If we stop, we have no life. Chapter 7.[33]

Luxury traps doubled as secular traps, a principle that applied to more than social media. One of the few things clergy and sociologists agreed on was that the accumulation of wealth made people more preoccupied with worldly things. The rule had a corollary. When the things were *designed* to be preoccupying, the process of secularization intensified. In fact, it became circular. In undermining religion, limbic capitalism undermined one of the most important historical barriers to its expansion and innovation. If God was dead, any product was possible. If any product was possible, the godly had less chance of recruiting.

And so nothing can impede limbic capitalism's progress. Your tragedy ends like Hamlet, *with bodies strewn about the stage.*

I did not say that. I said that it was a dangerous aspect of global capitalism that had deep pockets, technological momentum, fair historical winds, and following ideological seas. But regulation runs in cycles, threats prompt responses, and the political weather eventually turns. With sugar, the process has already begun. In 2012 New York City mayor Michael Bloomberg launched a campaign against large sodas, which he blamed for the costly increase in obesity and diabetes. Limbic-capitalist front groups like the Center for Consumer Freedom took out ads mocking Bloomberg for his pains: "New Yorkers need a Mayor, not a Nanny." Bloomberg's campaign fizzled. But his idea lived on. Five years later nine U.S. cities had enacted some form of sugary beverage tax. More than a dozen obesity-plagued nations in regions from Latin America to Oceania had passed similar legislation, which the WHO endorsed in 2016. Chile's National Congress imposed a tax, required junk food warning labels, and forbade cartoonish ads for sugary cereals. Adios Tony the Tiger. When lobbyists cried foul, Guido Girardi, a socialist senator trained as a pediatrician, called them modern-day "pedophiles."[34]

Whatever the weaknesses of organized religious opposition to vice, secular activism has remained alive and well. Public health reformers showed their mettle in the tobacco-control wars. Though they failed to rout the tobacco multinationals, they did fight them to a standstill over their most dangerous product, combustible cigarettes. Confronted with a rapid increase in adolescent vaping, they subjected the supposedly less dangerous e-cigarettes to new sales and marketing restrictions; by 2018, thirty countries had banned them altogether. These achievements, and the growing opposition to sugar-rich diets, showed that scientific evidence could still spark change. And it could protect existing regulations. In 1984 the U.S. government raised the legal drinking age to twenty-one, then a controversial move. The controversy faded when studies showed upwards of a thousand fewer traffic deaths a year. Teenagers still drank, but proportionately fewer of them blacked out or wrapped themselves around the steering wheel. There is another policy truth. The more dangerous a product is seen to be, particularly to the young, the likelier educational, regulatory, tax, and prohibition efforts are to succeed.[35]

You said prohibition had fallen from grace.

It has among secular progressives, who are more interested in harm reduction through treatment, taxation, regulation, and education. Those are long-haul strategies, unglamorous but cost-effective. Treatment makes life better and safer for addicts, though not always or often on their first try. Treatment requires money and time and, if it is to be available for all, political will.

Political will is also necessary for regulatory and tax policies that minimize consumption. Higher unit prices on, say, alcohol bring out lobbyists in droves. Much higher prices bring out bootleggers and smugglers. Yet medical studies and reviews have consistently found that boosting minimum prices reduces alcohol consumption and alcohol harms. The same applies to other potentially addictive products. Their demand may be relatively inflexible, but it is never absolutely so.[36]

The other arrow in the quiver of progressive coercion is regulation. Anyone who spends time in advertising archives will come away thinking that the regulatory bullseye is less vice than vice *marketing,* a view shared by social scientists. In 2001 a policy analyst and an economist, Robert Mac-Coun and Peter Reuter, surveyed vice regulation past and present. They concluded that commercial promotion mattered just as much as, or even more than, legal availability. The principle held for gambling houses as well as for cannabis shops.[37]

Let's concede that some legal products and services may be so dangerous as to deserve prohibition. That is the fate that many reformers envision for combustible cigarettes, and it is already the fate of tanning salons in most of melanoma-prone Australia. As a rule, though, the best approach to potentially addictive products and services is to worry less about their legal status and more about keeping prices high, advertisers at bay, and the young away. Pot is a prime example. Teens who take up regular smoking shed more IQ points than adults who do likewise. It is an inconvenient truth for a budding industry that forswears selling to underage customers but depends on daily stoners who disproportionately start the habit young.[38]

The same goes for digital addictions. One reason they have spread so rapidly is that, even granting the best of regulatory intentions and the fantasy of industry cooperation, it is practically impossible to keep kids out of the digital domain. Devices and apps are ubiquitous. Peer pressure is relentless. The hooks get planted early.

That leaves one last card to play, education. It is still possible to warn people, young and old, about the dangers of habituating products. The most effective warnings come wrapped in ridicule. In 1978 Australian anti-smoking activists founded Billboard Utilising Graffitists Against Unhealthy Promotions—BUGA UP, for short. The name was a pun on Aussie slang for screwing something up. BUGA UP screwed up billboard ads by "flipping" them with graffiti. A squirt of paint here and a squirt there on a sign advertising cigarettes, and "Have a Winfield" became "Have a Wank." Civil disobedience and cheeky populism, free of any taint of puritanism, was a winner. BUGA UP ignited a campaign that, in 1992, secured a national law outlawing all tobacco ads save for those at the point of sale.[39]

So, fill the subway escalator screens with satirical public service announcements rather than lasagna ads. Enlighten consumers, turn up the regulatory heat.

Just one problem, other than the obvious issue of commercial free speech. There are degrees of educability. Not everyone heeds the advice. Many of the same traits that make a person more vulnerable to addiction, such as

On October 1, 1983, the recently convicted BUGA UP surgeon-activist Arthur Chesterfield-Evans gave a defiant speech before a billboard in Sydney, Australia. "After six years of surgery, I could accept that people suffer and die," he said. "But I had real trouble coming to terms with the fact that cigarette diseases were the result of a cold-blooded and systematic campaign of deception waged by monied interests against less informed consumers." He climbed a ladder and spray-painted "Legal drug pushers the real criminals" on the sign. The cheering, placard-waving crowd joined in, covering the ad from top to bottom.

impulsivity, future-discounting, or stress-induced illness, render them less susceptible to public health messaging. Those who get the word—tobacco history again—tend to be better schooled and of higher social standing. When they quit or shun the habit others follow their example, partly because of the growing class stigma. But the reverse is also true. Because what we think about addiction depends on who is addicted, the dwindling remainder of the unreformed attracts less and less sympathy. People think they are stubborn fools who deserve their cancers and coronaries and overdoses.

Or their poverty, because who wants to give them jobs?

Or their freedom or even their lives. History takes strange turns. At the end of the Cold War almost no one foresaw the global rise of authoritarian populist nationalism. Yet it happened, and it affected policies toward vice and addiction. President Vladimir Putin pursued a hardline drug policy, later extended to alcohol abuse and smoking, the ball and chain of Russian life expectancy. In 2017 Putin declared that anyone born after 2015 would be banned from buying cigarettes, which amounted to a declaration of gradual prohibition. In 2016 the Philippine president, Rodrigo Duterte, denouncing a plague of crystal-meth "zombies" with shrunken brains, greenlighted an ugly campaign of extrajudicial murders of drug dealers and users. That same year Donald Trump won the presidency of the United States, promising a southwestern border wall to keep out drugs and immigrants. Meanwhile Chinese security police, wiser about the permeability of great walls, used high-tech surveillance to track drug users as well as dissidents. In 2018 Chinese censors and education officials, worried about a different sort of addiction, restricted the number of new videogame releases and promised to impose a digital verification system to limit how much and when minors could play. What happened next—Tencent's market value plummeted—is a reminder that vice and anti-vice have always been locked in a technological arms race. Victorian reformers exploited the high technology of their day. Latter-day authoritarians can do the same.[40]

The upshot is that limbic capitalism could—could, not necessarily will—be whipsawed by organized opposition from both the left and the right. Progressives and resurgent nationalists, together with moral conservatives, have made common cause against commercial vice before. They could do so again.

Should they?

It depends on how they go about it. The rationale for concerted action is clear. The addictive potential of commercial vice and, more broadly, the temptation to downshift the brain from disciplined, cortical pleasures to baser ones has never been more intense. Yet moralizing crusades eventually backfire, which is a big reason why vice regulation has historically moved in cycles of repression and toleration. To some degree, of course, all regulation is cyclical. Fear gets the upper hand first, and then greed, prompting a policy shift. But vice policy swings have been unusually wide, being intensified by the satisfaction of bashing enemies, whether libertine or puritanical. Mark Kleiman, a drug policy analyst, hit the nail on the head when he said that laws and programs ought to be judged by their results, not by the "warm feelings" generated in those who create them.

Kleiman said something else that bears repeating. The vice policy that yields the smallest sum of evils is often "grudging toleration." As in the Cold War, the aim should be containment. Smart containment means calculating and patiently applying the right mix of counterforce—taxes that bite, licenses for sale and consumption, strict age requirements, marketing bans, mass torts, satirical propaganda—at a series of continuously shifting points. Dumb containment means mindlessly punitive escalation, often at a single point: another Vietnam. But we get vice Vietnams because of yet another calculation: Which line maximizes my votes and placates my base? Engineered excess applies to vice policy as well as to vice commerce.[41]

YOU ASKED WHAT WE SHOULD DO. The answer is that, in politics as in life, we should be against excess.

ABBREVIATIONS

NOTES

ACKNOWLEDGMENTS

CREDITS

INDEX

ABBREVIATIONS

ADHS   Alcohol and Drugs History Society
FBIS   Foreign Broadcast Information Service Daily Reports
GAA   *Global Anti-Vice Activism, 1890–1950: Fighting Drinks, Drugs, and "Immorality,"* ed. Jessica R. Pliley, Robert Kramm, and Harald Fischer-Tiné. Cambridge: Cambridge U.P., 2016.
J.   *Journal*
JAMA   *Journal of the American Medical Association*
JKP   Jean Kilbourne Papers, Rubenstein Library, Duke University, Durham, North Carolina
JSAD   *Journal of Studies on Alcohol and Drugs*
JWT   J. Walter Thompson Company Collections, John W. Hartman Center for Sales, Advertising, and Marketing History, Duke University, Durham, North Carolina
LCMD   Library of Congress Manuscript Division, Washington, D.C.
NEJM   *New England Journal of Medicine*
NYRB   *New York Review of Books*
NYT   *New York Times*
PNAS   *Proceedings of the National Academy of Sciences of the United States of America*
Q.   *Quarterly*
SC-UNLV   Special Collections, Lied Library, University of Nevada, Las Vegas
SHAD   *Social History of Alcohol and Drugs*
TS   typescript
U.   University
U.P.   University Press

VF	Vertical Files, Drug Enforcement Administration Library, Arlington, Virginia
WHO	World Health Organization
WP	*Washington Post*
WSJ	*Wall Street Journal*
WWCTU	*World's Woman's Christian Temperance Union*

NOTES

INTRODUCTION

1. Five years later, when I contacted Berg to verify the accuracy of this account, he noted that he still had friends who were "quite compulsive gamers" (pers. comm., August 28, 2015).

2. Melanie Maier, "Wenn Porno zur Droge wird," *Stuttgarter Zeitung,* June 19, 2017 (translating *Einstiegsdroge* as "gateway drug"); James J. DiNicolantonio and Sean C. Lucan, "Sugar Season. It's Everywhere, and Addictive," *NYT,* editorial, December 22, 2014; Juliet Larkin, "Woman Drank Litres of Coke Every Day before Death," *New Zealand Herald,* April 19, 2012; Tom Phillips, "Chinese Teen Chops Off Hand to 'Cure' Internet Addiction," *Telegraph,* February 3, 2015; Lee Seok Hwai, "Taiwan Revises Law to Restrict Amount of Time Children Spend on Electronic Devices," *Straits Times,* January 24, 2015; Steve Sussman et al., "Prevalence of the Addictions: A Problem of the Majority or the Minority?" *Evaluation and the Health Professions* 34 (2011): 3–56.

3. Jon E. Grant et al., "Introduction to Behavioral Addictions," *American J. of Drug and Alcohol Abuse* 36 (2010): 233–241; Michael M. Vanyukov et al., "Common Liability to Addiction and 'Gateway Hypothesis': Theoretical, Empirical, and Evolutionary Perspective," *Drug and Alcohol Dependence* 123S (2012): S3–S17; American Psychiatric Association, *Diagnostic and Statistical Manual of Mental Disorders: DSM-5* (Washington, D.C.: American Psychiatric Publishing, 2013), 585, 795–798; WHO, "6C51 Gaming disorder," *ICD-11 for Mortality and Morbidity Statistics* (2018), https://icd.who.int/browse11/l-m /en#http%3a%2f%2fid.who.int%2ficd%2fentity%2f1448597234.

4. Michael J. Kuhar, *The Addicted Brain: Why We Abuse Drugs, Alcohol, and Nicotine* (Upper Saddle River, N.J.: Pearson, 2012), reviews brain effects, a subject I explore in more detail in Chapter 6.

5. Harry Emerson Fosdick, *The Prohibition Question: A Sermon Delivered . . . October 14, 1928* (New York: Park Avenue Baptist Church, n.d.), 5 (treat); Mark A. R. Kleiman, Jonathan P. Caulkins, and Angela Hawkin, *Drugs and Drug Policy: What Everyone Needs*

to Know (New York: Oxford U.P., 2011), 29; Jonathan P. Caulkins, "The Real Dangers of Marijuana," *National Affairs* no. 26 (Winter 2016): 22, 28.

6. David T. Courtwright, *Forces of Habit: Drugs and the Making of the Modern World* (Cambridge, Mass.: Harvard U.P., 2001).

7. Sterling Seagrave, *The Soong Dynasty* (New York: Harper and Row, 1985), 158–160; M. J.-J. Matignon, "À Propos d'un Pied de Chinoise," *Revue Scientifique* 62 (1898): 524.

8. Pathological learning: Steven E. Hyman, "Addiction: A Disease of Learning and Memory," *American J. of Psychiatry* 162 (2005): 1414–1422. Quotation: Markus Heilig, *The Thirteenth Step: Addiction in the Age of Brain Science* (New York: Columbia U.P., 2015), 77.

9. Kenneth Blum et al., "'Liking' and 'Wanting' Linked to Reward Deficiency Syndrome (RDS): Hypothesizing Differential Responsivity in Brain Reward Circuitry," *Current Pharmaceutical Design* 18 (2012): 113–118, typifies research on innate susceptibility.

10. Charles P. O'Brien, "With Addiction, Breaking a Habit Means Resisting a Reflex," *Weekend Edition,* NPR, October 20, 2013, http://www.npr.org/2013/10/20/238297311/with -addiction-breaking-a-habit-means-resisting-a-reflex.

11. Robert Weiss, "Sadly, Tech Addicts Have Taken a Page from Drug Abusers," *Huffington Post,* April 28, 2014, http://www.huffingtonpost.com/robert-weiss/tech-addiction _b_4808908.html. I have added advertising and anomie to the "Triple-A" formulation Weiss proposed.

12. The phrase is from Natasha Dow Schüll, *Addiction by Design: Machine Gambling in Las Vegas* (Princeton, N.J.: Princeton U.P., 2013).

1. NEWFOUND PLEASURES

1. Huw S. Groucutt et al., "*Homo Sapiens* in Arabia by 85,000 Years Ago," *Nature Ecology and Evolution* 2 (2018), https://www.nature.com/articles/s41559-018-0518-2; Yuval Noah Harari, *Sapiens: A Brief History of Humankind* (Toronto: McClelland and Stewart, 2015), chaps. 1, 4.

2. *Oxford English Dictionary,* s.v. "pleasure" (n. 1a), updated June 2006, http://www.oed .com/view/Entry/145578.

3. Andreas Wallberg et al., "A Worldwide Survey of Genome Sequence Variation Provides Insight into the Evolutionary History of the Honeybee *Apis mellifera,*" *Nature Genetics* 46 (2014): 1081–1088; Eva Crane, *The World History of Beekeeping and Honey Hunting* (New York: Routledge, 1999), parts 1 and 2.

4. Chris Clarkson et al., "Human Occupation of Northern Australia by 65,000 Years Ago," *Nature* 547 (2017): 306–310; Harari, *Sapiens,* 63–69; Jared Diamond, *Guns, Germs,*

and Steel: The Fates of Human Societies (New York: Norton, 1999), chap. 15; Angela Ratsch et al., "The Pituri Story: A Review of the Historical Literature Surrounding Traditional Australian Aboriginal Use of Nicotine in Central Australia," *J. of Ethnobiology and Ethnomedicine* 6 (2010), http://ethnobiomed.biomedcentral.com/articles/10.1186/1746-4269-6-26.

5. Peter T. Hurst, *Hallucinogens and Culture* (Novato, Calif.: Chandler and Sharp, 1976), 1–32; Edward F. Anderson, *Peyote: The Divine Cactus* (Tucson: U. of Arizona Press, 1980), 49.

6. Harari, *Sapiens,* chap. 2.

7. Ido Hartogsohn, "The American Trip: Set, Setting, and Psychedelics in 20th Century Psychology," in "Psychedelics in Psychology and Psychiatry," special edition, *MAPS Bulletin* 23, no. 1 (2013): 6–9; Norman E. Zinberg, *Drug, Set, and Setting: The Basis for Controlled Intoxicant Use* (New Haven: Yale U.P., 1984); Bee Wilson, *First Bite: How We Learn to Eat* (New York: Basic Books, 2015), 51–52; Adrian C. North, "Wine and Song: The Effect of Background Music on the Taste of Wine," http://www.wineanorak.com/musicandwine.pdf; Bob Holmes, *Flavor: The Science of Our Most Neglected Sense* (New York: Norton, 2017), 126–127.

8. Cara Feinberg, "The Placebo Phenomenon," *Harvard Magazine* (January–February 2013), http://harvardmagazine.com/2013/01/the-placebo-phenomenon; Fabrizio Benedetti, "Placebo-Induced Improvements: How Therapeutic Rituals Affect the Patient's Brain," *J. of Acupuncture and Meridian Studies* 5 (2012): 97–103; Tamar L. Ben-Shaanan et al., "Activation of the Reward System Boosts Innate and Adaptive Immunity," *Nature Medicine* 22 (2016): 940–944.

9. Miriam Kasin Hospodar, "Aphrodisiacs," in *The Oxford Companion to Sugar and Sweets,* ed. Darra Goldstein (New York: Oxford U.P., 2015), 20; Hillary J. Shaw, *The Consuming Geographies of Food: Diet, Food Deserts and Obesity* (London: Routledge, 2014), 59; David Stuart, *The Plants That Shaped Our Gardens* (Cambridge, Mass.: Harvard U.P., 2002), 78 (narwhal); Rajesh Nair et al., "The History of Ginseng in the Management of Erectile Dysfunction in Ancient China (3500–2600 BCE)," *Indian J. of Urology* 28 (January–March 2012): 15–20.

10. Wilson, *First Bite,* xxii, 9, 12, 19, 33; Jean Prescott and Paul Rozin, "Sweetness Preference," and Pascal Gagneux, "Sweets in Human Evolution," *Oxford Companion to Sugar and Sweets,* ed. Goldstein, 715–718, 718–721; Crane, *Beekeeping,* 29–30.

11. Daniel Kahneman, *Thinking, Fast and Slow* (New York: Farrar, Straus, and Giroux, 2011), chaps. 35–36; "Stoned Wallabies Make Crop Circles," *BBC News,* June 25, 2009, http://news.bbc.co.uk/2/hi/asia-pacific/8118257.stm.

12. Daniel E. Moerman, *Native American Ethnobotany* (Portland, Ore.: Timber Press, 1998), 356–357; Alexander von Gernet, "Nicotinian Dreams: The Prehistory and Early

History of Tobacco in Eastern North America," in *Consuming Habits: Drugs in History and Anthropology,* 2nd ed., ed. Jordan Goodman et al. (London: Routledge, 2007), 65–85.

13. Fray Bernardino de Sahagún, *Primeros Memoriales: Paleography of Nahuatl Text and English Translation,* trans. Thelma D. Sullivan (Norman: U. of Oklahoma Press, 1997), 288; Crane, *Beekeeping,* 507–512; John Maxwell O'Brien, *Alexander the Great: The Invisible Enemy: A Biography* (New York: Routledge, 1992); Stephen Hugh-Jones, "Coca, Beer, Cigars, and *Yagé*: Meals and Anti-Meals in an Amerindian Community," in *Consuming Habits,* ed. Goodman et al., 48.

14. Diamond, *Guns, Germs, and Steel,* part 2.

15. Maricel E. Presilla, "Chocolate, Pre-Columbian," in *Oxford Companion to Sugar and Sweets,* ed. Goldstein, 147–152; Deborah Cadbury, *Chocolate Wars: The 150-Year Rivalry between the World's Greatest Chocolate Makers* (New York: Public Affairs, 2010), 27, 135.

16. Andrew Lawler, *Why Did the Chicken Cross the World? The Epic Saga of the Bird That Powers Civilization* (New York: Atria, 2014), chap. 7.

17. Kurt Vonnegut, *Breakfast of Champions* (New York: Delta, 1973), 208.

18. David Carr, *The Night of the Gun: A Reporter Investigates the Darkest Story of His Life. His Own* (New York: Simon and Schuster, 2008), 106. Carr ended up dying of another addiction, to cigarettes.

19. Sarah Zielinski, "The Alcoholics of the Animal World," Smithsonian.com, September 16, 2011, http://www.smithsonianmag.com/science-nature/the-alcoholics-of-the-animal -world-81007700/; W. C. McGrew, "Natural Ingestion of Ethanol by Animals: Why?" *Liquid Bread: Beer and Brewing in Cross-Cultural Perspective,* ed. Wulf Schiefenhövel and Helen Macbeth (New York: Berghahn, 2011), 18.

20. Robert J. Braidwood et al., "Symposium: Did Man Once Live by Beer Alone?" *American Anthropologist* n.s. 55 (1953): 515–526; Michael Pollan, *Cooked: A Natural History of Transformation* (New York: Penguin, 2013), 385. I follow Harari, *Sapiens,* chap. 4, in dating the Neolithic Transition.

21. Greg Wadley and Brian Hayden, "Pharmacological Influences on the Neolithic Transition," *J. of Ethnobiology* 35 (2015): 568; Pollan, *Cooked,* 385 ("eating").

22. Wadley and Hayden, "Pharmacological Influences," 566–584.

23. Ibid.; Adam Kuper, *The Chosen Primate: Human Nature and Cultural Diversity* (Cambridge, Mass.: Harvard U.P., 1994), 93–96.

24. J. W. Purseglove, "The Origins and Migrations of Crops in Tropical Africa," in *Origins of African Plant Domestication,* ed. Jack R. Harlan et al. (The Hague: Mouton, 1976); Ian Hodder, *Entangled: An Archaeology of the Relationships between Humans and Things* (Chichester: Wiley-Blackwell, 2012), 18; Harari, *Sapiens,* 87. David T. Courtwright, *Forces*

of Habit: Drugs and the Making of the Modern World (Cambridge, Mass.: Harvard U.P., 2001), chap. 3, explains why some plant-drugs spread more rapidly than others.

25. Michael Pollan, *The Botany of Desire: A Plant's-Eye View of the World* (New York: Random House, 2001).

26. M. E. Penny et al., "Can Coca Leaves Contribute to Improving the Status of the Andean Population?" *Food and Nutrition Bulletin* 30 (2009): 205–216; Daniel W. Gade, "Inca and Colonial Settlement, Coca Cultivation and Endemic Disease in the Tropical Forest," *J. of Historical Geography* 5 (1979): 263–279; Joseph A. Gagliano, *Coca Prohibition in Peru: The Historical Debates* (Tucson: U. of Arizona Press, 1994), chaps. 1–3; Steven A. Karch, *A Brief History of Cocaine*, 2nd ed. (Boca Raton: Taylor and Francis, 2006), chap. 1. The next wave of conquerors, the Spanish, discovered other imperial uses. Despite ambivalence about the idolatrous "herb," they taxed coca to pay clerical salaries and grew rich from the commercial trade, which sustained exhausted workers in the Potosí mines. See, in addition to Gagliano and Karch, Garcilaso de la Vega, *Royal Commentaries of the Incas and General History of Peru,* part 1, trans. Harold V. Livermore (Austin: U. of Texas Press, 1966), 509.

27. Patricia L. Crown et al., "Ritual Black Drink Consumption at Cahokia," *PNAS* 109 (2012): 13944–13949; Keith Ashley, pers. comm., November 17, 2016.

28. Mark Nathan Cohen, *Health and the Rise of Civilization* (New Haven: Yale U.P., 1989), chap. 3; J. M. Roberts, *The New History of the World* (New York: Oxford U.P., 2003), chap. 2; and J. R. McNeill and William H. McNeill, *The Human Web: A Bird's-Eye View of World History* (New York: Norton, 2003), chap. 3.

29. *The Golden Age of King Midas* (Philadelphia: Penn Museum, 2016), 22–43.

30. Herodotus, *The Histories,* trans. Aubrey de Sélincourt, rev. by John Marincola (London: Penguin, 1996), 39; Suetonius, *The Twelve Caesars,* trans. Robert Graves, rev. by Michael Grant (London: Penguin, 1989), 94, 136.

31. Bert L. Vallee, "Alcohol in the Western World," *Scientific American* 278 (June 1998): 83; Mary Beard, *SPQR: A History of Ancient Rome* (New York: Liveright, 2015), 432–434, 455–459; Juvenal, *The Sixteen Satires,* trans. Peter Green (Harmondsworth, Middlesex: Penguin, 1967), 95; Suetonius, *Twelve Caesars,* trans. Graves, 206. Gambling bore a similar taint in Han China, yet remained irrepressibly popular among both the hoi polloi and top imperial officials. Desmond Lam, *Chopsticks and Gambling* (New Brunswick, N.J.: Transaction, 2014), 13–14.

32. Gina Hames, *Alcohol in World History* (London: Routledge, 2012), 9, 11, 20; Rod Phillips, *Alcohol: A History* (Chapel Hill: U. of North Carolina Press, 2014), 36; Sherwin B. Nuland, *Medicine: The Art of Healing* (New York: Macmillan, 1992), 70. The sweetened wines beloved of Roman aristocrats may also have been contaminated with lead, which aggravated gout and other health problems. Jerome O. Nriagu, "Saturnine

Gout among Roman Aristocrats—Did Lead Poisoning Contribute to the Fall of the Empire?" *NEJM* 308 (1983): 660–663.

33. Owen Jarus, "Ancient Board Game Found in Looted China Tomb," *Scientific American,* November 18, 2015, http://www.scientificamerican.com/article/ancient-board-game -found-in-looted-china-tomb1/.

34. David Parlett, *The Oxford History of Board Games* (Oxford: Oxford U.P., 1999), chap. 2; Herodotus, *Histories,* 40.

35. Object B16742, http://www.penn.museum/collections/object/22759; Beard, *SPQR,* 459.

36. David G. Schwartz, *Roll the Bones: The History of Gambling* (New York: Gotham, 2006), 19–21.

37. Nick Haslam and Louis Rothschild, "Pleasure," in *Encyclopedia of Human Emotions,* ed. David Levinson et al., vol. 2 (New York: Macmillan, 1999), 517.

38. Mihaly Csikszentmihalyi, *Beyond Boredom and Anxiety: Experiencing Flow in Work and Play* (San Francisco: Josey-Bass, 2000), quotations on p. 129; John Powell, *Why You Love Music: From Mozart to Metallica—The Emotional Power of Beautiful Sounds* (New York: Little, Brown, 2016), chap. 8.

39. "A Dialogue on Oratory," *The Complete Works of Tacitus,* trans. Alfred John Church and William Jackson Brodribb, ed. Moses Hadas (New York: Modern Library, 1942), 738–739.

40. Alison Gopnik, "Explanation as Orgasm," *Minds and Machines* 8 (1998): 101–118; Read Montague, *Why Choose This Book? How We Make Decisions* (New York: Dutton, 2006), 110–113; Teofilo F. Ruiz, *The Terror of History: On the Uncertainties of Life in Western Civilization* (Princeton, N.J.: Princeton U.P., 2011), part 4.

41. Vinod D. Deshmukh, "Neuroscience of Meditation," *TSW Holistic Health and Medicine* 1 (2006): 275–289.

42. Rob Iliffe, *Priest of Nature: The Religious Worlds of Isaac Newton* (New York: Oxford U.P., 2017), 66; Stefan Zweig, *Chess: A Novella,* trans. Anthea Bell (London: Penguin, 2011), 58 ("poisoning"), 65–76.

43. *Rig Veda,* X:34.

44. Schwartz, *Roll the Bones,* chap. 1; Deuteronomy 21:20–21; Plutarch, *Lives,* vol. 9, trans. Bernadotte Perrin (Cambridge, Mass.: Harvard U.P., 1920), 159–161.

45. Joseph Needham, *Science and Civilisation in China,* vol. 5, part 2 (Cambridge: Cambridge U.P., 1974), 287–294.

46. Phillips, *Alcohol,* 42–44, 187–191; Herodotus, *Histories,* 40; Mark David Wyers, *"Wicked" Instabul: The Regulation of Prostitution in the Early Turkish Republic* (Istanbul: Libra Kitapçılık ve Yayıncılık, 2012).

47. Margarete van Ess, "Uruk: The World's First City," in *The Great Cities in History,* ed. John Julius Norwich (London: Thames and Hudson, 2009), 20.

48. Peter Frankopan, *The Silk Roads: A New History of the World* (New York: Knopf, 2016), chaps. 1–12; Frances Wood, *The Silk Road: Two Thousand Years in the Heart of Asia* (Berkeley: U. of California Press, 2002), chaps. 1–4; Harari, *Sapiens,* 184; Mary Beard, *The Fires of Vesuvius: Pompeii Lost and Found* (Cambridge, Mass.: Harvard U.P., 2008), 24, 216–217.

49. Pierre-Arnaud Chouvy, *Opium: Uncovering the Politics of the Poppy* (Cambridge, Mass.: Harvard U.P., 2010), chap. 1; N. C. Shah and Akhtar Husain, "Historical Perspectives," in *The Opium Poppy,* ed. Akhtar Husain and J. R. Sharma (Lucknow: Central Institute of Medicinal and Aromatic Plants, 1983), 25–26; Frankopan, *Silk Roads,* 268.

50. Parlett, *Board Games,* chap. 16; Schwartz, *Roll the Bones,* chap. 3.

51. Robert Temple, *The Genius of China: 3,000 Years of Science, Discovery, and Invention* (New York: Simon and Schuster, 1986), 101 (quotation); Pollan, *Botany of Desire,* 21–23; Crane, *Beekeeping,* 358–361.

52. Phillips, *Alcohol,* chap. 6.

53. Fernand Braudel, *Civilization and Capitalism, 15th–18th Century,* vol. 1, trans. Siân Reynolds (New York: Harper and Row, 1982), 241–249; Mac Marshall and Leslie B. Marshall, "Opening Pandora's Bottle: Reconstructing Micronesians' Early Contacts with Alcoholic Beverages," in *Drugs and Alcohol in the Pacific,* ed. Juan F. Gaella (Aldershot, Hamphsire: Ashgate, 2002), 269.

54. Sander L. Gilman and Zhou Xun, "Introduction," in *Smoke: The Global History of Smoking,* ed. Gilman and Zhou (London: Reaktion, 2004), 9–15; David J. Linden, *The Compass of Pleasure* (New York: Viking, 2011), 50–51.

55. David Phillipson, *Band of Brothers: Boy Seamen in the Royal Navy* (Sutton: Stroud, Gloucestershire, 2003), 105; L. K. Gluckman, "Alcohol and the Maori in Historical Perspective," *New Zealand Medical J.* 79 (1974): 555.

56. Charles C. Mann, *1493: Uncovering the New World Columbus Created* (New York: Knopf, 2011), 17–19; John M. Riddle, *Quid Pro Quo: Studies in the History of Drugs* (Aldershot, Hampshire: Variorum, 1992), II-196 and XV-12.

57. Richard Evans Schultes et al., "Cannabis: An Example of Taxonomic Neglect," in *Cannabis and Culture,* ed. Vera Rubin (The Hague: Mouton, 1975), 22; Peter Maguire and Mike Ritter, *Thai Stick: Surfers, Scammers, and the Untold Story of the Marijuana Trade* (New York: Columbia U.P., 2014), 28; Isaac Campos, *Home Grown: Marijuana and the Origins of Mexico's War on Drugs* (Chapel Hill: U. of North Carolina Press, 2012), chap. 2; John Charles Chasteen, *Getting High: Marijuana through the Ages* (Lanham, Md.: Rowman and Littlefield, 2016), 50–58.

58. *Interwoven Globe: The Worldwide Textile Trade, 1500–1800,* ed. Amelia Peck (New York: Metropolitan Museum of Art, 2013), 177–178.

59. Lorna J. Sass, "Religion, Medicine, Politics and Spices," *Appetite* 2 (1981): 9; John Myrc, *Instruction for Parish Priests,* ed. Edward Peacock (London: Early English Text Society, 1868), 44; Jack Turner, *Spice: The History of a Temptation* (New York: Knopf, 2004), chap. 5. For examples of adulteration, see Shaw, *Consuming Geographies,* 65–67, and J. C. Drummond and Anne Wilbraham, *The Englishman's Food: A History of Five Centuries of English Diet,* rev. ed. (London: Jonathan Cape, 1957), chap. 17.

60. Sidney Mintz, *Sweetness and Power: The Place of Sugar in Modern History* (New York: Viking), 123; Drummond and Wilbraham, *Englishman's Food,* 54; Courtwright, *Forces of Habit,* 28; Johann Gottlob Krüger, *Gedancken vom Caffee, Thee, Toback und Schnuftoback* (Halle: Verlegt von Carl Hermann Hemmerde, 1746), 2–3; Hames, *Alcohol,* 67; Russell R. Menard and John J. McCusker, *The Economy of British America, 1607–1789* (Chapel Hill: U. of North Carolina Press, 1985), 121.

61. Niall Ferguson, *The Ascent of Money: A Financial History of the World* (New York: Penguin, 2008), 24–27; Mann, *1493,* chaps. 1, 4; Henry Hobhouse, *Seeds of Change: Five Plants That Transformed Mankind* (New York: Harper and Row, 1986), 116–119; Rudi Matthee, "Exotic Substances," in *Drugs and Narcotics in History,* ed. Roy Porter and Mikuláš Teich (Cambridge: Cambridge U.P., 1995), 45–47.

62. Harari, *Sapiens,* chap. 10.

2. MASS PLEASURES

1. Pierre Louÿs, *Biblys, Leda, A New Pleasure,* trans. M. S. Buck (New York: privately printed, 1920), 119–122.

2. Though "A New Pleasure" appeared in 1899, its opening refers to the Paris of "four years ago, perhaps five." A subsequent reference to Friday, June 9, dates the year more exactly to 1893. See also H. P. Clive, *Pierre Louÿs (1870–1925): A Biography* (Oxford: Clarendon Press, 1978), 212–213, 216. Shopping: Michael B. Miller, *The Bon Marché: Bourgeois Culture and the Department Store, 1869–1920* (Princeton, N.J.: Princeton U.P., 1981), chap. 5.

3. *Who's Who of Victorian Cinema,* ed. Stephen Herbert and Luke McKernan (London: BFI Publishing, 1996), 80, 106, 111–112; Patrick Robertson, *Robertson's Book of Firsts: Who Did What for the First Time* (New York: Bloomsbury, 2011), 9.

4. Edmondo de Amicis, *Studies of Paris,* trans. W. W. Cady (New York: G. P. Putnam's Sons, 1887), 16–17; Robertson, *Book of Firsts,* 227; Gina Hames, *Alcohol in World History* (London: Routledge, 2012), 70; Doris Lanier, *Absinthe: The Cocaine of the Nineteenth Century* (Jefferson, N.C.: McFarland, 1995), 21.

5. Ernest Hemingway, *The Sun Also Rises* (New York: Charles Scribner's Sons, 1926), 136, and *A Moveable Feast* (New York: Charles Scribner's Sons, 1964), 1, 14, 50.

6. Peter Stearns, "Teaching Consumerism in World History," http://worldhistoryconnected .press.illinois.edu/1.2/stearns.html.

7. *Autobiography of Mark Twain*, vol. 1, ed. Harriet Elinor Smith et al. (Berkeley: U. of California Press, 2010), 64–65.

8. George Rogers Taylor, *The Transportation Revolution, 1815–1860* (New York: Harper and Row, 1951), 136.

9. Ian R. Tyrrell, *Sobering Up: From Temperance to Prohibition in Antebellum America, 1800–1860* (Westport, Conn.: Greenwood, 1979), 26; W. J. Rorabaugh, *The Alcoholic Republic: An American Tradition* (New York: Oxford U.P., 1979), 69–75; Henry G. Crowgey, *Kentucky Bourbon: The Early Years of Whiskeymaking* (Lexington: U.P. of Kentucky, 1971), chap. 3; Henry H. Work: *Wood, Whiskey and Wine: A History of Barrels* (London: Reaktion, 2014), chap. 12; Reid Mitenbuler, *Bourbon Empire: The Past and Future of America's Whiskey* (New York: Viking, 2015), chaps. 7, 9; Robert Somers, *The Southern States since the War, 1870–71*, ed. Malcolm C. McMillan (University, Ala.: U. of Alabama Press, 1965), 79, 245.

10. Chantal Martineau, *How the Gringos Stole Tequila: The Modern Age of Mexico's Most Traditional Spirit* (Chicago: Chicago Review Press, 2015), 27, 59–60; George E. Snow, "Alcohol Production in Russia," in *The Supplement to the Modern Encyclopedia of Russian, Soviet and Eurasian History*, vol. 1, ed. George N. Rhyne (Gulf Breeze, Fla.: Academic International Press, 1995), 194; Mark Lawrence Schrad, *Vodka Politics: Alcohol, Autocracy, and the Secret History of the Russian State* (New York: Oxford U.P., 2014), 79.

11. Rod Phillips, *Alcohol: A History* (Chapel Hill: U. of North Carolina Press, 2014), chap. 9, statistics at p. 177.

12. Ulbe Bosma, *The Sugar Plantation in India and Indonesia: Industrial Production, 1770–2010* (New York: Cambridge U.P., 2013), chap. 5.

13. Niall Ferguson, *Empire: How Britain Made the Modern World* (London: Penguin, Allen Lane, 2002), 166; S. Robert Lathan, "Dr. Halsted at Hopkins and at High Hampton," *Baylor U. Medical Center Proceedings* 23 (January 2010): 35; Charles Ambler, "The Specter of Degeneration: Alcohol and Race in West Africa in the Early Twentieth Century," in *GAA*, 106.

14. H. G. Wells, *The World of William Clissold*, vol. 1 (New York: George H. Doran, 1926), 100, 101.

15. John Maynard Keynes, *The Economic Consequences of the Peace* (New York: Harcourt, Brace, 1920), 9, 11.

16. Jeffrey D. Sachs, "Twentieth-Century Political Economy: A Brief History of Global Capitalism," *Oxford Review of Economic Policy* 15 (Winter 1999): 90–101 (phases); "Morphin [sic] from Mail Order Houses," *JAMA* 48 (1907): 1280.

17. Arthur C. Verge, "George Freeth: King of the Surfers and California's Forgotten Hero," *California History* 80 (Summer–Fall 2001): 82–105.

18. Jürgen Osterhammel, *The Transformation of the World: A Global History of the Nineteenth Century,* trans. Patrick Camiller (Princeton, N.J.: Princeton U.P., 2014), 42, 911–912 (reference societies, quotation); Maria Misra, *Vishnu's Crowded Temple: India since the Great Rebellion* (New Haven: Yale U.P., 2008), 58, 175–176.

19. Andrei S. Markovits and Steven L. Hellerman, *Offside: Soccer and American Exceptionalism* (Princeton, N.J.: Princeton U.P., 2001), and Andrei S. Markovits and Lars Rensmann, *Gaming the World: How Sports Are Reshaping Global Politics and Culture* (Princeton, N.J.: Princeton U.P., 2010), explain the pecking order and why American favorites like baseball only partially penetrated global "sports spaces," which were largely filled during the crucial period of 1870–1930. However, in other respects—movies, popular music, radio, theme parks, and fast food—the United States assumed a vanguard role in the consumer pleasure revolution.

20. "Harvard in the 17th and 18th Centuries," http://hul.harvard.edu/lib/archives/h1718 /pages/highlights/highlight10.html; Peregrine Fitzhugh letter of solicitation, February 23, 1793, American Historical Manuscript Collection, New-York Historical Society, New York City. This section draws on David G. Schwartz, *Roll the Bones: The History of Gambling* (New York: Gotham, 2006), parts 2–6, and David T. Courtwright, "Learning from Las Vegas: Gambling, Technology, Capitalism, and Addiction," *UNLV Center for Gaming Research: Occasional Paper Series,* no. 25 (May 2014).

21. Reprinted in the *New York Times,* April 23, 1873, as "Monaco. Nice and Its Neighbors— The New Gambling-Place of the Old World."

22. Harry Brolaski, *Easy Money: Being the Experiences of a Reformed Gambler* (Cleveland: Searchlight Press, 1911), 116.

23. William F. Harrah, "My Recollections of the Hotel-Casino Industry . . ." (TS oral history, 2 vols., 1980), 175, SC-UNLV.

24. Utagawa Toyohiro, *Summer Party on the Bank of the Kamo River* (ca. 1800), Minneapolis Institute of Art, http://artstories.artsmia.org/#/0/122189; "Monte-Carlo's Most Prestigious Palatial Hotel," Monte-Carlo Legend, http://www.montecarlolegend.com /monte-carlos-most-prestigious-palace-the-hotel-de-paris/(Blanc); Warren Nelson, "Gaming from the Old Days to Computers" (TS, 1978), 61–62, and Harrah, "Recollections," 343–344, both SC-UNLV.

25. David J. Linden, *The Compass of Pleasure* (New York: Viking, 2011), 84; *General Catalogue of Noyes Bros. and Cutler, 1911–12* (St. Paul, Minn.: Pioneer Co., n.d.),

914; Susan Cheever, *My Name Is Bill* (New York: Washington Square Press, 2004), 73–75.

26. *Music, Sound, and Technology in America: A Documentary History of Early Phonograph, Cinema, and Radio,* ed. Timothy D. Taylor, Mark Katz, and Tony Grajeda (Durham: Duke U.P., 2012), part 2.

27. Gary S. Cross and Robert N. Proctor, *Packaged Pleasures: How Technology and Marketing Revolutionized Desire* (Chicago: U. of Chicago Press, 2014); John Pruitt, "Between Theater and Cinema: Silent Film Accompaniment in the 1920s," American Symphony Orchestra, http://americansymphony.org/between-theater-and-cinema-silent-film-accompaniment-in-the-1920s/. From a different angle, Robert J. Gordon's *The Rise and Fall of American Growth: The U.S. Standard of Living since the Civil War* (Princeton, N.J.: Princeton U.P., 2016) singled out the late nineteenth and early twentieth centuries as a unique period of technological innovation. Though Gordon argues that fewer transformative innovations occurred after 1970, he exempts "the sphere of entertainment, communications, and information technology" (p. 8)—which is precisely where the radical changes in digitized pleasure, vice, and addiction occurred. Whatever became of the *productivity* revolution, the *pleasure* revolution kept marching forward.

28. Cross and Proctor, *Packaged Pleasures,* chap. 3; Joseph Conrad to John Galsworthy, July 20, 1900, *The Collected Letters of Joseph Conrad,* vol. 2, ed. Frederick R. Karl and Laurence Davies (Cambridge: Cambridge U.P., 1986), 284; John Bain Jr. with Carl Werner, *Cigarettes in Fact and Fancy* (Boston: H. M. Caldwell, 1906), 132, 138–139.

29. Kerry Segrave, *Vending Machines: An American Social History* (Jefferson, N.C.: McFarland, 2002), chap. 1; George Akerlof and Robert J. Shiller, *Phishing for Phools: The Economics of Manipulation and Deception* (Princeton, N.J.: Princeton U.P., 2015), viii.

30. "A Crying Evil," *Los Angeles Times,* February 24, 1899, p. 8. Linden, *Compass of Pleasure,* chap. 5, describes how gambling uncertainty produces brain reward.

31. Robertson, *Book of Firsts,* 95, and Gary Krist, "The Blue Books," Wonders and Marvels, http://www.wondersandmarvels.com/2014/10/the-blue-books-guides-to-the-new-orleans-red-light-district.html.

32. James Harvey Young, *Pure Food: Securing the Federal Food and Drugs Act of 1906* (Princeton, N.J.: Princeton U.P., 1989), 117; Glenn Sonnedecker, "The Rise of Drug Manufacture in America," *Emory University Q.* 21 (1965): 80; Thomas Dormandy, *Opium: Reality's Dark Dream* (New Haven: Yale U.P., 2012), 120 (Pravaz).

33. David T. Courtwright, Herman Joseph, and Don Des Jarlais, *Addicts Who Survived: An Oral History of Narcotic Use in America before 1965* (Knoxville: U. of Tennessee Press, 2012), 237.

34. Melvin Wevers, "Blending the American Taste into the Dutch Cigarette," conference paper, American Historical Association, New York City, January 3, 2015; Nicolas

Rasmussen, *On Speed: The Many Lives of Amphetamine* (New York: NYU Press, 2008), chap. 4.

35. Brad Tolinksi and Alan di Perna, *Play It Loud: The Epic History of the Style, Sound, and Revolution of the Electric Guitar* (New York: Doubleday, 2016), chap. 1.

36. Thomas Gage, *A New Survey of the West-Indies* (London: M. Clark, 1699), 247; Hesther Lynch Piozzi, *Anecdotes of the Late Samuel Johnson . . .* , ed. S. C. Roberts (repr., Westport, Conn.: Greenwood, 1971), 68. This section also draws on *The Oxford Companion to Sugar and Sweets,* ed. Darra Goldstein (New York: Oxford U.P., 2015), 105–107, 142–158; Wolfgang Schivelbusch, *Tastes of Paradise: A Social History of Spices, Stimulants, and Intoxicants,* trans. David Jacobson (New York: Pantheon, 1992), chap. 3; and Cross and Proctor, *Packaged Pleasures,* chap. 4.

37. Deborah Cadbury, *Chocolate Wars: The 150-Year Rivalry between the World's Greatest Chocolate Makers* (New York: Public Affairs, 2010), chaps. 4–5. Import data: Dauril Alden, "The Significance of Cacao Production in the Amazon Region during the Late Colonial Period: An Essay in Comparative Economic History," *Proceedings of the American Philosophical Society* 120 (1976): 132.

38. "Conching and Refining," Chocolate Alchemy, http://chocolatealchemy.com /conching-and-refining/.

39. Michael D'Antonio, *Hershey: Milton S. Hershey's Extraordinary Life of Wealth, Empire, and Utopian Dreams* (New York: Simon and Schuster, 2006); Cadbury, *Chocolate Wars,* parts 2 and 3; Samuel F. Hinkle, *Hershey: Farsighted Confectioner, Famous Chocolate, Fine Community* (New York: Newcomen Society, 1964), 13–14.

40. U.S. Department of Commerce, Bureau of the Census, *Historical Statistics of the United States: Colonial Times to 1970,* part 1 (Washington, D.C.: Government Printing Office, 1975), 331; "Prohibition's Effect on Sugar," *Facts about Sugar* 15 (July 1, 1922): 8.

41. Ashley N. Gearhardt and William R. Corbin, "Interactions between Alcohol Consumption, Eating, and Weight," in *Food and Addiction: A Comprehensive Handbook,* ed. Kelly D. Brownell and Mark S. Gold (New York: Oxford U.P., 2012), 250; "Prohibition and Sugar Consumption," *New York Medical J.* 110 (1919): 724 (quotation); Cross and Proctor, *Packaged Pleasures,* 40–41, 126.

42. S. Dana Hubbard, "The New York City Narcotic and Differing Points of View on Narcotic Addiction," *Monthly Bulletin of the Department of Health, City of New York* 10 (February 1920): 36; David J. Mysels and Maria A. Sullivan, "The Relationship between Opioid and Sugar Intake: Review of Evidence and Clinical Applications," *J. of Opioid Management* 6 (2010): 445–452; Daniel M. Blumenthal and Mark S. Gold, "Relationships between Drugs of Abuse and Eating," in *Food and Addiction,* ed. Brownell and

Gold, 256–257; H. Richard Friman, "Germany and the Transformation of Cocaine," conference paper, Russell Sage Foundation, New York City, May 9–11, 1997, p. 6.

43. Stephan Guyenet, "By 2606, the US Diet Will Be 100 Percent Sugar," Whole Health Source, February 18, 2012, http://wholehealthsource.blogspot.com/2012/02/by-2606-us -diet-will-be-100-percent.html.

44. "Going Up in Smoke," *NYT,* September 24, 1925; Cassandra Tate, *Cigarette Wars: The Triumph of "The Little White Slaver"* (New York: Oxford U.P., 1999), 28–29, 49, 51, 56; Toine Spapens, "Illegal Gambling," in *The Oxford Handbook of Organized Crime,* ed. Letizia Paoli (New York: Oxford U.P., 2014), 405; *The White Slave Traffic: Speech of Hon. E. W. Saunders of Virginia* (Washington, D.C.: n.p., 1910), 4; Mike Alfred, *Johannesburg Portraits: From Lionel Phillips to Sibongile Khumalo* (Houghton, South Africa: Jacana, 2003), 12.

45. Kathryn Meyer, *Life and Death in the Garden: Sex, Drugs, Cops, and Robbers in Wartime China* (Lanham, Md.: Rowman and Littlefield, 2014).

46. Victor Fernández, "El burdel que inspiró a Picasso . . . ," *La Razón,* August 10, 2012; Brian G. Martin, *The Shanghai Green Gang: Politics and Organized Crime, 1919–1937* (Berkeley: U. of California Press, 1996), 32; Hans Derks, *History of the Opium Problem: The Assault on the East, ca. 1600–1950* (Leiden: Brill, 2012), 411–412.

47. Philip Thomas, "The Men's Quarter of Downtown Nashville," *Tennessee Historical Q.* 41 (Spring 1982): 48–66.

48. C. A. Bayly, *The Birth of the Modern World, 1780–1914: Global Connections and Comparisons* (Oxford: Blackwell, 2004), 180–189. The rounded, mid-range figure for 1600 is from "Historical Estimates of World Population," https://www.census.gov/data /tables/time-series/demo/international-programs/historical-est-worldpop.html.

49. Friedrich Engels, *The Condition of the Working Class in England,* trans. W. O. Henderson and W. H. Chaloner (New York: Macmillan, 1958), 115–116 (quotation), 143–144. Continental writers similarly tied alcoholism to joyless proletarian drudgery, e.g., Alfred Delrieu, *L'Alcoolisme en France et en Normandie* (Rouen: Julien Leclerf, 1900), 18–19.

50. Virginia Berridge, *Demons: Our Changing Attitudes to Alcohol, Tobacco, and Drugs* (Oxford: Oxford U.P., 2013), 46–48, 165–166; Gina Hames, *Alcohol in World History* (London: Routledge, 2012), 88–89.

51. Georg Simmel, "The Metropolis and Mental Life," in *The Blackwell City Reader,* ed. Gary Bridge and Sophie Watson (Malden, Mass.: Blackwell, 2002), 11–19; Hames, *Alcohol,* 73; Mayor LaGuardia's Committee on Marihuana, in *The Marihuana Problem in the City of New York* (repr., Metuchen, N.J., Scarecrow, 1973), 18; John C. Burnham, *Bad Habits: Drinking, Smoking, Taking Drugs, Gambling, Sexual Misbehavior, and Swearing in American History* (New York: NYU Press, 1993), 176; Stefan Zweig, *The World of*

Yesterday: Memories of a European, trans. Anthea Bell (London: Pushkin Press, 2011), 97, 105; Meyer, *Life and Death,* 138.

52. Phillips, *Alcohol,* 174; State of New York, *Second Annual Report of the Narcotic Drug Control Commission* (Albany: J. B. Lyon, 1920), 5; Burnham, *Bad Habits,* 175–177; Abraham Flexner, *Prostitution in Europe* (repr., Montclair, N.J.: Patterson Smith, 1969), 5; David T. Courtwright, *Violent Land: Single Men and Social Disorder from the Frontier to the Inner City* (Cambridge, Mass.: Harvard U.P., 1996), chaps. 3–9; Derks, *History of the Opium Problem,* chap. 17.

3. LIBERATING-ENSLAVING PLEASURES

1. Ernest Hemingway, *A Moveable Feast* (New York: Charles Scribner's Sons, 1964), 210.

2. Marshall Sahlins, "The Original Affluent Society," in *The Politics of Egalitarianism: Theory and Practice,* ed. Jacqueline Solway (New York: Berghahn, 2006), 79–98, quotations p. 80.

3. Debate: David Kaplan, "The Darker Side of the 'Original Affluent Society,'" *J. of Anthropological Research* 56 (2000): 301–324. Disease burden: Spencer Wells, *Pandora's Seed: The Unforeseen Cost of Civilization* (New York: Random House, 2010), height and longevity p. 23; Yuval Noah Harari, *Sapiens: A Brief History of Humankind* (Toronto: McClelland and Stewart, 2015), part 2, population figures p. 98; Mark Nathan Cohen, *Health and the Rise of Civilization* (New Haven: Yale U.P., 1989); A. R. Williams, "8 Mummy Finds Revealing Ancient Disease," *National Geographic News,* March 21, 2013, https://news.nationalgeographic.com/news/2013/03/130321-mummies-diseases-ancient -archaeology-science/.

4. Steven Pinker, *The Better Angels of Our Nature: Why Violence Has Declined* (New York: Viking, 2011), chap. 1 (violence); Robert W. Fogel, *Explaining Long-Term Trends in Health and Longevity* (Cambridge: Cambridge U.P., 2012), 141.

5. Wells, *Pandora's Seed,* 22; Harari, *Sapiens,* 79; Jared Diamond, "The Worst Mistake in the History of the Human Race," *Discover Magazine,* May 1987, 64–66.

6. Michael V. Angrosino, "Rum and Ganja: Indenture, Drug Foods, Labor Motivation, and the Evolution of the Modern Sugar Industry in Trinidad," in *Drugs, Labor, and Colonial Expansion,* ed. William Jankowiak and Daniel Bradburd (Tucson: U. of Arizona Press, 2003), 106; John Charles Chasteen, *Getting High: Marijuana through the Ages* (Lanham, Md.: Rowman and Littlefield, 2016), 56–57, 66, 69, 76, 84, 102, 109–110, 133–134.

7. Kātib Chelebi [also called Hajji Kalfa], *The Balance of Truth* [1656], trans. G. L. Lewis (London: George Allen and Unwin, 1957), 52.

8. Timothy Brook, *Vermeer's Hat: The Seventeenth Century and the Dawn of the Global World* (New York: Bloomsbury, 2008), 122–123, 140, 144 (quotation).

9. Chelebi, *Balance,* 52; Geoffrey Parker, *Global Crisis: War, Climate Change and Catastrophe in the Seventeenth Century* (New Haven: Yale U.P., 2013), 599–603; David T. Courtwright, *Forces of Habit: Drugs and the Making of the Modern World* (Cambridge, Mass.: Harvard U.P., 2001), 58–59; *Voices from the Ming-Qing Cataclysm: China in Tigers' Jaws,* ed. and trans. Lynn A. Struve (New Haven: Yale U.P., 1993), 1, 159–161.

10. Aldous Huxley, "Drugs That Shape Men's Minds," *Saturday Evening Post* 231 (October 18, 1958), 28 (quotation).

11. Daniel Lord Smail, *On Deep History and the Brain* (Berkeley: U. of California Press, 2008), de la Boétie on p. 173, and Smail, "An Essay on Neurohistory," in *Emerging Disciplines: Shaping New Fields of Scholarly Inquiry in and beyond the Humanities,* ed. Melissa Bailar (Houston: Rice U.P., 2010), 201–228; Simon Montefiore, *Jerusalem: The Biography* (New York: Knopf, 2011), 111–113 (crucifixion).

12. Jimmie Charters, *This Must Be the Place: Memoirs of Montparnasse,* as told to Morrill Cody (repr., New York: Collier, 1989), 12.

13. Thomas W. Laqueur, *Solitary Sex: A Cultural History of Masturbation* (New York: Zone Books, 2003), 238.

14. Ibid., figures 5.8a and 5.8b; Lawrence Stone, *The Family, Sex, and Marriage in England, 1500–1800* (New York: Harper and Row, 1977), 253–255; Stephen Greenblatt, "Me, Myself, and I," *NYRB* 51 (April 8, 2004), http://www.nybooks.com/articles/2004/04/08/me-myself-and-i/.

15. Pinker, *Better Angels of Our Nature,* chap. 4 (humanitarian revolution). Though Pinker uses different terminology, *Better Angels* amounts to a detailed account of the waning of the teletropic order, with striking parallels to *Deep History.*

16. *The Diaries of Evelyn Waugh,* ed. Michael Davie (London: Weidenfeld and Nicolson, 1976), 415.

17. Smail, *On Deep History,* 184–185; George Orwell, *The Collected Essays, Journalism, and Letters,* vol. 2, ed. Sonia Orwell and Ian Angus (New York: Harcourt, Brace and World, 1968), 14.

18. Stalin to Viacheslav [sic] Molotov, September 1, 1930, *Stalin's Letters to Molotov, 1925–1936,* ed. Lars T. Lih et al. (New Haven: Yale U.P., 1995), 208–209; Frank Dikötter, Lars Laamann, and Zhou Xun, *Narcotic Culture: A History of Drugs in China* (Chicago: U. of Chicago Press, 2004), 209.

19. Acts 12:23; George Whitefield, *The Heinous Sin of Drunkenness: A Sermon Preached on Board the* Whitaker (London: James Hutton, 1739), 5 and 6 (quotes), 16–18.

20. William Prynne, *The Unlovelinesse of Love-Lockes* (London: n.p., 1628), quotation p. A3; *The Diary of Ralph Josselin, 1616–1683,* ed. Alan Macfarlane (Oxford: Oxford U.P., 1991), 114; M. L. Weems, *God's Revenge against Gambling,* 4th ed. (Philadelphia: the author, 1822), 22–24. As recently as 2016 Grand Mufti Sheikh Abdulaziz Al-Sheikh issued a *fatwa* against chess as a waste of time and source of enmity. Ben Hubbard, "Saudi Arabia's Top Cleric Forbids Chess, but Players Maneuver," *NYT,* January 21, 2016.

21. "Chinese in New York," *NYT,* December 26, 1873; Samuel Hopkins Adams, "On Sale Everywhere," *Collier's* 68 (July 16, 1921): 8.

22. Prynne, *Unlovelinesse,* A3.

23. Didier Nourrisson, "Tabagisme et Antitabagisme en France au XIXe Siècle," *Histoire, Economie, et Société* 7 (1988): 545; Richard Leakey, "Past, Present, and Future of Life on Earth," lecture, University of North Florida, April 21, 2015 (pariahs).

24. Samuel Tenney, "Whiskey Triumphant over Turner" (MS, 1778), New-York Historical Society, Mss Collection; Schrad, *Vodka Politics,* chap. 11, quotation p. 168.

25. H. J. Anslinger to Secretary of the Treasury, September 3, 1936, "Heroin—History," VF; Adam Derek Zientek, "Affective Neuroscience and the Causes of the Mutiny of the French 82nd Infantry Brigade," *Contemporary European History* 23 (2014): 518–519.

26. "Society for the Suppression of Vice," *The Leisure Hour,* no. 1046 (January 13, 1872), 32.

27. Craig Heron, *Booze: A Distilled History* (Toronto: Between the Lines, 2003), chap. 4, quotation p. 103; John Walruff to L. W. Clay, May 22, 1882, History—Prohibition, MS 138, and William P. Ferguson to J. E. Everett, February 12, 1902, History—Temperance, MS 645, Kansas Historical Society, Topeka; Harry Emerson Fosdick, *The Prohibition Question: A Sermon . . . October 14, 1928* (New York: Park Avenue Baptist Church, 1928), 7 (quotation), 11–12; Virginia Berridge, *Demons: Our Changing Attitudes to Alcohol, Tobacco, and Drugs* (Oxford: Oxford U.P., 2013), 45.

28. Cigarette girls: Photograph in Edward James Parrish Papers, box 3, Rubenstein Library, Duke University, Durham, North Carolina. Google Ngram searches show phrases like "*tráfico de licores*" and "*trafic d'alcool*" appearing with much greater frequency in the early twentieth century than in the mid-nineteenth.

29. H. A. Depierris, *Physiologie Sociale: Le Tabac . . .* (Paris: E. Dentu, 1876), chap. 21; Auguste Forel, *La Question Sexuelle: Exposée aux Adultes Cultivés* (Paris: G. Steinheil, 1906), 292–298; "Relation of Alcohol to Insanity," *JAMA* 13 (1889): 816; James Nicholls, *The Politics of Alcohol: A History of the Drink Question in England* (Manchester: Manchester U.P., 2009), 171–173; Nikolay Kamenov, "A Question of Social Medicine or Racial Hygiene: The Bulgarian Temperance Discourse and Eugenics in the Interwar Period, 1920–1940," *GAA,* 129–138, "idiot" p. 137; Lawson Crowe, "Alcohol and Heredity: Theories about the Effects of Alcohol Use on Offspring," *Social Biology* 32 (1985):

146–161; Victor Cyril and E. Berger, *La "Coco": Poison Moderne* (Paris: Ernest Flammarion, 1924), 93.

30. Claude Quétel, *History of Syphilis*, trans. Judith Braddock and Brian Pike (Baltimore: Johns Hopkins U.P., 1990), French percentage p. 199, "machine-gun" p. 219; Christian Henriot, "Medicine, VD and Prostitution in Pre-Revolutionary China," *Social History of Medicine* 5 (1992): 106–107.

31. Andrew Roberts, *Napoleon: A Life* (New York: Viking, 2014), 597–598; Leonard F. Guttridge, *Icebound: The Jeannette Expedition's Quest for the North Pole* (Annapolis: Naval Institute Press, 1986), 329; Nienke Bakker et al., *On the Verge of Insanity: Van Gogh and His Illness* (Amsterdam: Van Gogh Museum, 2016), 97–98, 125; Michael D'Antonio, *Hershey: Milton S. Hershey's Extraordinary Life of Wealth, Empire, and Utopian Dreams* (New York: Simon and Schuster, 2006), 93–94; "Hershey, Catherine Sweeney; 1871–1915," Hershey Community Archives, http://www.hersheyarchives.org/essay/printable.aspx ?EssayId=11; V. Lerner, Y. Finkelstein, and E. Witztum, "The Enigma of Lenin's (1870– 1924) Malady," *European J. of Neurology* 11 (2004): 371–376; C. J. Chivers, "A Retrospective Diagnosis Says Lenin Had Syphilis," *NYT*, June 22, 2004.

32. Warren S. Walker, "Lost Liquor Lore: The Blue Flame of Intemperance," *Popular Culture* 16 (Fall 1982): 17–25, and John Allen Krout, *The Origins of Prohibition* (New York: Russell and Russell, 1967), 232.

33. Carole Shamas, "Changes in English and Anglo-American Consumption from 1550 to 1800," in *Consumption and the World of Goods*, ed. John Brewer and Roy Porter (London: Routledge, 1993), 185; Elizabeth Abbott, "Slavery," in *The Oxford Companion to Sugar and Sweets*, ed. Darra Goldstein (New York: Oxford U.P., 2015), 617–618; John E. Crowley, "Sugar Machines: Picturing Industrialized Slavery," *American Historical Review* 121 (2016): 436.

34. Courtwright, *Forces of Habit*, chap. 7; Jay Coughtry, *The Notorious Triangle: Rhode Island and the African Slave Trade, 1700–1807* (Philadelphia: Temple U.P., 1981), 85–86; S. T. Livermore, *A History of Block Island* (Hartford, Conn.: Case, Lockwood, and Brainard, 1877), 60; Frederick H. Smith, *Caribbean Rum: A Social and Economic History* (Gainesville: U.P. of Florida, 2005), 103.

35. Juan de Castro, *Historia de las Virtudes y Propiedades del Tabaco* (Córdoba: Salvador de Cea Tesa, 1620), 19; *The Diary of Colonel Landon Carter of Sabine Hall, 1752–1778*, ed. Jack P. Greene, vol. 2 (Richmond: Virginia Historical Society, 1987), 870; [Anthony Benezet,] *Serious Considerations on Several Important Subjects* (Philadelphia: Joseph Crukshank, 1778), 42; Nathan Allen, *An Essay on the Opium Trade* (Boston: John P. Jewett, 1850), 25.

36. *Oxford English Dictionary*, s.v. "addiction," updated November 2010, http://www .oed.com/view/Entry/2179; John Lawson, *A New Voyage to Carolina . . .* (London: n.p.,

1709), 172, 202; Samuel Johnson, *A Dictionary of the English Language,* vol. 1 (London: W. Strahan, 1755), http://johnsonsdictionaryonline.com/?page_id=7070&i=80, italics in original.

37. Jessica Warner, "'Resolv'd to Drink No More': Addiction as a Preindustrial Construct," *J. of Studies on Alcohol* 55 (1994): 685–691; Reshat Saka, *Narcotic Drugs* (Istanbul: Cumhuriyet, 1948), TS translation in "Marijuana—History," VF; Matthew Warner Osborn, *Rum Maniacs, Alcoholic Insanity in the Early American Republic* (Chicago: U. of Chicago Press, 2014), chap. 1, Rush quotation p. 34; Brian Vale and Griffith Edwards, *Physician to the Fleet: The Life and Times of Thomas Trotter, 1760–1832* (Woodbridge, Suffolk: Boydell, 2011), chap. 13, quotations p. 169.

38. Harry Gene Levine, "The Discovery of Addiction: Changing Conceptions of Habitual Drunkenness in America," *J. of Studies on Alcohol* 39 (1978): 143–174; Hasso Spode, "Transubstantiations of the Mystery: Two Remarks on the Shifts in the Knowledge about Addiction," *SHAD* 20 (2005): 125; Friedrich-Wilhelm Kielhorn, "The History of Alcoholism: Brühl-Cramer's Concepts and Observations," *Addiction* 91 (1996): 121–128; Jean-Charles Sournia, *A History of Alcoholism,* trans. Nick Hindley and Gareth Stanton (Oxford: Basil Blackwell, 1990), 44–48. The special issue of *SHAD* 28 (Winter 2014) provides an overview and country-specific analyses of changing European addiction terminology.

39. Edwin Van Bibber-Orr, "Alcoholism and Song Literati," in *Behaving Badly in Early and Medieval China,* ed. N. Harry Rothschild and Leslie V. Wallace (Honolulu: U. of Hawai'i Press, 2017), 135–153.

40. "Walnut Lodge Hospital," *Geer's Hartford City Directory,* no. 63 (July 1900): 777; U.S. census schedule, Hartford County (MS, June 5, 1900), roll 137, Connecticut Historical Society, Hartford; Leslie E. Keeley, *The Non-Heredity of Inebriety* (Chicago: Scott, Foresman, 1896), 191 ("education"); T. D. Crothers, "The Significance of a History of Alcoholic Addiction," *Medical Record* 79 (1911): 770 (crucifix).

41. Berridge, *Demons,* chap. 4; David T. Courtwright, "Mr. ATOD's Wild Ride: What Do Alcohol, Tobacco, and Other Drugs Have in Common," *SHAD* 20 (2005): 105–124, "social" p. 111. Although Google Ngram searches reflect medical as well as informal usages, it is noteworthy that the frequency of "inebriety" peaked in American English in 1894, and in British English in 1912.

42. Arthur Hill Hassall, "The Great Tobacco Question: Is Smoking Injurious to Health," *Lancet,* part 1 (1857): 198; Depierris, *Le Tabac,* chap. 20; Harvey W. Wiley, "The Alcohol and Drug Habit and Its Prophylaxis," *Proceedings of the Second Pan American Scientific Congress,* vol. 9 (Washington, D.C.: Government Printing Office, 1917), 159; "Smokers' Palates Painted in Court," *NYT,* January 22, 1914; R. M. Blanchard, "Heroin and Soldiers," *Military Surgeon* 33 (1913): 142; David T. Courtwright, Herman Joseph, and Don

Des Jarlais, *Addicts Who Survived: An Oral History of Narcotic Use in America before 1965* (Knoxville: U. of Tennessee Press, 2012), 174; Robert N. Proctor, "The Nazi War on Tobacco: Ideology, Evidence, and Possible Cancer Consequences," *Bulletin of the History of Medicine* 71 (1997): 435–488, quotation p. 441.

43. Keith McMahon, *The Fall of the God of Money: Opium Smoking in Nineteenth-Century China* (Lanham, Md.: Rowman and Littlefield, 2002), 36; Zheng Yangwen, *The Social Life of Opium in China* (Cambridge: Cambridge U.P., 2005), 87–92; Sander L. Gilman, "Jews and Smoking," in *Smoke: A Global History of Smoking*, ed. Sander L. Gilman and Zhou Xun (London: Reaktion, 2004), 282–283; J. B. Jeter, "The Evils of Gaming," *Virginia Baptist Preacher* 1 (March 1842): 48.

44. Robert Bailey, *The Life and Adventures of Robert Bailey . . .* (Richmond: J. & G. Cochran, 1822), 216; Patricia C. Glick, "The Ruling Passion: Gambling and Sport in Antebellum Baltimore, Norfolk, and Richmond," *Virginia Cavalcade* 39 (Autumn 1989): 62–69; Weems, *God's Revenge against Gambling*, 11; Charles Dickens, *The Old Curiosity Shop* (London: Chapman and Hall, 1841).

45. *Letters from Liselotte*, trans. and ed. Maria Kroll (London: Victor Gollancz, 1970), 69; Lorne Tepperman et al., *The Dostoevsky Effect: Problem Gambling and the Origins of Addiction* (Don Mills, Ontario: Oxford U.P., 2013), chaps. 2–3; Mike Dash, "Crockford's Club: How a Fishmonger Built a Gambling Hall and Bankrupted the British Aristocracy," Smithsonian.com, November 29, 2012, http://www.smithsonianmag.com/history/crockfords-club-how-a-fishmonger-built-a-gambling-hall-and-bankrupted-the-british-aristocracy-148268691/.

46. Ira M. Condit, *The Chinaman as We See Him* (Chicago: Fleming H. Revell, 1900), 60; Markus Heilig, *The Thirteenth Step: Addiction in the Age of Brain Science* (New York: Columbia U.P., 2015), 139; Ernest Poole, *The Village: Russian Impressions* (New York: Macmillan, 1918), 154.

47. Linda Carroll, "Fetal Brains Suffer Badly from Effects of Alcohol," *NYT*, November 4, 2003; Nathalie E. Holz et al., "The Long-Term Impact of Early Life Poverty on Orbitofrontal Cortex Volume in Adulthood: Results from a Prospective Study over 25 Years," *Neuropsychopharmacology* 40 (2015): 996–1004; Natalie H. Brito and Kimberly G. Noble, "Socioeconomic Status and Structural Brain Development," *Frontiers in Neuroscience* 8 (2014): 1–11; Pilyoung Kim et al., "Effects of Childhood Poverty and Chronic Stress on Emotion Regulatory Brain Function in Adulthood," *PNAS* 110 (2013): 18442–18447; W. K. Bickel et al., "A Competing Neurobehavioral Decision Systems Model of SES-Related Health and Behavioral Disparities," *Preventive Medicine* 68 (2014): 37–43; Warren K. Bickel et al., "Behavioral and Neuroeconomics of Drug Addiction: Competing Neural Systems and Temporal Discounting Processes," *Drug and Alcohol Dependence* 90S (2007): S85–S91; Jim Orford, *Power, Powerlessness*

and Addiction (Cambridge: Cambridge U.P., 2013), chaps. 4–5; Harold Winter, *The Economics of Excess: Addiction, Indulgence, and Social Policy* (Stanford: Stanford U.P., 2011), 4, 44, 57–59, 125, 146–147; Dan I. Lubman et al., "Cannabis and Adolescent Brain Development," *Pharmacology and Therapeutics* 148 (2015): 1–16; and Heilig, *Thirteenth Step,* chaps. 9, 12.

48. Richard P. Feynman, *"Surely You're Joking, Mr. Feynman!": Adventures of a Curious Character* (New York: Norton, 1985), 204; David E. Johnson, *Douglas Southall Freeman* (Gretna, La.: Pelican, 2002), 218–219; Orford, *Power,* 110–113; Robert A. Caro, *The Years of Lyndon Johnson: Master of the Senate* (New York: Knopf, 2002), 631; Gene M. Heyman, *Addiction: A Disorder of Choice* (Cambridge, Mass.: Harvard U.P., 2009), 85–86.

49. Bruce K. Alexander, *The Globalisation of Addiction: A Study in the Poverty of Spirit* (Oxford: Oxford U.P., 2008), 131–137, and related web site, http://www.brucekalexander .com/; Orford, *Power,* 106–110; Courtwright, *Forces of Habit,* 147–148; Peter C. Mancall, *Deadly Medicine: Indians and Alcohol in Early America* (Ithaca: Cornell U.P., 1995); Benjamin Rush, *Essays, Literary, Moral and Philosophical* (Philadelphia: Thomas and Samuel F. Bradford, 1798), 258; Kimberly Johnston-Dodds, *Early California Laws and Policies Related to California Indians* (Sacramento: California Reference Bureau, 2002), 8. "Bootlegger" has other possible origins, described in *The Encyclopedia of Alcoholism,* ed. Robert O'Brien and Morris Chafetz (New York: Facts on File, 1982), 52–53.

50. Jeanne Schaver, "Nurse's Narrative Report" (TS, April 1952), M/V Health Collection, Anchorage Museum, Anchorage, Alaska.

4. ANTI-VICE ACTIVISM

1. Anon., *The Skilful Physician,* ed. Carey Balaban, Jonathon Erlen, and Richard Siderits (1656; repr., Amsterdam: Harwood, 1997), 5 (quotation); Thomas Short, *Discourses on Tea, Sugar, Milk, Made-Wines, Spirits, Punch, Tobacco, &c.* (London: T. Longman and A. Millar, 1750), 165.

2. Ian Tyrrell, *Reforming the World: The Creation of America's Moral Empire* (Princeton, N.J.: Princeton U.P., 2010), 76.

3. George A. Akerlof and Robert J. Shiller, *Phishing for Phools: The Economics of Manipulation and Deception* (Princeton, N.J.: Princeton U.P., 2015), vii–11.

4. Wilbur F. Crafts, *Familiar Talks on That Boy and Girl of Yours: Sociology from Viewpoint of the Family* (New York: Baker and Taylor, 1922), 374 (famines, quoting J. J. Davis).

5. Doris Kearns Goodwin, *The Bully Pulpit: Theodore Roosevelt, William Howard Taft, and the Golden Age of Journalism* (New York: Simon and Schuster, 2013), 193 (Lease).

6. Steven Pinker, *The Better Angels of Our Nature: Why Violence Has Declined* (New York: Viking, 2011), 174–177.

7. Charles S. Maier, "Consigning the Twentieth Century to History: Alternative Narratives for the Modern Era," *American Historical Review* 105 (2000): 807–831; Johan Edman, "Temperance and Modernity: Alcohol Consumption as a Collective Problem, 1885–1913," *J. of Social History* 49 (2015): 20–52; S. G. Moore, "The Relative Practical Value of Measures against Infant Mortality," *Lancet* 187, no. 4836 (1916): 944; Josephus Daniels, *Men Must Live Straight If They Would Shoot Straight* (Washington, D.C.: Navy Department Commission on Training Camp Activities, 1917), 1, 15.

8. Rod Phillips, *Alcohol: A History* (Chapel Hill: U. of North Carolina Press, 2014), 214–215.

9. Wennan Liu, "'No Smoking' for the Nation: Anti-Cigarette Campaigns in Modern China, 1910–1935" (Ph.D. diss., U. of California, Berkeley, 1999); Sherman Cochran, *Big Business in China: Sino-Foreign Rivalry in the Cigarette Industry, 1890–1930* (Cambridge, Mass.: Harvard U.P., 1980), 28; David T. Courtwright, "Global Anti-Vice Activism: A Postmortem," *GAA,* 317 (addiction authority); Norman Ohler, *Blitzed: Drugs in Nazi Germany,* trans. Shaun Whiteside ([London]: Allen Lane, 2016), 23 (quotation); Hasso Spode, "The 'Alcohol Question' in Central Europe between Science and Civic Religion," ADHS conference, Buffalo, N.Y., June 24, 2011 (30,000). Spode adds that the total number of German alcoholics subjected to all forms of coercion is not known.

10. Nolan R. Best, *Yes, "It's the Law" and It's a Good Law* (New York: George H. Doran, 1926), 22; U.S. Dept. of Justice, Bureau of Prohibition, *The Value of Law Observance: A Factual Monograph* (Washington, D.C.: Government Printing Office, 1930), 34.

11. David M. Fahey and Padma Manian, "Poverty and Purification: The Politics of Gandhi's Campaign for Prohibition," *The Historian* 67 (2005): 503; Chantal Martineau, *How the Gringos Stole Tequila: The Modern Age of Mexico's Most Traditional Spirit* (Chicago: Chicago Review Press, 2015), 10; Ronny Ambjörnsson, "The Honest and Diligent Worker" (Skeptron Occasional Papers 5, Stockholm, 1991), http://www.skeptron.uu.se /broady/sec/ske-5.htm; Annemarie McAllister, "The Alternative World of the Proud Non-Drinker: Nineteenth-Century Public Displays of Temperance," *SHAD* 28 (2014): 168; "A Counter-Attraction," *Brotherhood of Locomotive Engineers Monthly J.* 8 (1874): 627; Edward C. Leonard Jr., "The Treatment of Philadelphia Inebriates," *American J. on Addictions* 6 (1997): 3.

12. *Municipal Drink Traffic* (London: Fabian Society, 1898), 18; Remarks of William Storr, *The Official Report of the Church [of England] Congress, Held at Portsmouth . . . 1885,* ed. C. Dunkley (London: Bemrose and Sons, 1885), 581 (quotation).

13. Courtwright, "Global Anti-Vice Activism."

14. Crafts, *Familiar Talks,* 376–377 (Sunday); Gaines M. Foster, "Conservative Social Christianity, the Law, and Personal Morality: Wilbur F. Crafts in Washington," *Church*

History 71 (2002): 799–819; Tyrrell, *Reforming the World*, 25 ("international"), 33–34; "Dr. Wilbur F. Crafts, Crusader, Dies at 73," *NYT*, December 28, 1922.

15. Harald Fischer-Tiné, "Eradicating the 'Scourge of Drink' and the 'Un-pardonable Sin of Illegitimate Sexual Enjoyment': M. K. Gandhi as Anti-Vice Crusader," *Interdisziplinäre Zeitschrift für Südasienforschung* 2 (2017), http://www.hsozkult.de/journals /id/zeitschriften-748?title=interdisziplinaere-zeitschrift-fuer-suedasienforschung-2 -2017; "Introduction," *GAA*, 1–9 ("peripatetic" p. 1); Stephen Legg, "Anti-Vice Lives: Peopling the Archives of Prostitution in Interwar India," *GAA*, 253; M. K. Gandhi, *Key to Health*, trans. Sushila Nayar, http://www.mkgandhi.org/ebks/key_to_health.pdf, 21–24; *The Collected Works of Mahatma Gandhi*, vol. 27 (New Delhi: India Ministry of Information and Broadcasting, 1968), 347 ("women," "power"); Joseph Lelyveld, *Great Soul: Mahatma Gandhi and His Struggle with India* (New York: Knopf, 2011), 30, 48, 51 (filth). Native leaders, missionaries: John Abbey, *The Church of God and the Gates of Hell* (London: R. J. James, 1911), 33–35; *Temperance and Prohibition in New Zealand*, ed. J. Cocker and J. Malton Murray (London: Epworth Press, 1930), chap. 10.

16. "'Gandhi Cigarettes'!" *Young India*, January 12, 1921.

17. Josiah P. Rowe Jr., *Letters from a World War I Aviator*, ed. Genevieve Bailey Rowe and Diana Rowe Doran (Boston: Sinclaire, 1986), 25–26.

18. Charles Bamberger memoirs (TS, 1943), box 14, Ralph Ginzburg Papers, State Historical Society of Wisconsin, Madison, Wisc.; John C. Burnham, *Bad Habits: Drinking, Smoking, Taking Drugs, Gambling, Sexual Misbehavior, and Swearing in American History* (New York: NYU Press, 1993), 197; David T. Courtwright, Herman Joseph, and Don Des Jarlais, *Addicts Who Survived: An Oral History of Narcotic Use in America before 1965* (Knoxville: U. of Tennessee Press, 2012), 174–175, 180.

19. Algot Niska, *Over Green Borders: The Memoirs of Algot Niska*, trans. J. Jerry Danielsson (New York: Vantage, 1953), vii.

20. W. L. Treadway to Lyndon Small, September 22, 1932, correspondence 1929–1955, Lyndon Frederick Small Papers, National Library of Medicine, Bethesda, Maryland (burglary).

21. William Cabell Bruce, "Is Prohibition a Success after Five Years? No!" *Current History* reprint (August 1925): 11 (cloakroom); Jeffrey A. Miron and Jeffrey Zwiebel, "Alcohol Consumption during Prohibition," *American Economic Review* 81 (1991): 242–247; Jack S. Blocker Jr., "Did Prohibition Really Work? Alcohol Prohibition as a Public Health Innovation," *American J. of Public Health* 96 (2006): 233–243, breweries p. 236; Lisa McGirr, *The War on Alcohol: Prohibition and the Rise of the American State* (New York: Norton, 2016), 50 (beer prices).

22. W. J. Rorabaugh, *Prohibition: A Concise History* (New York: Oxford U.P., 2018), 61–62 (half); McGirr, *War on Alcohol*, 50 (wife); Foreign Policy Association, "Prohibition

and Drug Addiction" (TS, 1925), 3, "Addiction—Incidence—[to] 1959," VF (Bellevue); Mark H. Moore, "Actually, Prohibition Was a Success," *NYT,* October 16, 1989; Austin Kerr, "American Dream," *New Scientist* 164 (November 1999): 94–95.

23. Holly M. Karibo, *Sin City North: Sex, Drugs, and Citizenship in the Detroit-Windsor Borderland* (Chapel Hill: U. of North Carolina Press, 2015), 37; Mabel Willebrandt, "'It Can't Be Done'" (TS speech, September 24, 1928), 8, Willebrandt Papers, LCMD.

24. Blocker, "Prohibition," 240.

25. "36 Individuals and 6 Corporations Indicted in Largest Bootleg Ring since Prohibition," *NYT,* July 16, 1937; "A Survey of Illegal Distilling in the U.S. Today" (TS, 1951), John W. Hill Papers, folder 11, box 96, State Historical Society of Wisconsin. The WHO estimated that, in 2005, illicit manufacturing accounted for 29 percent of global alcohol consumption, with bootlegging most common in poorer countries. *Global Status Report on Alcohol and Health* (Geneva: WHO, 2011), 5.

26. Fahey and Manian, "Poverty and Purification," 489–506, "easy" p. 503; Fischer-Tiné, "Eradicating" (champagne); David T. Courtwright, *Forces of Habit: Drugs and the Making of the Modern World* (Cambridge, Mass.: Harvard U.P., 2001), 156–159; Peter Evans and Sean McLain, "Diageo Makes $1.9 Billion Offer for Control of India's United Spirits," *WSJ,* April 15, 2014.

27. Gerald Posner, *God's Bankers: A History of Money and Power at the Vatican* (New York: Simon and Schuster, 2015), 17; Thembisa Waetjen, "Poppies and Gold: Opium and Law-Making on the Witwatersrand, 1904–1910," *J. of African History* 57 (2016): 391–416; "Use of Narcotics in Siam," *Boston Medical and Surgical J.* 31 (1844): 341; Thaksaphon Thamarangsi, "Thailand: Alcohol Today," *Addiction* 101 (2006): 783; W. A. Penn, *The Soverane Herbe: A History of Tobacco* (London: Grant Richards, 1902), 213–214.

28. Mary C. Neuburger, *Balkan Smoke: Tobacco and the Making of Modern Bulgaria* (Ithaca: Cornell U.P., 2013), 143 (German statistics).

29. Ibid., quotation p. 200.

30. "Meeting in Richmond," *Richmond Enquirer,* November 1, 1833; *Report of the Committee of Twenty-Four . . . for the Purpose of Devising Means to Suppress the Vice of Gambling in This City* (Richmond: T. W. White, 1833), "taxed" p. 25.

31. *Report of the Minority of the Committee of Twenty-Four, on the Subject of Gambling in the City of Richmond* (Richmond: T. W. White, 1833), "moralists" p. 4. The dissenters were German-born merchant Gustavus Lucke, Episcopalian attorney Henry L. Brooke, and newspaper editor Edward V. Sparhawk.

32. Harry M. Ward, *Children of the Streets of Richmond, 1865–1920* (Jefferson, N.C.: McFarland, 2015), 109.

33. T. D. Crothers, "A Review of the History and Literature of Inebriety . . . ," *J. of Inebriety* 33 (1912): 143; Crafts to Wesley Jones, January 16, 1922, U. of Washington Digital Collections, http://digitalcollections.lib.washington.edu/cdm/ref/collection/pioneerlife /id/19937; Jacob M. Appel, "'Physicians Are Not Bootleggers': The Short, Peculiar Life of the Medicinal Alcohol Movement," *Bulletin of the History of Medicine* 82 (2008): 355–386.

34. A. E. Moule, "The Use of Opium and Its Bearing on the Spread of Christianity in China," in *Records of the General Conference of the Protestant Missionaries in China Held at Shanghai, May 10–24, 1877* (Shanghai: Presbyterian Missionary Press, 1878), 353.

35. C. Vann Woodward, *Origins of the New South, 1877–1913* (Baton Rouge: Louisiana State U.P., 1971), 389–391; Boyd P. Doty, ed., *Prohibition Quiz Book,* 2nd ed. (Westerville, Ohio: Anti-Saloon League, 1929), map p. 78 (Louisiana); Walter J. Decker to Mrs. E. W. Root, January 13, 1933, and Earle K. James to Mrs. E. W. Root, January 7, 1933, box 1, Women's Organization for National Prohibition Reform, LCMD (Bolivia and Chile).

36. Meta Remec, "Sexual Diseases between Science and Morality," paper, Global Anti-Vice Activism conference, Monte Verità, Switzerland, April 2, 2012.

37. Mark Lawrence Schrad, *The Political Power of Bad Ideas: Networks, Institutions, and the Global Prohibition Wave* (New York: Oxford U.P., 2010), 33; Samuel Hopkins Adams, "On Sale Everywhere," *Collier's* 68 (July 16, 1921): 8 (class).

38. Petre Matei, "De la 'Iarba Dracului' la Drog. Aspecte ale Condamnării Tutunului în Spațiul Românesc," *Archiva Moldaviae* 8 (2016): 29–50.

39. Elizabeth Dorn Lublin, "Controlling Youth and Tobacco in Meiji-Period Japan," ADHS conference, London, June 21, 2013.

40. "America and the Living Death" (TS, n.d.), box 56, and Hobson to Rockefeller, April 23, 1928, box 56, Hobson Papers, LCMD. Similar shifts away from religious and moral arguments and toward individual and collective health, order, efficiency, and preparedness occurred in West Africa, Europe, and Latin America. See *GAA,* chaps. 5–9.

41. "AHR Conversation: Religious Identities and Violence," *American Historical Review* 112 (2007): 1465 (Miles); George Creel, *Rebel at Large: Recollections of Fifty Crowded Years* (New York: G. P. Putnam's Sons, 1947), 52; Ethel S. Ellis, "Valentine Note of 37 Years Ago," *Topeka Journal,* February 14, 1940; Alexandra Popoff, *Sophia Tolstoy: A Biography* (New York: Free Press, 2010), 135, 176 ("crime").

42. Anthony Taylor, "'Godless Edens': Surveillance, Eroticized Anarchy, and 'Depraved Communities' in Britain and the Wider World, 1890–1930," *GAA,* 53–73, "marriages" p. 62, "Edens" p. 65.

43. Alexander C. Zabriskie, *Bishop Brent: Crusader for Christian Unity* (Philadelphia: Westminster Press, 1948), 41; Brent diary, August 17 and 18, 1923, box 3, Charles Henry Brent Papers, LCMD ("mess").

44. William B. McAllister, *Drug Diplomacy in the Twentieth Century: An International History* (London: Routledge, 2000), 28; Lida Thornburgh to Elizabeth Jessup, October 29, 1929, box 55 ("saint") and Brent diary ("too full"), March 11, 1929, box 3, Brent Papers; "Bishop Brent Defends Right of Dry Law Opponents 'With Clean Hands' to Seek Modification of Prohibition," *Buffalo Courier,* February 8, 1926. This sketch also draws on the biographical materials in boxes 54–55 of the Brent Papers; Zabriskie, *Bishop Brent;* and "Bishop Brent Dies at 66 in Lausanne," *NYT,* March 28, 1929.

45. Zabriskie, *Bishop Brent,* 196.

46. Donald Day, "Whoopee Spree; Prohibition Ends," *Chicago Tribune,* April 5, 1932.

47. J. Buks to Mrs. E. W. Root, December 5, 1932, box 1, Women's Organization for National Prohibition Reform, LCMD.

48. Phillips, *Alcohol,* 274 (quotation), 275; Corinne Pernet, "The Limits of Global Biopolitics: The Question of Alcoholism and Workers' Leisure at the League of Nations," paper, Global Anti-Vice Activism conference, Monte Verità, Switzerland, April 2, 2012.

49. David G. Schwartz, *Roll the Bones: The History of Gambling* (New York: Gotham, 2006), chap. 10; Ernest Hemingway, *A Moveable Feast* (New York: Charles Scribner's Sons, 1964), 201.

50. Schwartz, *Roll the Bones,* 316–319; S. Jonathan Wiesen, *Creating the Nazi Marketplace: Commerce and Consumption in the Third Reich* (New York: Cambridge U.P., 2011), 48–49.

51. Treasury Department, "In re: Alphonse Capone" (TS, December 21, 1933), comp. Frank J. Wilson, https://www.irs.gov/pub/irs-utl/file-2-report-dated-12211933-in-re -alphonse-capone-by-sa-frank-wilson.pdf.

52. Jessica R. Pliley, "The FBI's White Slave Division," *GAA,* 233–234; Tyrrell, *Reforming the World,* 138–139.

53. Laurie Bernstein, *Prostitutes and Their Regulation in Imperial Russia* (Berkeley: U. of California Press, 1995), 46; Abraham Flexner, *Prostitution in Europe* (repr., Montclair, N.J.: Patterson Smith, 1969), chap. 1.

54. Vern Bullough and Bonnie Bullough, *Women and Prostitution: A Social History* (Buffalo: Prometheus, 1987), chap. 13; W. T. Stead, "The Maiden Tribute of Modern Babylon . . . I," *Pall Mall Gazette,* July 6, 1885.

55. Joel Best, *Controlling Vice: Regulating Brothel Prostitution in St. Paul, 1865–1883* (Columbus: Ohio State U.P., 1998).

56. Andrew Roberts, *Napoleon: A Life* (New York: Viking, 2014), 685–686.

57. Catherine Carstairs, *Jailed for Possession: Illegal Drug Use, Regulation, and Power in Canada, 1920–1961* (Toronto: U. of Toronto Press, 2006); Isaac Campos, *Home Grown:*

Marijuana and the Origins of Mexico's War on Drugs (Chapel Hill: U. of North Carolina Press, 2012); Vera Rubin and Lambros Comitas, *Ganja in Jamaica: A Medical Anthropological Study of Chronic Marijuana Use* (The Hague: Mouton, 1975); Howard Padwa, *Social Poison: The Culture and Politics of Opiate Control in Britain and France, 1821–1926* (Baltimore: Johns Hopkins U.P., 2012); "History of Heroin," *Bulletin on Narcotics* 5 (1953): 8–10 (Egypt); Anton Werkle, "French-Speaking Countries of Africa South of the Sahara" (TS, 1974), "Laws and Legislation—Countries," VF; Alisher B. Latypov, "The Soviet Doctor and the Treatment of Drug Addiction: 'A Difficult and Most Ungracious Task,'" *Harm Reduction J.* 8 (2011), https://harmreductionjournal.biomedcentral.com /articles/10.1186/1477-7517-8-32. McAllister, *Drug Diplomacy,* describes key international treaties.

58. Bullough and Bullough, *Women and Prostitution,* chap. 14; Louis Berg, *Prison Doctor* (New York: Brentano's, 1932), 64 ("dunghill").

59. Pavel Vasilyev, "Medical and Criminological Constructions of Drug Addiction in Late Imperial and Early Soviet Russia," *GAA,* 189 (quoting Aleksandr Sholomovich); Thomas Gleaton, "A Man of Our Time: Gabriel G. Nahas" (TS, n.d.), biographical file, Gabriel G. Nahas Papers, Archives and Special Collections, A. C. Long Health Sciences Library, Columbia University (reference to Dr. Selim Nahas, Gabriel's uncle); Rodrigues Doria, "The Smokers of *Maconha:* Effects and Evils of the Vice" (TS translation, n.d.), 2, "Marijuana Effects—[to] 1950," VF; Carlos Gutiérrez Noriega, "El Hábito de la Coca en Sud América," *América Indígena* 12 (1952): 117; Kazuo Kenmochi, *Devilish Drug: Narcotic Photographic Document* (Tokyo: n.p., 1963), 124–125.

60. Li Zhisui, *The Private Life of Chairman Mao: The Memoirs of Mao's Personal Physician,* trans. Tai Hung-chao (New York: Random House, 1994), 67–68, 108; Courtwright, *Forces of Habit,* 183–185; Miriam Kingsberg, *Moral Nation: Modern Japan and Narcotics in Global History* (Berkeley: U. of California Press, 2014), 186; Andrew G. Walder, *China under Mao: A Revolution Derailed* (Cambridge, Mass.: Harvard U.P., 2015), 2, 7, 8, 62, 64, 67–69; Dan Washburn, *The Forbidden Game: Golf and the Chinese Dream* (London: Oneworld, 2014), xi, 5. Though they seldom filled the full death quotas, officials everywhere carried out high-profile executions following mass rallies and public trials. The killing peaked in late 1952. Zhou Yongming, *Anti-Drug Crusades in Twentieth-Century China: Nationalism, History, and State Building* (Lanham, Md.: Rowman and Littlefield, 1999), chap. 6, quotation p. 107.

5. PRO-VICE ACTIVISM

1. John C. Burnham, *Bad Habits: Drinking, Smoking, Taking Drugs, Gambling, Sexual Misbehavior, and Swearing in American History* (New York: NYU Press, 1993), "everybody" p. 139; David G. Schwartz, *Roll the Bones: The History of Gambling* (New York:

Gotham, 2006), 378 (bingo); Pat Frank, *The Long Way Round* (Philadelphia: J. B. Lippincott, 1953), 19 (Friday); "Chesterfield" (TS, November 13, 1961), Liggett and Myers Minutes, box 19, Review Board Records, JWT (*Playboy* readership).

2. David T. Courtwright, *No Right Turn: Conservative Politics in a Liberal America* (Cambridge, Mass.: Harvard U.P., 2010), chaps. 2, 5, 10–11; Dave Palermo, "Slot Machines Big Business for Military," *Las Vegas Review-Journal/Sun,* October 18, 1992.

3. *Civilization: The West and The Rest with Niall Ferguson,* part 2, documentary produced by Chimerica Media Limited, the BBC and Channel 13 in association with WNET, aired on PBS in May 2012 (quote); Tibor Frank, "Supranational English, American Values, and East-Central Europe," *Publications of the Modern Language Association of America* 119 (2004): 80–91; Michael Anderson, "China's 'Great Leap' toward Madison Avenue," *J. of Communication* 31 (Winter 1981): 11; Wolf Lieschke, "Winston-Spain Briefing" (TS, May 29, 1984), n.p., box 36, Burt Manning Papers, JWT.

4. "World War II Fast Facts," CNN, http://www.cnn.com/2013/07/09/world/world-war-ii-fast-facts/(70 million); Burnham, *Bad Habits,* 220 ("not polite"); Mary Louise Roberts, *What Soldiers Do: Sex and the American GI in World War II France* (Chicago: U. of Chicago Press, 2013), 61–63, 122.

5. Stephen G. Fritz, *Frontsoldaten: The German Soldier in World War II* (Lexington: U.P. of Kentucky, 1995), 79; Sönke Neitzel and Harald Welzer, *Soldaten: On Fighting, Killing, and Dying,* trans. Jefferson Chase (New York: Knopf, 2012), 171 (quotes).

6. Vincent Milano, "Wehrmacht Brothels," Der Erste Zug (2005), http://www.dererstezug.com/WehrmachtBrothels.htm.

7. Norman Ohler, *Blitzed: Drugs in Nazi Germany,* trans. Shaun Whiteside ([London]: Allen Lane, 2016), "delight" p. 43; Nicolas Rasmussen, *On Speed: The Many Lives of Amphetamine* (New York: NYU Press, 2008), chap. 3; Łukasz Kamieński, *Shooting Up: A Short History of Drugs and War* (New York: Oxford U.P., 2016), chap. 7, Finns pp. 137–138, "holiday" p. 139.

8. J. H. Reid, *Heinrich Böll: A German for His Time* (Oxford: Oswald Wolff, 1988), 32; Neitzel and Welzer, *Soldaten,* 160; Peter Steinkamp, "Zur Devianz-Problematik in der Wehrmacht: Alkohol- und Rauschmittelmissbrauch bei der Truppe" (Ph.D. dissertation, Albert-Ludwigs-Universität Freiburg, 2008), chap. 2 (a third); Andreas Ulrich, "The Nazi Death Machine: Hitler's Drugged Soldiers," *Spiegel Online,* May 6, 2005, http://www.spiegel.de/international/the-nazi-death-machine-hitler-s-drugged-soldiers-a-354606.html ("blind eye").

9. Phil Richards and John J. Banigan, *How to Abandon Ship* (New York: Cornell Maritime Press, 1942), 101–102; Ohler, *Blitzed,* 49–51, and Ohler recounting his interview with Böll's son, *Fresh Air,* NPR, March 7, 2017, http://www.npr.org/programs/fresh-air/2017/03/07/519035318/fresh-air-for-march-7-2017; Kamieński, *Shooting*

Up, 128–132; Akihiko Sato, "Narrative on Methamphetamine Use in Japan after World War II," ADHS conference, University of Guelph, August 10–12, 2007; Mark Gayn, *Japan Diary* (Rutland, Vt.: Charles E. Tuttle, 1981), 13, 47, 49; John W. Dower, *Embracing Defeat: Japan in the Wake of World War II* (New York: Norton, 1999), 62–63, 107–108.

10. Esteban Ortiz-Ospina et al., "Trade and Globalization" (2018), Our World in Data, https://ourworldindata.org/international-trade; David T. Courtwright, *Sky as Frontier: Aviation, Adventure, and Empire* (College Station: Texas A&M U.P., 2004), 125–131, 196–201, 130.

11. James H. Mills, *Cannabis Nation: Control and Consumption in Britain, 1928–2008* (Oxford: Oxford U.P., 2013), quotation p. 76.

12. David Owen, "Floating Feasts," *New Yorker* 90 (Nov. 3, 2014): 52–57; "Viking Cruises: History," https://www.vikingcruises.com/about-us/history.html#noscroll.

13. Courtwright, *Sky as Frontier,* 142, 154, 202; Carl Solberg, *Conquest of the Skies: A History of Commercial Aviation in America* (Boston: Little, Brown, 1979), 378–379; Aimée Bratt, *Glamour and Turbulence—I Remember Pan Am, 1966–91* (New York: Vantage, 1996), 102.

14. Mike Brunker, "In-flight Gambling Ready for Takeoff," ZDNet, November 14, 1997, http://www.zdnet.com/article/in-flight-gambling-ready-for-takeoff/; Jenifer Chao, "From Gambling to Retail, Airports Competing for Profits," *Las Vegas Review-Journal,* January 27, 1997 ("time"); Nicole Winfield, "Redefining the Secret Shopper," *Florida Times-Union,* December 24, 2012.

15. John D. Kasarda and Greg Lindsay, *Aerotropolis: The Way We'll Live Next* (New York: Farrar, Straus and Giroux, 2011), 264.

16. Jim Krane, *City of Gold: Dubai and the Dream of Capitalism* (New York: St. Martin's Press, 2009), 215, 220, 253–254; Jad Mouawad, "Dubai, Once a Humble Refueling Stop, Is Crossroad to the Globe," *NYT,* June 18, 2014; Ashraf Dali, "Arabian 'Sex' Nights in the Gulf States," Asian Next News Network, January 23, 2017, http://www.theasian .asia/archives/97883; Misha Glenny, *McMafia: A Journey through the Global Criminal Underworld* (New York: Vintage, 2009), chap. 6.

17. Philip Jacobson, "Saudi Men Flout Muslim Laws in Bars of Bahrain," *Telegraph,* March 4, 2001; Yaroslav Trofimov, "Upon Sober Reflection, Bahrain Reconsiders the Wages of Sin," *WSJ,* June 9, 2009 (quote); "Tactful Solutions Cure Liquor Advertisers' Ailments," *Advertising Age,* August 18, 1980; Joost Hiltermann and Toby Matthiesen, "Bahrain Burning," *NYRB* 58 (August 18, 2011), 49–51.

18. Jonathan Rabinovitz, "Can the Man Who Made Sun City Make It in Atlantic City?" *NYT,* September 21, 1997; Paul Vallely, "The Great Casino Cash-In: The Sun King (and

His Shady Past)," *Independent,* February 1, 2007; Graham Boynton, "Mandela's Favourite Multi-Billionaire," *Telegraph,* August 23, 2005 (quote).

19. Tim Walker, "Walt Disney's Chain-Smoking Habit," *Independent,* November 18, 2013; Dewayne Bevil, "Disney's Magic Kingdom Will Serve Beer, Wine in New Fantasyland Restaurant," *Orlando Sentinel,* September 13, 2012 (quote); Lauren Delgado, "Four More Magic Kingdom Restaurants to Serve Wine, Beer," *Orlando Sentinel,* December 16, 2016. Like Disney, Viking Cruises avoided gambling for reasons of branding.

20. Charles Passy, "Gay Orlando Steps Out," *NYT,* May 13, 2005; Scott Powers, "Mickey Welcomes Gay Ceremonies," *Florida Times-Union,* April 7, 2007 ("money").

21. Schwartz, *Roll the Bones,* 354–355; Sam Boyd, oral history interview (TS, 1977), 8 (Honolulu), Airlines Vertical File, and Jimmy Newman, oral history interview (TS, 1978), 19, SC-UNLV; Phillip I. Earl, "Veiling the Tiger: The Crusade against Gambling, 1859–1910," *Nevada Historical Q.* 29 (1985): 175–204.

22. Schwartz, *Roll the Bones,* 420. The specs are from Stern's 1968 proposal, *Las Vegas International Hotel,* available at http://d.library.unlv.edu/digital/collection/sky/id/1945 /rec/3. Stern's career is documented at http://digital.library.unlv.edu/skyline/architect /martin-stern. I have also consulted Stern's wartime correspondence at SC-UNLV and interviewed his son, Leonard Stern.

23. Author interview with Leonard Stern, May 1, 2013.

24. Mark H. Haller, "Bootleggers as Businessmen: From City Slums to City Builders," in *Law, Alcohol, and Order: Perspectives on National Prohibition,* ed. David E. Kyvig (Westport, Conn.: Greenwood Press, 1985), 153; John Handley, "Las Vegas: A Posh Playground for Adults, a Wagering Wonderland," *Chicago Tribune,* June 13, 1976 (Hope); Larry Gragg, *Bright Light City: Las Vegas in Popular Culture* (Lawrence: U.P. of Kansas, 2013); Bob Colacello, *Holy Terror: Andy Warhol Close Up* (New York: HarperCollins, 1990), 333.

25. Author interview with John Acres, May 3, 2013; Dave Palermo and Warren Bates, "Prostitution Often Linked to Casinos," *Las Vegas Review-Journal,* June 6, 1995; Gragg, *Bright Light City,* 2.

26. Schwartz, *Roll the Bones,* 482, and "The Conjuring of the Mirage," *Vegas Seven,* April 23, 2014, http://vegasseven.com/2014/04/30/the-conjuring-of-the-mirage/; Howard Stutz, "Wynn Las Vegas: The Unveiling," *Las Vegas Gaming Wire,* April 27, 2005.

27. "Steve Wynn: The Biggest Winner," *60 Minutes,* CBS News, April 12, 2009, http:// www.cbsnews.com/videos/steve-wynn-the-biggest-winner/; *Tales from the Pit: Casino Table Games Managers in Their Own Words,* ed. David G. Schwartz (Las Vegas: UNLV Gaming Press, 2016), 209 ("adult"), 223 ("amenities"); Bob Shemeligian, "Recalling Old Vegas," *Las Vegas Sun,* November 1, 1993; Christina Almeida, "Vegas's Safe Bet: Visitors

Will Drop Money in Stores," *WP,* January 2, 2005; Josh Eells, "Night Club Royale," *New Yorker* 89 (September 30, 2013), 36–41; Chris Kirkham, "In Las Vegas, Drinks Flow a Little Less Freely," *WSJ,* April 19, 2017 (gambling revenue).

28. Quotes: Kirkham, "In Las Vegas"; Marc Cooper, *The Last Honest Place in America: Paradise and Perdition in the New Las Vegas* (New York: Nation Books, 2004), 10.

29. Dave Palermo, "Crossing the World's Borders: Gaming Not Only in U.S.," *Las Vegas Sun and Review-Journal,* April 10, 1994; Barry Chamish, "Israel Likely to Approve Casinos," *Euroslot* 5 (January 1995): 101.

30. Steve Friess, "A Vegas-Size Bet on China," *Newsweek* 148 (September 4, 2006): 52; Kasarda and Lindsay, *Aerotropolis,* 378–379.

31. Muhammad Cohen, "Sands Macao: The House that Built Sheldon Adelson," Forbes Asia, May 15, 2014, https://www.forbes.com/sites/muhammadcohen/2014/05/15/sands -macao-the-house-that-built-sheldon-adelson/#35a415ac5d1c; "Fact Sheet: The Sands Macao" (TS, 2004), Gambling Vertical File—Foreign: Macau, SC-UNLV; Desmond Lam, *Chopsticks and Gambling* (New Brunswick: Transaction, 2014), 133–134 (6 percent); "Macau 2015 Annual Research: Key Facts," World Travel and Tourism Council, https:// www.wttc.org/-/media/files/reports/economic%20impact%20research/countries%20 2015/macau2015.pdf; Kate O'Keeffe, "China Tightens Reins on Macau," *WSJ,* December 4, 2012; Kelvin Chan, "Asian Casino Boom Aims to Lure Region's New Rich," Inquirer .Net, September 13, 2012, http://business.inquirer.net/81896/asian-casino-boom-aims -to-lure-regions-new-rich.

32. George A. Akerlof and Robert J. Shiller, *Phishing for Phools: The Economics of Manipulation and Deception* (Princeton, N.J.: Princeton U.P., 2015), xi; Cass R. Sunstein, "Why Free Markets Make Fools of Us," *NYRB* 62 (October 22, 2015): 40–42; "BofA Pulls Out of Nevada's Brothel Business," *Las Vegas Sun,* November 3, 1993.

33. "Population Pyramids of the World from 1950 to 2100," http://www.populationpyramid .net/world/1960/; Ulrike Thoms, "The Contraceptive Pill, the Pharmaceutical Industry and Changes in the Patient-Doctor Relationship in West Germany," and Agata Ignaciuk, Teresa Ortiz-Gómez, and Esteban Rodriguez-Ocaña, "Doctors, Women and the Circulation of Knowledge of Oral Contraceptives in Spain, 1960s–1970s," in *Gendered Drugs and Medicine: Historical and Socio-Cultural Perspectives,* ed. Teresa Ortiz-Gómez and María Jesús Santesmases (Farnham: Ashgate, 2014), respectively 153–174 and 133–152.

34. Burnham, *Bad Habits,* 162; Matthew Vaz, "'We Intend to Run It': Racial Politics, Illegal Gambling, and the Rise of Government Lotteries in the United States, 1960–1985," *J. of American History* 101 (2014): 88–89, 95.

35. Henry M. Stevens, "The Position of Beer in American Life" (TS, 1950), 1–4, box 33, Writings and Speeches Collection, JWT; "Beer Marketing" (TS, 1984), 9, Miller Brewing— General, box 12, "The Everyday Hero" (TS, 1984), n.p., Scripts and Proposals—1984, box

14, and "The Million Dollar Minute" (TS, 1985), Super Bowl XIX, box 46, all in Burt Manning Papers, JWT; "Special Report: Beer on College Campuses," undated clipping, and Robert McBride, "Competition, Marketing, and Regulatory Issues in the Beer Industry," draft paper, National Council on Alcoholism, Detroit, Michigan, April 12–15, 1984, pp. 7, 19–20, both in box 26, JKP; Murray Sperber, *Beer and Circus: How Big-Time College Sports Is Crippling Undergraduate Education* (New York: Henry Holt, 2000), 172–174, 184–185; Leonard Shapiro, "This Bud Bowl Is Not for You," *WP,* January 1, 1991; William L. White, "Taking on Alcohol, Pharmaceutical, and Tobacco Advertising: An Interview with Dr. Jean Kilbourne" (2014), 10, Selected Papers of William L. White, http://www.williamwhitepapers.com/pr/2014%20Dr.%20Jean%20 Kilbourne.pdf; Henry M. Stevens, "Alcohol Ads Increase Drinking," Marin Institute, n.v. (August 1997), 1–3.

36. Teoh Mei Mei, "High Point in Liquor Promotion Raises Ire," *New Straights Times,* July 27, 1995; David Jernigan, "Global Alcohol Is Big, Profitable and Powerful," *Institute of Alcohol Studies,* no. 1 (1997), http://www.ias.org.uk/What-we-do/Alcohol-Alert/Issue -1-1997/Global-alcohol-is-big-profitable-and-powerful.aspx; David Jernigan and James O'Hara, "Alcohol Advertising and Promotion," in *Reducing Underage Drinking: A Collective Responsibility,* ed. Richard J. Bonnie and Mary Ellen O'Connell (Washington, D.C.: National Academies Press, 2004), 631.

37. "Underage Drinking Rampant in Delhi: Survey," *India Today,* February 1, 2009; Sally Casswell, "Alcohol Harm—The Urgent Need for a Global Response," *Addiction* 106 (2011): 1205–1206; Peter Mehlman, "A Fan Throws in the Towel and Hangs Up His Spikes," *NYT,* January 4, 2004 (rethinking); Peter Evans, "Thirsty for Growth, Liquor Giant Taps Africa," *WSJ,* July 31, 2015; Olabisi A. Odejide, "Alcohol Policies in Africa," *African J. of Alcohol and Drug Studies* 5 (2006): 27–39.

38. WHO, *Global Status on Alcohol and Health, 2014* (Geneva: WHO, 2014), figure 12, http://apps.who.int/iris/bitstream/10665/112736/1/9789240692763_eng.pdf; Ogochukwu Odeigah et al., "Nigeria: A Country in Need of an Alcohol Strategy," *JSAD* 79 (2018): 318.

39. Casswell, "Alcohol Harm," 1206.

40. David T. Courtwright, "Mr. ATOD's Wild Ride: What Do Alcohol, Tobacco, and Other Drugs Have in Common," *SHAD* 20 (2005): 118–120 sketches the history of "gateway" drug literature, to which controlled studies were subsequently added, e.g., Michael T. Lynskey, Jacqueline M. Vink, and Dorret I. Boomsma, "Early Onset Cannabis Use and Progression to Other Drug Use in a Sample of Dutch Twins," *Behavior Genetics* 36 (2006): 195–200. "Enormous": Malcolm C. Hall, "Illicit Drug Abuse in Australia—A Brief Statistical Picture," *J. of Drug Issues* 7 (1977): 316.

41. Virginia Berridge, *Demons: Our Changing Attitudes to Alcohol, Tobacco, and Drugs* (Oxford: Oxford U.P., 2013), 143, 145, 150; William F. McDermott, "McDermott on

Smoking," *Cleveland Plain Dealer,* June 23, 1954 (snatched); Larry Collins and Dominique Lapierre, *Is Paris Burning?* (New York: Simon and Schuster, 1965), 324; Diego Armus, "Cigarette Smoking in Modern Buenos Aires," *GAA,* 205; Andrew Lycett, *Ian Fleming: The Man behind James Bond* (Atlanta: Turner Publishing, 1995), 172, 442.

42. Michael Schwalbe, *Smoke Damage: Voices from the Front Lines of America's Tobacco Wars* (Madison, Wisc.: Borderland Books, 2011), 1–7, 67.

43. Robert Proctor, *Golden Holocaust: Origins of the Cigarette Catastrophe and the Case for Abolition* (Berkeley: U. of California Press, 2011), chaps. 21, 25.

44. Nick Sim, "5 Elements of the Original Disneyland That Would Look Weirdly Out of Place Today," *Theme Park Tourist,* December 9, 2014, http://www.themeparktourist .com/features/20141209/29726/5-elements-original-disneyland; Allan M. Brandt, *The Cigarette Century: The Rise, Fall, and Deadly Persistence of the Product That Defined America* (New York: Basic, 2007), 496.

45. Barbara Forey et al., *International Smoking Statistics Web Edition: United Kingdom* (March 17, 2016), 21, http://www.pnlee.co.uk/Downloads/ISS/ISS-UnitedKingdom _160317.pdf; Patricia A. Mahan to Salem, July 10, 2000, Truth Tobacco Industry Documents, https://www.industrydocumentslibrary.ucsf.edu/tobacco/docs/#id=kgkn0083.

46. Patrick Peretti-Watel et al., "Cigarette Smoking as Stigma: Evidence from France," *International J. of Drug Policy* 25 (2014): 285; Nicholas A. Christakis and James H. Fowler, "The Collective Dynamics of Smoking in a Large Social Network," *NEJM* 358 (2008): 2249–2258; Keith J. Winstein, "Ability to Quit Smoking Is Affected by Friendships," *WSJ,* May 22, 2008 (Christakis); Ronald Bayer and Jennifer Stuber, "Tobacco Control, Stigma, and Public Health: Rethinking the Relations," *American J. of Public Health* 96 (2006): 47–50; Daniel Buchman, "Tobacco Denormalization and Stigma," Neuroethics at the Core, May 2, 2010, https://neuroethicscanada.wordpress.com/2010/05/02/tobacco -denormalization-and-stigma/; Laura D. Hirschbein, *Smoking Privileges: Psychiatry, the Mentally Ill, and the Tobacco Industry in America* (New Brunswick, N.J.: Rutgers U.P., 2015). Those with psychiatric disorders are also significantly likelier to be prescription opioid users. Matthew A. Davis et al., "Prescription Opioid Use among Adults with Mental Health Disorders in the United States," *J. of the American Board of Family Medicine* 30 (July–August 2017): 407–414.

47. Heather Wipfli, *The Global War on Tobacco: Mapping the World's First Public Health Treaty* (Baltimore, Md.: Johns Hopkins U.P., 2015), chap. 2; Neil Carrier and Gernot Klantschnig, *Africa and the War on Drugs* (London: Zed Books, 2012), 28; Thomas Bollyky and David Fidler, "Has a Global Tobacco Treaty Made a Difference?" *Atlantic,* February 28, 2015.

48. Marie Ng et al., "Smoking Prevalence and Cigarette Consumption in 187 Countries, 1980–2012," *JAMA* 311 (2014): 186; Proctor, *Golden Holocaust,* 53–54, 540 (4 billion); The

Tobacco Atlas: Consumption, https://tobaccoatlas.org/topic/consumption/ (5.7 trillion); Paul Geitner, "EU Signs Deal to Resolve Cigarette Smuggling," *Florida Times-Union,* July 10, 2004.

49. United Nations, Department of Economic and Social Affairs, "World Urbanization Prospects, 2018 revision," May 16, 2018, https://www.un.org/development/desa /publications/2018-revision-of-world-urbanization-prospects.html.

50. Anqi Shen, Georgios A. Antonopoulos, and Klaus Von Lampe, " 'The Dragon Breathes Smoke': Cigarette Counterfeiting in the People's Republic of China," *British J. of Criminology* 50 (November 2010): 239–258; Michael Eriksen et al., *The Tobacco Atlas,* 5th rev. ed. (Atlanta: American Cancer Society, 2015), 30–31.

51. Wipfli, *Global War,* 132 (Uruguay); Mike Esterl, "America's Smokers: Still 40 Million Strong," *WSJ,* July 16, 2014; Sabrina Tavernise, "A Hot Debate over E-Cigarettes as a Path to Tobacco, or from It," *NYT,* February 22, 2014, and "Use of E-Cigarettes Rises Sharply among Teenagers, Report Says," *NYT,* April 16, 2015. Some companies also developed heat-don't-burn cigarettes, ideal for those who wanted (or needed) tobacco vapor but wished to shun carcinogen-rich smoke. Tripp Mickle, "Reynolds's New Cigarette Will Heat, Not Burn, Tobacco," *WSJ,* November 18, 2014.

52. Jennifer Maloney and Saabira Chaudhuri, "Tobacco's Surprise Rebound," *WSJ,* April 24, 2017; *Credit Suisse Global Investment Returns Yearbook 2015* (Zurich: Credit Suisse AG, 2015), 20, available at https://psc.ky.gov/pscecf/2016-00370/rateintervention%40ky .gov/03312017050856/Dimson_et_al_-_Credit_Suisse_-_2015_Investment_Returns _Yearbook.pdf. The figure of $300 million is the inflation-adjusted estimate of the cost of a minimum-efficient-scale plant, from Kim Warren, "A Strategic Analysis of BAT's Tobacco Business" (TS, 1993), 5, Truth Tobacco Industry Documents, https://www .industrydocumentslibrary.ucsf.edu/tobacco/docs/#id=nhxc0039.

53. Casswell, "Alcohol Harm," 1206; Orville Schell, *Discos and Democracy: China in the Throes of Reform* (New York: Pantheon, 1988), 380; Daniel Southerl, "Capitalist Chicken Goes to Beijing," *WP,* November 13, 1987.

54. George Wehrfritz, "Joining the Party," *Newsweek* 127 (April 1, 1996): 46–49; David Eimer, "The Sexual Revolution Sweeps across China," *The Independent,* December 11, 2005; "Nation Becomes World's Biggest Sex-Toy Producer," *People's Daily Online,* July 10, 2010, http://en.people.cn/90001/90778/90860/7060276.html; Mian Mian, *Candy,* trans. Andrea Lingenfelter (New York: Little, Brown, 2003).

55. Rebecca MacKinnon, "Flatter World and Thicker Walls? Blogs, Censorship and Civic Discourse in China," *Public Choice* 134 (2008): 32 (Deng); Liu Qian, "Guangdong Declares War against Drugs," *Hong Kong Liaowang Overseas Edition,* September 9, 1991, and "Casinos, Brothels Prohibited in Shenzhen," *Hong Kong Hsin Wan Pao,* June 27, 1985, both in FBIS; Shaozhen Lin and Yong-an Zhang, "Risk Control and Rational Recreation:

A Qualitative Analysis of Synthetic Drug Use among Young Urbanites in China," *International J. of Drug Policy* 25 (2014): 772–773 (Shanghai).

56. Austin Ramzy, "China Cracks Down on Golf, the 'Sport for Millionaires,'" *NYT*, April 18, 2015; Simon Zekaria and Ruth Bender, "Liquor Makers Warn of Drier Sales in Asia," *WSJ*, April 19, 2013.

57. "68 Drug Traffickers Hanged Nationwide," IRNA news bulletin, February 14, 1989, FBIS.

58. Nazila Fathi, "As Liquor Business Booms, Bootleggers Risk the Lash," *NYT*, April 4, 2006 ("hard"); D. Khatinoglu, "Three Consuming Alcohol Iranians Sentenced to Death [sic]," Trend News Agency (Azerbaijan) brief, June 24, 2012; Marketa Hulpachova, "Tehran—The Secret Party Town," *Guardian*, April 17, 2014 ("life"). Islamists fared just as poorly in Tunisia, a country with ancient traditions of viticulture and brewing and the highest per capita alcohol consumption in the Maghreb. "WHO: Tunisians, Heaviest Alcohol Drinkers in the Region," *Morocco World News*, December 24, 2014, https://www.moroccoworldnews.com/2014/12/148071/who-tunisians-heaviest-alcohol-drinkers-in-the-region/.

59. N. Umid, "Iran to Inaugurate Alcohol Addiction Treatment Centre," Trend News Agency (Azerbaijan) brief, August 25, 2013; Youssef M. Ibrahim, "Iran Puts Addicts in Its Labor Camps," *NYT*, July 22, 1989; Ramita Navai, "Breaking Bad in Tehran: How Iran Got a Taste for Crystal Meth," *Guardian*, May 13, 2014; "The Latest Scourge Plaguing Iran's Youth—Meth Addiction," *Jerusalem Post*, April 10, 2017; United Nations Office on Drugs and Crime, *Transnational Organized Crime in East Asia and the Pacific: A Threat Assessment* (April 2013), 68, http://www.unodc.org/res/cld/bibliography/transnational-organized-crime-in-east-asia-and-the-pacific-a-threat-assessment_html/TOCTA_EAP_web.pdf. Iran's pseudoephedrine imports rose from five metric tons in 2006 to fifty-five in 2012.

60. Jeffrey D. Sachs, "Twentieth-Century Political Economy: A Brief History of Global Capitalism," *Oxford Review of Economic Policy* 15 (Winter 1999): 90–101; Ortiz-Ospina and Roser, "International Trade," using upper-bound estimates.

61. Christopher Walker, "Opponents Unite to Outlaw Sex-Aid Pill," *The Times*, May 27, 1998; Monica Rohr, "Nearly Undetectable Cocaine Found," *Chicago Tribune*, June 27, 1991; Valentina Pop, "Busy Belgian Port Becomes Cocaine Gateway," *WSJ*, March 2, 2018; Misha Glenny, *McMafia: A Journey through the Global Criminal Underworld* (New York: Vintage, 2009), "Route" p. xviii; "DEA Sensitive: Pakistan" (TS, 1999), 21–22, "Pakistan," VF; John F. Burns, "Heroin Becomes Scourge for 1.5 Million in Pakistan," *NYT*, April 5, 1995; Sam Quinones, *Dreamland: The True Tale of America's Opiate Epidemic* (New York: Bloomsbury, 2015), 103–104; Mark Schoofs, "As Meth Trade Goes Global, South Africa Becomes a Hub," *WSJ*, May 21, 2007. Glenny estimated that criminal transactions accounted for 15 to 20 percent of global GDP. Judging from the fact that the number of $100 bills in circulation rose 79 percent between 2009 and the end of

2016, the criminal share of GDP may well have increased since Glenny published. Adam Creighton, "Despite Global Curbs, Cash Still Rules," *WSJ,* April 10, 2017.

62. Johannes P. Jütting and Juan R. de Laiglesia, "Forgotten Workers," *OECD Observer,* no. 274 (October 2009), http://oecdobserver.org/news/archivestory.php/aid/3067/Forgotten_workers.html (half); "Troops Quit Rio Drug Slums after Weekend of Searches," *International Herald Tribune,* November 22, 1994; William Finnegan, "Silver or Lead," *New Yorker* 86 (May 31, 2010): 39–51; *Cartel Land,* documentary directed by Matthew Heineman, 2015 (quotes).

63. U.S. State Department, *Trafficking in Persons Report* (June 2012), 7–10, https://www.state.gov/documents/organization/210737.pdf; International Labour Organization, "Forced Labour, Modern Slavery and Human Trafficking," March 2017, http://www.ilo.org/global/topics/forced-labour/lang—en/index.htm; United Nations Office on Drugs and Crime, *Global Report on Trafficking in Persons* (New York: United Nations, 2012), 7, https://www.unodc.org/documents/data-and-analysis/glotip/Trafficking_in_Persons_2012_web.pdf; Carolyn Nordstrom, *Global Outlaws: Crime, Money, and Power in the Contemporary World* (Berkeley: U. of California Press, 2007), 186–187; Harold Heckle, "Spanish Police Arrest 'Bar Code Pimps' Gang," *Oakland News,* March 24, 2012; "Sex Trafficker Used African Witchcraft to Smuggle Children for Prostitution," *Telegraph,* October 29, 2012.

64. Iain Gately, *Tobacco: The Story of How Tobacco Seduced the World* (New York: Grove, 2001), 358 (one-third); Albert Stridsberg to Ellen Gartrell, January 29, 2001, letters folder, box 4, Albert B. Stridsberg Papers, JWT (blue seal); Nordstrom, *Global Outlaws,* xv–24.

65. Nuria Romo-Avilés, Carmen Meneses-Falcón, and Eugenia Gil-García, "Learning to Be a Girl: Gender, Risks, and Legal Drugs amongst Spanish Teenagers," in *Gendered Drugs and Medicine,* ed. Ortiz-Gómez and Santesmases, 224 (quotes); Nadja Vietz, "Marijuana in Spain: Our On the Ground Report," Canna Law Blog, March 10, 2016, http://www.cannalawblog.com/marijuana-in-spain-our-on-the-ground-report/.

66. Toine Spapens, "Illegal Gambling," in *The Oxford Handbook of Organized Crime,* ed. Letizia Paoli (New York: Oxford U.P., 2014), 408; Phil Williams, "Organizing Transnational Crime: Networks, Markets and Hierarchies," in *Combating Transnational Crime: Concepts, Activities and Responses,* ed. Phil Williams and Dimitri Vlassis (London: Frank Cass, 2001), 66–67.

6. FOOD ADDICTIONS

1. Alan I. Leshner, "Addiction Is a Brain Disease, and It Matters," *Science* 278 (1997): 45–47.

2. Bill Snyder, "Nora Volkow: Two Paths to the Future," *Lens* (February 2006), http://www.mc.vanderbilt.edu/lens/article/?id=129&pg=0; John Gregory, "Dr. Nora Volkow of

the National Institute on Drug Abuse," Kentucky Educational Television, May 9, 2016, https://www.ket.org/opioids/dr-nora-volkow-of-the-national-institute-on-drug-abuse/ (alcoholism); Stanton Peele, "Why We Need to Stop Nora Volkow from Taking Over the World," *Substance.com*, January 17, 2015, http://www.substance.com/stop-nora-volkow -late/2720/.

3. Nora Volkow, "Why Do Our Brains Get Addicted?" TEDMED 2014, https:// www.tedmed.com/talks/show?id=309096. For a formal review of the evidence, see Volkow et al., "Addiction: Beyond Dopamine Reward Circuitry," *PNAS* 108 (2011): 15037–15042.

4. Paul Bloom, *How Pleasure Works: The New Science of Why We Like What We Like* (New York: Norton, 2010), chap. 6, "lite" p. 169; Fyodor Dostoevsky, *The Gambler,* trans. Victor Terras (Chicago: U. of Chicago Press, 1972), 188; Martin Lindstrom, *Buyology: Truth and Lies about Why We Buy* (New York: Doubleday, 2008), 14–15 (labels); Alfred R. Lindesmith, *Addiction and Opiates* (1968; repr., New Brunswick, N.J.: Aldine, 2008), 34–38; Peter Gzowski, "How to Quit Smoking in Fifty Years or Less," in *Addicted: Notes from the Belly of the Beast,* ed. Lorna Crozier and Patrick Lane, 2nd ed. (Vancouver: Greystone, 2006), 81.

5. Volkow, "Why Do Our Brains Get Addicted?"

6. Mark Lawrence Schrad, *Vodka Politics: Alcohol, Autocracy, and the Secret History of the Russian State* (New York: Oxford U.P., 2014), 218 (Trotsky).

7. Judit H. Ward et al., "Re-Introducing Bunky at 125: E. M. Jellinek's Life and Contributions to Alcohol Studies," *JSAD* 77 (2016): 375–383; Nancy Campbell, *Discovering Addiction: The Science and Politics of Substance Abuse Research* (Ann Arbor: U. of Michigan Press, 2007), chap. 3.

8. Solomon H. Snyder, "Historical Review: Opioid Receptors," *Trends in Pharmacological Sciences* 24 (2003): 198–205; Teresa Pollin and Jack Durell, "Bill Pollin Era at NIDA (1979–1985)," *Drug and Alcohol Dependence* 107 (2010): 88–91; David T. Courtwright, "The NIDA Brain Disease Paradigm: History, Resistance, and Spinoffs," *BioSocieties* 5 (2010): 137–147; Campbell, *Discovering Addiction,* 211 (Kuhar).

9. Campbell, *Discovering Addiction,* 213 ("beyond"); Michael J. Kuhar, *The Addicted Brain: Why We Abuse Drugs, Alcohol, and Nicotine* (Upper Saddle River, N.J.: Pearson, 2012), 74–77.

10. Adrian Meule, "Back by Popular Demand: A Narrative Review of the History of Food Addiction Research," *Yale J. of Biology and Medicine* 88 (2015): 296–297; Emily Aronson, "Renowned Psychologist Bart Hoebel . . . Dies," press release, Princeton University, June 14, 2011, https://www.princeton.edu/news/2011/06/14/renowned -psychologist-bart-hoebel-who-studied-addiction-behavior-dies; Linda Bartoshuk,

"Addicted to Food: An Interview with Bart Hoebel," APS *Observer* (November 2009), https://www.psychologicalscience.org/observer/addicted-to-food-an-interview-with-bart-hoebel; "Yale Hosts Historic Conference on Food and Addiction," *Yale News,* July 9, 2007; *Food and Addiction: A Comprehensive Handbook,* ed. Kelly D. Brownell and Mark S. Gold (New York: Oxford U.P., 2012).

11. David A. Kessler, *The End of Overeating: Taking Control of the Insatiable American Appetite* (New York: Rodale, 2009); Michael Moss, *Salt Sugar Fat: How the Food Giants Hooked Us* (New York: Random House, 2013); Cécile Bertrand, "Êtes-vous 'Addict' au Sucre? Les Signes qui Doivent Vous Alerter," *Madame Figaro,* January 25, 2017, http://madame.lefigaro.fr/bien-etre/etes-vous-addict-au-sucre-les-signent-qui-doivent-vous-alerter-230117-129301; Mark S. Gold, "Introduction," in *Eating Disorders, Overeating, and Pathological Attachment to Food: Independent or Addictive Disorders?* ed. Mark S. Gold (Binghamton, N.Y.: Haworth Press, 2004), 3; Oprah Winfrey, "How Did I Let This Happen Again?" *Oprah.com* (January 2009), http://www.oprah.com/spirit/Oprahs-Battle-with-Weight-Gain-O-January-2009-Cover/2.

12. "Food Addicts in Recovery Anonymous," Shaw TV Lethbridge, January 16, 2014, https://www.youtube.com/watch?v=toCIbYqYdVk; "A Conversation with Margaret Bullitt-Jonas about Her Memoir, *Holy Hunger,*" Reviving Creation, http://revivingcreation.org/holy-hunger/; Caitlin Moran, "I Know Why the Fat Lady Sings," *WSJ,* June 16–17, 2012. There are at least two other AA-style food addiction organizations: Overeaters Anonymous, founded in 1960, and Food Addicts Anonymous, founded in 1987.

13. Béatrice Lauby-Secretan et al., "Body Fatness and Cancer—Viewpoint of the IARC Working Group," *NEJM* 375 (2016): 794–798; Markku Peltonen and Lena M. S. Carlsson, "Body Fatness and Cancer," *NEJM* 375 (2016): 2007–2008; Rory Jones, "Diabetes 'Disaster' Jolts Persian Gulf," *WSJ,* February 11, 2014; Jesus Alegre-Díaz et al., "Diabetes and Cause-Specific Mortality in Mexico City," *NEJM* 375 (2016): 1961–1971; The GBD 2015 Obesity Collaborators, "Health Effects of Overweight and Obesity in 195 Countries over 25 Years," *NEJM* 377 (2017): 13–27.

14. "Obesity among Adults . . . ," NCHS Data Brief, December 4, 2007, https://www.cdc.gov/nchs/data/databriefs/db01.pdf; Eric A. Finklestein et al., "Annual Medical Spending Attributable to Obesity: Payer- and Service-Specific Estimates," *Health Affairs* 28 (2009): 822–831 (using price-adjusted 2008 dollars). The one-quarter estimate is explained at the end of this chapter.

15. Kevin Helliker, "Food May Be Addicting for Some," *WSJ,* April 5, 2011; Gene-Jack Wang et al., "Similarity between Obesity and Drug Addiction as Assessed by Neurofunctional Imaging," *J. of Addictive Diseases* 23 (2004): 39–53; Marcia Levin Pelchat, "Food Addiction in Humans," *J. of Nutrition* 139 (2009): 620–662; Scott Vrecko, "'Civilizing

Technologies' and the Control of Deviance," *BioSocieties* 5 (2010): 36–51; Kessler, *End of Overeating*, 31–41, 143.

16. Mark S. Gold, Kimberly Frost-Pineda, and William S. Jacobs, "Overeating, Binge Eating, and Eating Disorders as Addictions," *Psychiatric Annals* 33 (February 2003): 117–122; Katie Kleiner et al., "Body Mass Index and Alcohol Use," *J. of Addictive Diseases* 23 (2004): 105–117; Mark S. Gold, "From Bedside to Bench and Back Again: A 30-Year Saga," *Physiology and Behavior* 104 (2011): 157–161; "Jelly Belly Jelly Beans and Ronald Reagan," Ronald Reagan Presidential Library and Museum, January 2013, https://www.reaganlibrary.gov/sreference/jelly-belly-jelly-beans-and-ronald-reagan; David Carr, *The Night of the Gun: A Reporter Investigates the Darkest Story of His Life. His Own* (New York: Simon and Schuster, 2008), 196.

17. Bill Moyers's interview of George Koob from "The Hijacked Brain," *Moyers on Addiction: Close to Home*, March 29, 1998, edited transcript at http://www.thetherapist.com/PBS_Article_03.html; Roy A. Wise and George F. Koob, "The Development and Maintenance of Drug Addiction," *Neuropsychopharmacology* 39 (2014): 254–262; Markus Heilig, *The Thirteenth Step: Addiction in the Age of Brain Science* (New York: Columbia U.P., 2015), chap. 8.

18. Wendy C. King et al., "Prevalence of Alcohol Use Disorders before and after Bariatric Surgery," *JAMA* 307 (2012): 2516–2525; Gold, "From Bedside to Bench," 157–158.

19. Abigail Zuger, "A General in the Drug War," *NYT,* June 13, 2011 (move together); Kenneth Blum et al., "'Liking' and 'Wanting' Linked to Reward Deficiency Syndrome (RDS): Hypothesizing Differential Responsivity in Brain Reward Circuitry," *Current Pharmaceutical Design* 18 (2012): 113–118; Heilig, *Thirteenth Step,* 73; David J. Linden, *The Compass of Pleasure* (New York: Viking, 2011), 78–82; Gene-Jack Wang, Nora D. Volkow, et al., "Brain Dopamine and Obesity," *Lancet* 357 (2001): 354–357. Melissa A. Munn-Chernoff et al., "A Twin Study of Alcohol Dependence, Binge Eating, and Compensatory Behaviors," *JSAD* 74 (2013): 664–673, found heritability estimates for alcoholism and eating disorders ranging from 38 to 53 percent.

20. Caroline Davis, "Maternal Diet and Offspring Development," *Addiction* 106 (2011): 1215–1216; G. H. Gudjonsson et al., "An Epidemiological Study of ADHD Symptoms among Young Persons and the Relationship with Cigarette Smoking, Alcohol Consumption and Illicit Drug Use," *J. of Child Psychology and Psychiatry* 53 (2012): 304–312; Ju-Yu Yen et al., "The Comorbid Psychiatric Symptoms of Internet Addiction: Attention Deficit and Hyperactivity Disorder (ADHD), Depression, Social Phobia, and Hostility," *J. of Adolescent Health* 41 (2007): 93–98. For a detailed discussion of genetic and epigenetic factors, see *Food and Addiction,* ed. Brownell and Gold, chaps. 3–4. In an April 25, 2013, interview with the author, Gold speculated that early exposure to addictive foods and drugs has become a peculiarly unhealthful aspect of modern life. The

problem is not so much parental genes but "genes that are changed in the intrauterine environment and early childhood environment" through exposure to mass-produced substances like fructose and nicotine.

21. Davis, "Maternal Diet," 1216. Recent evidence suggests that the original fetal spectrum disorder, alcohol, may also be more widespread and damaging than supposed. Philip A. May et al., "Prevalence of Fetal Alcohol Spectrum Disorders in 4 US Communities," *JAMA* 319 (2018): 474–482.

22. I have drawn the arguments from the food addiction proponents cited above and such thoughtful critics and commentators as Gene M. Heyman, *Addiction: A Disorder of Choice* (Cambridge, Mass.: Harvard U.P., 2009), chap. 6; Bennett Foddy, "Addiction and Its Sciences—Philosophy," *Addiction* 106 (2010): 25–31; Howard I. Kushner, "Historical Perspectives of Addiction," in *Addiction Medicine: Science and Practice,* ed. Bankole A. Johnson, vol. 1 (New York: Springer, 2011), 75–93; Sally Satel and Scott O. Lilienfeld, *Brainwashed: The Seductive Appeal of Mindless Neuroscience* (New York: Basic Books, 2013), chap. 3, and Satel and Lilienfeld, "Calling It a 'Brain Disease' Makes Addiction Harder to Treat," *Boston Globe,* June 22, 2017; Rachel Hammer et al., "Addiction: Current Criticism of the Brain Disease Paradigm," *American J. of Bioethics Neuroscience* 4 (2013): 27–32; Suzanne Frazer, David Moore, and Helen Keane, *Habits: Remaking Addiction* (New York: Palgrave Macmillan, 2014), chaps. 6–7; Wayne Hall, Adrian Carter, and Cynthia Forlini, "The Brain Disease Model of Addiction: Is It Supported by the Evidence and Has It Delivered on Its Promises?" *Lancet Psychiatry* 2 (2015): 105–110; and Maia Szalavitz, *Unbroken Brain: A Revolutionary New Way of Understanding Addiction* (New York: St. Martin's Press, 2016). An earlier version of the dialogue appears in "Food as a Drug: How Good Is the Analogy?" Addictions Old and New Conference, University of Richmond, October 23, 2015, https://www.youtube.com/watch?v=QOfYwHkCIZA.

23. In addition to the sources cited above, I have drawn illustrations, statistics, and quotations from Tara Parker-Pope, "Craving an Ice-Cream Fix," *NYT,* September 20, 2012 (Cheetos); Victorino Matus, "Taste the Science in Every Bite," *WSJ,* May 23–24, 2015 (Doritos); Robert Lustig, "The Sugar-Addiction Taboo," *Atlantic,* January 2, 2014 (fructose); Charles Duhigg, *The Power of Habit: Why We Do What We Do in Life and Business* (New York: Random House, 2014), 92–93 (overcome); Maia Szalavitz, "Can Food Really Be Addictive?" *Time,* April 5, 2012 (20 percent); Mark A. R. Kleiman, Jonathan P. Caulkins, and Angela Hawkin, *Drugs and Drug Policy: What Everyone Needs to Know* (New York: Oxford U.P., 2011), 29 (10 percent); Ashley Gearhardt, "Addiction," in *The Oxford Companion to Sugar and Sweets,* ed. Darra Goldstein (New York: Oxford U.P., 2015), 1–4 (subclinical); "Obesity and Overweight," WHO Fact Sheet, February 16, 2018, http://www.who.int/news-room/fact-sheets/detail/obesity-and-overweight (more than half); John E. Blundell and Graham Finlayson, "Food Addiction Is Not Helpful: The Hedonic Component—Implicit Wanting—Is Important," *Addiction* 106 (2011):

1216–1217 (culture); Warren Belasco, *Food: The Key Concepts* (Oxford: Berg, 2008), 88–96 (multiple sources of obesity); Stanton Peele, "The Meaning of Addiction: Is Eating Addictive?" *Huffington Post*, September 12, 2011 ("fulfill"); A. Agrawal et al., "The Genetics of Addiction—A Translational Perspective," *Translational Psychiatry* 2 (2012), e140, doi:10.1038 / tp.2012.54; Jacqueline M. Vink, "Genetics of Addiction: Future Focus on Gene x Environment Interaction," *JSAD* 77 (2016): 684–687; Jesse J. Prinz, *Beyond Human Nature: How Culture and Experience Shape the Human Mind* (New York: Norton, 2012), 24–29 (genes and environment); Timothy P. Condon, "Reflecting on 30 Years of Research . . . ," *Behavioral Healthcare* 26, no. 5 (2006): 14, 16; Xiaoyun Shen et al., "Anti-Addiction Vaccines," *F1000 Medicine Reports* 3 (2011), https://f1000.com/prime/reports/m/3/20, and Douglas Quenqua, "An Addiction Vaccine, Tantalizingly Close," *NYT*, October 3, 2011 (limitations); Kent C. Berridge and Morten L. Kringleback, "Pleasure Systems in the Brain," *Neuron* 86 (2015): 646–664, and Aldo Badiani et al., "Addiction Research and Theory: A Commentary on the Surgeon General's Report on Alcohol, Drugs, and Health," *Addiction Biology* 23 (2017): 3–5 (etiological debates); and "Definition of Addiction," April 12, 2011, American Society of Addiction Medicine, https://www.asam.org/quality-practice/definition-of -addiction, emphasis added.

24. For a summary and review of the critical literature, see David T. Courtwright, "Addiction and the Science of History," *Addiction* 107 (2012): 486–492, with rejoinders in "Addiction, History, and Historians: A Symposium," Points blog, March 2, 2012, https://pointsadhsblog.wordpress.com/2012/03/02/addiction-and-historians-a -symposium/. Colors: Timothy A. Hickman, "Target America: Visual Culture, Neuroimaging, and the 'Hijacked Brain' Theory of Addiction," *Past and Present* 222, suppl. 9 (2013): 213.

25. Nora D. Volkow and George Koob, "Brain Disease Model of Addiction: Why Is It So Controversial?" *Lancet Psychiatry* 2 (2015): 677–679.

26. Richard A. Rawson et al., "The Globalization of Addiction Research: Capacity Building Mechanisms and Selected Examples," *Harvard Review of Psychiatry* 23 (2015): 147–156; Leshner, "Addiction," 46; Griffith Edwards, *Matters of Substance: Drugs—And Why Everyone's a User* (New York: St. Martin's Press, 2004), xxxvii–xxxviii; Judit H. Ward and William Bejarno, "Broad Thinking: An Interview with Harold Kalant," *JSAD* 78 (2017): 161.

27. Michelle M. Mello, Eric B. Rimm, and David M. Studder, "The McLawsuit: The Fast-Food Industry and Legal Accountability for Obesity," *Health Affairs* 22 (2003): 207–216; Kessler, *End of Overeating*, 242 (Puck); Bart Hoebel, "Sugar Addiction: Bingeing, Withdrawal, and Craving," conference presentation, Obesity and Food Addiction Summit, Bainbridge Island, Washington. April 25, 2009, http://foodaddictionsummit .org/webcast/hoebel.html; Moss, *Salt Sugar Fat*, "mouthfeel" 154, burst, 287; Annie Gas-

parro and Jesse Newman, "The New Science of Taste: 1,000 Banana Flavors," *WSJ*, October 31, 2014.

28. Steve Steinberg, "Industry Turns Flavor into a Science," *Chicago Tribune*, January 30, 1986 (one in ten); Moss, *Salt Sugar Fat*, 311 (Lin). Genetically modified yeast cells have also been used to turn sugar into opioids, further blurring the food / pharma line. Stephanie Galanie et al., "Complete Biosynthesis of Opioids in Yeast," *Science* 349 (2015): 1095–1100.

29. Michael Pollan, *The Botany of Desire: A Plant's Eye View of the World* (New York: Random House, 2001), chap. 4, and Daniel Akst, *We Have Met the Enemy: Self-Control in an Age of Excess* (New York: Penguin, 2011), 23 (potatoes); Moss, *Salt Sugar Fat*, 60 (Mortimer); Michael Specter, "Freedom from Fries," *New Yorker* 91 (November 2, 2015): 56–65 (cheap food); Sarah Tracy, pers. comm., September 14, 2017 (Lay's). Addictiveness has since become a common food-marketing gambit, e.g., Firehouse Subs' slogan, "One bite. One taste. You're hooked."

30. Charles Spence, "Auditory Contributions to Flavour Perception and Feeding Behaviour," *Physiology and Behavior* 107 (2012): 507–508.

31. Nicola Twilley, "Accounting for Taste," *New Yorker* 91 (November 2, 2015): 50–55 (coffee, sodas); Moss, *Salt Sugar Fat*, 320, and "25 Unique Potato Chip Flavors from around the World You Probably Never Heard Of," October 12, 2014, http://list25.com /25-unique-potato-chip-flavors-from-around-the-world-you-probably-never-heard-of /; Harry Rothschild, pers. comm., September 18, 2017 (extensions).

32. Bert C. Goss confidential memorandum, January 10, 1956, p. 4, folder 4, box 93, John W. Hill Papers, State Historical Society of Wisconsin, Madison (Coca-Cola); "New Croissan'wich TV Scripts and Storyboards" (TS, 1984), "general" folder, box 2, Burt Manning Papers, JWT; David Segal, "Grilled Chicken, That Temperamental Star," *NYT*, October 8, 2011 ("Pavlovs").

33. Charles Spence, "From Instagram to TV Ads: What's the Science behind Food Porn?" *Guardian*, March 19, 2017.

34. Kessler, *End of Overeating*, 243 ("happy," citing unpublished Heath McDonald paper); Hal Friedman to Burger King Creative Team, December 17, 1986, "general" folder, box 2, Burt Manning Papers, JWT ("music"); Rumy Doo, "Silent Mukbang Brings Focus Back to Food," *Korea Herald*, August 18, 2016; "'Meokbang' Emerges as New Way to Relieve Stress," *Korea Times*, February 17, 2017; Euny Hong, "Why Some Koreans Make $10,000 a Month to Eat on Camera," *Quartz*, January 16, 2016, https://qz.com /592710/why-some-koreans-make-10000-a-month-to-eat-on-camera/. The sources differ slightly over when *mukbang* first emerged.

35. "Creative Direction: Children's Advertising" (TS, 1976), 1, 4, Advertising to Children, box 2, Burt Manning Papers, JWT; Paul M. Fischer et al., "Brand Logo Recognition by

Children Aged 3 to 6 Years," *JAMA* 266 (1991): 3145–3148; Amanda S. Bruce et al., "Branding and a Child's Brain: An fMRI Study of Neural Responses to Logos," *Social Cognitive and Affective Neuroscience* 9 (2014): 118–122; Harry Varley, "Dealing in Futures," *Printer's Ink* 108 (August 14, 1919): 162–172; Moss, *Salt Sugar Fat,* 77–80.

36. John Willem to Robert Urban et al., August 8, 1955, Anheuser-Busch, box 18B, Dan Seymour Papers (Budweiser); "Thompson T-Square" (TS, 1966), 5, Miscellaneous Reports, box 4, Albert B. Stridsberg Papers, JWT (heavy users). Representative product analyses and surveys are in Chunky Chocolate Corp. (whence "gustatory"), box 18; Mrs. Butterworth's Syrup minutes and attachments, box 19; Liggett and Meyers— Chesterfield, box 19 ("full satisfaction"); and United States Brewers Association, box 32, Review Board Records, all in JWT. "Lift" from Goss confidential memorandum, p. 3, box 93, John W. Hill Papers, State Historical Society of Wisconsin, Madison.

37. David W. Ellwood, *The Shock of America: Europe and the Challenge of the Century* (Oxford: Oxford U.P., 2012), 404–405; Albert Stridsberg, "The Next Thirty Years of American Advertising . . ." (TS, December 18, 1969), 1, 4, international marketing folder, box 4, Stridsberg Papers, JWT (Kraft, quotation); Lawrence Wallack and Kathryn Montgomery, "Advertising for All by the Year 2000: Public Health Implications for Less Developed Countries," *J. of Public Health Policy* 13 (1992): 205; Barbara Sundberg Baudot, *International Advertising Handbook* (Lexington, Mass.: Lexington Books, 1989), 11, 15–16n20 (percentages).

38. Andrew Jacobs and Matt Richtel, "How Big Business Got Brazil Hooked on Junk Food," *NYT,* September 16, 2017; Michele Simon, "Nestle Stoops to New Low, Launches Barge to Peddle Junk Food on the Amazon River to Brazil's Poor," *Alternet,* July 8, 2010, http://www.alternet.org/story/147446/nestle_stoops_to_new_low,_launches_barge_to _peddle_junk_food_on_the_amazon_river_to_brazil's_poor/.

39. April Fulton, "McDonald's Goes Vegetarian—In India," NPR, September 4, 2012, http://www.npr.org/sections/thesalt/2012/09/04/160543754/mcdonalds-goes-vegetarian -in-india; Ronald A. Lukens-Bull, "Ronald McDonald as a Javanese Saint and an Indonesian Freedom Fighter: Reflections on the Global and the Local," *Crossroads* 17 (2003): 114–117.

40. *McDonaldization: The Reader,* 2nd edition, ed. George Ritzer (Thousand Oaks, Calif.: Pine Forge, 2006), provides an introduction and representative studies.

41. Coca-Cola, "Per Capita Consumption of Company Beverage Products," https:// www.coca-colacompany.com/annual-review/2011/pdf/2011-per-capita-consumption.pdf; Amy Guthrie et al., "Companies Brace for Mexican Food Fight," *WSJ,* October 19–20, 2013; Margot Sanger-Katz, "Sales Fall Again in Mexico's Second Year of Taxing Soda," *NYT,* February 22, 2017; Bartow J. Elmore, *Citizen Coke: The Making of Coca-Cola Capitalism* (New York: Norton, 2015), 187.

42. Victoria de Grazia, *Irresistible Empire: America's Advance through Twentieth-Century Europe* (Cambridge, Mass.: Harvard U.P., 2005), 469–471 (McDonald's) and Mark Bittman, "The True Cost of a Burger," *NYT*, July 15, 2014 (emissions). Elmore, *Citizen Coke*, and James Walvin, *Sugar: The World Corrupted: From Slavery to Obesity* (New York: Pegasus, 2018) survey environmental and other externalities.

43. Ashley N. Gearhardt, William R. Corbin, and Kelly D. Brownell, "Preliminary Validation of the Yale Food Addiction Scale," *Appetite* 52 (2009): 430–436. One quarter or more / 150 million: Caroline Davis et al., "Evidence That 'Food Addiction' Is a Valid Phenotype of Obesity," *Appetite* 57 (2011): 711–717; Nicole M. Avena et al., "Tossing the Baby Out with the Bathwater after a Brief Rinse? The Potential Downside of Dismissing Food Addiction on Limited Data," *Nature Reviews Neuroscience* 13 (2012): 514; and WHO, "Obesity and Overweight." Steve Sussman, *Substance and Behavioral Addictions: Concepts, Causes, and Cures* (Cambridge: Cambridge U.P., 2017), 115, proposes a figure of 2 percent of the general adult population, which would yield a 2014 total closer to 100 million. Sussman warns, however, that the percentage is tentative and "it is possible that the prevalence of food addiction is much higher."

7. DIGITAL ADDICTIONS

1. Carol Cling, "Slot Machines City's Most Popular Form of Gaming," *Las Vegas Review-Journal*, April 5, 1994 ("excited"); Marc Cooper, *The Last Honest Place in America: Paradise and Perdition in the New Las Vegas* (New York: Nation Books, 2004), 134 ("trendy").

2. Cooper, *Last Honest Place*, 95, 140 (quotation), 141–142.

3. Lynn Waddell, "Do Locals Gamble? You Bet!" *Las Vegas Sun*, April 9, 1991; Andrés Martinez, *24/7: Living It Up and Doubling Down in the New Las Vegas* (New York: Villard, 1999), 239–240.

4. Natasha Dow Schüll, *Addiction by Design: Machine Gambling in Las Vegas* (Princeton, N.J.: Princeton U.P., 2012), quotation p. 2.

5. Ibid., 1–19, 223–226, quotation p. 226, original italicized.

6. Gary Rivlin, "The Chrome-Shiny . . . Bandit," *NYT Magazine*, May 9, 2004, 81 ("losers"); Schüll, *Addiction by Design*, 21 ("creative"), 295 ("bomb"), italics in original.

7. M. P. Davis, "A 'Virtual' Success," *Gaming and Wagering Business* 5 (October 1984): 14.

8. Mark Maremont and Alexandra Berzon, "The Real Odds on Gambling," *WSJ*, October 12–13, 2013; Schüll, *Addiction by Design*, 16–18, 69, 293; Patrick Roberts, "Table Dances," *RD&E: Retail, Dining and Entertainment in the Gaming and Hospitality Industry* 2 (2008): 15.

9. Schüll, *Addiction by Design*, 119–120 (Australia), 300–302 (globalization); "What Is Pachinko?" (n.d., ca. 1992–1993), Gambling Vertical File—Games: Pachinko, SC-UNLV; Misha Glenny, *McMafia: A Journey through the Global Criminal Underworld* (New York: Vintage, 2009), 308; Pablo Gorondi, "Hungary's Gambling Issue," *Florida Times-Union*, October 5, 2012; Victoria Coren Mitchell, "A Stupid Gamble on Evil Machines," *Guardian*, August 19, 2017.

10. Schüll, *Addiction by Design*, 119–120; Alexandra Berzon and Mark Maremont, "Researchers Bet Casino Data Can Identify Gambling Addicts," *WSJ*, August 3–4, 2013; Adam Baidawi, "Australians Are the World's Biggest Gambling Losers . . . ," *NYT*, April 4, 2018; Sean Nicholls, "Account Limit Lift to $5000 'Dangerous' for Gamblers," *Sydney Morning Herald*, June 9, 2015.

11. Natasha Dow Schüll, "Addiction by Design: From Slot Machines to Candy Crush," Addictions Old and New Conference, University of Richmond, October 23, 2015, https://www.youtube.com/watch?v=TazssD6L7wc.

12. Hilarie Cash et al., "Internet Addiction: A Brief Summary of Research and Practice," *Current Psychiatry Reviews* 8 (2012): 294. For drug language parallels (e.g., "It was the most intense nothingness there ever was"; "It anesthetizes the whole damn ugly world") see Gene M. Heyman, *Addiction: A Disorder of Choice* (Cambridge, Mass.: Harvard U.P., 2009), 46–52.

13. Cash et al., "Internet Addiction," 292–298; Aviv Weinstein and Michel Lejoyeux, "Internet Addiction or Excessive Internet Use," *American J. of Drug and Alcohol Abuse* 36 (2010): 277–283; Tiffany Hsu, "Video Game Addiction Tries to Move from Basement to Doctor's Office," *NYT*, June 17, 2018.

14. Excerpts with minor format changes from International Center for Media and Public Agenda and Salzburg Academy on Media and Global Change, "Going 24 Hours without Media," The World Unplugged, 2011, https://theworldunplugged.wordpress.com/. U.S. (23 percent) and Chinese students (22 percent) were the most likely to mention addiction, Argentinian (12 percent) and Ugandan (14 percent) students the least likely, findings that suggest that internet accessibility affected self-perceptions of media addiction.

15. Hormesis ordinarily applies to the biphasic dose response of an environmental agent like ionizing radiation or a chemical compound. But the concept has been extended to such behaviors as eating and exercise, and I see no reason why it should not also cover autotropic digital behaviors, which are beneficial if infrequent but injurious and teletropic (others gain control over your emotions and beliefs) if frequent and habitual. On hormesis, see Mark P. Mattson, "Hormesis Defined," *Ageing Research Reviews* 7 (2008): 1–7. On beneficial digital use, see Greg Wadley, "Mood-Enhancing Technology," in *OzCHI '16: Proceedings of the 28th Australian Conference on Computer-Human Interaction* (Launceston, Australia, 2016), https://dl.acm.org/citation.cfm?id=3010954.

16. Kimberly S. Young, "A Therapist's Guide to Assess and Treat Internet Addiction," http://www.netaddiction.com/articles/practitioners.pdf; Amanda Lenhardt, "Teens, Social Media and Technology: Overview 2015," *Pew Research Center Report,* April 9, 2015, http://www.pewinternet.org/2015/04/09/teens-social-media-technology-2015/; Donald W. Black, "A Review of Compulsive Buying Disorder," *World Psychiatry* 6 (2007): 1–18.

17. Eric Bellman, "Internet's Next Users: More Video, Less Typing," *WSJ,* August 8, 2017.

18. John C. Burnham, *Bad Habits: Drinking, Smoking, Taking Drugs, Gambling, Sexual Misbehavior, and Swearing in American History* (New York: NYU Press, 1993), chap. 8; "Trolling," Urban Dictionary, http://www.urbandictionary.com/define.php?term=trolling.

19. Adam Alter, *Irresistible: The Rise of Addictive Technology and the Business of Keeping Us Hooked* (New York: Penguin, 2017), 3 (Harris); Steve Henn, "How Video Games Are Getting Inside Your Head—and Wallet," *Morning Edition,* NPR, October 29, 2013, http://www.npr.org/sections/alltechconsidered/2013/10/30/241449067/how-video-games-are-getting-inside-your-head-and-wallet; Sarah E. Needleman, "Game Developers Are Making It Hard for Players to Stop," *WSJ,* August 21, 2018; David Barboza, "Ogre to Slay? Outsource It to Chinese," *NYT,* December 9, 2005; Sarah E. Needleman, "Mobile-Game Makers Hunt for 'Whales,'" *WSJ,* May 11, 2015. By the 2010s casino owners and gambling machine designers feared that their internet rivals, unencumbered by brick-and-mortar facilities, would succeed in monopolizing young gamers' time or, worse yet, in moving gambling online, leaving half-empty casinos to aging baby boomers and rock-and-roll nostalgia acts. What to do about the trend divided the industry. Innovators proclaimed adapt or die, while stand-patters like Sheldon Adelson threatened to spend whatever it took to stop internet gambling. Hannah Dreier, "Gambling Industry Fights Self on Internet Gambling," *Washington Examiner,* February 10, 2014.

20. Nancy Jo Sales, *American Girls: Social Media and the Secret Lives of Teenagers* (New York: Knopf, 2016), 10 (self-reported addiction), 192 ("no life"), 271 ("porn all day").

21. "Going 24 Hours without Media"; Emily Rauhala, "These Viral Selfie Apps with 1 Billion Downloads Are Shaping China's Start-Up Culture," *WP,* August 3, 2016; Heather Chen, "Asia's Smartphone Addiction," BBC News, September 7, 2015, http://www.bbc.com/news/world-asia-33130567; "Net Addiction a Growing Problem," *Japan Times,* September 3, 2013. I draw also on Ian Hodder, *Entangled: An Archaeology of the Relations between Human and Things* (Chichester: Wiley-Blackwell, 2012), 103–105, whose account of "taut" material and social entanglements leading to human entrapment fits smartphones and social media perfectly.

22. Amanda Lenhart, "Teens, Social Media and Technology Overview 2015," Pew Research Center, April 9, 2015, http://www.pewinternet.org/2015/04/09/teens-social-media-technology-2015/.

23. Sales, *American Girls*, 240. Brian Y. Park et al., "Is Internet Porn Causing Sexual Dysfunctions? A Review with Clinical Reports," *Behavioral Sciences* 6, no. 3 (2016), https://doi.org/10.3390/bs6030017, reviews the international literature and provides case studies. Gary Wilson's TEDx talk, "The Great Porn Experiment," May 16, 2012, https://www.youtube.com/watch?v=wSF82AwSDiU, offers a primer on pornography addiction and argues for neuropathological commonalities with food and drug addiction.

24. Norbert Elias, *The Civilizing Process: Sociogenetic and Psychogenetic Investigations*, rev. ed., trans. Edmund Jephcott (Oxford: Blackwell, 2000); Steven Pinker, *The Better Angels of Our Nature: Why Violence Has Declined* (New York: Viking, 2011), chap. 3; Mark Regnerus, "Cheap Sex and the Decline of Marriage," *WSJ*, September 29, 2017; Sales, *American Girls*, 197.

25. Anna North, review of *American Girls*, by Nancy Jo Sales, *NYT*, March 25, 2016; Zoë Heller, "'Hot' Sex and Young Girls," *NYRB* 63 (August 18, 2016): 22–23; Pinker, *Better Angels*, 477.

26. Alter, *Irresistible*, 4.

27. According to the WHO, 16.2 million adults die annually as a result of tobacco, alcohol, salty diets, and physical inactivity. To this sum I have added another 2.7 million 2014 deaths from four sources: (1) distracted driving (estimated as 10 percent of total road accident deaths); (2) infections that originated from unprotected extra-marital sex or drug injection (estimated, very conservatively, as 50 percent of all HIV / AIDS, syphilis, and hepatitis C deaths); (3) drug overdose deaths; and (4) deaths directly caused by diabetes, such as kidney failure. Result: In 2014 approximately 18.9 million persons died, the vast majority prematurely, from conditions caused or exacerbated by "bad habits." That same year "bad blood"—wars and homicides—claimed the lives of 0.624 million persons, yielding a ratio of 30 to 1. The calculation has limits. Neither the WHO's data nor my assumptions are sacrosanct, and the ratio varies from year to year as wars begin or end. But the exercise makes the point that unhealthful habits, encouraged and facilitated by legal and illegal global enterprises, have come to exact a far higher annual toll than the world's armies, tyrants, banditti, and brawlers. WHO, *Noncommunicable Diseases*, fact sheet, June 2017 edition, http://www.who.int/mediacentre/factsheets/fs355/en/; "World Rankings—Total Deaths," 2014, http://www.worldlifeexpectancy.com/world-rankings-total-deaths (WHO data); WHO, *Diabetes*, fact sheet, November 2017 edition, http://www.who.int/mediacentre/factsheets/fs312/en/.

28. Kit Smith, "47 Incredible Facebook Statistics and Facts for 2016," *Brandwatch*, May 12, 2016, https://www.brandwatch.com/blog/47-facebook-statistics-2016/; Alter, *Irresistible*, 5, 7, 10; Nir Eyal with Ryan Hoover, *Hooked: How to Build Habit-Forming Products* (New York: Portfolio / Penguin, 2014), 131 ("tribe"); Tamara Lush, "At War with World

of Warcraft: An Addict Tells His Story," *Guardian,* August 29, 2011. School teachers who read a draft of this chapter remarked on the similarities between digital reinforcement and effective pedagogy. SRA Reading Labs, for example, rely on the same six principles. Limbic capitalists appropriate more than addicts' brains. They appropriate the learning process itself.

29. Nick Bilton, "Instagram Quickly Passes 1 Million Users," *NYT,* December 21, 2010 ("hooked"); Josh Constine, "Instagram's Growth Speeds Up as It Hits 700 Million Users," *TechCrunch,* April 26, 2017, https://techcrunch.com/2017/04/26/instagram-700-million -users/; Ellen McCarthy, "Breaking Up with Your Smartphone . . . ," *WP,* February 8, 2018 (quotation).

30. Eyal with Hoover, *Hooked,* 17, 39 ("unleashed"), 48 ("quell").

31. Kashmir Hill, "10 Reasons Why Facebook Bought Instagram," *Forbes,* April 11, 2012, https://www.forbes.com/sites/kashmirhill/2012/04/11/ten-reasons-why-facebook -bought-instagram/#7366140bd1b1; David Batty, "Instagram Acts after BBC Finds Site Users Are Advertising Illegal Drugs," *Guardian,* November 7, 2013; "1 Million Porn Videos on Instagram Hidden in Arabic Hashtags: Report," *Times of India,* March 15, 2016.

32. Sherry Turkle, *Alone Together: Why We Expect More from Technology and Less from Each Other* (New York: Basic Books, 2011); Nicholas Carr, *The Shallows: What the Internet Is Doing to Our Brains* (New York: Norton, 2010); Nicholas Carr, "How Smartphones Hijack Our Minds," *WSJ,* October 7–8, 2017; Tamar Lewin, "If Your Kids Are Awake, They're Probably Online," *NYT,* January 20, 2010; Matt Richtel, *A Deadly Wandering: A Tale of Tragedy and Redemption in the Age of Attention* (New York: William Morrow, 2014); Leonard Sax, *Boys Adrift: The Five Factors Driving the Growing Epidemic of Unmotivated Boys and Underachieving Young Men* (New York: Basic Books, 2007), chaps. 2–3; "Mexico," The World Unplugged, https://theworldunplugged.wordpress .com/countries/mexico/.

33. Zadie Smith, "Generation Why?" *NYRB* 57 (November 25, 2010): 58; Carl Wilkinson, "Shutting Out a World of Digital Distraction," *Telegraph,* September 6, 2012 (Franzen); Adrian F. Ward et al., "Brain Drain: The Mere Presence of One's Own Smartphone Reduces Available Cognitive Capacity," *J. of the Association for Consumer Research* 2 (2017): 140–154.

34. "Time suck," Urban Dictionary, https://www.urbandictionary.com/define.php ?term=time%20suck; Jean M. Twenge, "Have Smartphones Destroyed a Generation?" *Atlantic* (September 2017), https://www.theatlantic.com/magazine/archive/2017/09 /has-the-smartphone-destroyed-a-generation/534198/; Melinda Beck, "The Effects of Chronic Heavy Drinking on Brain Function Are Underdiagnosed," *WSJ,* December 21, 2015 (Koob).

35. Pinker, *Better Angels,* chaps. 3, 5, 9, and 10.

36. Ibid., 673, 682; Steven Pinker, *Enlightenment Now: The Case for Reason, Science, Humanism, and Progress* (New York: Viking, 2018), 12–13, 83–84; Robert Wright, "Progress Is Not a Zero-Sum Game," TED talk, February 2006, https://www.ted.com/talks/robert_wright_on_optimism#t-524840.

37. Nir Eyal, "Opening Remarks," 2014 Habit Summit, https://www.youtube.com/watch?v=QxD3LQrJpBw; Haley Sweetland Edwards, "The Masters of Mind Control," *Time* 191 (April 23, 2018): 36.

38. Nir Eyal, "The Promise and Peril of Persuasive Technology," 2017 Habit Summit, https://www.youtube.com/watch?v=EuAYOhSKOwk.

39. "Tencent Announces 2016 Fourth Quarter and Annual Results," March 22, 2017, pp. 1, 3–4 (quotations), https://www.tencent.com/en-us/articles/15000591490174029.pdf; Timothy McDonald, "Honour of Kings: China's Most Vilified Online Game," BBC News, July 7, 2017, http://www.bbc.com/news/business-40516125.

40. Paul Lewis, "'Our Minds Can Be Hijacked': The Tech Insiders Who Fear a Smartphone Dystopia," *Guardian,* October 5, 2017; "Chamath Palihapitiya . . . on Money as an Instrument of Change," Stanford Graduate School of Business, November 13, 2017, https://www.youtube.com/watch?v=PMotykwoSIk&feature=youtu.be&t=21m21s.

41. Nick Bilton, "Steve Jobs Was a Low-Tech Parent," *NYT,* September 10, 2014; Alter, *Irresistible,* 2; "Chamath Palihapitiya"; Lewis, "Our Minds Can Be Hijacked."

42. Author interview with Leonard Stern, May 1, 2013.

43. Murray Melbin, *Night as Frontier: Colonizing the World after Dark* (New York: Free Press, 1987); Jane Brox, *Brilliant: The Evolution of Artificial Light* (Boston: Houghton Mifflin Harcourt, 2010), 30; "Crimes Related to Awakening Drugs a Worry," *Mainichi Shimbun,* TS translation in "Addiction—Incidence, Countries, 1976–1977," VF.

44. "Fly TWA Las Vegas" ad, "Facts about McCarran" (TS news release, n.d.), and "Aviation History in the Las Vegas Valley" (TS news film transcript, n.d.), p. 3, Aviation Vertical File, SC-UNLV.

45. David T. Courtwright, *No Right Turn: Conservative Politics in a Liberal America* (Cambridge, Mass.: Harvard U.P., 2010), 117–119, 252–256.

46. Bill Tancer, *Click: What Millions of People Are Doing Online and Why It Matters* (New York: Hyperion, 2008), 19–26, 110–114.

47. David T. Courtwright, Herman Joseph, and Don Des Jarlais, *Addicts Who Survived: An Oral History of Narcotic Use in America before 1965* (Knoxville: U. of Tennessee Press, 2012), 257 ("life"); Pinker, *Enlightenment Now,* 260 (Caravaggio, Callas); Google search April 2018.

48. Susan E. Foster et al., "Alcohol Consumption and Expenditures for Underage Drinking and Adult Excessive Drinking," *JAMA* 289 (2003): 989–995 (20 percent);

John Carroll, "DOE Symposium" (TS, September 9, 1995), 5, box 1, JKP; Center for Media Education, "ABSOLUTe Web: Tobacco and Alcohol Industries Launch Into Cyberspace," *InfoActive* (Winter 1997): 1–16; Sarah Mart, Jacob Mergendoller, and Michele Simon, "Alcohol Promotion on Facebook," *J. of Global Drug Policy and Practice* 3, no. 3 (2009), http://www.eatdrinkpolitics.com/wp-content/uploads /AlcoholPromotionFacebookSimon.pdf; "How Alcohol Brands Are Advertising with Social Media Influencers," Mediakix, March 17, 2016, http://mediakix.com/2016/03 /alcohol-advertising-social-media-influencers/#gs.HwTAiQU; Patricia A. Cavazos-Rehg et al., "'Hey Everyone, I'm Drunk.' An Evaluation of Drinking-Related Twitter Chatter," *JSAD* 76 (2015): 635–639; Sarah A. Stoddard et al., "Permissive Norms and Young Adults' Alcohol and Marijuana Use: The Role of Online Communities," *JSAD* 73 (2012): 968–975; Craig MacAndrew and Robert B. Edgerton, *Drunken Comportment: A Social Explanation* (Chicago: Aldine, 1969).

49. "Commentator [sic] on Pornography, Illegal Publications," *Beijing Renmin Ribao,* November 24, 1995, FBIS; Dan Levin, "In China, Illegal Drugs Are Sold Online in an Unbridled Market," *NYT,* June 21, 2015.

50. Michael Flood and Clive Hamilton, "Youth and Pornography in Australia: Evidence on the Extent of Exposure and Likely Effects," discussion paper no. 52, Australia Institute, February 2003, 53, http://www.tai.org.au/sites/default/files/DP52_8.pdf; "Iceland Considers Pornography Ban," *Telegraph,* February 13, 2013; Jeremiah Kiplangat, "Internet Unlocks a World of Sexual Fantasy," *Standard Digital,* February 9, 2009, https://www.standardmedia .co.ke/article/1144006137/internet-unlocks-a-world-of-sexual-fantasy ("craved").

51. Kit R. Roane, "Prostitutes on Wane in New York Streets but Take to Internet," *NYT,* February 23, 1998; John D. McKinnon, "Web Freedom's Role in Sex Trafficking," *WSJ,* July 12, 2016 (quotations).

52. Robert Weiss, "Hyperstimulation and Digital Media: Sex and Tech Addictions," Addictions Old and New Conference, University of Richmond, October 23, 2015, https:// www.youtube.com/watch?v=oHTtuewZePE; Gardiner Harris, "Cellphones Reshape Prostitution in India, and Complicate Efforts to Prevent AIDS," *NYT,* November 24, 2012.

53. Sabrina Tavernise, "F.D.A. Warns 5 Producers of Powdered Caffeine," *NYT,* September 1, 2015; Zolan Kanno-Youngs and Jeanne Whalen, "Gangs Cut Out Middlemen," *WSJ,* June 9, 2017; Jeff Elder, "Icann, Regulators Clash over Illegal Online Drug Sales," *WSJ,* October 27, 2014 (estimate); Anna Lembke, *Drug Dealer, M.D.* (Baltimore: Johns Hopkins U.P., 2016), 78.

54. Bari Weiss, "Thank You for Smoking—Marijuana," *WSJ,* March 15–16, 2014 (Hartfield). When checked in November 2017, both Amazon.de and Amazon.fr offered Screeny ~~eny refills.

55. David Weinberger, "Criminal Networks and Indoor Cannabis in Europe: Has the Phenomenon Reached France?" *Drugs, International Challenges,* no. 1 (May 2011): 1–5; National Drug Intelligence Center, *Indoor Cannabis Cultivation Operations: An Intelligence Brief* (Washington, D.C.: U.S. Department of Justice, 2000), v, 1–13.

56. Yuval Noah Harari, *Homo Deus: A Brief History of Tomorrow* (New York: Harper-Collins, 2017).

8. AGAINST EXCESS

1. Lydia Leavitt, "69gadget's OhMiBod Freestyle Review," *TechCrunch,* October 24, 2009, https://techcrunch.com/2009/10/24/69gadgets-ohmibod-freestyle-review/.

2. William B. McAllister, pers. comm.

3. Charles E. Rosenberg, "Disease in History: Frames and Framers," *Millbank Memorial Fund Q.* 67 suppl. 1 (1989): 1. The criticisms and questions were raised by several readers listed in the Acknowledgments.

4. Robin L. Hornung and Solmaz Poorsattar, "Tanning Addiction: The New Form of Substance Abuse," Skin Cancer Foundation, August 2, 2013, https://www.skincancer.org/prevention/tanning/tanning-addiction.

5. Jerod L. Stapleton, Elliot J. Coups, and Joel Hillhouse, "The American Suntanning Association: A 'Science-First Organization' with a Biased Scientific Agenda," *JAMA Dermatology* 149 (2013): 523–524; Steven Reinberg, "1 in 5 Young Women Who Tan Indoors Get Addicted," WebMD, October 19, 2017, https://www.webmd.com/skin-problems-and-treatments/news/20171019/1-in-5-young-women-who-tan-indoors-get-addicted#1 (quotation).

6. "Metallurgy," *London Q. Review* [American ed.] 120 (July 1866): 53–54; Douglas Alan Fisher, *The Epic of Steel* (New York: Harper and Row, 1963), chaps. 11–12.

7. Jan Sundin and Sam Willner, *Social Change and Health in Sweden: 250 Years of Politics and Practice* (Solna: Swedish National Institute of Public Health, 2007), 25, https://www.diva-portal.org/smash/get/diva2:17729/FULLTEXT01.pdf.

8. Sully Ledermann, *Alcool, Alcoolisme, Alcoolisation,* vol. 1: *Données Scientfiques de Caractère Physiologique, Économique et Social* and vol 2: *Mortalité, Morbidité, Accidents du Travail* (Paris: Presses Universitaires de France, 1956, 1964); M. Craplet, "Policies and Politics in France: 'From Apéritif to Digestif,'" in *From Science to Action? 100 Years Later—Alcohol Policies Revisited,* ed. Richard Müller and Harald Klingemann (New York: Kluwer, 2004), 127; Virginia Berridge, *Demons: Our Changing Attitudes to Alcohol, Tobacco, and Drugs* (Oxford: Oxford U.P., 2013), 190–191; Alex Mold, "'Everybody Likes a Drink. Nobody Likes a Drunk': Alcohol, Health Education and the Public in 1970s Britain," *Social History of Medicine* 30 (2017): 612–636.

9. Ana Regina Noto et al., "The Hidden Role of the Alcohol Industry in Youth Drinking in Brazil," *JSAD* 76 (2015): 981; Jean Kilbourne to Ace Bushnell, August 7, 1986, box 26, JKP (annuities).

10. Richard H. Thaler and Cass R. Sunstein, *Nudge: Improving Decisions about Health, Wealth, and Happiness,* rev. ed. (New York: Penguin, 2009), introduction and part 1.

11. Ibid., 49; Khushbu Shah, "How Cinnabon Tricks You with Its Cinnamon Smells," Eater, May 21, 2014, https://www.eater.com/2014/5/21/6220567/how-cinnabon-tricks-you -with-its-cinnamon-smells.

12. Robert N. Proctor, *Golden Holocaust: Origins of the Cigarette Catastrophe and the Case for Abolition* (Berkeley: U. of California Press, 2011), 398–403; Alix M. Freedman, "'Impact Booster': Tobacco Firm Shows How Ammonia Spurs Delivery of Nicotine," *WSJ,* October 18, 1995; "Expert: Ammonia Added to Cigarettes," CNN, February 4, 1998, http:// www.cnn.com/US/9802/04/minnesota.tobacco/index.html?_s=PM:US (10 million); Anonymous, "Response to Wall Street Journal on Ammonia and Nicotine" (TS, October 13, 1995), Truth Tobacco Industry Documents, https://www.industrydocumentslibrary .ucsf.edu/tobacco/docs/#id=kndy0082 ("flavorants," "naturally").

13. National Center for Responsible Gaming, *1998 Annual Report,* Gambling Vertical File—Associations: National Center for Responsible Gaming, SC-UNLV (checks); Brett Pulley, "Study Finds Legality Spreads the Compulsion to Gamble," *NYT,* December 7, 1997; Eliza Strickland, "Gambling with Science," *Salon,* June 16, 2008, https://www.salon .com/2008/06/16/gambling_science/.

14. Cristin E. Kearns, Laura A. Schmidt, and Stanton A. Glantz, "Sugar Industry and Coronary Heart Disease Research: A Historical Analysis of Internal Industry Documents," *JAMA Internal Medicine* 176 (2016): 1680–1685.

15. Amanda Reiman, Mark Welty, and Perry Solomon, "Cannabis as a Substitute for Opioid-Based Pain Medication: Patient Self-Report," *Cannabis and Cannabinoid Research* 2 (2017): 160–166.

16. "Anheuser-Busch Company Profile" (TS, 1997), box 1, JKP.

17. Kathryn Meyer, *Life and Death in the Garden: Sex, Drugs, Cops, and Robbers in Wartime China* (Lanham, Md.: Rowman and Littlefield, 2014), 55.

18. "Investors Win Big with Bet on Chinese Lottery Firm's Shares," *South China Morning Post,* updated ed., January 7, 2014, http://www.scmp.com/business/china-business /article/1399019/investors-win-big-bet-chinese-lottery-firms-shares.

19. *Pursue Perfection* (Copenhagen: Carlsberg Foundation, 2014), 25, 28.

20. "OxyContin Press Release, 1996," TS, reproduced in *Los Angeles Times,* May 5, 2016, http://documents.latimes.com/oxycontin-press-release-1996/, 1, 2, 8, scare quotes in original.

21. This account draws on Barry Meier, *Pain Killer: An Empire of Deceit and the Origin of America's Opioid Epidemic* (New York: Random House, 2018); Sam Quinones, *Dreamland: The True Tale of America's Opiate Epidemic* (New York: Bloomsbury, 2015); Christopher Glazek, "The Secretive Family Making Billions from the Opioid Crisis," *Esquire,* October 16, 2017, http://www.esquire.com/news -politics/a12775932/sackler-family-oxycontin/; Andrew Kolodny et al., "The Prescription Opioid and Heroin Crisis: A Public Health Approach to an Epidemic of Addiction," *Annual Review of Public Health* 36 (2015): 559–574; Harriet Ryan, Lisa Girion, and Scott Glover, "OxyContin Goes Global—'We're Only Just Getting Started,'" *Los Angeles Times,* December 18, 2016; Jeanne Whalen, "U.S. Lifespans Fall Again," *WSJ,* December 21, 2017; and Keith Humphreys, Jonathan P. Caulkins, and Vanda Felbab-Brown, "Opioids of the Masses: Stopping an American Epidemic from Going Global," *Foreign Affairs* 97 (May / June 2018): 118–129.

22. Patrick Radden Keefe, "Empire of Pain," *New Yorker* 93 (October 30, 2017): 34–49, quotation p. 36.

23. Ibid., 43 (whales).

24. Jeanne Whalen and Laura Cooper, "Private Equity Invests in Rehab Centers," *WSJ,* September 6, 2017; Leslie Scism and Nicole Friedman, "Smartphone Use Lifts Car-Insurance Rates," *WSJ,* February 21, 2017.

25. Micha Berman et al., "Estimating the Cost of a Smoking Employee," *Tobacco Control* 23 (2014): 428–433.

26. Jon Evans, "Drug Testing: Technologies and Global Markets," *BCC Research,* May 2017, https://www.bccresearch.com/market-research/pharmaceuticals/drug-testing -technologies-markets-report-phm013g.html; "Weight Management Market Analysis," *Grand View Research* (February 2017), https://www.grandviewresearch.com/industry -analysis/weight-management-market.

27. Denise Grady, "Lung Cancer Patients Live Longer with Immune Therapy," *NYT,* April 16, 2018 ($100,000); C. M. Durmand et al., "The Drug Overdose Epidemic and Deceased-Donor Transplantation in the United States: A National Registry Study," *Annals of Internal Medicine* 168 (2018): 702–711; Jeanne Whalen, "After Addiction Comes Families' Second Blow: The Crushing Cost of Rehab," *WSJ,* March 8, 2018; Elisabeth Rosenthal, "The $2.7 Trillion Medical Bill," *NYT,* June 1, 2013.

28. Ronald P. Formisano, *The Tea Party: A Brief History* (Baltimore, Md.: Johns Hopkins U.P., 2012), 87 ("benefits").

29. Salil Panchal, "Ragpickers—Biggest Drug Addicts' Group," *Times of India,* August 20, 1990.

30. Bruce Alexander, *The Globalisation of Addiction: A Study in Poverty of the Spirit*

(Oxford: Oxford U.P., 2008), "addictive faith" p. 258. Alexander elaborates and illustrates his views at http://www.brucekalexander.com/.

31. Quinones, *Dreamland*.

32. *Catechism of the Catholic Church* (Ligouri, Mo.: Ligouri Press, 1994), 551–552.

33. Laurie Goodstein, "Evangelicals Fear the Loss of the Teenagers," *NYT*, October 6, 2006. Ultra-Orthodox Jews face a similar challenge. Yair Ettinger, "Gerrer Hasidim Declare War on Computers," *Haaretz*, May 21, 2007.

34. Ron Dicker, "'Nanny Bloomberg' Ad . . . ," *Huffington Post*, December 6, 2017, https://www.huffingtonpost.com/2012/06/04/nanny-bloomberg-ad-in-new_n_1568037.html; Lester Wan, Elaine Watson, and Rachel Arthur, "Sugar Taxes: The Global Picture in 2017," Beveragedaily.com, December 20, 2017, https://www.beveragedaily.com/Article /2017/12/20/Sugar-taxes-The-global-picture-in-2017; Mike Esterl, "Coca-Cola Deepens Its Push into Africa," *WSJ*, February 1, 2016; Andrew Jacobs, "In Sweeping War on Obesity, Chile Slays Tony the Tiger," *NYT*, February 7, 2018.

35. Dusita Maneemuang, "Call to Overturn Ban on E-cigarettes in Thailand," *Asia Times*, http://www.atimes.com/article/call-to-overturn-ban-on-e-cigarettes-in-thailand /(thirty); William DeJong and Jason Blanchette, "Case Closed: Research Evidence on the Positive Public Health Impact of the Age 21 Minimum Legal Drinking Age in the United States," *JSAD* supplement no. 17 (2014): 108–115.

36. Representative studies of the effectiveness of treatment and minimum unit pricing are Institute of Medicine, *Treating Drug Problems*, ed. Dean R. Gerstein and Henrick J. Harwood, 2 vols. (Washington, D.C.: National Academy Press, 1990, 1992), and Sadie Boniface, Jack W. Scannell, and Sally Marlow, "Evidence for the Effectiveness of Minimum Pricing of Alcohol: A Systematic Review and Assessment Using the Bradford Hill Criteria for Causality," *BMJ Open* 7 (2017), http://bmjopen.bmj.com/content/bmjopen /7/5/e013497.full.pdf.

37. Robert J. MacCoun and Peter Reuter, *Drug War Heresies: Learning from Other Vices, Times, and Places* (Cambridge: Cambridge U.P., 2001).

38. Substance Abuse and Mental Health Services Administration, *TEDS Report*, August 13, 2013, https://www.samhsa.gov/data/sites/default/files/MarijuanaAdmissionsAg ed18to30EarlyVsAdult/MarijuanaAdmissionsAged18to30EarlyVsAdult/Marijuana%20 AdmissionsAged18to30EarlyVsAdult.htm; Jonathan P. Caulkins, "The Real Dangers of Marijuana," *National Affairs*, no. 26 (Winter 2016): 21–34.

39. Simon Chapman, "Civil Disobedience and Tobacco Control: The Case of BUGA UP," *Tobacco Control* 5 (1996): 179–185. On the power of ridicule, see Steven Pinker, *The Better Angels of Our Nature: Why Violence Has Declined* (New York: Viking, 2011), 163–165, 247–248, 633–634.

40. Peter Orszag, "Putin's Other War: Fighting Russian Binge Drinking," *Chicago Tribune,* August 12, 2015; Jon Rogers, "Putin's Plan to Stub Out Smoking," *Express,* January 10, 2017; Mike Ives, "Methamphetamine Abuse Colors Politics in the Philippines," *NYT,* October 13, 2016 ("zombies"); Maya Wang, "China's Dystopian Push to Revolutionize Surveillance," *WP,* August 18, 2017; Shan Li, "Beijing Tightens Screws on Makers of Videogames," "Game Freeze Stretches On," and "Tencent Tells Young Gamers to Hit 'Pause,'" *WSJ,* September 1–2, October 25, and November 6, 2018.

41. Mark A. R. Kleiman, *Against Excess: Drug Policy for Results* (New York: Basic Books, 1992), 19, 69, 387.

ACKNOWLEDGMENTS

In 2001 I published *Forces of Habit,* a global history of psychoactive drug use, commerce, and regulation. Over the next seventeen years I became convinced that drug history was part of a larger history of brain reward and habituating commerce. Reading Daniel Lord Smail's *On Deep History and the Brain* (2008) and Gary S. Cross and Robert N. Proctor's *Packaged Pleasures: How Technology and Marketing Revolutionized Desire* (2014) reinforced the conviction. So did Natasha Dow Schüll's *Addiction by Design: Machine Gambling in Las Vegas* (2012) and Michael Moss's *Salt Sugar Fat: How the Food Giants Hooked Us* (2013). These and other accounts made it plain that digitized gambling and highly palatable food could have drug-like effects, an insight that dovetailed with research in neuroscience and behavioral economics. Psychologically informed works like George A. Akerlof and Robert J. Shiller's *Phishing for Phools: The Economics of Manipulation and Deception* (2015) and Adam Alter's *Irresistible: The Rise of Addictive Technology and the Business of Keeping Us Hooked* (2017) further strengthened my belief that the basic story was one of limbic capitalists versus kludgy consumer brains.

To tell that story I decided to write an interdisciplinary history of pleasure, vice, and addiction. I began at the beginning and framed my account as a natural and accelerating quest to ameliorate the human condition that assumed a more artificial and sinister aspect under the conditions of late modernity. Along the way I found myself contemplating Yuval Noah Harari's *Sapiens: A Brief History of Humankind* (2015), from which I took the notion of luxury traps; Ian Hodder's *Entangled: An Archaeology of the*

Relationships between Humans and Things (2012), which helped me more fully understand pleasure commodities' liberating-enslaving nature; and Steven Pinker's two histories of human progress, *The Better Angels of Our Nature: Why Violence Has Declined* (2011) and *Enlightenment Now: The Case for Reason, Science, Humanism, and Progress* (2018). As noted in Chapters 3 and 7, I came to see my narrative as Pinker with the warts left on. The worse angels of our nature had piggybacked on our better ones.

The historian John Burnham inspired piggybacking of another sort. In *Bad Habits: Drinking, Smoking, Taking Drugs, Gambling, Sexual Misbehavior, and Swearing in American History* (1993), Burnham explained the political fall and commercial resurrection of his subtitular vices. But he did so only for the United States and he published before processed food and digital technology featured in discussions of addiction. Seeing an opportunity to update and globalize Burnham's work, I determined to make this book a sequel, not only to *Forces of Habit,* but to the master's *Bad Habits,* to which my subtitle pays homage.

Another opportunity presented itself when historians Jessica R. Pliley, Robert Kramm, and Harald Fischer-Tiné edited a timely anthology, *Global Anti-Vice Activism, 1890–1950: Fighting Drinks, Drugs, and "Immorality"* (2016). Chapter 4 owes much to its contributors. Chapter 5 extends their work by describing pro-vice activism during and after World War II. No thesis without an antithesis, I thought, especially when the antithesis seemed to be winning.

Chapters 6 and 7 push, I trust congenially, the boundaries of the Alcohol and Drugs History Society (ADHS). Founded in 1979 as an alcohol and temperance history study group, the ADHS evolved into an international scholarly organization whose brief included licit and illicit drugs. To it I would add other habituating substances and behaviors, a case I have made in papers presented at ADHS meetings and elaborate here by resituating alcohol and drugs in a larger history of pleasure, vice, and addiction.

Chapter 8, "Against Excess," nods to Mark A. R. Kleiman. I reread his *Against Excess: Drug Policy for Results* (1992) while wrestling with the what-is-to-be-done question. I found that many of his "grudging-toleration" drug policy recommendations applied to larger issues of commercial vice and designer addiction. This insight would not have surprised Robert J. MacCoun and Peter Reuter, whose *Drug War Heresies: Learning from Other Vices, Times, and Places* (2001) explored parallels between the regulation of drugs and the regulation of activities like gambling and prostitution. To borrow a phrase from Jonathan Caulkins, another historically minded analyst, we face more than a drug problem. We face a problem of "temptation commodities with habituating tendencies." That these commodities form a unified field of interdisciplinary inquiry and understanding is the central argument of this book.

I cannot say whether I have succeeded in persuading anyone of this argument. I can say that I had help in trying. Michael Acord, Peter Andreas, Daniel Berg, Alison Bruey, Claire Clark, Andrew Courtwright, Keith Humphreys, David Jaffee, Chau Kelly, Jennifer Lieberman, William and David McAllister, Shelby Miller, Eric Moller, James P. Olsen, Harry Rothschild, Deborah Rudacille, Daniel Lord Smail, and Greg Wadley commented on various drafts, as did graduate students Kara Barker, Nick Iorio, Victoria Jones, Roberta Miller, Kyle Morgan, Courteney Papczynski, Will Pate, Imani Phillips, Kyle Reagan, Jamie Smith, Stephanie Smith, Taylor Youngling, and Andrea Zabala. My editor, Kathleen McDermott, assisted at every stage of the process. Louise E. Robbins provided meticulous copyediting, and Michael Russem oversaw the book's interior design.

External funding for this project came from a National Endowment for the Humanities Public Scholar Award and a UNLV Center for Gaming Research Fellowship. Daniel Sack assisted me in applying for the former, David G. Schwartz the latter. Chapters 2, 5, and 6 build on ideas first presented in my UNLV paper, "Learning from Las Vegas: Gambling, Technology, Capitalism, and Addiction," *UNLV Center for Gaming Research: Occasional Paper Series* no. 25 (May 2014). I am grateful for the chance to begin work on these concepts in that publication.

Additional support came from the University of Richmond's Douglas Southall Freeman Professorship. This position included generous funding for a conference, "Addictions Old and New," held on October 22–23, 2015.

I have drawn on several of the presentations and, with the help of Hugh West, Deborah Govoruhk, and Mark Kwolek, made edited versions available at https://history.richmond.edu/addiction-conference/.

My home institution, the University of North Florida, provided research funding and a fellowship supplement. David Fenner, Charles Closmann, David Sheffler, and George Rainbolt helped with leaves and course releases, Marianne Roberts with travel. Elizabeth Curry and Jennifer Bibb sheltered me in Carpenter Library; Alisa Craddock gathered research materials from far afield. Michael Boyles assisted with the illustrations. I thank them and the many other administrators, colleagues, archivists, librarians, and students who helped me in my quest. There is surprisingly little pleasure to be had in writing the history of pleasure. There is this, though: The unalloyed gratitude one feels in being able to acknowledge the kindness and generosity of others.

CREDITS

INDEX

Page numbers in italics refer to illustrations.

and military vices, 129–131, 146; and methamphetamine, 130; and alcohol, 131, *132*; and tourism, 134, *135*, 136; and contraception, 147

Globalization: and limbic capitalism, 8–10, 45, 159–163, 189–192, 228–229, 236–239; of new pleasures, 18, 30–38, 44–47; of tourism, 134–137; of casino gambling, 139–146; of alcohol industry, 150–151; of tobacco industry, 154–155; and urbanization, 155; after Cold War, 159; of obesity, 173–174; of addiction neuroscience, 182–183; and internet, 202

Golf, 118, 126, 137, 158

Great Depression: and Prohibition, 108–109; and vice, 127, 139–140, 163, 237

Habits: and vice, 7–8, 29, 77, 85, 202; of elites, 110, 115; in wartime, 130–131; and conditioning, 167, 208, 239; and food addiction, 177; and limbic capitalism, 189, 191, 208, 211–212, 228, 231. *See also* Addiction; Alcoholism; Internet; Young people; *and specific habits*

Harari, Yuval Noah, 21–22, 220, 305

Harrah, William, 50–51, 52, 140, 143, 145

Hefner, Hugh, 127–128

Heroin: and addiction, 3, 7, 116–117, 157, 178, 234; and set and setting, 15; blending of, 55, 229; prohibition of, 79, 116–117; and cigarettes, 90; adulterated, 105–106; and gateway theory, 151–152; trafficking of, 152, 159, 160, 234, 239

Hershey, Milton, 58–59, 61, 82

Hinduism, 29, 69, 76, 102

Hitler, Adolf, 75, 97

HIV / AIDS, 219, 233, 296n27

Holland. *See* Netherlands

Homo sapiens: migrations of, 12–14; imagination of, 14, 26, 168; unique pleasures of, 26–28; population of, 68; life expectancy of, 69; obsolescence of, 220–221

Honey, 13–14, 16, 17, 24, 31, 33, 34

Hormesis: defined, 19, 224, 294n15; and arsenic, 29; and capitalism, 67; and alcohol, 95, 226–227; and digital media, 199

Huxley, Aldous, 72

Hypodermic syringes, 48, 55, 87, 168, 175, 211

Ice cream, 52, 59–60, 190

Immigration: and cuisine, 35; and cities, 42, 63; and prostitution, 61, 160–162; and opium, 64, 77, 110; and poverty, 97; and cannabis, 133

Imperialism: and spread of pleasure, 8, 45; and opium trade, 31, 64, 116, 190; and monetized trade, 37; and alcohol trade, 102, 116; and tobacco taxes, 116; and regulated prostitution, 122; and drug policy, 124; and globalization, 159; decline of, 240; and coca, 255n26

India: and honey, 13; and aphrodisiacs, 16, 29; and yoga, 28; and gambling, 29; and chess, 31; and long-distance trade, 31, 44, 102; and opiates, 31, 102, 238, 239; and curries, 35; sugar imports to, 44; and alcohol, 102, 110; and prostitution, 102, 219; and tobacco, 102–103; Western views of, 116, 117; and social media, 200

Indians (American): and tobacco, 14, 17, 85; and trade, 23; and gambling, 25, 29; and alcohol, 36, 83, 85, 93–95, 217; mortality of, 83

Taxes: on intoxicants, 6, 237; and civilization, 23; on opium, 31, 110–111, 118; on alcohol, 34, 43, 63, 100, 108–110, 120, 127, 226; on gambling, 49–50, 62, 111, 113, 122, 144, 148; from plantation agriculture, 83; to discourage use, 97, 105, 181, 242, 246; and modernizing states, 110–111, 116; on tobacco, 111, 116, 124, 162; on prostitution, 123; avoidance of, 162–163; on sugar, 191, 241

Tea, 15, 18, 37, 45

Telephones: and consumerism, 45; and prostitution, 55, 219; and bootlegging, 65; and transnational crime, 160. *See also* Smartphones

Television: and advertising, 127, 148, 150, 189; and Walt Disney, 138; and product placement, 186; and digitized gambling, 194–195; via cable, 215

Temperance: and Gothenburg system, 63, 100, 169; international meetings, *88*; criticisms of, 96; and WWCTU, 96, 101, 240; literature, 97; and drinking fountains, 98; and recreation, 100; and *Lebensreform*, 117–118; propaganda for, 126. *See also* Activism; Prohibition of alcohol

Theaters: for live performances, 51, 73, 91, 102; for movies, 52; for pornography, 137; food in, 186

Tobacco: spread of, 14, 21, 32, 34, 70, 152–156; addiction to, 17, 85, 153, 157, 229–230; blending of, 34, 52, 53, 56; price of, 37, 42, 70, *71*, 103, 111; campaigns against, 70, 90, 114, 116, 152–156, 243–244; and health, 80, 90, 93, 102–103, 152–153, 207, 231, 235; and slavery, *84*; and crime, 91; in military, 92, 129, 130, 152; on airplanes, 134;

and mental illness, 154; and stigma, 154, 244; profitability of, 156. *See also* Cigarettes; Smoking; Taxes; *and specific nations*

Tourism: declining cost of, 45, 133; and gambling, 50–51, 122, 142–145, 214, 231; and pleasure meccas, 133–146, 158, 214–215; democratization of, 136; and vice normalization, 136, 163; and gay people, 139. *See also specific destinations*

Trade: and pleasures and vices, 8, 18, 23, 30–38, 159–164; shift to ocean-going, 31; monetization of, 36–38, 160; and industrialization, 42–46; as progressive force, 66, 210–211, 225. *See also* Columbian Exchange; Globalization; Silk Roads; Transportation

Transportation: steam revolution in, 42–47, 101, 225; and industrialization, 66, 133; and anti-vice activism, 100–101, 163; and containerization, 159. *See also* Automobiles; Aviation; Railroads; Tourism; Trade

Trotsky, Leon, 165, 169

Trotter, Thomas, 85–86

United States: widespread addiction in, 2, 236–237; and spirits, 42, 43; and tobacco, 42, *53*, *84*, 153; as reference society, 46–48, 128–129, 157, 189, 237, 238, 261n27; and gambling, 50, 112–114, 148; and narcotics, 55, 105–106; and chocolate production, 57, 59–61; in World War I, 59, 98; and sugar, 59–60, 61; and obesity, 61, 174; and prostitution, 98, 217–219; and pornography, 105, 203–205, 216; and normalized vice, 127–129, 148, 164, 202; in World War II, 129, *132*; and